REA's Test Prep Books Are The Best!

(a sample of the <u>hundreds of letters</u> REA receives each year)

" REA's AP Statistics book is well-organized and has an excellent selection of test questions. "
An AP Statistics Test-Taker, South Carolina

" My students report your chapters of review as the most valuable single resource they used for review and preparation. "
Teacher, American Fork, UT

" Your book was such a better value and was so much more complete than anything your competition has produced — and I have them all! "
Teacher, Virginia Beach, VA

" Compared to the other books that my fellow students had, your book was the most helpful in helping me get a great score. "
Student, North Hollywood, CA

" Your book was responsible for my success on the exam, which helped me get into the college of my choice... I will look for REA the next time I need help. "
Student, Chesterfield, MO

" Just a short note to say thanks for the great support your book gave me in helping me pass the test... I'm on my way to a B.S. degree because of you! "
Student, Orlando, FL

(more on next page)

(continued from front page)

" I did well because of your wonderful prep books... I just wanted to thank you for helping me prepare for these tests. "
Student, San Diego, CA

" The [REA] book is great for independent study for the exam... From [it], I gained test confidence and a positive attitude. "
Student, Jackson, MS

" I'm a student at a Canadian high school. I really wanted to go to school in the U.S., so I got this book. I was really going into it without knowing what to expect. This product really helped. I went into the test confident. "
Student, Winnipeg, Manitoba

" The best thing about this book is that it's updated and the information is accurate... I would rate it an 11 out of 10. "
Student, Chicago, IL

" The [REA] practice tests are very much like the real thing... [and] are stated in a logical manner [that is] superior [to the competition]. "
Student, Freeville, NY

" I am fond of your books and have found them to be of tremendous assistance in preparing for all classes. "
Student, Spartanburg, SC

AP STATISTICS

4th Edition

TestWare® Edition

Robin Levine-Wissing
Instructional Supervisor for Mathematics
and AP Statistics Instructor
Glenbrook North High School
Northbrook, Illinois

David W. Thiel
Mathematics Specialist
Southern Nevada Regional Professional
Development Program
Adjunct Professor, Department of Economics
University of Nevada–Las Vegas

Research & Education Association
Visit our website at: www.rea.com

Research & Education Association
61 Ethel Road West
Piscataway, New Jersey 08854
E-mail: info@rea.com

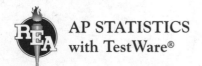

AP STATISTICS
with TestWare®

Printed in the United States of America

Library of Congress Control Number 2009937487

ISBN-13: 978-0-7386-0790-0
ISBN-10: 0-7386-0790-8

Windows® is a registered trademark of Microsoft Corporation.

REA® and TestWare® are registered trademarks of Research & Education Association, Inc.

CONTENTS

Chapter 4

STATISTICAL INFERENCE

ABOUT OUR AUTHORS

Robin Levine-Wissing is currently the Instructional Supervisor for Mathematics and an AP Statistics Instructor at Glenbrook North High School in Northbrook, Illinois. She holds a bachelor's degree in Mathematics and Education from American University, in Washington, D.C., a master's degree in Communication Sciences from Kean University of New Jersey, and an Educational Leadership certificate from North Central College in Naperville, Illinois.

She has been teaching mathematics for 28 years, AP Statistics for 10 years, and has been a reader of the AP Statistics exams for 6 years. Beginning in June 2006, Robin will be a table leader for the College Board. She has been an AP College Board Faculty Consultant and workshop presenter since 2000. Robin is also a current Teachers Teaching with Technology (T^3) National Instructor, training teachers on handheld and computer technology for mathematics classes. She has presented workshops across the United States, Hawaii, and Canada for teachers of mathematics and statistics.

Robin was the 1993 recipient of the Presidential Award for Excellence in Mathematics Teaching, a 1998 Tandy Technology Scholar, and 1996 Clark County Teacher of the Year.

Robin lives with her husband Ed and dog Sydney in suburban Chicago, Illinois. They enjoy travel and foreign films.

—I wish to thank my wonderful husband, Ed, for all of his support and encouragement with this project. I could not have completed this work without you by my side. Thank you, Sydney, my dog, who often jumped up on the desk chair and sat on my lap while I was typing away, working on this book. Lastly, to Rocky and Lightning, I miss you more and more each day. I will always love you.

David Thiel is a 20-year teacher of mathematics and physics in Las Vegas, Nevada, and has a passion for probability and statistics. He has been teaching statistics for 15 years and has been involved in the Advanced Placement Statistics Program since its inception in 1996. He is a College Board consultant for AP Statistics and has been an exam reader for 6 years.

David presently spends his days as a K-12 mathematics specialist for the Southern Nevada Regional Professional Development Program, where he provides training to teachers of all levels in mathematics content and pedagogy. David is also an adjunct professor in the Department of Economics at the University of Nevada-Las Vegas, where he teaches courses in introductory statistics.

David has earned several honors in his teaching career, including the Presidential Award for Excellence in Mathematics Teaching, the Tandy Technology Scholars Award, and Outstanding Part-time Instructor at UNLV. He is a graduate of Montana State University, from which he holds both a B.S. and an M.S. in Mathematics.

David and his wife have one son and one Labrador retriever. He enjoys playing strategy games and watching baseball. He believes there is no better place in the world to study probability than Las Vegas.

—For Kim, Alex, and Franklin. Thank you for all of your patience and support.

—Special thanks to Steve Goodman of Glenbrook North High School for his assistance in scrutinizing the practice exams and in creating their solutions.

About Research & Education Association

Founded in 1959, Research & Education Association (REA) is dedicated to publishing the finest and most effective educational materials—including software, study guides, and test preps—for students in middle school, high school, college, graduate school, and beyond.

REA's test preparation series includes books and software for all academic levels in almost all disciplines. REA publishes test preps for students who have not yet entered high school, as well as high school students preparing to enter college. Students from countries around the world seeking to attend college in the United States will find the assistance they need in REA's publications. For college students seeking advanced degrees, REA publishes test preps for many major graduate school admission examinations in a wide variety of disciplines, including engineering, law, and medicine. Students at every level, in every field, with every ambition can find what they are looking for among REA's publications.

REA's series presents tests that accurately depict the official exams in both degree of difficulty and types of questions. REA's practice tests are always based upon the most recently administered exams, and include every type of question that can be expected on the actual exams.

REA's publications and educational materials are highly regarded and continually receive an unprecedented amount of praise from professionals, instructors, librarians, parents, and students. Our authors are as diverse as the subject matter represented in the books we publish. They are well known in their respective disciplines and serve on the faculties of prestigious colleges and universities throughout the United States and Canada.

We invite you to visit us at *www.rea.com* to find out how "REA is making the world smarter."

STAFF ACKNOWLEDGMENTS

In addition to our author, we would like to thank Larry B. Kling, Vice President, Editorial, for supervising development; Pam Weston, Vice President, Publishing, for setting the quality standards for production integrity and managing the publication to completion; John Cording, Vice President, Technology, for coordinating the design and development of REA's TEST*ware*® software; Diane Goldschmidt, Senior Editor, for project management and preflight editorial review; Christine Reilley and Anne Winthrop Esposito, Senior Editors, for editorial contributions; Amy Jamison, Heena Patel and Michelle Boykins, Technology Project Managers, for their design contributions and software testing efforts; Christine Saul, Senior Graphic Artist, for cover design; and Jeff LoBalbo, Senior Graphic Artist, for post-production file mapping.

We also gratefully acknowledge the team at Aquent Publishing Services, for typesetting this edition.

AP STATISTICS

Independent Study Schedule

The following study schedule allows for thorough preparation for the AP Statistics Examination. Although it is designed for 6 weeks, it can be condensed into a 3-week course by collapsing each 2-week period into a single week. Be sure to set aside at least 2 hours each day to study. Bear in mind that the more time you spend studying, the more prepared and relaxed you will feel on the day of the exam.

Week	Activity
1	Read and study the Introduction, which will acquaint you with the AP Statistics Examination. Become familiar with the content and format of the AP Statistics Exam. Take and score Practice Test 1 on CD-ROM to determine your strengths and weaknesses. Ideally, someone with knowledge of statistics should score your free-response questions. After grading your exam, determine which types of questions caused you the most difficulty. This will help you pinpoint which review areas you should study most thoroughly.
2 & 3	Carefully read and study the Statistics Review included in Chapters 1–4 of this book.
4	Take AP Statistics Practice Test 2 on CD-ROM. After scoring your exam, carefully review all incorrect answer explanations. If there are any types of questions or particular subjects that seem difficult to you, review those subjects by referring back to the appropriate section of the Statistics Review.
5	Take Practice Test 3 in this book. and after scoring your exam, carefully review all incorrect answer explanations. If there are any types of questions or particular subjects that seem difficult to you, review those subjects by referring back to the appropriate section of the Statistics Review.
6	Take Practice Test 4 in this book. After scoring it, review all incorrect answer explanations. Study any areas in which you consider yourself to be weak by using the Statistics Review and any other reliable sources you have on hand. Review our practice tests again to be sure you understand the problems that you originally answered incorrectly.

INSTALLING REA's TEST*ware*®

SYSTEM REQUIREMENTS

Pentium 75 MHz (300 MHz recommended) or a higher or compatible processor; Microsoft Windows 98 or later; 64 MB Available RAM; Internet Explorer 5.5 or higher.

INSTALLATION

1. Insert the AP Statistics TEST*ware*® CD-ROM into the CD-ROM drive.
2. If the installation doesn't begin automatically, from the Start Menu choose the RUN command. When the RUN dialog box appears, type d:\setup (where *d* is the letter of your CD-ROM drive) at the prompt and click OK.
3. The installation process will begin. A dialog box proposing the directory "Program Files\REA\APStatistics" will appear. If the name and location are suitable, click OK. If you wish to specify a different name or location, type it in and click OK.
4. Start the AP Statistics TEST*ware*® application by double-clicking on the icon.

REA's AP Statistics TEST*ware*® is **EASY** to **LEARN AND USE**. To achieve maximum benefits, we recommend that you take a few minutes to go through the on-screen tutorial on your computer. The "screen buttons" are also explained there to familiarize you with the program.

TECHNICAL SUPPORT

REA's TEST*ware*® is backed by customer and technical support. For questions about **installation or operation of your software**, contact us at:

> **Research & Education Association**
> **Phone: (732) 819-8880 (9 a.m. to 5 p.m. ET, Monday–Friday)**
> **Fax: (732) 819-8808**
> **Website: www.rea.com**
> **E-mail: info@rea.com**

Note to Windows XP Users: In order for the TEST*ware*® to function properly, please install and run the application under the same computer-administrator level user account. Installing the TEST*ware*® as one user and running it as another could cause file-access path conflicts.

▼
INTRODUCTION

MAKING THE GRADE ON THE AP STATISTICS EXAM

ABOUT THE BOOK AND TEST*ware*®

This book and the accompanying software provides an accurate and complete representation of the Advanced Placement Statistics Examination. The four full-length practice exams included are based on the most recently administered AP Statistics Exam. Each of our practice tests is designed within the official timeframe of a 3-hour administration and includes every type of question that you can expect to encounter on the actual exam. Following each of our practice exams is an answer key complete with detailed explanations designed to clarify and contextualize the material for you. Practice Tests 1 and 2 are included in two formats: in printed form in this book and in TEST*ware*® format on the enclosed CD. **We recommend that you begin your preparation by first taking the computerized version of your test.** The software provides timed conditions and instantaneous, accurate scoring, which makes it all the easier to pinpoint your strengths and weaknesses.

In addition, to help make your preparation for the exam more realistic and to aid you in brushing up on areas of weakness, the following are provided at the end of this book:

- Actual formula sheets and statistical tables that you will be given to use during the AP Statistics Examination. (Appendix A)
- A glossary of key terms. (Appendix B)
- A cross-reference of the practice exam problems and the topics in the AP Statistics Topic Outline they test. (Appendix C)

By studying the review section, completing all four practice exams, and studying our step-by-step explanations, you will pinpoint your strengths and weaknesses and, above all, put yourself in the best possible position to master the AP Statistics Examination.

ABOUT THE EXAM

The Advanced Placement Statistics Examination is offered each May at participating schools and multischool centers throughout the world.

The Advanced Placement Program is designed to provide high school students with the opportunity to pursue college-level studies while still attending high school. The results of these exams are used by colleges and universities in the awarding of credit for introductory courses and placement in programs of study.

The Advanced Placement Statistics Course is designed to be the equivalent of an introductory college course. The AP Statistics Exam covers material in the following areas:

1. Exploring Data: Describing patterns and departures from patterns (20–30%);
2. Sampling and Experimentation: Planning and conducting a study (10–15%);
3. Anticipating Patterns: Exploring random phenomena using probability and simulation (20–30%);
4. Statistical Inference: Estimating population parameters and testing hypotheses (30–40%);

Each review chapter in this book covers one of the four content areas.

FORMAT OF THE EXAM

The AP Statistics Exam consists of two 90-minute sections:

- Section I consists of 40 multiple-choice questions, each with five possible answers. This section counts 50% of the examination grade.
- Section II counts 50% of the examination grade and is made up of two parts.
  - (a) Part A is five free-response questions. Each question is designed to be answered in approximately 12 minutes. This part counts for 75% of the Section II score.
  - (b) Part B is one question known as the "investigative task." It tests several concepts and procedures from multiple content areas in the context of a single problem. This investigative task is designed to be answered in about 30 minutes and counts as 25% of the Section II score.

In Section I, you will earn one point for each correct answer and lose one-fourth of a point for each incorrect answer.

In Section II, each problem is scored holistically on a 0–4 scale. These scores can be generally interpreted as follows:

- 4 = Complete Response
- 3 = Substantial Response
- 2 = Developing Response
- 1 = Minimal Response
- 0 = No Credit

Each problem in Section II is scored for accuracy and completeness of statistical methods, and on the strength of communication. About half of the score on any problem can be considered to be how well you communicate about the concepts involved and the conclusions you reach. Calculations alone will not earn full credit.

For more information about the scoring of the free-response and investigative task sections of the exam, visit the College Board website at *www.collegeboard.com.*

THE USE OF CALCULATORS

Graphing calculators with statistical capabilities can be used during the AP Statistics Exam. Each student is expected to bring his or her own on exam day. Although it is possible to do well on the exam without a calculator, not having one is a disadvantage. In fact, you are allowed to bring two calculators, if you wish.

Each student should have a working calculator to aid in computation and performing statistical procedures. Know how to use it before going into the exam. An unfamiliar calculator will be a hindrance during the exam. Practice using it.

Only certain calculators are allowed on the AP Statistics Exam. Calculators with QWERTY-type keyboards or those with paper tape printers are not allowed. A complete list of those allowed and disallowed can be found on College Board's Web site at www.collegeboard.com/student/testing/ap/sub_stats.html?stats.

This book has calculator instructions for the Texas Instruments TI-84 series calculators. Nearly all instructions can be used for the TI-83 series, but some commands on TI-84 are not available on TI-83. If you have questions about the capabilities of your calculator, consult your owner's manual.

Finally, the calculator is a tool and not a substitute for knowledge. You must be able to communicate clearly and demonstrate your understanding of statistics. Simply writing down a computation from the calculator may earn little or no credit. Remember, although this book has calculator instruction so that you can use it as a tool on the exam, this book also takes you through the steps to be successful without a calculator.

HOW TO USE THIS BOOK AND TEST*ware*®

What do I study first?

To begin your studies, read over this introduction and the suggestions for test taking. Take Practice Test 1 on CD-ROM. This will allow you to determine your strengths and weaknesses. Next, study the course review material focusing on your specific problem areas. The course review includes the information you need to know when taking the exam. Then take Practice Test 2 on CD-ROM and Practice Tests 3 and 4 in this book. To best utilize your study time, follow our Independent Study Schedule, which you will find in the front of this book.

SSD accommodations for students with disabilities

Many students qualify for extra time to take the AP Exams and our TEST*ware*® can be adapted to accommodate your time extension. This allows you to practice under the same extended time accommodations that you will receive on the actual test day. To customize your TEST*ware*® to suit the most common extensions, visit our website at *www.rea.com/ssd*.

SCORING THE EXAM

How Do I Score My Practice Tests?

The multiple-choice section of the exam is scored by crediting each correct answer with one point and deducting one-fourth of a point for each incorrect answer. Unanswered questions receive neither credit nor deduction.

The free-response questions are graded by readers chosen from around the country for their familiarity with the AP Program. Each free-response question is read and scored with the reader providing the score on a 0-to-4 (0 being the lowest and 4 the highest) scale. The free-response questions are scored on the basis of the statistical knowledge and communication the student used to answer the question. The statistical knowledge criteria include identifying the important concepts of the problem and demonstrating statistical concepts and techniques that result in a correct solution of the problem. The communication criteria include an explanation of what was done and why, along with a statement of conclusions drawn. Once the free-response questions have been graded by all of the readers, the scores are converted. The open-ended questions count as 75% of the free-response score; the investigative-task question counts as 25%.

SCORING THE MULTIPLE-CHOICE SECTION

For the multiple-choice section, use the following formula to calculate your raw score:

$$\underset{\substack{\text{number} \\ \text{right}}}{\rule{3cm}{0.4pt}} - (\underset{\substack{\text{number} \\ \text{wrong}}}{\rule{3cm}{0.4pt}} \times 1/4) = \underset{\substack{\text{raw score (round to the} \\ \text{nearest whole number)}}}{\rule{3cm}{0.4pt}}$$

Note: Do not include unanswered questions in the formula.

SCORING THE FREE-RESPONSE QUESTIONS

For the free-response section, use the following formula to calculate your raw score:

$$\underset{\substack{\text{5 open-ended} \\ \text{questions (75\%)}}}{\rule{3cm}{0.4pt}} + \underset{\substack{\text{1 investigative-task} \\ \text{question (25\%)}}}{\rule{3cm}{0.4pt}} = \underset{\text{raw score}}{\rule{2cm}{0.4pt}}$$

THE COMPOSITE SCORE

To obtain your composite score, use the following method:

$$\underset{\substack{\text{Multiple-choice} \\ \text{raw score}}}{\rule{3cm}{0.4pt}} + \underset{\substack{\text{Free-response} \\ \text{raw score}}}{\rule{3cm}{0.4pt}} = \underset{\text{raw score}}{\rule{2cm}{0.4pt}}$$

Your score on the multiple-choice section and your grade on the free-response section are combined and converted to the program's 5-point scale:

5—extremely well-qualified   2—possibly qualified
4—well-qualified   1—no recommendation
3—qualified

Most colleges grant students who earn at least a "3" college credit and/or advanced placement. You should check with your school guidance office about specific college requirements.

STUDYING FOR YOUR AP EXAMINATION

It is never too early to start studying. The earlier you begin, the more time you will have to sharpen your skills. Do not procrastinate! Cramming is not an effective way to study, since it does not allow you the time needed to learn the test material.

It is very important for you to choose the time and place for studying that works best for you. Some students may set aside a certain number of hours every morning to study, while others may choose to study at night before going to sleep. Other students may study during the day, while waiting in a line, or even while eating lunch. Only you can determine when and where your study time will be most effective. But be consistent and use your time wisely. Work out a study routine and stick to it!

When you take the practice exam(s), try to make your testing conditions as much like the actual test as possible. Turn your television and radio off, and sit down at a quiet table free from distraction. Make sure to time yourself.

Complete the practice test(s), score your test(s), and thoroughly review the explanations for the questions you answered incorrectly. However, do not review too much during any one sitting. Concentrate on one problem area at a time by reviewing the question and explanation, and by studying our review(s) until you are confident that you completely understand the material.

Since you will be allowed to write in your test booklet during the actual exam, you may want to write in the margins and spaces of this book when practicing. However, do not make miscellaneous notes on your answer sheet. Mark your answers clearly and make sure the answer you have chosen corresponds to the question you are answering.

Keep track of your scores! This will enable you to gauge your progress and discover general weaknesses in particular sections. You should carefully study the reviews that cover the topics causing you difficulty, as this will build your skills in those areas.

To get the most out of your studying time, we recommend that you follow the Study Schedule. It details how you can best budget your time.

WHAT YOU MAY AND MAY NOT BRING TO THE EXAM

You should bring the following to the exam:

- A good supply of #2 pencils.
- An eraser.
- An approved graphing calculator with statistical capabilities. You may have two. Fresh batteries are suggested.
- A watch without a calculator. Turn off any alarms.
- A photo ID.
- A light jacket or sweatshirt to deal with cool testing rooms.
- If the testing site allows it, a snack. An energy bar and fruit juice are good choices.
- You should also consult with your test administrator before the exam to confirm other materials you are expected to bring.

You may NOT bring the following to the exam:

- Highlighters
- text-correction fluid
- Rulers
- Books
- Statistical tables or formulas (they are provided)
- Papers of any kind, including scratch paper
- Laptop or hand-held computers
- PDAs
- Cameras
- Cell phones, two-way radios, or pagers
- Portable televisions, stereos, or radios
- text-correction fluid
- Highlighters

(Yes, those last two were listed again for a very good reason. Do not bring them!)

TEST TAKING TIPS

The Multiple-Choice Section

You have 90 minutes to do 40 questions in this section, a little over 2 minutes per question. Most students find this to be an ample amount of time. It is recommended that you go through the questions one at a time; answering those you know how to do. If you are not sure about a question, skip it and go on. You have time. Just make sure that you are marking the answer sheet for the question you are answering.

After you have gone through the test once, go back again and do the questions you skipped. You may need to read a question several times to understand it. You may be able to eliminate several of the choices. Do not panic, you still have time. Keep a steady pace and do not get hung up on a single question.

The scoring system for the multiple-choice section gives no advantage or disadvantage to blind guessing. However, if you can eliminate choices that you know are wrong, you increase your chance of guessing the correct answer. In that case, go for it! Narrowing the correct answer down to two or three choices gives you an advantage if you must now guess.

The Free-Response Section

You have 90 minutes to complete six free-response questions in this section. Question 6 is worth about double what the other five questions are worth and therefore demands more time. It is recommended that you read through all of the questions before you begin working. Then first attempt the questions that you know how to do.

Watch your time. It is easy to get caught up in a question and spend a lot of time on it. Also realize that because Question 6 is worth about double each of the other five, you shouldn't save it for last when you may run out of time. You should begin this question with at least 45 minutes left in the exam. It is important to get something down for Question 6. Once you have completed those questions you know how to do, and have tackled Question 6, go back and do those you skipped. Try to at least answer each part of all six questions. You cannot earn credit for leaving a question blank.

Some questions will have several parts. Sometimes one part leads to another; sometimes it will not. If you are having trouble with one part, you should still attempt the next part. Even if you miss one part, you may still get credit for the next.

Communicate clearly and succinctly. Explain what you are doing and why. Answer the question in the context of the scenario provided. Answer the question as if you were teaching the grader the concept or procedure. Graders want to give you credit, but they are not mind readers.

Do not ramble. Say what you need to say to answer the question and stop. You may have extra space on the paper—do not feel compelled to fill it up. Many a student has written more than was needed, made a contradictory statement, and lost credit.

Write legibly. If graders cannot read it, you may not get credit. If you have poor penmanship, practice that too in the months before the exam.

Do not provide calculator syntax as your explanation of a procedure. If you use the calculator, explain what you did statistically, in words, while providing the results of the calculator output.

CONTACTING THE AP PROGRAM

For registration bulletins or more information about the AP Statistics exam, contact

AP Services
P.O. Box 6671
Princeton, NJ 08541-6671
Phone: (609) 771-7300 or (888) 225-5427
Web site: www.collegeboard.com

Good luck on your AP Statistics exam!

CHAPTER 1
Exploring Data

EXPLORING DATA

A. CONSTRUCTING AND INTERPRETING GRAPHICAL DISPLAYS OF DISTRIBUTIONS OF UNIVARIATE DATA

Variables

When data are collected from a group of individuals, the characteristics under study are called **variables**. The variables could be heights in feet of 15 mountains in North America, the number of cars owned by a family, or the colors of silk blouses on sale in 12 stores in Los Angeles.

Variables can be either **categorical** or **quantitative** (numerical). Categorical variables are those whose values take on names or labels, such as the colors of blouses. Quantitative variables are those that show quantity and come from counting or measuring.

Quantitative variables can be further classified as **discrete** or **continuous**. Discrete numerical variables usually come from counting and can take on only certain values, such as the number of cars owned by a family. A family can have 2 cars or 3 cars, but cannot have 2.5 cars. The height of a mountain is an example of a continuous variable—one from measuring. It could take on practically any value, such as 1000 feet, 1001 feet, or 1000.437 feet.

Data are often classified by the number of variables under study. **Univariate** data are data where only one variable is being considered at a time. This variable may be from a single group or from multiple groups being compared. When two variables are being studied simultaneously, the data are called **bivariate**. Bivariate data are covered in Section D of this chapter.

Describing Distributions of Quantitative Data

Data can be organized by listing or plotting the **observed values** of the variable in a **frequency table** or graph. Below is an example of a frequency table.

Scores of AP Statistics Students					
Score	1	2	3	4	5
Frequency	10	18	38	28	17

Graphical displays include the **bar chart**, **dotplot**, **stemplot**, **box-and-whisker plot**, **histogram**, and **cumulative frequency graph**. Each of the graphs listed will be discussed in detail momentarily. (Bar charts are used for categorical data and are covered in Section E.)

Center, shape, and spread are characteristics that describe the distribution of univariate data. The center can be estimated by locating the middle of the distribution. Estimate the point where about half of the data are on either side of that point. You may have learned that the **mean** and **median** are measures of center. They will be discussed in more detail in Section B. For now, to find the center of a distribution from a graph, estimate as described above.

To describe the shape of the distribution, we use the terms such as symmetric, bell- or mound-shaped, skewed, uniform, unimodal, and bimodal. When examining the shape of the data, we also look for gaps, outliers, or any other unusual features.

Symmetric graphs appear to have mirror images about their center. If a graph has only one clear peak, it is called **unimodal**; if it has two, it is **bimodal**. Symmetric, unimodal graphs may sometimes be referred to as **mound-shaped**, or **bell-shaped**, because they look like a mound or bell.

Skewed graphs are unimodal graphs that tend to slant—most of the data are clustered on one side of the distribution and "tails" off on the other side. If the tail is on the left, we call the distribution left-skewed. If the tail is on the right, it is right-skewed.

A **uniform** distribution is symmetric where the data are distributed fairly evenly across the graph. There are no clear peaks and the data do not seem to cluster in one area or another.

Below are some examples of graphs and their shapes.

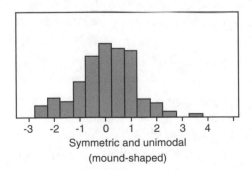

Symmetric and unimodal
(mound-shaped)

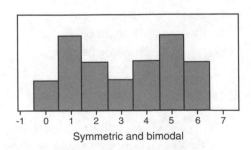

Symmetric and bimodal

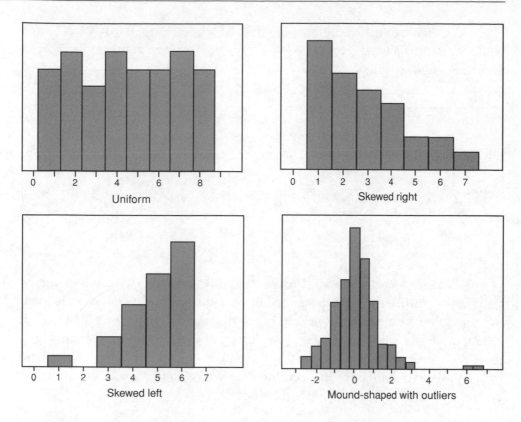

The spread describes the **variability** of the distribution of the data.

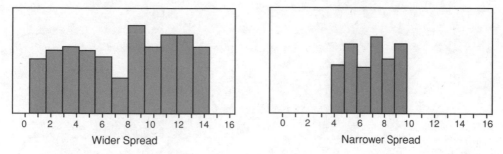

The histogram on the left is more variable than the one on the right. Note that they are graphed on the same scale and it is clear which graph has more spread.

When interpreting the spread of a graphical display consider the **range**—the **maximum** minus the **minimum** value—as a starting point. If there seem to be values outside of the general pattern, you would do well to also look at how variable the data are without them. You may have learned that the **standard deviation** and **interquartile range** are also used to measure the variability of the data. These will be discussed in more detail in Section B. For now, look at the overall spread of the data, both with and without any unusual observations.

Look again at the histograms below. The range on the left is 14 − 1 = 13 while the range on the right is 10 − 4 = 6. The smaller range indicates less spread and, thus, less variability.

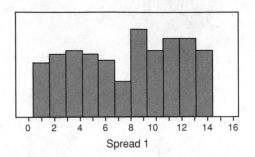

Spread 1

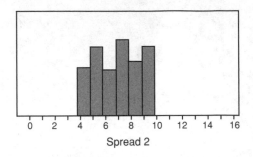

Spread 2

When we speak of unusual features of a distribution, we are looking for **gaps** and/or **outliers**. Gaps are spaces between clusters of data. Outliers are values that fall out of the overall pattern of the distribution. In the graph on the left below, there is a clear gap between two clusters of data. In the graph on the right, there are a couple of observations that are outliers—they fall outside the overall pattern of the distribution. In Section B we will quantify what constitutes an outlier. For now, "eyeballing" it will suffice.

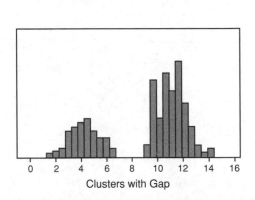

Clusters with Gap

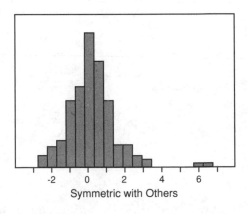

Symmetric with Others

Remember, when describing distributions think *center*, *spread*, *shape*, and *outliers/unusual features*.

Constructing Displays of Quantitative Data

A **dotplot** is a quick method to plot small sets of data, usually discrete, that are not too spread out. Computer software can make dotplots of large sets of data, but doing so by hand takes time. The dotplot below represents the number of people living in a house for 15 residences on a particular block in a small town.

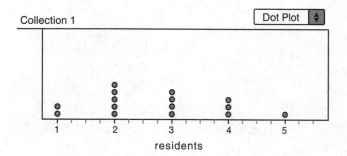

Each dot represents one house, and the number of dots in each column represents how many houses have a certain number of residents. There are two houses with one resident in the house, five houses with two residents, and so on.

Example: Describe the distribution below of the number of people living in the 15 residences.

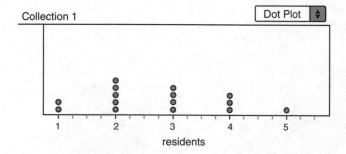

Answer: The distribution has a shape slightly skewed to the right with a peak at two residents. The data seem to be centered at three residents and the range of the data is four residents. There are no extreme values present or gaps within the data.

A **histogram** is an appropriate display for quantitative data. It is used primarily for continuous data, but may be used for discrete data that have a wide spread. The horizontal axis is broken into intervals or **bins**. Histograms are also good for large data sets. The histogram below shows the amount of money spent by passengers on a board ship during a recent cruise to Alaska.

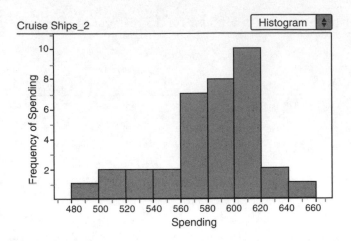

The bins have widths of $20. One person spent between $480 and $500, two spent between $500 and $520, and so on. We cannot tell from the graph the precise amounts each individual spent.

Example: Describe the distribution below of the amount spent by passengers on board a ship during a recent cruise to Alaska.

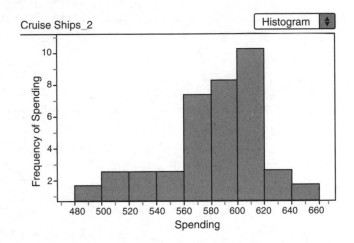

Answer: The distribution has a shape skewed to the left with a peak around $600 to $620. The data are centered at about $590—this is about where half of the observations will be to the left and half to the right. The range of the data is about $180, but the clear majority of passengers spent between $560 and $620. There are no extreme values present or gaps within the data.

The vertical axis on the previous histogram is of count or frequency. It can also be a relative frequency or percentage. This is often useful if a data set is very large. Below is an example of a relative frequency histogram.

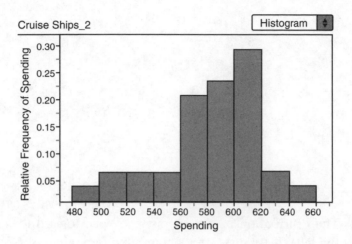

A **stemplot**, also called stem-and-leaf plot, can be used to display univariate data as well. It is good for small sets of data (about 50 or less) and forms a plot much like a histogram. The stemplot below represents test scores for a class of 32 students.

```
  3 | 3
  4 |
  5 |
  6 | 3 7 9
  7 | 2 2 5 7
  8 | 1 2 6 8 8 8 9 9 9
  9 | 0 0 0 1 3 3 4 5 5 6 7
 10 | 0 0 0 0
Key: 6 | 3 represents a score of 63
```

The values on the left of the vertical bar are called the stems; those on the right are called leaves. Stems and leaves need not be tens and ones—they may be hundreds and tens, ones and tenths, and so on. A good stemplot always includes a key for the reader so that the values may be interpreted correctly.

Example: Describe the distribution of test scores for students in the class using the stemplot below.

```
 3 | 3
 4 |
 5 |
 6 | 3 7 9
 7 | 2 2 5 7
 8 | 1 2 6 8 8 8 9 9 9
 9 | 0 0 0 1 3 3 4 5 5 6 7
10 | 0 0 0 0
```
Key: 6 | 3 represents a score of 63

Answer: The distribution of test scores is skewed toward lower values (to the left). It is centered at about 89 with a range of 67. There is an extreme low value at 33, which appears to be an outlier. Without it, the range is only 37, about half as much.

Sometimes, the shape of a stemplot is hard to describe because one has only a few stems but many leaves. Consider the plot below.

```
1 | 0 0 1 4 4 5 6 6 8 8 9
2 | 2 2 3 3 7 7 8
3 | 0 0 1 1 1 3 3 4 5 5 5 6 6 7 7 7 7 9
4 | 0 0 0 0 1 1 1 2 2 3 3 4 5 6 6 6 8 8 8 8 8 9 9 9
```

A split-stem plot is the solution. "Split" the stems by having two stems of "1," two of "2," and so on. Leaves with values 0–4 would be placed in the first of the split stems and values 5–9 would be placed in the second of the split stems.

```
1 | 0 0 1 4 4
1 | 5 6 6 8 8 9
2 | 2 2 3 3
2 | 7 7 8
3 | 0 0 1 1 1 3 3 4
3 | 5 5 5 6 6 7 7 7 7 9
4 | 0 0 0 0 1 1 1 2 2 3 3 4
4 | 5 6 6 6 8 8 8 8 8 9 9 9
```

If we did not split the stems, it would be more difficult to view the shape of the distribution.

Calculator Tip:

Many graphs and functions for univariate data can be done on the graphing calculator, but the observations must be first entered into a list. We will use the test scores of the 32 students from a previous example: 33, 63, 67, 69, 72, 72, 75, 77, 81, 82, 86, 88, 88, 88, 89, 89, 89, 90, 90, 90, 91, 93, 93, 94, 95, 95, 96, 97, 100, 100, 100, 100.

From the home screen, press $\boxed{\text{STAT}}$.

```
EDIT CALC TESTS
1:Edit...
2:SortA(
3:SortD(
4:ClrList
5:SetUpEditor
```

Choose 1:**Edit**. This brings you into the main list editor.

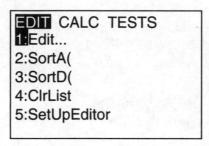

Enter the data into the list that you are going to use. For now, use L1. Press $\boxed{\text{ENTER}}$ after each entry to move to the next line.

```
L1       L2       L3       1
 33      ------   ------
 63
 67
 69
 72
 72
L1(7)=
```

Continue to type in values until the list is complete. Note that the cursor is on the last entry, which in this case is 100, that is the 32nd entry into this list.

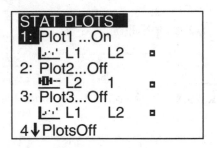

Calculator Tip:

Histograms can be made from data in lists. From the home screen, press $\boxed{2^{nd}}$ $\boxed{\text{STAT PLOT}}$, and then choose 1:Plot1....

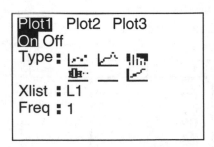

Turn on the plot by pressing $\boxed{\text{ENTER}}$ when the cursor is over On. Arrow right to the third type of plot, which is a histogram. Press $\boxed{\text{ENTER}}$ so that it is highlighted. Arrow down to Xlist: and press $\boxed{2^{nd}}$ $\boxed{\text{L1}}$. On the Freq: line, enter 1, if it is not already so. (This is the frequency of each value in Xlist and is used if two lists act as a frequency table.)

Press ZOOM 9 to see the graph. The calculator will sometimes choose bin widths that are hard to use.

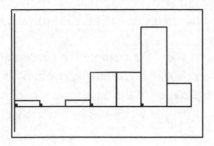

Press WINDOW . A bin width of 5 or 10 may make more sense in this situation than the one of 11.16. Change Xmin, Xmax, Xscl, Ymin, Ymax, and Yscl to the values shown below on the right. Xscl is the width of your bins, beginning at Xmin. An appropriate window for these data is shown on the screen below.

```
WINDOW
 Xmin=33
 Xmax=111.16666...
 Xscl=11.166666...
 Ymin=-4.20966
 Ymax=16.38
 Yscl=.1
 Xres=1
```

```
WINDOW
 Xmin=30
 Xmax=105
 Xscl=5
 Ymin=-4
 Ymax=15
 Yscl=1
 Xres=1
```

Press GRAPH to view the histogram.

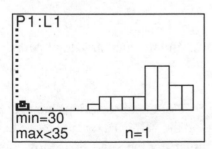

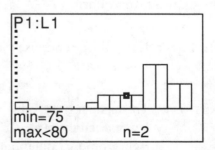

You can use the TRACE button and arrows to view the frequencies of each bin.

Note: Before making a plot, it is good practice to make sure that any function entered into the Y= editor is turned off or deleted so that it does not interfere with the plots that will be graphed. You can turn off a function by pressing Y= ; arrow to the function you want turned off by placing the cursor over "=" next to that function, and then press ENTER to deselect it. Now, it will not interfere with your plot.

The display used to show the cumulative percentage of values in a distribution is a **cumulative relative frequency graph**. This type of plot shows the sums of the relative frequencies of the data from smallest to largest. The display below shows the ages of people who took a river cruise.

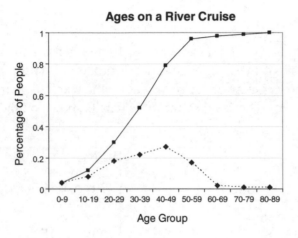

The dotted line represents the percentage of passengers in each age group; the solid line represents the cumulative percentage up to and including that age group. The last age group (80–89) has a cumulative percentage of 100, which means that all of the people on the cruise were aged 89 and below. A cumulative relative frequency graph helps us locate what percentage of a distribution is at or below a given value.

Example: Using the river cruise plot above, find the median age of people on this cruise.

Answer: The median is the value where 50% of the observations are at or below it. Find the 50% (0.5) mark on the vertical axis, and move to the right from that point until you intersect the solid line. Move down from that point to the horizontal axis, which shows the age group on the cruise. In this case the median is in the age group from 30 to 39. We cannot be sure exactly where it is in that interval.

Trial Run

1. A plant manager records the number of times an assembly line is shut down each day for 25 days. A dotplot of the data is shown below.

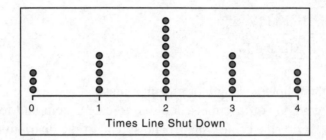

    Describe the shape of the distribution.

    (A) Skewed right

    (B) Symmetric

    (C) Skewed left

    (D) Uniform

    (E) Bimodal

2. Which of the following types of data are categorical?

    (A) Heights of students in your class

    (B) Colors of the vehicles in the school parking lot

    (C) Ages of major league baseball players

    (D) Number of pets in each household in a neighborhood

    (E) Scores on a final exam

3. In which of the situations listed would a histogram be an appropriate data display?

    I.   The data are categorical.

    II. The data are quantitative.

III. The data are discrete.

IV. The data are continuous.

(A) I only

(B) II and III only

(C) II and IV only

(D) II, III, and IV only

(E) I, II, III, and IV

4. Given the following length of time in minutes it takes 20 students to get to school who do not take the school bus, create a stem-and-leaf plot of the data. Describe the center, shape, and spread of the distribution.

15	13	17	16	35	27	5	16	18	21
37	12	25	7	23	50	2	36	59	5

Trial Run Solutions

1. B. The distribution is symmetric.

2. B. Colors are categorical as they are not counts or measures.

3. D. Histograms are used to display the distribution of quantitative data, either discrete or continuous.

4.

```
0 | 2 5 5 7
1 | 2 3 5 6 6 7 8
2 | 1 3 5 7
3 | 5 6 7
4 |
5 | 0 9
```
Key: Stem—tens, leaf—ones

The distribution is skewed to the right (toward the higher values). The distribution is centered around 17 or 18 minutes. The range is 57 minutes, and it seems to take most students less than 30 minutes to get to school. There is a gap between 37 and 50 that should be investigated—two students need 50 or more minutes; these are extreme values. Without those extremes, the range is 35 minutes.

B. SUMMARIZING DISTRIBUTIONS OF UNIVARIATE DATA

Measuring Center: Mean and Median

The mean and median are **measures of center**. They locate the middle or the center of a distribution.

The **mean** is the average of a data set. The mean is calculated by the formula, $\bar{x} = \dfrac{\sum x_i}{n}$, where n is the number of observations in the data set, and x_i represents individual observations counting from 1 to n. The summation symbol, Σ, is the command to add up the expression following it.

Example: The weights (in pounds) of 10 jockeys that are going to race at Arlington Park are 113, 117, 112, 113.5, 115.8, 114, 114.6, 113.5, 112.4, and 113. Calculate the mean weight of the jockeys.

Answer:
$$\bar{x} = \frac{\sum x_i}{n}$$
$$= \frac{113+117+112+113.5+115.8+114+114.6+113.5+112.4+113}{10}$$
$$= \frac{1138.8}{10}$$
$$= 113.88 \text{ pounds.}$$

The **median** is the middle number of a data set that has been arranged from the smallest to largest value or vice versa. If there is an even number of values in the data set, the median is the mean of the two in the middle.

Example: What is the median of the data set 4, 5, 5, 6, 6, 7, 7, 7, 9?

Answer: The median is 6 since it is the middle value.

Example: What are the mean and median of the set 4, 5, 5, 6, 6, 7, 7, 7, 9, 10?

Answer: The median is 6.5 since the mean of the middle two numbers, 6 and 7, is 6.5. Note that the median does not have to be one of the data points. The mean is the sum of the data divided by the number of data, or $\dfrac{66}{10} = 6.6$.

The median is a better measure of center if the data set has outliers or is skewed in any way. The maximum value in the previous example was 10. If it were larger, the median would not be affected, but the mean would, since the mean is computed using the actual values of the data.

Example: What are the mean and median of the set 4, 5, 5, 6, 6, 7, 7, 7, 9, 30?

Answer: The median is still 6.5, as it was in the previous example. The median is not affected by extreme values or outliers. The mean for the data set is 8.6.

The shape of a distribution can tell us about the relationship between the mean and median. In symmetric distributions, the mean and median are close to the same. In skewed distributions, the mean is "pulled" away from the median toward the tail. Since the mean is based on the values of the data, it tends to go toward more extreme values, which in skewed distributions are located in the tail.

Example: Estimate the median of each distribution shown below and describe how the mean compares to it.

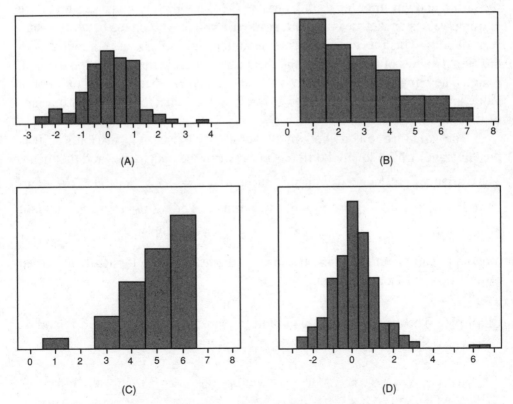

Answer: Graph (a) is symmetric with a median at about 0. The mean will also be about 0. Graph (b) is right-skewed with a median of about 3. The mean will be pulled more toward the values of 4–7 than it will be toward 1–2, so the mean will be greater than 3. Graph (c) is left-skewed with a median of 5. The mean will be pulled toward the lower values, so it is less than 5. Graph (d) is symmetric with a few extreme high values. The median is about 0, and the mean will be just slightly larger because of the outliers.

Measuring Spread: Range, Interquartile Range, Standard Deviation, Variance, and Outliers

In addition to measures of center, distributions need to be described with measures of **variability**. It is not enough to know where the middle of a distribution is, but also how spread out it is. A manufacturer of light bulbs would like small variability in the amount of hours the bulbs will likely burn. A coach who needs to decide which athletes go on to the finals may want larger variability in heat times because it will be easier to decide who are truly the fastest runners.

For data that are fairly **symmetric** and not affected by outliers, **standard deviation** and **variance** are useful measures of variability. For data sets that have extreme values or skewness, the **interquartile range** would be a better measure of variability. This is because standard deviation and variance are computed with the actual values of the data, like the mean. Interquartile range, like the median, is not. The **range** of a data set is simply the difference between the maximum value and the minimum value, and is rarely a good choice, especially because of it being affected by outliers.

The **variance** tells us how much variability exists in a distribution. It is the "average" of the squared differences between the data values and the mean. The variance is calculated with the formula $s^2 = \dfrac{1}{n-1}\sum (x_i - \bar{x})^2$. The standard deviation is the square root of the variance. The formula for the standard deviation is therefore $s = \sqrt{\dfrac{1}{n-1}\sum (x_i - \bar{x})^2}$. The standard deviation is used for most applications in statistics. It can be thought of as the typical distance an observation lies from the mean.

Example: The average monthly rainfall in inches in Birmingham, England, is shown in the table below.

Jan	Feb	Mar	Apr	May	Jun	Jul	Aug	Sep	Oct	Nov	Dec
2.3	1.9	2.1	1.8	2.2	2.2	2.0	2.8	2.2	2.1	2.5	2.6

Compute the variance and standard deviation of the monthly rainfall.

Answer: To compute the variance and standard deviation, the mean must first be computed. In this data set, $\bar{x} = \dfrac{26.7}{12} = 2.225$. The variance is computed as follows:

$$\begin{aligned}
s^2 &= \frac{1}{n-1}\sum(x_i - \bar{x})^2 \\
&= \frac{1}{12-1}(2.3-2.225)^2 + (1.9-2.225)^2 + (2.1-2.225)^2 + \cdots + (2.6-2.225)^2 \\
&= \frac{1}{11}(0.9225) \\
&\approx 0.084.
\end{aligned}$$

The standard deviation is the square root of the variance, or $\sqrt{0.084} \approx 0.290$. The monthly mean rainfall in Birmingham is 2.225 inches and it varies by about 0.29 inches from that each month, sometimes more, sometimes less.

The **five-number summary** is composed of the minimum, maximum, median, **first quartile** (Q_1), and **third quartile** (Q_3) of a data set. The quartiles and the median (which is the second quartile or Q_2) break the data into four equally sized groups. These groups may not have the same spreads, though.

To find Q_1, determine the middle value of all observations below the median in an ordered data set. The value of Q_3 is found at the middle value of all observations above the median of a data set.

The **interquartile range (IQR)** is a measure of variability that works well for data that are skewed or have outliers. The IQR is the spread of the middle 50% of the data and not affected by extreme values. The IQR is calculated by $Q_3 - Q_1$. The interquartile range is a single value, like the range.

Example: Find the five-number summary and interquartile range of the data set 4, 5, 5, 6, 6, 7, 7, 7, 9, 30.

Answer: The minimum value is 4, the maximum is 30, and the median is 6.5. The first quartile is the middle of the five values below the median, or 5. The third quartile is the middle of the five values above the median, or 7. The five-number summary is min = 4, Q_1 = 5, median = 6.5, Q_3 = 7, max = 30.

The interquartile range is $Q_3 - Q_1 = 7 - 5 = 2$

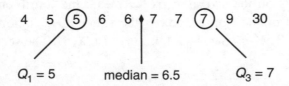

Calculator Tip:

Summary statistics can be computed using the graphing calculator. We will compute these values for the rainfall data from Birmingham, England.

Jan	Feb	Mar	Apr	May	Jun	Jul	Aug	Sep	Oct	Nov	Dec
2.3	1.9	2.1	1.8	2.2	2.2	2.0	2.8	2.2	2.1	2.5	2.6

From the home screen, press $\boxed{\text{STAT}}$. Choose 1:Edit. Enter the data into L1.

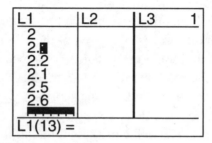

Press $\boxed{\text{2nd}}$ $\boxed{\text{QUIT}}$ to return to the home screen.

Press $\boxed{\text{STAT}}$, arrow right to CALC, and then choose 1:Var Stats. Press $\boxed{\text{2nd}}$ $\boxed{\text{L}_1}$ and then press $\boxed{\text{ENTER}}$.

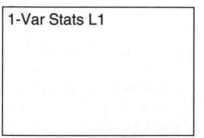

The first entry on the screen, $\bar{x}$, is the mean; the fourth entry Sx is the standard deviation of the sample. (σx is the standard deviation if this is an entire population.) The sample size, n, is also displayed. The second and third values, Σx and Σx^2, are the sum of the data and the sum of the squared data, respectively.

```
1-Var Stats
  x̄=2.225
  Σx=26.7
  Σx²=60.33
  Sx=.2895921897
  σx=.2772634127
↓ n=12
```

Arrowing down gives the five-number summary.

```
1-Var Stats
↑ n=12
  minX=1.8
  Q1=2.05
  Med=2.2
  Q3=2.4
■ maxX=2.8
```

Outliers are extreme values that do not fall within the general pattern of the data. A common rule for determining whether an observation is an outlier is the 1.5*IQR* rule. If an observation is farther than 1.5*IQR* above the third quartile, or farther than 1.5*IQR* below the first quartile, it is considered an outlier. Those boundaries at $Q_1 - 1.5IQR$ and $Q_3 + 1.5IQR$ are called "fences." Outliers are points lying outside the fences.

Example: The salaries of the New York Yankees (in thousands of dollars) can be summarized by the five-number summary:

Minimum	Q_1	Median	Q_3	Maximum
323	2,375	5,667	12,678	26,000

Would the maximum or minimum salaries be considered outliers?

Answer: The interquartile range of the salaries is $12{,}678 - 2{,}375 = 10{,}303$. The lower outlier fence is located at
$Q_1 - 1.5IQR = 2{,}375 - 1.5(10{,}303) = -13{,}709.5$.
The upper outlier fence is located at
$Q_3 + 1.5IQR = 12{,}678 + 1.5(10{,}303) = 28{,}132.5$.
Neither the minimum nor the maximum values are beyond the fences, and are therefore not considered outliers.

Constructing Box-and-Whisker Plots

A **box-and-whisker plot**, or more simply a **boxplot**, is a graphical display of the five-number summary and any outliers. The "box" of the boxplot is drawn from the first quartile to the third quartile and then is split into two sections by the median. The box shows the spread of the middle half of the data. Whiskers are usually extended from the ends of the box to the minimum and maximum values. If outliers are present, as determined by the $1.5IQR$ rule, the whiskers only extend to the most extreme values inside the fences. Outliers are then plotted as points by themselves.

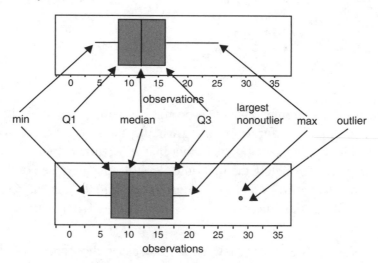

Example: The salaries of the New York Yankees (in thousands of dollars) can be summarized by the five-number summary:

Minimum	Q_1	Median	Q_3	Maximum
323	2,375	5,667	12,678	26,000

Construct a box-and-whisker plot for the distribution and describe its shape.

Answer: We saw in the previous example that there are no outliers. So, we merely need to plot these five values to scale.

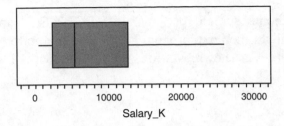

The shape of the distribution is skewed right. Each quarter of the data, moving from low salaries to high salaries, has a wider spread than the previous one. The data cluster toward the left and spread out toward the right—a right skew.

A graphing calculator boxplot and histogram are shown below to emphasize this point.

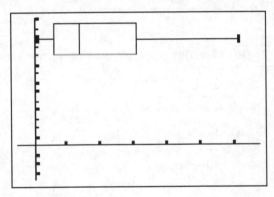

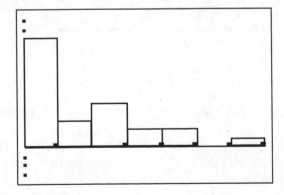

Calculator Tip:

Boxplots can be created on the graphing calculator. The Birmingham weather data have been entered into L1.

Jan	Feb	Mar	Apr	May	Jun	Jul	Aug	Sep	Oct	Nov	Dec
2.3	1.9	2.1	1.8	2.2	2.2	2.0	2.8	2.2	2.1	2.5	2.6

From the home screen, press 2nd STAT PLOT and then choose 1:Plot1.... Highlight the boxplot icon, leftmost in the bottom row. Complete the rest of the entries as shown. Mark: is the symbol that will show outliers, if any exist.

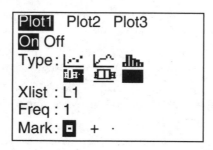

Press ZOOM 9 to see the graph in an appropriate viewing window.

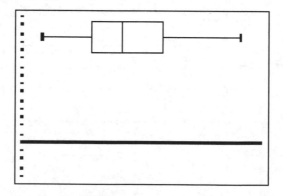

Measuring Position: Quartiles, Percentiles, Standardized scores

Quartiles (discussed previously) are measures of **position**. They give information relating the location of a point in a data set or population to the rest of the group. Recall that quartiles divide the data into four equally sized parts.

Percentiles are another measure of position. They divide the data set into 100 equal parts. An observation at the Pth percentile is higher than P percent of all observations. If you took a standardized test and your score was in the 83rd percentile, 83% of the people that took the same test scored lower than you. If you scored in the 83rd percentile on another standardized test, you were still in the same position relative to everyone else on *that* test. The size of the population that took the test may have changed, but that is not indicated in the percentile score.

Standardized scores, or **z-scores,** are a way to measure where an individual in a population stands relative to the mean by using the standard deviation as a unit of measure. z-scores measure how many standard deviations away from the mean (in either direction) an observation is.

A z-score is calculated by the formula $z = \dfrac{\text{observation} - \text{mean}}{\text{standard deviaton}}$. z-scores that are positive represent observations that are greater than the mean; negative z-scores represent observations that are less than the mean.

Example: You scored an 87 on a test in your Statistics class where the mean was 85 and the standard deviation was 3. Your best friend is in a different Statistics class and scored a 90 where the mean in her class was 88 and the standard deviation was 4. Who had the better score relative to their own class?

Answer: For you, $z = \dfrac{87 - 85}{3} = 0.667$. For your friend, $z = \dfrac{90 - 88}{4} = 0.5$. You scored better relative to your class since your z-score is larger. The z-scores represent how many standard deviations from the mean each of your scores were.

Computer Printout of Summary Statistics

You will sometimes be given a computer printout summarizing a set of data. The output is fairly easy to read, but there are some things of which you should be aware. Below is a sample computer printout.

N	Mean	Median	TrMean	StDev	SEMean
80	4.58	4.04	4.37	2.99	0.33

Min	Max	Q1	Q3
0.46	13.63	2.15	6.56

The sample size (N), mean, median, standard deviation (StDev), mininum, maximum, first quartile, and third quartile are easily identified. The two values we have not covered in this section are TrMean and SEMean.

TrMean is the "trimmed mean." It is usually the mean of the middle 90% of the observations—potential outliers have been "trimmed" off. SEMean is the "standard error of the mean." It will be covered in more detail in Chapters 3 and 4.

The Effect of Changing Units on Summary Measures

Changing units will change measures of center and spread by the same ratio as the multiplier.

Example: The weights (in pounds) of 10 jockeys that are going to race at Arlington Park are 113, 117, 112, 113.5, 115.8, 114, 114.6, 113.5, 112.4, and 113. Summary statistics are as follows: mean = 113.88, standard deviation = 1.54, median = 113.5, IQR = 1.6.
If the jockey's weights were converted from pounds to kilograms (2.2 pounds = 1 kilogram), what would the new summary measures be?

Answer: Converting each observation from pounds to kilograms (dividing by 2.2), we get

Pounds	113	117	112	113.5	115.8	114	114.6	113.5	112.4	113
Kilograms	51.4	53.2	50.9	51.6	52.6	51.8	52.1	51.6	51.1	51.3

The new summary measures are as follows:

	Pounds	Kilograms
Mean	113.88	51.76
Standard deviation	1.54	0.70
Median	113.5	51.6
IQR	1.6	0.73

Each of the summary measures in kilograms is the equivalent measure in pounds divided by 2.2. It is not necessary to convert the individual observations. One only need convert the summary measures.

Adding or subtracting the same constant to or from each will change measures of center in a similar manner, but will not change measures of spread.

Example: Each jockey's clothes and saddle add about 4 pounds to the weight placed on the horse. What are the summary statistics for the weight of the 10 jockeys plus their equipment?

Answer: One need not add 4 pounds to each jockey's weight and recompute the summary statistics. Measures of center will increase by

4 pounds, and measures of spread will not change. The summary measures are as follows:

	Jockey	Jockey plus equipment
Mean	113.88	117.88
Standard deviation	1.54	1.54
Median	113.5	117.5
IQR	1.6	1.6

Trial Run

1. The computer printout of summary statistics for a set of data is given below.

N	Mean	Median	TrMean	StDev	SEMean
80	4.58	4.04	4.37	2.99	0.33

Min	Max	Q1	Q3
0.46	13.63	2.15	6.56

Which of the following is true of the distribution of the data?

(A) It is symmetric with no outliers.

(B) It is right-skewed with at least one outlier.

(C) It is left-skewed with at least one outlier.

(D) It is right-skewed with no outliers.

(E) The distribution's shape cannot be determined without having the original data.

2. Math placement tests for a certain state university system are approximately normally distributed with a mean of 78 and a standard deviation of 6.5. If John's z-score is 1.69, what was his score on the test?

(A) 68

(B) 78

(C) 84

(D) 86

(E) 89

3. We know that the mean weight of nine body-builders is 265 pounds. We have the following list of weights for the first eight athletes but have lost the weight for Big Ned. What does Ned weigh?

    Weights: 250, 282, 260, 245, 237, 291, 249, 291, ?

    (A) 210

    (B) 233

    (C) 265

    (D) 280

    (E) 295

4. If the mean for a college entrance examination is currently 34 and the standard deviation is 1.7, what would the new mean and standard deviation be if each individual's score is increased by 1.5?

    (A) 34, 1.7

    (B) 34, 2.2

    (C) 35.5, 1.7

    (D) 35.5, 2.2

    (E) 35.5, 3.2

5. Which of the following distributions will have the smallest standard deviation, assuming that none contain outliers?

    (A) A uniform distribution of integers with a mean of 5 and a range of 10.

    (B) A bell-shaped distribution of integers with a mean of 5 and a range of 10.

    (C) A right-skewed distribution of integers with a mean of 4 and a range of 10.

    (D) All three distributions have equal standard deviations.

    (E) The answer cannot be determined from the information given.

6. The mean monthly rainfall (in inches) for Las Vegas, Nevada, is listed below.

Jan	Feb	Mar	Apr	May	Jun	Jul	Aug	Sep	Oct	Nov	Dec
0.48	0.47	0.42	0.21	0.28	0.12	0.35	0.49	0.28	0.21	0.43	0.38

    Compute the mean, variance, and standard deviation of the monthly rainfall.

7. Consider the length of time (in minutes) it takes 20 students to get to school who do not take the school bus. 15, 13, 17, 16, 35, 27, 5, 16, 18, 21, 5, 37, 12, 25, 7, 23, 50, 2, 36, 59

   (a) One student takes 59 minutes to get to school. Would you consider this an outlier? Provide statistical support for your conclusion.

   (b) Construct the boxplot for this set of data.

   (c) Describe the distribution.

8. Max is in Mrs. Jones' first-period science class. Allison is in Mrs. Jones' second-period science class. Max earned an 80% on the last test where the mean in that class was 77% and the standard deviation was 5. Allison earned a 79% on the same test but the mean in her class was also 77% with a standard deviation of 4. Who scored better relative to their own class? Show statistical support for your conclusion.

Trial Run Solutions

1. B. It is right-skewed with at least one outlier. The *IQR* is $6.56 - 2.15 = 4.41$. There are clearly no low outliers, since the minimum value is less than the *IQR* below Q_1. The upper fence is at $Q_3 + 1.5IQR = 6.56 + 1.5(4.41) = 13.175$. The maximum value of 13.63 is greater than this fence; this value is an outlier. There may be more, but we cannot tell without the raw data. Also, a boxplot would look

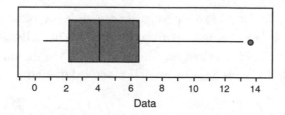

something like this. Clearly, this is a right-skewed distribution. Finally, the mean is greater than the median, which gives evidence, but not certainty, that the distribution is skewed right.

2. E. Set up the equation $1.69 = \dfrac{x - 78}{6.5}$ and solve for *x*;

   $x = 1.69 (6.5) + 78 = 88.985$.

3. D. The mean is the sum of the eight known weights plus Ned's, all divided
    by 9. Set up the equation $\dfrac{2105+x}{9} = 265$ and solve for x; $x = 280$.

4. C. The mean would change by 1.5 units but the standard deviation would
    remain the same. Adding or subtracting only affects center, not spread.

5. B. The distributions would look something like this.

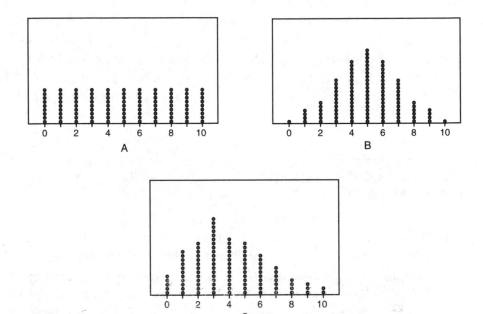

Standard deviation is a measure of spread. It is a measure of the typical
distance an observation lies from the mean. The bell-shaped distribution
has more of the distribution near the mean than the uniform or skewed
distributions, so it has the smaller standard deviation.

6. Entering the 12 data values into a list on the graphing calculator and
    using the 1-Var Stats function, gives $\bar{x} = 0.343$ and $s = 0.122$. The vari-
    ance is $s^2 = 0.015$.

7. (a) Calculate the five-number summary using your calculator. The inter-
    quartile range is $IQR = Q_3 - Q_1 = 31 - 12.5 = 18.5$. The upper fence
    is $Q_3 + 1.5IQR = 31 + 1.5(18.5) = 58.75$. The observation 59 minutes
    is greater than the upper fence, so it is an outlier.

(b) The boxplot is a graph of the five-number summary drawn to scale. The box sets between 12.5 minutes and 31 minutes, with the median dividing it at 17.5 minutes. The lower whisker extends to the minimum of 2 minutes; the upper whisker extends to the largest nonoutlier, which is 50 minutes. The outlier at 59 minutes is marked as a single point.

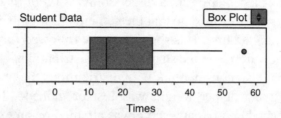

(c) The distribution is right-skewed, centered at 17.5 minutes, with an interquartile range of 18.5 minutes. The middle half of the data lie between 12.5 minutes and 31 minutes. There is one outlier at 59 minutes. Most students made it to school in 18 minutes or less; about 75% took a half hour or less.

8. Set up standardized score calculations: $z = \dfrac{80 - 77}{5} = 0.6$ and $z = \dfrac{79 - 77}{4} = 0.5$. The standard score of 0.6 is larger and further to the right of the mean, so Max scored better relative to his own class.

C. COMPARING DISTRIBUTIONS OF UNIVARIATE DATA (DOT-PLOTS, BACK-TO-BACK STEMPLOTS, PARALLEL BOXPLOTS)

When comparing two or more sets of univariate data it is important to look at similarities and differences between the groups as well as any interesting features within the groups. When making comparisons, be clear about your statements. If you mention that one distribution has a center of 16 and the other distribution has a center of 20, a direct comparison of that relationship should be stated. In other words, state that the center is four units larger for the second distribution than the first. This should also be followed for measures of spread, measures of location, and the shapes of the distributions.

You must also consider that both distributions may be compared to some benchmark, like whether weight was lost or gained—the benchmark is no change—or whether a passing score was attained on an exam. Sometimes this benchmark may be subtly implied; sometimes it will be explicitly stated.

The keys to remember: *center, spread, shape,* and *outliers/unusual features*.

Example: The weight loss of 30 people for 1 week on Diet Plan X is shown in the first dotplot and the weight loss of 30 people for 1 week on Diet Plan Y is shown in the second dotplot. A positive value represents a loss in weight; a negative value represents a gain in weight. Compare the two diet plans.

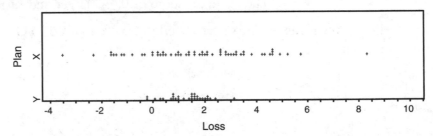

Answer: Both distributions are fairly symmetric with Diet Plan X having an average weight loss of around 1.8 pounds while Diet Plan Y has an average weight loss of around 1.4 pounds. People on Plan X lost an average of 0.4 pounds more than Plan Y.

There is more variability in Plan X than in Plan Y. The overall spread of Plan X is about three times that of Plan Y, and Plan X has one extremely high value. Even though the average loss for Plan Y is less than Plan X, Plan Y only had 2 people actually gain weight whereas Plan X had 10 people gain weight, and Plan Y's gains were much smaller. More people lost larger amounts of weights with Plan X than with Plan Y.

Note: You may be asked on the exam which diet plan you would consider using for weight loss. It would be important to mention the fact that even though Plan Y had only a few people that lost small amounts of weights as compared to Plan X, you still might consider Plan X since many people lost larger amounts of weights. No matter which you choose, you must complete your reasoning with reference to *both* diet plans, not just the one you are choosing.

Example: Below are parallel boxplots representing pretest and posttest scores for a written driving learner's permit test where 8 represents the score needed to receive a learner's permit. Students took a weekend class on driver safety before taking the posttest. Compare the two distributions.

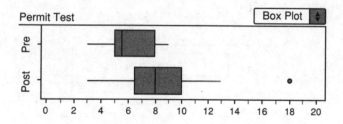

Answer: Both distributions are fairly symmetric overall, but the middle half of the pretest scores may have some skew. The posttest scores contain a high outlier at 18. The average on the posttest was about 2.5 points higher than the pretest—8 vs. 5.5. The posttest scores are more variable than the pretest scores, having nearly double the spread, not counting the outlier. Only one-fourth of the test takers scored well enough on the pretest to get a permit whereas half of the test takers on the posttest scored well enough to get a permit. It appears that the training course improved scores on the test overall.

Calculator Tip:

The graphing calculator can display parallel boxplots. Two sets of data have been entered into the following lists:

L1: 13, 15, 15, 15, 16, 18, 19, 20, 20, 22, 25, 28, 30, 31, 31, 35, 38, 39, 40, 43

L2: 28, 30, 33, 34, 36, 36, 37, 39, 40, 43, 43, 44, 44, 46, 47, 48, 48, 49, 52, 53

From the home screen, press 2nd STAT PLOT . Set up Plot1 and Plot2 for boxplots where Plot1 will display the data in L1 and Plot2 will display the data in L2.

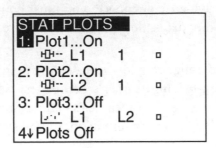

Press ZOOM 9 to view both plots on the same scale of an appropriate viewing window.

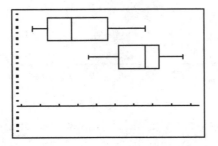

Trial Run

1. Which of the following four sets of data have the smallest and largest standard deviations?

I	II	III	IV
1	1	1	1
2	5	1	3
3	5	1	3
4	5	1	3
5	5	5	5
6	5	9	7

7	5	9	7
8	5	9	7
9	9	9	9

(A) Smallest II; largest I

(B) Smallest II; largest III

(C) Smallest II; largest IV

(D) Smallest III; largest I

(E) Smallest IV; largest I

2. Which histogram represents the same set of data as the boxplot below?

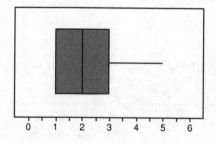

(A)

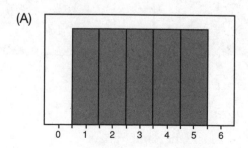

(B)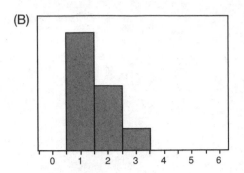

(C)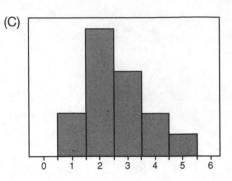

(D)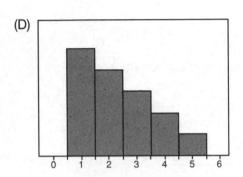

(E)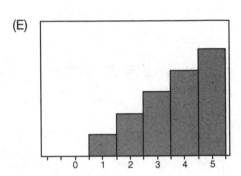

3.   Given the histograms of the distributions of integers below:

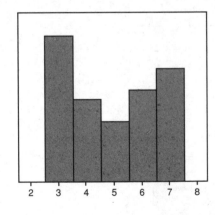 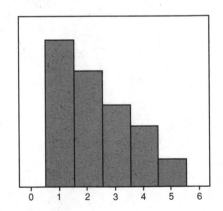

Which of the following statements is true?

I.   Both data sets have the same range.

II.   Both distributions have the same shape.

III.   Both distributions have means greater than the medians.

    (A) I only

    (B) II only

    (C) I and III only

    (D) II and III only

    (E) I, II, and III

4.   The back-to-back stemplot shown below shows the number of compact discs owned by random samples of teenagers that live in the United States and Canada.

United States		Canada
3	1	
9 8 6 5 5 5	1	
2 0 0	2	
8 5	2	8
1 1 0	3	0 3 4
9 8 5	3	6 6 7 9
3 0	4	0 3 3 4 4
	4	6 7 8 8 9
	5	2 3

Which of the following is true of the distributions of the number of CDs owned by teenagers in the two countries?

    (A) There is more variation in the number of CDs owned by teenagers in the United States than Canada.

    (B) The mean is larger than the median for both groups.

    (C) The U.S. group has an outlier and the Canadian group does not.

    (D) Teenagers in the United States own more CDs overall.

    (E) The median of the U.S. group is greater than the median of the Canadian group.

5.   The home game attendance for the first 20 games and the last 20 games of the season for a baseball team are shown below.

First 20 Games	Last 20 Games
33,000	30,000
34,000	30,600

34,400	33,200
36,900	34,600
37,500	34,800
40,100	35,100
41,200	36,000
44,500	39,900
46,200	40,000
46,500	40,200
46,600	41,700
49,100	43,800
51,200	44,000
53,200	44,400
53,400	45,000
53,700	47,000
54,100	47,600
54,400	48,000
54,700	51,700
55,900	54,300

(a)   Construct parallel boxplots of the two distributions. Compare the distributions.

(b)   Construct back-to-back stemplots of the two distributions. Compare the distributions.

(c)   Compare the two types of plots. What information can be obtained from the stemplots that might not be easily obtained from the box-plots and vice versa.

Trial Run Solutions

1.   B. One need not compute the standard deviations to have an idea which is the greatest and which is the least. Standard deviation is a measure of variability from the mean. All four sets have a mean of 5. Set II has the most data clustering around the mean; Set III has the least. The actual standard deviations are 2.7, 2.0, 4.0, and 2.6.

2.   D. The distribution is right-skewed, so choices A and E are incorrect. The minimum is 1 and the maximum is 5, so choice B is incorrect. The boxplot has no low whisker, so the minimum and first quartile are the same. This cannot be choice C, as the minimum is 1, but the first quartile is 2. Choice D has both a minimum and first quartile of 1.

3.   A. The histogram on the right is skewed right whereas the one on the left is more symmetrical. In right-skewed distributions, the mean is greater than the median. The mean of the histogram on the left is less than the median—the median is 5, but there are more data with values of 3 and 4 than 6 or 7, so the mean will be less than 5. Both sets have a range of 4.

4.   A. The range for U.S. teenagers is 30, which is larger than the range for Canadian teenagers, which is 25. Also, the United States has more skewness in its distribution than Canada, which would mean a larger standard deviation in distributions with similar ranges. Both sets have the same number of observations, and the center of the U.S. distribution is visibly lower, so the United States will also have a lower total number of CDs. Neither group has an outlier.

5.   (a) Five-number summaries for the two distributions are as follows:

First 20 games—33,000; 38,800; 46,550; 53,550; 55,900

Last 20 games—30,000; 34,950; 40,950; 46,000; 54,300

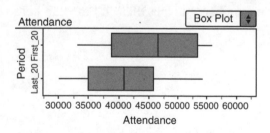

The distribution of the first 20 games has a slight left skew; the distribution of the last 20 games is symmetric. On average, there were about 5,600 more people in attendance per game during the first 20 games of the season than the last 20 games of the season. Overall, the variability of the two groups is almost the same, although the interquartile range of the first 20 games' attendance is about half again as much as the last 20 games.

Three-fourths of the attendance values for the last 20 games are less than the median for the first 20 games. Clearly, the attendance has dropped at the end of the season as compared to the beginning.

(b)

	First 20 Games		Last 20 games
	4 4 3	3	0 1 3
	8 7	3	5 5 5 6
	1 0	4	0 0 0 2 4 4 4
	9 7 7 6 5	4	5 7 8 8
	4 4 4 3 3 1	5	2 4
	6 5	5	

Stem: ten thousands

Leaf: thousands

(attendance rounded to the nearest thousand)

Neither plot shows any extreme values. The last 20 games shows a symmetric shape while the first 20 games has a slight skew to the lower values (left). The average attendance for the first 20 games is greater than the last 20, and the attendance for the first 20 games is more spread out.

(c) The stemplots allow you to view the actual data points whereas the boxplots do not. Some of the detail is lost with boxplots. Also, certain elements of shape or unusual features can be discerned from the stemplot. (Gaps and bimodality do not show up in a boxplot—these characteristics are not present here, however.) Parallel boxplots give a clearer view of where various locations in the data fall relative to each other. For instance, it is easier to compare the quartiles and median in the boxplot than it is in the stemplot.

D. EXPLORING BIVARIATE DATA

Analyzing Patterns in Scatterplots

Bivariate data consist of two variables, between which one is typically looking for an association. The variables may be categorical or quantitative; in this section we will focus on quantitative bivariate data.

The two variables under study are referred to as the **explanatory variable** (*x*) and the **response variable** (*y*). The explanatory variable *explains* or *predicts* the response variable. The response variable measures the outcomes that have been observed.

Example: Data collected from snack foods included the number of grams of fat per serving and the total number of calories in the food. Identify the explanatory and response variables when looking for a relationship between fat grams and calories.

Answer: The explanatory variable is grams of fat and the response variable is calories. The number of grams of fat would be a predictor of the number of calories in the snack.

Scatterplots are used to visualize quantitative bivariate data. These plots can tell us if and how two variables are related. When examining univariate data we described a distribution's shape, center, spread, and outliers/unusual features. In a scatterplot, we will focus on its shape, direction, and strength, and look for outliers and unusual features. Below is a scatterplot of the top 30 leading scorers in the National Basketball Association (NBA). Each point represents 1 of the 30 players. Michael Jordan, who scored 32,292 points in 1,072 games, is noted.

The **shape** of a plot is usually classified as linear or nonlinear (curved). The **direction** of a scatterplot tells what happens to the response variable as the explanatory variable increases. This is the slope of the general pattern of the data. The **strength** describes how tight or spread out the points of a scatterplot are.

The table below shows comparisons of scatterplots of various shapes, directions, and strengths.

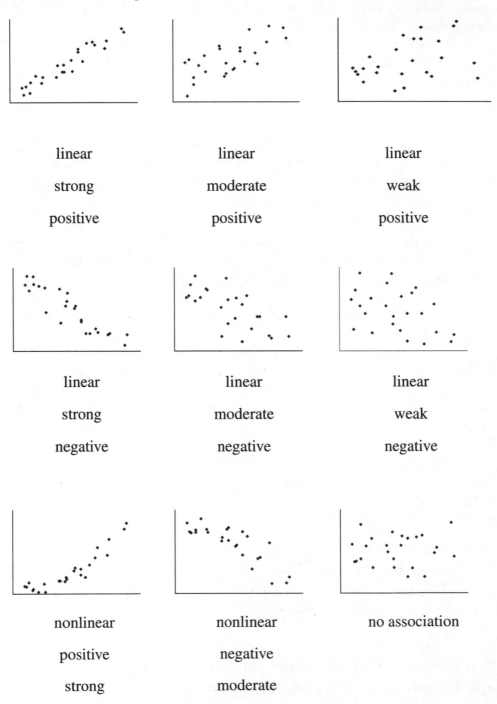

linear	linear	linear
strong	moderate	weak
positive	positive	positive

linear	linear	linear
strong	moderate	weak
negative	negative	negative

nonlinear	nonlinear	no association
positive	negative	
strong	moderate	

When analyzing a scatterplot it is also a good idea to look for outliers, clusters, or gaps in the data. The scatterplot below has an obvious gap. There is an overall positive, linear association but we should find out the reason for the gap.

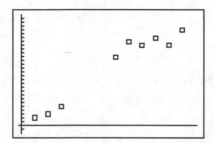

The scatterplot below has an obvious outlier. An outlier falls outside the general pattern of the data. There could be several possible reasons for the outlier and it merits investigation.

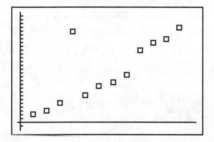

Example: A scatterplot of the top 30 scorers in NBA history is shown below. Identify the explanatory variable and the response variable. Describe the association between the two variables.

NBA Leading Scorers

Answer: The explanatory variable is the number of games played. The response variable is the number of points scored. The relationship is linear, strong, and positive. There are no outliers, but there is a large gap between 1,100 and 1,400 games. The two extreme points, perhaps a couple of players with very long careers, appear to follow the general pattern of the data.

Calculator Tip:

A scatterplot can be viewed on the graphing calculator. First, the data must be entered into lists. Recall that you access the list editor by pressing STAT and then choosing 1:Edit... .

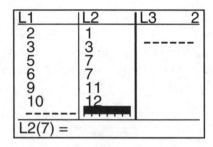

Press 2nd STAT PLOT and choose 1:Plot 1. Turn on the plot, select the scatterplot icon, and enter the appropriate lists for Xlist: and Ylist:.

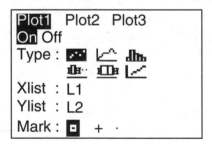

Press ZOOM 9 to see the scatterplot.

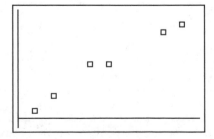

Correlation

The strength of a *linear* association can be measured by the **correlation coefficient**. This notation for correlation is r and is calculated using the following formula: $r = \dfrac{1}{n-1} \sum \left(\dfrac{x_i - \bar{x}}{s_x} \right) \left(\dfrac{y_i - \bar{y}}{s_y} \right)$.

The correlation coefficient is based on the means and standard deviations of the two variables. It is the average product of the standardized scores of x and y for each point. There are several important characteristics of the correlation coefficient.

- Correlation can only be calculated with quantitative variables.

- The value of r has a maximum of 1 and a minimum of –1. When r is exactly 1 or –1, all of the data points fit exactly on a line. A correlation of 0 indicates no linear association. The sign of the correlation indicates the direction of the relationship.

- Correlation does not change when the variables are interchanged, i.e., when the explanatory becomes the response and the response becomes the explanatory.

- Since r is calculated using standardized values, the correlation value will not change if the units of measure are changed (changing pounds to kilograms, for example).

- Correlation only measures strengths of *linear* relationships and is not an appropriate measure for nonlinear data.

- Correlation is not a resistant measure. It is affected by outliers.

Correlation is a unitless number that has no direct interpretation. However, some benchmarks can help us get a feel for the strength of a linear association. Ignoring the sign, correlations less than 0.5 are considered weak, those between 0.5 and 0.8 are considered moderate, and those greater than 0.8 are considered strong. These are not absolute rules, but do give us a frame of reference.

Example: Match each scatterplot below with the correlation that best describes the linear association between the explanatory and response variables.

$r = 0.468$ $r = 0.998$ $r = -0.503$

$r = 0.069$ $r = -0.940$

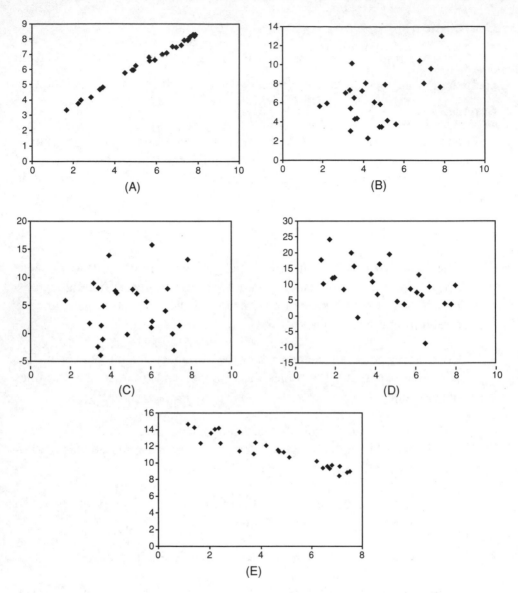

Answer: A. 0.998 B. 0.468 C. 0.069 D. −0.503 E. −0.94
Graph A has the strongest correlation; graph C has the weakest correlation. Graphs B and D have about the same strength; it is only the direction that is different.

Calculator Tip:

The graphing calculator can compute the correlation coefficient.

When using the TI family of graphing calculators, it is important to make sure that the diagnostics feature is turned on in order to view the correlation. You only need to do this once. (You will have to do it again if the calculator is reset or the batteries are changed.)

Press 2nd Catalog and arrow down to DiagnosticOn .

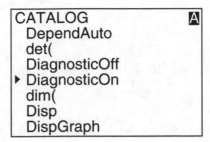

Press ENTER ENTER and the command is done.

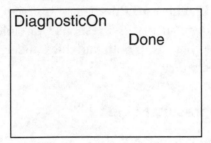

To compute the correlation coefficient the data must be in lists. (This tip uses the data from the previous calculator tip on scatterplots.)

Press STAT , arrow right to CALC, and then choose 8: LinReg (a+bx).

```
EDIT CALC TESTS
5↑QuadReg
6: CubicReg
7: QuartReg
8: LinReg(a+bx)
9: LnReg
0: ExpReg
A↓ PwrReg
```

Enter the list containing x (in this case L1), a comma, and then the list holding y (in this case L2). Press ENTER .

```
LinReg(a+bx) L1,
L2
```

The correlation coefficient is the value of r.

```
LinReg
  y=a+bx
  a=-.9508196721
  b=1.33442623
  r²=.9750654855
  r=.9874540422
```

A strong correlation does *not* mean that there is a cause–effect relationship between the two variables. You need an experiment to justify a cause–effect relationship. There may be other variables that contribute to the relationship seen. One such variable is a **lurking variable**. This is a variable that has a simultaneous effect on both the explanatory and response variables, but was not part of the study. It may cause changes in both variables under study and therefore be the reason for the association.

Least-Squares Regression Line

Linear regression is a method of finding the best model for a linear relationship between the explanatory and response variables. This method calculates the best-fit line by minimizing the sum of the squares of the differences between the observed values and the predicted values from the line. This line is called the **least-squares regression line** or LSRL.

The LSRL has the equation $\hat{y} = b_0 + b_1 x$, where b_0 is the y-intercept of the line and b_1 is the slope. The symbol $\hat{y}$ is read "y-hat" and is the *predicted* value of the response variable y for the explanatory variable x.

The slope and intercept are calculated by the following formulas: $b_1 = r\dfrac{s_y}{s_x}$ and $b_0 = \bar{y} - b_1 \bar{x}$, where $\bar{x}$ and $\bar{y}$ are the means of the explanatory and response variables, respectively; s_x and s_y are the respective standard deviations.

Notation alert! The formulas provided on the AP Statistics Exam use b_0 for the intercept and b_1 for the slope. Graphing calculators and some textbooks use a for intercept and b for slope. You must be able to use these interchangeably.

The least-squares regression line is an *average*. It predicts the mean value of y for a given value of x. This property also means that the least-squares regression line *always* goes through the point $(\bar{x}, \bar{y})$.

Example: The heights (in inches) and shoe sizes for 15 women were recorded. The equation of the least-squares regression line is $\hat{y} = -17.7 + 0.390x$, where x is the height and y is the shoe size. What is the predicted shoe size for a woman 63 inches tall?

Answer: Substitute 63 for height (x) into the equation. The predicted shoe size is $\hat{y} = -17.7 + 0.390x = -17.7 + 0.390\,(63) = 6.87$. Since this is not an actual shoe size, we might conclude that a woman 63 inches tall would wear a shoe of size 6.5 or 7. However, the least-squares regression model predicts the *average* shoe size for 63-inch-tall women to be 6.87.

We would not want to use this model to predict the shoe size of a woman 78 inches tall. Seventy-eight inches is outside the range of the data that were used to fit the model. Using the model to predict that shoe size is called **extrapolation**. Responses predicted in this way could be unreasonable. Shoe sizes may not necessarily increase at the same rate for people over 6 feet tall and under 5 feet tall. Be careful of extrapolation in any model.

The slope of the least-squares regression line is also an average. It describes the mean change in the predicted value of the response variable for a one-unit change in the explanatory variable.

Example: The heights (in inches) and shoe sizes for 15 women were recorded. The equation of the least-squares regression line is $\hat{y} = -17.7 + 0.390x$, where x is the height and y is the shoe size. Interpret the slope of the LSRL.

Answer: The slope is 0.390, which means that for every increase of 1 inch in women's heights, their shoe sizes increase by an average of 0.39.

The **coefficient of determination** or r^2 is another way of indicating how well the linear model fits the data. It is computed by squaring the correlation r. Unlike correlation, though, it does have an interpretation. The value of r^2 is the percent of variation in the response variable that can be explained by its linear relationship with the explanatory variable.

Example: A scatterplot of the heights (in inches) and shoe sizes for 15 women is shown below, along with the least-squares regression line. The value of r^2 is 0.851. Interpret r^2.

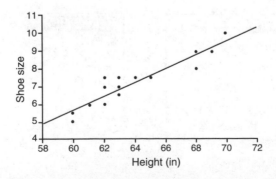

Answer. There is variability in the shoe sizes and there is variability in the heights. In this case, about 85.1% of the variability in the shoe size can be explained by its linear relationship with the height. The other 14.9% is due to other variables not under consideration.

Calculator tip:

The least-squares regression model can be computed with the graphing calculator. This tip uses the previous data lists as shown below.

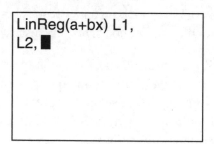

Press, STAT arrow right to CALC, and then choose 8: LinReg (a+bx). Enter the list containing x (in this case L1), a comma, and then the list holding y (in this case L2). *Do not* press ENTER yet.

```
LinReg(a+bx) L1,
L2, ■
```

Now, enter a comma, press VARS, arrow right to Y-VARS, and choose 1:Function…. Then, choose 1:Y1. This will store the equation of the LSRL in Y1.

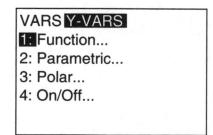

```
LinReg(a+bx) L1,
L2,Y1
```

Press ENTER now. The intercept, slope, coefficient of determination, and correlation are displayed.

```
LinReg
  y=a+bx
  a=-.9508196721
  b=1.33442623
  r²=.9750654855
  r=.9874540422
```

If you press ZOOM 9, you will see the scatterplot and the least-squares regression line overlaid.

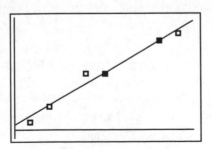

Computer Printout of Least-Squares Regression

On the exam, you may be provided with computer output to interpret. The output below is of the women's height and shoe size data.

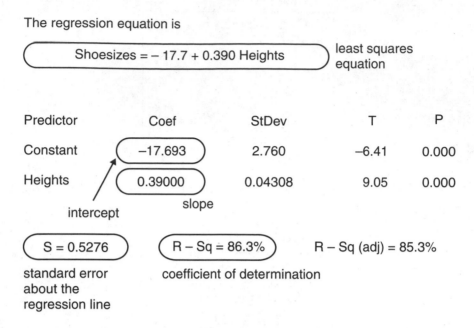

The regression equation is

Shoesizes = − 17.7 + 0.390 Heights   least squares equation

Predictor	Coef	StDev	T	P
Constant	−17.693	2.760	−6.41	0.000
Heights	0.39000	0.04308	9.05	0.000

intercept   slope

S = 0.5276   R − Sq = 86.3%   R − Sq (adj) = 85.3%

standard error about the regression line   coefficient of determination

Note that the correlation coefficient r does not show up on the printout. It can be found by taking the square root of R-Sq(uared): $r = \sqrt{0.863} = 0.929$. Do not forget that the sign of the correlation is the same as the slope, which is positive in this case. Also, it would be best to ignore R-Sq(adj), as its use is not part of the AP Statistics curriculum.

Finally, the value of s is the standard error about the regression line. Like standard deviation is the typical distance a value lies from the mean, the value of s here is the typical vertical distance a point is from the LSRL. If you were to make a prediction, it would give you an estimate of about how much you might over- or underpredict.

Residual Plots, Outliers, and Influential Points

Residuals are the differences between the observed values of the response variable y and the predicted values $\hat{y}$ from the regression model. There is one residual for each point, which is calculated as

residual = observed value − predicted value = $y - \hat{y}$.

After you have fit a model to the data, it is best to examine the graph of the residuals. This is done by plotting the residuals on the vertical axis against the explanatory variable. If the residual graph shows no curve or "U-shaped" pattern, a linear model is appropriate for the data. However, if a linear model is not appropriate, the residual graph will have some sort of pattern or curved feature.

The graph below is the residual plot for the height and shoe size data. There is no curved pattern in the plot, so a linear model is appropriate for these data.

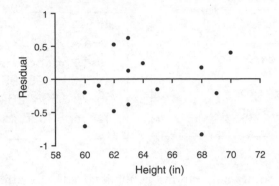

The residual plot below is from a data set that is clearly not linear. Even though the correlation coefficient may be high, implying that any linear association would be strong, the residuals tell us that the pattern of the data is not truly linear. This graph gives us reason to believe that the data are not well modeled by the line.

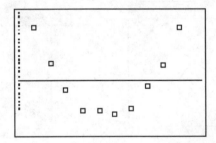

A residual plot can also reveal possible outliers. **Outliers** have large residuals since those points are far from the least-squares regression line (in the *y*-direction). An outlier usually does not have a great effect on the slope of a least-squares regression line, but does have influence on the correlation.

The scatterplots below represent a data set with an outlier (left) and with the outlier removed (right). The least-squares regression is shown for both sets. Note that the slope (*b*) did not significantly change when removing the outlier, but the correlation (*r*) increased substantially.

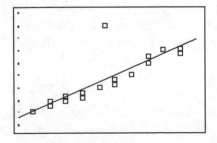 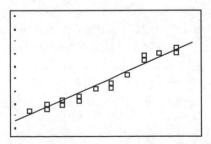

```
LinReg
  y=a+bx
  a=4.513412275
  b=.5837636452
  r²=.6748459211
  r=.8214900614
```

```
LinReg
  y=a+bx
  a=4.256366874
  b=.5841495993
  r²=.9615631264
  r=.9805932523
```

Influential points are extreme points that radically affect the slope of a LSRL. For example, consider the scatterplots below of men's heights and shoe sizes with their regression lines and values of r^2. The graph on the left shows data for 15 randomly selected men. The graph on the right shows the same men plus Shaquille O'Neal, an 85-inch tall basketball player with a shoe of size 22.

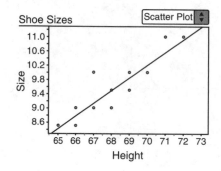

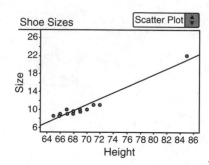

If O'Neal's point were removed from the data, the slope would drop from $0.676 \frac{\text{sizes}}{\text{inch}}$ to $0.357 \frac{\text{sizes}}{\text{inch}}$. Therefore, O'Neal is an influential observation. Note also that the removal of O'Neal would reduce r^2 from 0.94 to 0.79. This is also a characteristic of extreme points that seem to be in the general pattern of the data—they artificially strengthen correlation and r^2.

Calculator Tip:

Residual plots can be made easily on the graphing calculator. We will use the lists **L1** and **L2** defined previously in this section. Run the linear regression function **LinReg (a+bx)**; then prepare to create a scatterplot. Both tasks were outlined earlier in this section.

Enter the appropriate list for **Xlist:**. For **Ylist:** press [2nd] [LIST], arrow down, and then choose the list identified at **RESID**.

```
Plot1  Plot2  Plot3          NAMES  OPS  MATH
On Off                       1: L1
Type : ▰▰  ⌁  ⅊             2: L2
        ⅏  ⊞  ⌇             3: L3
Xlist : L1                   4: L4
Ylist : RESID                5: L5
Mark : ▫  +  ·               6: L6
                             7: RESID
```

Press ZOOM 9 to see the residual plot.

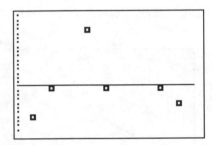

Transformations to Achieve Linearity: Logarithmic and Power Transformations

When the regression calculations and residual plots indicate that a linear model is not appropriate, we must find another model for the data. This involves transforming the response variable and in some cases the explanatory variable, as well. Remember that regression and correlation are used when describing and analyzing linear data only. When we transform data to achieve linearity, we can use the regression techniques as defined in the previous section. At that point, predictions can be made and the prediction can be transformed back to terms of the original data.

A common method of transforming data is a **logarithmic transformation.** This is done by taking the logarithm of a variable and using it in place of the original variable when creating a scatterplot and finding the least-squares regression model. Two models that can be obtained by logarithmic transformations are the **exponential model** $\hat{y} = ab^x$ and the **power model** $\hat{y} = ax^b$. For an exponential model, only the response variable is transformed; for the power model, both are transformed.

A certain bacteria's population has been recorded as follows over time (hours) as shown below. The original data show a curved pattern. Populations can often be modeled by an exponential function of the form $\hat{y} = ab^x$.

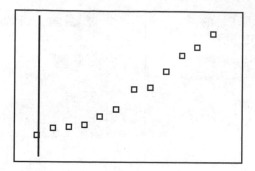

The logarithm of the *y*-values was taken. A scatterplot of (log *y*) versus *x* is shown below along with its least-squares regression line.

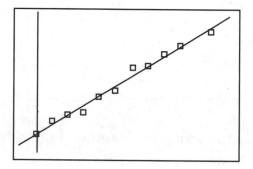

The graph of the residuals from the transformed linear regression shows that a linear model is appropriate for the transformed data.

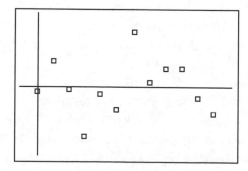

Since a linear model is acceptable for the transformed data, the original data fit an exponential model. You can now use the transformed linear model to make predictions.

Example: The linear model of log y on x is given by the equation log $\hat{y} = 1.85 + 0.065x$, where x is the time in hours and y is the population of bacteria in thousands. Predict the number of bacteria at time $x = 16$ hours.

Answer: Substitute $x = 16$ into the equation

log $\hat{y} = 1.85 + 0.065x = 1.85 + 0.065(16) = 2.89$. Since log $\hat{y} = 2.89$, then $y = 10^{2.89} \approx 776$. The number of bacteria is about 776 thousand.

The equation log $\hat{y} = 1.85 + 0.065x$ is written iterms of log $\hat{y}$ and not $\hat{y}$. It can be **back-transformed** by solving for $\hat{y}$.

$$
\begin{aligned}
\log \hat{y} &= 1.85 + 0.065x \\
10^{\log \hat{y}} &= 10^{1.85 + 0.065x} \\
\hat{y} &= 10^{1.85} \cdot 10^{0.065x} \\
\hat{y} &= 70.8 \, (1.161)^x .
\end{aligned}
$$

Predictions using this exponential function will yield the same values as with the transformed linear model. That is, $\hat{y} = 70.8 \, (1.161)^x = 70.8 \, (1.161)^{16} \approx 771$. (The difference is due to the round-off error.)

We also use logarithmic transformations for power models. A power model has a curved look to it just as the exponential model. The power model is written as $\hat{y} = ax^b$.

The scatterplot below shows the relationship between x and y.

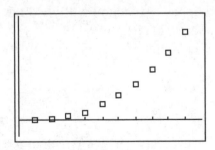

Assume that simply doing a logarithmic transformation of y did not straighten the plot. We may take the logarithm of *both* the explanatory and response variables. A scatterplot of (log y) versus (log x) is shown below along with its residual plot.

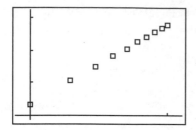
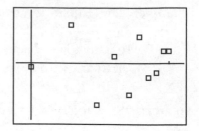

Since there is no U-shaped pattern in the residual graph, a power model was appropriate. You can now use the transformed linear model to make predictions.

Example: The linear model of log y on log x is given by the equation $\log \hat{y} = -0.356 + 1.484\,(\log x)$, where x is a planet's distance from the Sun (in millions of miles) and y is its orbital period (in years). Predict the orbital period of Mars, a planet 141 million miles from the Sun.

Answer: Substitute $x = 141$ into the equation.
$\log \hat{y} = -0.356 + 1.484\,(\log 141) \approx 2.83$. Since, $\log \hat{y} = 2.83$, then $y \approx 681$. The orbital period of Mars is about 681 days.

The equation $\log \hat{y} = -0.356 + 1.484\,(\log x)$ is written in terms of $\log \hat{y}$ and $\log x$, not y and x. It can be back-transformed by solving for $\hat{y}$.

$$
\begin{aligned}
\log \hat{y} &= -0.356 + 1.484\,(\log x) \\
10^{\log \hat{y}} &= 10^{0.356 + 1.484(\log x)} \\
\hat{y} &= 10^{0.356} \cdot 10^{1.484(\log x)} \\
\hat{y} &= 0.441 x^{1.484}.
\end{aligned}
$$

Predictions using this power function will yield the same values as with the transformed linear model. That is, $\hat{y} = 0.441 x^{1.484} = 2.270\,(141)^{1.484} \approx 682$. (The difference is due to the round-off error.)

Trial Run

1. A residual graph of a data set is shown. Which of the following statements is correct?

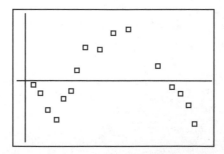

(A)   The pattern in the residual graph indicates that a linear model is appropriate.

(B)   The pattern in the residual graph indicates that a nonlinear model is appropriate.

(C)   The pattern in the residual graph indicates that the model will look exactly like the residual graph.

(D)   The pattern in the residual graph indicates that there is an error in the data.

(E)   The pattern in the residual graph indicates that one point is an outlier.

2.   A regression model is found for two variables, percent scored on a final exam vs. number of hours studied. The correlation was calculated to be 0.89. Which is the correct interpretation of this value?

(A)   For each additional hour studied, the score increased by 0.89 percent.

(B)   For each additional percent scored on the test, about one more hour of study is required.

(C)   If a linear association exists between the number of hours studied for a final exam and the percent scored on the exam, it is strong.

(D)   Eighty-nine percent of the variability in exam scores can be explained by its linear relationship to the number of hours studied.

(E)   There is no association between the number of hours studied for a final exam and the percent scored on the exam.

3.   A positive residual indicates that

(A)   the regression line overpredicted the response variable

(B)   the regression line underpredicted the response variable

(C)   the regression line overpredicted the explanatory variable

(D)   the regression line underpredicted the explanatory variable

(E)   the predicted value of the variable is the same as the actual value of the variable

4.   A dentist found that the coefficient of correlation between the time patients spend brushing their teeth and the whiteness of those teeth is 0.8. This suggests that

(A)   80% of people who brush their teeth have white teeth

(B)   80% of the variation in the whiteness of people's teeth can be explained by variation in the time they spend brushing their teeth

(C)   36% of the variation in the whiteness of people's teeth can be explained by variation in the time they spend brushing their teeth

(D)   64% of the variation in the time people spend brushing their teeth can be explained by variation in the degree of whiteness in their teeth

(E)   64% of the variation in the whiteness of people's teeth can be explained by variation in the time they spend brushing their teeth

5.   A small college admitted 25 students to its new mathematics program last fall. Each prospective student was required to take a diagnostic test upon entry to the program. Possible scores on the test range from a minimum of 20 to a maximum of 40.

The chair of the department is interested in whether or not the diagnostic test score can predict a student's achievement in the program as measured by grade point average (GPA). After 1 year in the program, students' GPAs were recorded and plotted against their diagnostic test scores (DTS).

The following is a computer printout of the scatterplot, residual plot, and least-squares regression model of GPA versus DTS.

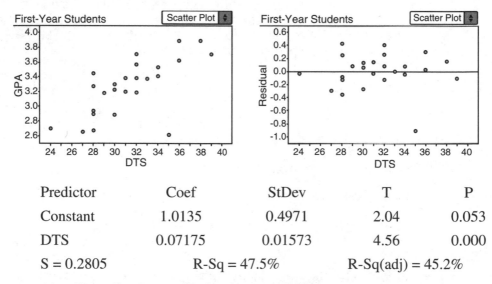

Predictor	Coef	StDev	T	P
Constant	1.0135	0.4971	2.04	0.053
DTS	0.07175	0.01573	4.56	0.000

S = 0.2805   R-Sq = 47.5%   R-Sq(adj) = 45.2%

(a)   Describe the association between the first-year grade point average (GPA) of the mathematics students and their diagnostic test score (DTS) taken upon admission.

(b) Does it appear that the least-squares regression line is a reasonable model to predict GPA from DTS? Justify your answer.

(c) One student had a DTS of 35 and a GPA of 2.62. Compute the residual for this observation.

(d) Compute the value of the correlation coefficient. If the outlier at (35, 2.62) were removed, how would the value of the correlation coefficient be affected? Justify your answer.

6. The graph below is the residual graph created from the regression analysis of the data collected from an AP Statistics class. The explanatory variable was midterm exam scores, and the response variable was final exam scores.

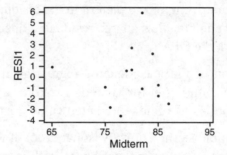

(a) The regression equation is *Final* = 11.7 + 0.882 (*Midterm*). What was the approximate final exam score for the student whose midterm score was 65?

(b) There were three scores that had a residual value of zero. What does this mean?

(c) About how many scores were underpredicted by the regression line?

Trial Run Solutions

1. B. The curved patterns in the residual plot indicates that a linear model is not appropriate and further investigation is needed to determine the best model for the data.

2. C. Correlation indicates the strength of the linear association between two variables. It is a unitless number and has not formal interpretation.

We do not have a scatterplot, so we do not know if the relationship is indeed linear, but a correlation of 0.89 indicates that the data would fit tightly around the least-squares regression line.

3. B. When the residual is positive, the line is below that point, therefore underpredicting the value of the response variable.

4. E. Since $r = 0.8$, therefore $r^2 = 0.64$. The statement in E is the correct interpretation of r^2.

5. (a) There is a moderate, positive, linear association between first-year grade point average of the mathematics students and their diagnostic test score taken upon admission. There appears to be one outlier at about (35, 2.6).

    (b) There does not seem to be a pattern in the residual graph even though there is one point that has a large residual; a linear model is appropriate to predict the GPA from DTS.

    (c) The equation of the least-squares regression line is $y = 1.0135 + 0.0175x$. Substituting in for x yields 1.626 for a predicted GPA. The residual is observed value – predicted value = $2.62 - 1.626 = 0.994$.

    (d) The correlation coefficient is the square root of R-sq. Since the slope is positive, the correlation coefficient will be positive. The value is 0.689. If the outlier were removed, the association would become slightly stronger and the value of 0.689 would increase toward 1.

6. (a) For a score of 65, the model predicts a final exam score of $11.7 + 0.882(65) = 69.03$. The residual for this score is 1. Since observed score – predicted score = residual, observed score $-69.03 = 1$, so the observed score is about 70.03. The student earned a score of 70 on his or her final exam.

    (b) A residual value of zero means that the actual and predicted values were the same. The three points would fall right on the least-squares regression line.

    (c) There are seven scores with positive residuals. These scores were underpredicted by the regression line.

E. EXPLORING CATEGORICAL DATA

Categorical data are data that are labels, names, or other nonnumerical outcomes. Gender (male, female), car color (white, red, blue, etc.), and one's response to a survey question (yes, no, maybe) are all categorical variables.

Categorical data are typically organized into a table, known as a **frequency table**. A frequency table summarizes how many times a particular category of a variable occurred.

Example: A survey of 12 adults asked, "Of chocolate, strawberry, and vanilla, which is your favorite ice cream flavor." The results were as follows:

Flavor

vanilla	strawberry	vanilla
chocolate	vanilla	strawberry
vanilla	chocolate	chocolate
vanilla	chocolate	vanilla

Create a frequency table that summarizes these data.

Answer:

Flavor	Chocolate	Strawberry	Vanilla
Frequency	4	2	6

Note: A frequency table of one variable, such as the one above, is sometimes called a **one-way table**.

The quantity of each response can be expressed as a **relative frequency**, which is a percentage or proportion of the whole number of data. A table of relative frequencies is known as a **relative frequency table**.

Example: A survey of 12 adults asked, "Of chocolate, strawberry, and vanilla, which is your favorite ice cream flavor." The results were as follows:

Flavor

vanilla	strawberry	vanilla
chocolate	vanilla	strawberry
vanilla	chocolate	chocolate
vanilla	chocolate	vanilla

Create a relative frequency table that summarizes these data. Round relative frequencies to three decimal places.

Answer: The relative frequencies of chocolate, strawberry, and vanilla are $\dfrac{4}{12}, \dfrac{2}{12},$ and $\dfrac{6}{12}$ respectively.

Flavor	Chocolate	Strawberry	Vanilla
Frequency	0.333	0.167	0.500

OR

Flavor	Chocolate	Strawberry	Vanilla
Frequency	33.3%	16.7%	50.0%

As with numerical data, categorical data can be represented visually in graphs or charts. One method is a **bar chart**. A bar chart displays the distribution of a categorical variable, with each bar's length proportional to the frequency of its represented category.

Example: Create a bar chart showing the frequencies of responses as given in the following frequency table.

Flavor	Chocolate	Strawberry	Vanilla
Frequency	4	2	6

Answer:

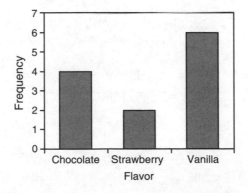

Answer:

A bar graph can display relative frequencies as well.

Example: Create a bar chart showing the relative frequencies of responses as given in the following relative frequency table.

Flavor	Chocolate	Strawberry	Vanilla
Relative Frequency	33.3%	16.7%	50.0%

Answer:

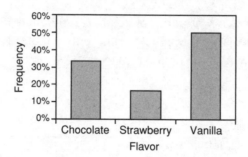

Two-Way Tables

When two categorical variables are under consideration (or one variable from several different populations), a **two-way table** or **contingency table** is created. The table shows the distribution of data for each variable.

Example: A survey of 12 adults asked, "Of chocolate, strawberry, and vanilla, which is your favorite ice cream flavor." Each respondent's gender was also recorded. The results were as follows:

Flavor	Gender	Flavor	Gender
vanilla	male	chocolate	female
chocolate	female	chocolate	male
vanilla	male	vanilla	female
vanilla	male	strawberry	male
strawberry	female	chocolate	female
vanilla	male	vanilla	male

Answer:

		Flavor			
		Chocolate	Strawberry	Vanilla	Total
	Female	3	1	1	5
Gender	Male	1	1	5	7
	Total	4	2	6	12

Frequencies for each cell are called **joint frequencies** or the **joint distribution**. Two-way tables may or may not have a total row and a total column. It is recommended that they be included. These totals are called **marginal frequencies** or the **marginal distribution**.

Two-way (or contingency) tables can also display relative frequencies. These relative frequencies can be of the entire table, of rows, or of columns.

Example: Create a two-way table of relative frequencies, with each cell being the relative frequency of the entire table. Round each relative frequency to three decimal places.

Answer:

Relative Frequency of the table		Flavor			
		Chocolate	Strawberry	Vanilla	Total
Gender	Female	$\frac{3}{12} = 0.250$	$\frac{1}{12} \approx 0.083$	$\frac{1}{12} \approx 0.083$	$\frac{5}{12} \approx 0.417$
	Male	$\frac{1}{12} \approx 0.083$	$\frac{1}{12} \approx 0.083$	$\frac{5}{12} \approx 0.417$	$\frac{7}{12} \approx 0.583$
	Total	$\frac{4}{12} \approx 0.333$	$\frac{2}{12} \approx 0.167$	$\frac{6}{12} = 0.500$	$\frac{12}{12} = 1$

OR

Relative Frequency of the table		Flavor			
		Chocolate	Strawberry	Vanilla	Total
Gender	Female	25.0%	8.3%	8.3%	41.7%
	Male	8.3%	8.3%	41.7%	58.3%
	Total	33.3%	16.7%	50.0%	100%

Example: Create a two-way table of relative frequencies, with each cell being the relative frequency of the row. Round each relative frequency to three decimal places.

Answer:

Relative Frequency of the row		Flavor			
		Chocolate	Strawberry	Vanilla	Total
Gender	Female	$\frac{3}{5} = 0.600$	$\frac{1}{5} = 0.200$	$\frac{1}{5} = 0.200$	$\frac{5}{5} = 1$
	Male	$\frac{1}{7} \approx 0.143$	$\frac{1}{7} \approx 0.143$	$\frac{5}{7} \approx 0.714$	$\frac{7}{7} = 1$
	Total	$\frac{4}{12} \approx 0.333$	$\frac{2}{12} \approx 0.167$	$\frac{6}{12} = 0.500$	$\frac{12}{12} = 1.$

OR

Relative Frequency of the row		Flavor			
		Chocolate	Strawberry	Vanilla	Total
Gender	Female	60.0%	20.0%	20.0%	100%
	Male	14.3%	14.3%	71.4%	100%
	Total	33.3%	16.7%	50.0%	100%

The relative frequencies for each cell are called **conditional frequencies** or the **conditional distribution**. In this case, it is the conditional distribution for gender. For example, given that a respondent has the condition *gender is female*, the percentages that like chocolate, strawberry, or vanilla are 60%, 20%, and 20%, respectively.

Example: Create a two-way table of relative frequencies, with each cell being the relative frequency of the column. Round each relative frequency to three decimal places.

Answer:

Relative Frequency of the column		Flavor			
		Chocolate	Strawberry	Vanilla	Total
Gender	Female	$\frac{3}{4} = 0.750$	$\frac{1}{2} = 0.500$	$\frac{1}{6} \approx 0.167$	$\frac{5}{12} \approx 0.417$
	Male	$\frac{1}{4} = 0.250$	$\frac{1}{2} = 0.500$	$\frac{5}{6} \approx 0.833$	$\frac{7}{12} \approx 0.583$
	Total	$\frac{4}{4} = 1$	$\frac{2}{2} = 1$	$\frac{6}{6} = 1$	$\frac{12}{12} = 1$

OR

Relative Frequency of the column		Flavor			
		Chocolate	Strawberry	Vanilla	Total
Gender	Female	75.0%	50.0%	16.7%	100%
	Male	25.0%	50.0%	83.3%	100%
	Total	100%	100%	100%	100%

This table shows the conditional distribution for flavor. For example, given that a respondent has the condition *preferred flavor is chocolate*, the percentages by gender are 75% female and 25% male.

The purpose of creating two-way tables with conditional distributions is to look for an **association** between two categorical variables of a single population, or one categorical variable of several populations. In the previous examples, one may be assessing whether there is an association between gender and preferred ice cream flavor.

Relative Frequency of the row		Flavor			
		Chocolate	Strawberry	Vanilla	Total
Gender	Female	60.0%	20.0%	20.0%	100%
	Male	14.3%	14.3%	71.4%	100%
	Total	33.3%	16.7%	50.0%	100%

In this instance, females are more likely to prefer chocolate to vanilla— 60% to 20%. Males, on the other hand, prefer vanilla to chocolate—71.4% to 14.3%. The likelihood of preferring strawberry is about the same for either gender. There does seem to be an association between gender and flavor (or there are differences in flavor preference between males and females).

An association (or difference) such as this can be represented in a graphical form. The method of graphing a conditional distribution is with a **relative frequency segmented bar chart.** In a relative frequency segmented bar chart, one bar is drawn for each category of the conditional variable. Each bar is segmented into parts whose length is proportional to the percentage of categories of the other second variable.

Example: Make a relative frequency segmented bar chart for the conditional distribution shown below.

Relative Frequency of the row		Flavor			
		Chocolate	Strawberry	Vanilla	Total
Gender	Female	60.0%	20.0%	20.0%	100%
	Male	14.3%	14.3%	71.4%	100%
	Total	33.3%	16.7%	50.0%	100%

Answer:

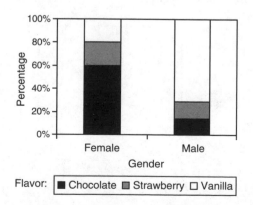

Note: The conditional variable is gender, so one bar exists for each category of the conditional variable. The segments correspond to the categories of the other variable: flavor.

It is clear from the graph that females prefer chocolate over vanilla and in a greater percentage than males. The same can be said of males preferring vanilla over chocolate and in a greater percentage than females. Strawberry was preferred about equally between the two genders.

Example: Make a relative frequency segmented bar chart for the two-way table below, conditional on the variable *flavor*.

		Flavor			
		Chocolate	Strawberry	Vanilla	Total
Gender	Female	3	1	1	5
	Male	1	1	5	7
	Total	4	2	6	12

Answer: The conditional distribution on the variable flavor is shown below.

Relative Frequency of the column		Flavor			
		Chocolate	Strawberry	Vanilla	Total
Gender	Female	75.0%	50.0%	16.7%	100%
	Male	25.0%	50.0%	83.3%	100%
	Total	100%	100%	100%	100%

Its corresponding relative frequency segmented bar graph is

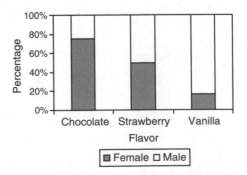

Note: The conditional variable is flavor, so one bar exists for each category of the conditional variable. The segments correspond to the categories of the other variable: gender.

It is clear from the graph that those who prefer chocolate tend to be female and those preferring vanilla tend to be male.

Trial Run

1. Marketing managers at various department stores that are housed in malls are studying the types of people that might be shopping in their stores. They want to make sure that they are catering to the clientele coming to their store. Vehicles parked within 200 feet of various types of "anchor" stores at a mall were categorized as shown in the table below. The data were collected on a Saturday in May.

		Classification of Vehicle				
		Compact	Family/SUV	Luxury	Sport	Total
Store Class	Discount	130	198	12	32	372
	Mid-range	108	210	42	64	424
	High-end	64	178	53	73	368
	Total	302	586	107	169	1,164

What percentage of those vehicles parked within 200 feet of Mid-range stores are Family/SUV?

(A) 18.0%

(B) 35.8%

(C) 36.4%

(D) 49.5%

(E) 50.3%

2. The table below shows the number of people from different age ranges enrolled in day and evening programs at a local community college.

	Time of Program		
	Day	Evening	Total
Under 25 years	850	400	1,250
25–30 years	750	475	1,225
Over 30 years	300	560	860
Total	1,900	1,435	3,335

(Age Range)

(a) Create an appropriate graphical display to compare the distribution of ages for evening vs. day programs.

(b) Does there appear to be an association between the age and the time of the program?

Trial Run Solutions

3. D. The question asks about vehicles parked near Mid-range stores, of which there are 424. Of those 424 cars, 210 are of the Family/SUV class. Thus, $\frac{210}{424} \approx 0.495$, or 49.5% of cars near Mid-range stores are Family/SUV.

4. (a) First, the table needs to be converted to a conditional distribution. Since the distribution of ages for each program time is desired, the conditional distribution for time (for columns) is computed.

	Time of Program		
	Day	Evening	Total
Under 25 years	44.7%	27.8%	37.5%
25–30 years	39.5%	33.1%	36.7%
Over 30 years	15.8%	39.0%	25.8%
Total	100%	100%	100%

(Age Range)

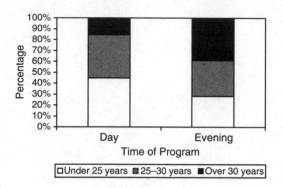

A segmented bar chart looks like this.

(b) Comparing the age groups' proportions between the two program times, there does appear to be an association between the two variables. While the distribution of ages in the evening is fairly even, nearly half of daytime attendees are in the Under 25 classification and only about 15% are over 30 years of age. A smaller percentage of evening students are in the youngest category than during the daytime; evening programs have a much higher percentage of the oldest students than day programs. The percentage of the middle group of students is about the same between the two programs.

Essentially, it can be said that younger students tend to attend during the day and older students tend to take programs in the evenings.

CHAPTER 2
Sampling and Experimentation

SAMPLING AND EXPERIMENTATION

A. OVERVIEW OF METHODS OF DATA COLLECTION

There are four methods of data collection with which you should be familiar: census, sample survey, experiment, and observational study.

A **census** is a study that observes, or attempts to observe, every individual in a population. The **population** is the collection of all individuals under consideration in the study.

A **sample survey** is a study that collects information from a sample of a population in order to determine one or more characteristics of the population. A **sample** is a selected subset of a population from which data are gathered.

An **experiment** is a study where the researcher deliberately influences individuals by imposing conditions and determining the individuals' responses to those conditions.

An **observational study** attempts to determine relationships between variables, but the researcher imposes no conditions like an experiment. Surveys are a form of observational study.

Sample surveys and experiments are discussed in greater detail later in this chapter.

Example: The principal of a new school wants to know what mascot the incoming students would prefer. He summons each of the student body into his office and asks what the new mascot should be. What type of study is this?

Answer: This is a census. The principal has collected data from every individual in the population, in this case, the population of all school students.

Example: The principal of the new school is also interested in what type of dress code the school should have. He telephones the parents of every tenth student summoned to his office and asks their opinions about school dress codes. What type of study is this?

Answer: This is a sample survey. The principal has collected data from only a subset of the population, in this case, the population of all school parents.

Example: A pharmaceutical company wishes to test a new medication it thinks will reduce cholesterol. A group of 20 volunteers is formed and each has his or her cholesterol level measured. Half is randomly assigned to take the new drug and the other half is given a dummy pill, a pill with no active ingredients. After 6 months the volunteers' cholesterol is measured again and any change from the beginning of the study recorded. What type of study is this?

Answer: This is an experiment. The company is imposing conditions (new drug, dummy pill) on the participants in the study to determine their response (change in cholesterol) to the conditions.

Example: A health studies research lab is interested in the effect of certain vegetables on cholesterol level. A group of 20 volunteers is formed and each keeps a diary of his or her food consumption for the next 6 months, after which time the diaries are collected and cholesterol level is measured. The researchers then examine the relationship between the rate of consumption of certain vegetables and cholesterol level. What type of study is this?

Answer: This is an observational study. The researchers are imposing no conditions on the participants in the study.

Trial Run

1. A supervisor is trying to improve sales at an insurance company. The supervisor asks all agents to turn in their logs from the past month, which record how much time each of them spent with individual prospective

customers. The supervisor examines each agent's average time spent with customers and the number of policies the agent sold. What kind of study is this?

(A)   An observational study using a sample

(B)   An observational study using a census

(C)   An experiment using a sample

(D)   An experiment using a census

(E)   A census, but whether it is an experiment or an observational study cannot be determined

Trial Run Solution

1.   B. The supervisor has *all* agents turn in their logs; thus it is a census. It is an observational study because no conditions were imposed on the agents before data were collected.

B. PLANNING AND CONDUCTING SURVEYS

The purpose of a sample survey is to determine one or more characteristics about a population from the results of the sample. The characteristic of the population is a **population parameter**. The result of the sample survey used to estimate the parameter is a **sample statistic**. There are many methods to obtain a sample from a population.

Sampling Methods

A **voluntary response sample** is composed of individuals who choose to respond to a survey because of interest in the subject, particularly those with strong opinions or attraction.

A **convenience sample** is composed of individuals who are easily accessed or contacted.

Example: A journalism class prints a survey in their school newspaper. Readers are asked to clip the survey from the paper, complete it, and return it to a drop box in the school cafeteria. What type of sample is this?

Answer: This is a voluntary response sample. It is likely that only students interested in the survey's subject matter will take the time to respond.

Example: A journalism class stations pollsters in front of the stadium during a football game. They ask each student who enters his or her opinion of the quality of the school's athletics program. What type of sample is this?

Answer: This is a convenience sample. The site was likely chosen because of the ease of gathering data there.

A **random sample (or probability sample)** is composed of individuals selected by chance. There are several types of random samples.

A **simple random sample (SRS)** is a sample where n individuals are selected from a population in a way that every possible combination of n individuals is equally likely. In general, one may think of an SRS as having all individuals of the population in a hat and selecting n individuals, without replacement, from the hat.

Note: Not only is it required of a simple random sample that each *individual* has an equally likely chance of being chosen, but also each possible group must be equally likely. That is, if an SRS is to have a size of $n = 5$, no possible group of five individuals can be any more or less likely to be selected than any other group.

A **stratified random sample** is a sample in which simple random samples are selected from each of several homogeneous subgroups of the population, known as **strata** (singular, **stratum**).

Note: In a stratified random sample, every individual in each subgroup has an equally likely chance of being chosen, but every individual in the population may not. Additionally, each possible group of individuals from the population will not have the same chance of being chosen.

A **cluster sample** is a sample in which a simple random sample of heterogeneous subgroups of the population is selected. The subgroups are known as **clusters**. The selected clusters may also themselves be subject to random sampling, or a census done for each.

A **multistage sample** is a sample resulting from multiple applications of cluster, stratified, and/or simple random sampling.

A **systematic random sample** is a sample where every kth individual is selected from a list or queue. The first selection is randomly chosen from the first k individuals.

Example: A media research firm is conducting a poll on an upcoming election for city council. The firm obtains a list of all 15,000 registered voters in the council ward under consideration. The voters' ID numbers are entered into a computer and 500 are chosen at random, without replacement, to comprise the sample. What type of sampling design is this?

Answer: This is a simple random sample. Individuals are chosen at random, without replacement, from a list of the entire population. This is a "select n from a hat"-type of sampling.

Note: In this scenario, every possible group of 500 individuals has an equally likely chance of being selected, as does every individual.

Example: A media research firm is conducting a poll on an upcoming election for city council. The firm obtains a list of all 15,000 registered voters in the council ward under consideration. The voters' ID numbers and party affiliations (Democrat, Republican, Independent) are entered into a computer. The firm randomly selects, without replacement,

200 Democrats, 200 Republicans, and 100 Independents to comprise the sample. What type of sampling design is this?

Answer: This is a stratified random sample. Individuals were first placed in strata, in this case, party affiliation. Then, simple random samples from each stratum were selected to make up the final sample.

Note: In this scenario, all individuals within their respective strata have an equally likely chance of being chosen, but all individuals in the population may not. If there are more Democrats than Republicans, then it is more likely that a particular Republican voter will be in the sample than a particular Democrat voter. Additionally, every possible group of 500 individuals from the population does not have an equally likely chance of being chosen, since samples of 500 Democrats, or 250 Democrats and 250 Republicans, for example, are not possible.

Example: A media research firm is conducting a poll on an upcoming election for city council. The firm obtains a list of all 15,000 registered voters in the council ward under consideration. The voters' ID numbers and voting precinct numbers (01–75) are entered into a computer. The firm first randomly selects 20 of the voting precincts. Then, from each of the chosen precincts, 25 voters are chosen with simple random samples. What type of sampling design is this?

Answer: This is a cluster sample. Individuals were first grouped into clusters by voting precinct, of which several were selected. Then, simple random samples from each cluster were selected to make up the final sample.

Note: An additional step could have been added to the previous example. If voters in the selected precincts were then grouped by party affiliation, and an SRS taken from each group, the result would have been a multistage sample.

Example: A media research firm is conducting a poll on an upcoming election for city council. The firm obtains a list of all 15,000 registered voters in the council ward under consideration. The list is sorted by voter ID number. The firm randomly selects one person from the first 100 on the list; then it selects every 100th person after that. The sample size is 150. What type of sampling design is this?

Answer: This is a systematic random sample. One of the first k individuals on the list is randomly selected—in this case $k = 100$—and every kth individual on the list is selected after that.

Note: Even though each individual has an equally likely chance of being selected in the systematic random sample, it is *not* equivalent to a simple random sample.

Each of the described designs has advantages and disadvantages.

The advantage of convenience samples and voluntary response samples is that gathering data is easy. Respondents are either close at hand, in the case of a convenience sample, or a portion of the initiative in data collection is up to the respondent, in the case of a voluntary response sample. Both of these can be poor designs, as they are subject to bias.

Bias and Sampling Error

Bias is the term for systematic deviation from the truth, in this case, the characteristic of the population (parameter) one wishes to estimate from the sample (statistic). A sampling method is biased if it tends to produce samples that do not represent the population. There are several terms used to describe bias.

Undercoverage occurs when some individuals of a population are not included in the sampling process.

Voluntary response bias is present in voluntary response samples. It occurs because people with strong opinions or interest in the survey topics tend to respond more frequently. Voluntary response bias is a form of undercoverage.

Example: A journalism class prints a survey in their school newspaper about the school charging students for parking. Readers are asked to clip the survey from the paper, complete it, and return it to a drop box in the school cafeteria. Why is this sample biased?

Answer: This survey is subject to voluntary response bias, as it is likely that only students who drive to school now, or will drive soon, will take the time to respond. Nondrivers will tend to leave themselves out. Even if the population of interest were only driving students, those opposed to parking fees would be more likely to respond.

Example: A journalism class stations pollsters in front of the stadium during a football game. They ask each student who enters his or her opinion of the quality of the school's athletics program. Why is this sample biased?

Answer: This convenience sample is subject to undercoverage. Only those students attending the football game will be able to register their opinions, potentially leaving out a large portion of the population.

Random sampling, when done properly, tends to reduce the effects of undercoverage by giving each individual in the population a chance to be selected for the survey. This is its greatest advantage—it helps produce samples that resemble the population. *Random sampling is a necessary part of a well-designed survey or sampling procedure.*

Simple random samples are, in practice, very difficult to produce. The advantage of cluster sampling and multistage sampling is that using these methods it can be easier to obtain a sample than using a simple random sample. In the previous example about the polling firm, were the surveys being conducted door to door, it would be easier to go to several houses in a few randomly selected voting precincts than to many houses scattered about the entire council ward. This saves resources—time and potentially money.

Another problem with random samples is variability. Each possible SRS from a population will generate a different sample statistic. The differences among these statistics are called **sampling variability** or **sampling error**. Sampling variability is a natural part of the random sampling process and should not be confused with bias. It is not the result of a poorly designed study.

The advantage of stratified random sampling is that it reduces sampling variability if there are differences between the strata in how they respond. It takes away the chance that one may get a disproportionate number of individuals from a stratum in the sample than exist in the population.

Even surveys conducted by using properly executed random sampling techniques are still subject to bias. **Nonresponse bias** is the situation where an individual selected to be in the sample is unwilling, or unable, to provide data. **Response bias** occurs when because of the manner in which an interview is conducted, because of the phrasing of questions, or because of the attitude of the respondent, inaccurate data are collected.

Example: A media research firm is conducting a poll on an upcoming election for city council. The firm obtains a list of all 15,000 registered voters in the council ward under consideration and a simple random sample of 500 voters is chosen. Over a 24-hour period, telephone calls are placed to the voters, with follow-up calls made to those voters who do not answer the phone on the first attempt. Pollsters could not reach 37 of the 500 voters selected. What sources of bias could exist in this survey?

Answer: This survey could be subject to nonresponse bias. Thirty-seven voters could not be reached. Their opinions could affect the results of the survey, and the data gathered may not accurately represent the views of the population.

Example: A journalism class conducts a simple random sample of students at their school. They ask each student, "Given the fact that our school has won seven championships in the last five years, do you favor or oppose reducing funding for athletic programs?" What sources of bias could exist in this survey?

Answer: The question is clearly leading the respondent to answer in opposition to reducing funding because of its mention of the school's recent athletic prowess. This is a form of response bias. A better question would be to ask, "Do you favor or oppose reducing funding for the school's athletic programs?"

Sampling with Random Digit Tables

A random digit table can be used to select a random sample from a population. Each member of the population is assigned an identification number, with the length of the number in digits determined by the size of the population. For populations of 10 or less, one digit is needed. Populations of 11–100 require two-digit numbers. Three digits are required for populations of size 101–1,000, and so on. Note that if one has 100 individuals in a population, assigning 01–100 is *not* correct. The number 100 has three digits and all of the others from 01 to 99 have two. However, 00 is a two-digit number that will work for 100.

Random numbers of the same length are selected from the random digit table by reading across the lines of the table. Each consecutive group of digits will either select one of the individuals in the population, or be ignored because it has already been selected, if sampling without replacement, or because it does not correspond with any member of the population.

Example: Select a simple random sample of size $n = 6$ from the population of names below using the random digit table provided:

Anita	Billy	Carol	Doug	Elmer
Francine	Glenda	Hector	Ivy	Jose
Kelly	Lynn	Melvin	Nicole	Olive
Paul	Quincy	Rae	Sue	Tom

01401	49913	20134	96010
16290	33843	95945	04834
37520	93015	93615	03413

Answer: First, assign two-digit identification numbers to the members of the population.

01 Anita	02 Billy	03 Carol	04 Doug	05 Elmer
06 Francine	07 Glenda	08 Hector	09 Ivy	10 Jose
11 Kelly	12 Lynn	13 Melvin	14 Nicole	15 Olive
16 Paul	17 Quincy	18 Rae	19 Sue	20 Tom

Next, take consecutive two-digit numbers from the random number table, excluding values 21–99 and 00, and those that have already been selected.

0 1 4 0 1	4 9 9 1 3	2 0 1 3 4	9 6 0 1 0
1 6 2 9 0	3 3 8 4 3	9 5 9 4 5	0 4 8 3 4
3 7 5 2 0	9 3 0 1 5	9 3 6 1 5	0 3 4 1 3

The first five two-digit numbers (single underline) are 01, 40, 14, 99, and 13. These correspond to Anita, no selection, Nicole, no selection, and Melvin. So far, three of the sample have been selected. Continuing, the next several two-digit numbers (double underline) are as follows: 20—Tom; 13—Melvin, but he is a repeat and is not selected again; 49—no selection; 60—no selection; 10—Jose; and (skipping to the next line) 16—Paul.

The simple random sample of size $n = 6$ is Anita, Nicole, Melvin, Tom, Jose, and Paul.

Trial Run

1. A certain high school has 2,350 students. The student body officers are interested in creating activities to have the freshmen become more involved. Which is the best method that will give the appropriate representation of the freshmen at that school?

   (A) During the lunch hour, ask some freshmen their choice of activities.

   (B) Take a simple random sample of the entire student body and ask their choice of activities.

   (C) Take a simple random sample of the freshmen class only and ask their choice of activities.

(D) Take a simple random sample of nonfreshmen and ask which activities they would have liked when they were freshmen.

(E) The student body officers should make the decision based on their experiences as freshmen.

2. What is the purpose of stratification in sampling?

(A) To reduce variability in the response

(B) To increase the sample size

(C) To restrict which members of the population can be sampled

(D) To reduce response bias

(E) To ensure an equal probability of a particular individual being sampled

3. A machine stamps out metal pieces. An inspector checks every 20th piece for defects and size. This is an example of

(A) random sampling

(B) systematic sampling

(C) stratified sampling

(D) cluster sampling

(E) quota sampling

4. The state board of education wishes to study the attitudes of parents whose children are taking an experimental curriculum. The state consists of urban, suburban, and rural communities of different cultural backgrounds. Which sampling method is likely to yield the most reliable measure of parents' attitudes?

(A) Simple random sample

(B) Stratified random sample

(C) Cluster sample

(D) Voluntary response sample

(E) Convenience

5. Which of the following is NOT a result of a study's design process?

(A) Undercoverage

(B) Voluntary response bias

(C) Response bias

(D) Sampling error

(E) Nonresponse bias

6. A popular resort hotel in Hawaii is contemplating changing their status to become "all-inclusive." This means that the price guests would pay includes all meals and activities throughout their stay. To determine if this new status would increase their occupancy rate, the hotel management sends out questionnaires to all guests who stayed at the hotel in the last 12 months.

(a) Explain any limitations to this survey method.

(b) What would be a better method of obtaining information about changing the hotel's status to "all-inclusive."

Trial Run Solutions

1. C. A well-designed survey will sample randomly from the population, in this case, the freshman class. The other four choices either lack randomization, or sample individuals not in the desired population.

2. A. The purpose of stratification is to reduce variability in the response variable due to inherent differences in subgroups of the population.

3. B. Systematic sampling involves taking every kth individual from a list or queue of the population. In this case, whether the first piece was selected randomly—as it should be—is unknown.

4. B. Since the subgroups (urban, suburban, rural) have different cultural backgrounds, their attitudes toward an experimental curriculum may vary significantly from group to group. To reduce this variability, a stratified sample should be taken.

5. D. Sampling error is natural variability due to the random sampling process. The other four choices are biases that systematically steer the response variable away from the truth.

6.   (a) The survey conveniently samples from people who have stayed at the hotel, and perhaps are already enamored with it. This could lead to undercoverage and may generate results that are more positive than the population of all potential guests would provide. Voluntary response bias is an issue, as people with strong feelings about the hotel, particularly positive, are more likely to respond.

   (b) If a survey were what is needed, obtaining lists of visitors from the local Chamber of Commerce, tourist agencies, or airlines/cruise lines would provide a larger sampling frame from which to draw.

C. PLANNING AND CONDUCTING EXPERIMENTS

Recall that an **experiment** is a study where the researcher deliberately influences individuals by imposing conditions and determining the individuals' responses to those conditions. The individuals in an experiment are referred to as **experimental units**, or if they are people, **subjects**. Experimental units could be people, animals, plots of land, batteries, or any number of things on which conditions are imposed.

In an experiment, the researcher is interested in the response variable and how it is related to one or more explanatory variables called **factors**. Each factor has one or more **levels**, different quantities or categories of the factor. Combinations of different levels of the factors are called **treatments**. Sometimes, human subjects are given a faux treatment, known as a **placebo**, that resembles the real treatments under consideration.

Example: A pharmaceutical company wishes to test a new medication it thinks will reduce cholesterol. A group of 20 volunteers is formed and each has his or her cholesterol level measured. Half is randomly assigned to take the new drug and the other half is given a placebo. After 6 months the volunteers' cholesterol is measured again and any change from the beginning of the study recorded. Identify the experimental units, factors and their levels, treatments, and response variable in this experiment.

Answer: The experimental units (subjects) in this study are the 20 volunteers. There is one factor, the medication, and it has two levels, the active pill and the placebo. Thus, there are only two treatments, the active pill and the dummy pill. The response variable is the change in cholesterol over the period of the study.

A diagram can assist visualizing the experiment's design.

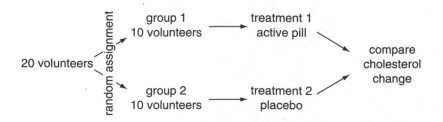

Example: An agricultural researcher is interested in determining how much water and fertilizer are optimum for growing a certain plant. Twenty-four plots of land are available to grow the plant. The researcher will apply three different amounts of fertilizer (low, medium, and high) and two different amounts of water (light and heavy). These will be applied at random in equal combination to each of four plots. After 6 weeks, the plants' heights in each plot will be recorded. Identify the experimental units, factors and their levels, treatments, and response variable in this experiment.

Answer: The experimental units in this study are plots of land. There are two factors, fertilizer and water. Fertilizer has three levels: low, medium, and high. Water has two levels: light and heavy. There are total six treatments of fertilizer–water combinations: low–light, low–heavy, medium–light, medium–heavy, high–light, and high–heavy. The response variable is the height of the plants at the end of the study.

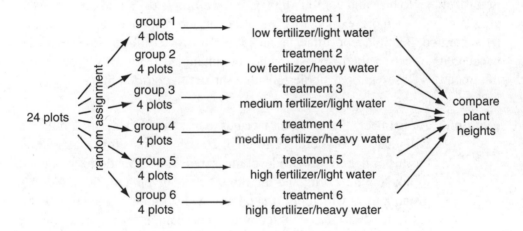

Characteristics of a Well-Designed Experiment

A well-designed comparative experiment has the following characteristics: control, randomization, and replication.

Control is the principle that potential sources of variation due to variables not under consideration must be reduced. These other variables are often called **lurking variables**. Control is achieved by making the experimental conditions as identical as possible for all experimental units.

One form of control in a comparative experiment is creating a baseline group or **control group**. A control group may be given no treatment, a faux treatment like a placebo, or an accepted treatment that is to be compared to another. In studies involving human subjects, controls are important to reduce a phenomenon known as the **placebo effect**, where subjects show a response to a treatment merely because the treatment is imposed regardless of its actual effect.

Another type of control is **blinding**. Blinding is the practice of denying knowledge to subjects of which treatment is being imposed upon them. This reduces the chances that the subjects will alter their behavior and introduce unwanted variability into the response. Sometimes, those collecting data in the experiment can introduce variability into the response, particularly when the response variable has a degree of subjectivity. When both subjects and evaluators are ignorant about which treatment a subject received, the study is called **double-blind**.

Randomization is the process by which treatments are assigned by a chance mechanism to the experimental units. It "averages out" variation due to variables that cannot be controlled.

Replication is the practice of reducing chance variation by assigning each treatment to many experimental units.

An experiment that does not include control, randomization, and replication is subject to bias and confounding. **Confounding** is the situation where the effects of two or more explanatory variables on the response variable cannot be separated. The placebo effect is an example of a **confounding variable**, because its effect on the response cannot be untangled from the effects of the treatment(s). Observational studies are also subject to confounding.

Example: A pharmaceutical company wishes to test a new medication it thinks will reduce cholesterol. A group of 20 volunteers is formed and each has his or her cholesterol level measured. Half is randomly assigned to take the new drug and the other half is given a placebo. Neither group knows which pill it is taking. After 6 months the volunteers' cholesterol is measured again and any change from the beginning of the study recorded. Explain where control, randomization, and replication are present in this study.

Answer: Control is first implemented by having a control group—the group receiving the placebo. All subjects are alike in that all are taking a pill. The second form of control is by blinding the subjects. The subjects are less likely to introduce unwanted variability by changing their behavior, as they may if they knew which pill they were given. Randomization is provided by the random assignment of the two treatments to the subjects. Replication is present in that each treatment is imposed 10 times. (More would be better.)

Example: A health studies research lab is interested in the effect of certain vegetables on cholesterol level. A group of 20 volunteers is formed and each keeps a diary of his food consumption for the next 6 months, after which time the diaries are collected and cholesterol level is measured. The researchers then examine the relationship between the rate of consumption of certain vegetables and cholesterol level. What confounding variables could be present in this observational study?

Answer: Sources of confounding could be exercise, diet outside of the vegetables being considered, or other health-related variables. Those who eat more vegetables may eat lower-fat diets, be less likely to smoke, or more likely to exercise, all variables that affect cholesterol level.

Experiment Designs

There are two major types of experimental designs. The first is a **completely randomized design**. A completely randomized design is one in which all experimental units are assigned treatments solely by chance. No grouping of experimental units is done prior to assignment of treatments.

The second major design is the **randomized block design**. If a researcher has reason to believe that subgroups of the experimental units will respond differently to treatments because of some characteristic, the units are sorted into those subgroups before treatments are assigned. In an experiment, these subgroups are called **blocks**. Once units are assigned to blocks, treatments are randomly assigned to the units in each block. Blocking is a form of control to reduce unwanted variability in the response variable due to some variable other than the treatment(s). Experimental units may be sorted into blocks by one or more characteristics.

When only two treatments exist, experimental units are sometimes placed into pairs. These pairs may be units related by some variable, or may be single unit that receives each treatment at different times (known as reuse). This is a form of block design called **matched pairs**. If the pair consists of two experimental units, one is randomly assigned one of the two treatments with second unit receiving the other. If the pair is the same unit to be reused, one treatment is randomly assigned first, completed, and then the other treatment follows.

(Note: Do not confuse **blocking** and **stratification**. They perform similar functions in experiments and sampling, respectively, but blocks are part of an experimental design and strata are part of a sampling process.)

Example: A pharmaceutical company wishes to test a new medication it thinks will reduce cholesterol. A group of 20 volunteers is formed and each has his or her cholesterol level measured. Half is randomly assigned to take the new drug and the other half is given a placebo. Neither group knows which pill it is taking. After 6 months the volunteers' cholesterol is measured again and any change from the beginning of the study recorded. What type of experimental design is this?

Answer: This is a completely randomized design.

Example: A pharmaceutical company wishes to test a new medication it thinks will reduce cholesterol. A group of 20 volunteers is formed and each has his or her cholesterol level measured. After 6 months the volunteers' cholesterol is measured again and any change from the beginning of the study recorded. The researcher believes that regular exercise may influence the change in cholesterol level. Create a randomized block design that takes account of subjects who exercise regularly.

Answer: First, divide the subjects into two blocks: those who exercise regularly and those who do not. Then, randomly assign the treatments within each block, with half of each block receiving each treatment. A diagram is given as follows.

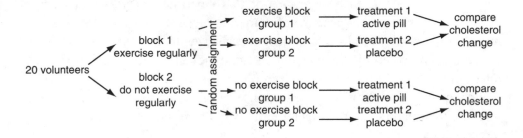

Example: A pharmaceutical company wishes to test a new medication it thinks will reduce cholesterol. A group of 20 volunteers is formed and each has his or her cholesterol level measured. After 6 months the volunteers' cholesterol is measured again and any change from the beginning of the study recorded. The researcher believes that initial cholesterol level may influence the change in cholesterol level. Create a matched pairs design that takes account of subjects' initial cholesterol level.

Answer: Pair the subjects by initial cholesterol level, making the two with the highest levels a pair, then the third and fourth highest levels the next pair, and so on. Randomly assign one of each pair one of the treatments, with the other subject in the pair receiving the other treatment.

Trial Run

1. When performing an experiment using an experimental group and a control group, which of the following is important?

   (A) The control group and experimental group are similar.

   (B) The control group and the experimental group have different backgrounds.

   (C) The experimental group is more interested in the research than the control group.

   (D) The control group's interest in the experiment is maintained.

   (E) The experimental group and control group should communicate with each other as much as possible.

2. The placebo effect refers to changes in subjects caused by

   (A) the administration of an active treatment

   (B) separation from real-life conditions

   (C) evaluating the response variable

   (D) the attention of the experiment itself

   (E) lack of randomization of treatments

3. What is the purpose of blocking in the design of an experiment?

   (A) To reduce variability within treatment groups

   (B) To reduce variability between treatment groups

   (C) To make randomization of treatments more efficient

   (D) To blind subjects as to which treatment group they are in

   (E) To decrease the chance of the placebo effect

4. A manufacturer of tires wants to conduct an experiment with a new type of tread design. This tread is supposed to last longer in hot climates than the existing tread design. The tire company wants to conduct the experiment in Phoenix, Arizona, during the months of April through September. One hundred taxicabs will be used in the experiment, and only the front wheels will have the new tires.

   Design an experiment to determine if the new type of tire will last longer than the existing tire.

Trial Run Solutions

1. A. In a well-designed experiment, it is important that the different treatment groups be as alike as possible so that any difference in response is due to the treatment and not other variables.

2. D. The placebo effect is a response to a treatment merely because one is imposed, whether or not the treatment is meant to produce a response.

3. A. Variability of the response variable within treatment groups makes it more difficult to see differences because of the treatments. It is between group variability that one desires in order to compare treatments. Blinding and blocking are separate procedures. The placebo effect can be addressed with control groups.

Note: Do not confuse *blocks* and *treatment groups*. *Blocks* are homogeneous collections of experimental units, created due to other variables that may affect the response variable. Treatments are randomly assigned to units in each block. *Treatment groups* are collections of experimental units that receive the same treatment.

4. One choice would be to use a completely randomized design. Assign the 100 taxicabs two-digit numbers from 00 to 99. Choose two-digit random numbers from a random number table, without duplication, until 50 have been selected. Place the new tires on the front wheels of those taxicabs; place the old tires on the front wheels of the remaining taxicabs. At the end of the experiment's time period, evaluate the two tread designs for wear. Compare the difference in mean tread wear between the two designs. It would be best if the taxicab owners were blinded to which tread design they are using.

A better choice would be to use a blocked design, in this case a matched-pairs design. (The blocks are the individual taxicabs themselves.) Use the same number assignment and random selection method outlined above. This time, the 50 selected cabs will have a new tire on the left-front wheel and an old tire on the right-front. The tire assignments are reversed on the remaining 50 cabs. This design has the advantage that it filters out any unwanted variability due to how the cabs are driven. At the end of the experiment, evaluate both tires for wear and determine if the mean difference of (new–old) is less than zero. Again, blinding is important.

D. GENERALIZABILITY OF RESULTS AND TYPES OF CONCLUSIONS THAT CAN BE DRAWN FROM OBSERVATIONAL STUDIES, EXPERIMENTS, AND SURVEYS

When individuals are selected at random from a population, inferences to the population can be made. Without this random selection, inference is inappropriate. This typically applies to observational studies and surveys.

When treatments are randomly assigned to groups, cause–effect relationships between explanatory and response variables can be made. Without this random assignment, causal relationships cannot be drawn. This typically applies to experiments.

It is difficult in practice to draw cause–effect relationships from observational studies and surveys because possible confounding variables are not controlled. It is also difficult to make population-wide inferences from experiments because experimental units are infrequently a random sample of the population.

Trial Run

1. To study a cause–effect relationship between variables, which of the following types of studies should be employed?

   (A) Simple random sample

   (B) Stratified random sample

   (C) Observational study

   (D) Comparative experiment

   (E) Census

2. To ensure that the results of an experiment can be generalized from a sample to a population, a researcher should

   (A) use blocking

   (B) use a control group

   (C) conduct it on a random sample of the population

   (D) repeat the study several times

   (E) use blinding

Trial Run Solutions

1. D. Well-designed experiments can allow cause–effect inferences. Surveys and observational studies, even one using a census, cannot allow this because of the lack of control for confounding variables.

2. C. Either experiments or observational studies allow inference from the sample to the population provided that the participants in the study are a random sample of the population.

CHAPTER 3
Anticipating Patterns

Chapter 3

ANTICIPATING PATTERNS

A. PROBABILITY

Probability describes the chance that a certain outcome of a random phenomenon will occur. **Random phenomena** are those where their outcomes are unpredictable in the short term, but a long-term pattern emerges. One can determine the probability of a particular event of a random phenomenon by considering a set of equally likely outcomes or by examining its long-term relative frequency. In either case, the probability of an event is always a value between 0 and 1. This is noted as $0 \leq P(\text{Event}) \leq 1$.

The probability of an event given *equally likely* outcomes is determined by the formula

$$\text{probability of event } A = P(A) = \frac{\text{number of successful outcomes}}{\text{total number of possible } equally\ likely \text{ outcomes}}$$

Example: A small high school has 16 freshmen, 15 sophomores, 12 juniors, and 17 seniors. If a student from the school is selected at random, what is the probability that the student is a junior?

Answer: When choosing a student at random, there are $16 + 15 + 12 + 17 = 60$ total equally likely outcomes of which 12 are juniors (a successful outcome). Therefore, $P(\text{junior}) = \dfrac{12}{60} = 0.2$.

Probabilities of events can also be determined by examining the long-term relative frequency of their occurrence. The principle behind this is the **law of large numbers**. The law of large numbers states: The long-term relative frequency of an event gets closer to the true relative frequency as the number of trials of the random phenomenon increases.

Example: A thumbtack is tossed onto the floor. What is the probability of it landing with its point up?

Answer: Even though there are two outcomes, "point up" and "point down," they may not be equally likely. However, one could approximate the true probability by tossing a tack many times and determining its long-term relative frequency. The graph below indicates that the probability of a tack landing "point up" is about 0.42.

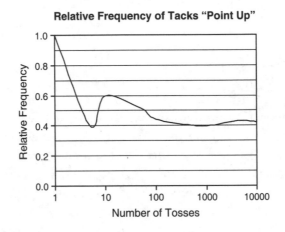

The **complement** of an event is an event *not* occurring. The following formula is used to describe complementary events.

For **complementary events**: $P(\text{not} A) = 1 - P(A)$

Example: A thumbtack is tossed onto the floor. What is the probability of it *not* landing with its point up?

Answer: From the previous example we determined that $P(\text{point up}) = 0.42$. Thus, $P(\text{not point up}) = 1 - P(\text{point up}) = 1 - 0.42 = 0.58$

On occasion, two (or more) events from a random phenomenon are considered at the same time. If those events cannot occur simultaneously, we call them **disjoint** (or **mutually exclusive**). For example, when considering a randomly selected high school student, the events "freshman" and "sophomore" are disjoint since the student cannot be both a freshman and a sophomore. The events "boy" and "sophomore" are not disjoint because the student could be both a sophomore and a boy.

The **addition rule** for probability aids in computing the chances of one or several events occurring at a given time.

Addition rule: $P(A \cup B) = P(A) + P(B) - P(A \cap B)$. (Note: $\cup$ is the symbol for *union* or the word "or"; $\cap$ is the symbol for *intersection* or the word "and.") If events A and B are disjoint, $P(A \cap B) = 0$.

Example: The table below shows the breakdown of students in a small school by class and gender. What is the probability that a randomly selected student will be a sophomore or a junior?

	Freshmen	Sophomores	Juniors	Seniors	Total
Boys	9	7	5	7	28
Girls	7	8	7	10	32
Total	16	15	12	17	60

Answer: $P(\text{sophomore}) = \dfrac{15}{60}$, $P(\text{junior}) = \dfrac{12}{60}$, so,

$$P(\text{sophomore} \cup \text{junior}) = P(\text{sophomore}) + P(\text{junior}) = \frac{15}{60} + \frac{12}{60} = \frac{27}{60} = 0.45.$$

Example: What is the probability that a randomly selected student will be a sophomore or a girl?

Answer: $P(\text{sophomore}) = \dfrac{15}{60}$, $P(\text{girl}) = \dfrac{32}{60}$, so,

$$P(\text{sophomore} \cup \text{girl}) = P(\text{sophomore}) + P(\text{girl}) - P(\text{sophomore} \cap \text{girl})$$

$$= \frac{15}{60} + \frac{32}{60} - \frac{8}{60} = \frac{39}{60} = 0.65.$$

A **Venn diagram** is a graphical representation of sets or outcomes and how they intersect. A Venn diagram for two events A and B is shown below. The black oval corresponds to the outcomes in event A; the light gray oval does the same for event B. The intersection is seen as dark gray. The outcomes belonging to neither event are in the white area.

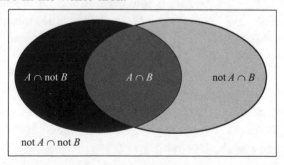

Consider the previous example. Sophomores are 15 of the students and are within the black oval—8 girls and 7 boys. Girls are 32 of the students and are in the light gray oval—8 sophomores and 24 from other classes. There are 8 sophomore girls, so there are 8 in the intersection. Twenty-one students are neither sophomores nor girls (freshman boys, junior boys, and senior boys). The $P(\text{sophomore} \cup \text{girl})$ is equal to the number of students that fall into either the sophomore or girl ovals or both, which is $7 + 8 + 24 = 39$, divided by the total number of students, which is 60.

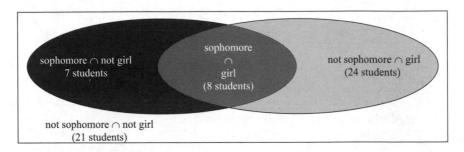

Sometimes we are interested in the probability of an event occurring given that another event has occurred. This is called **conditional probability**.

Conditional probability: $P(B \mid A) = \dfrac{P(A \cap B)}{P(A)}$. (Note: the vertical bar I is the symbol for "given that" and precedes the condition that has occurred.)

Example: What is the probability that a randomly selected student is a girl *given that* the student is a sophomore?

Answer: ~$P(\text{sophomore}) = \dfrac{15}{60}$, $P(\text{girl} \cap \text{sophomore}) = \dfrac{8}{60}$, so,

$$P(\text{girl} \mid \text{sophomore}) = \frac{P(\text{girl} \cap \text{sophomore})}{P(\text{sophomore})} = \frac{8/60}{15/60} = \frac{8}{15} \approx 0.533.$$

Another way to see this is that once it is established that the student is a sophomore, there are only 15 students it could possibly be and 8 of those are girls.

When two events are related, and the fact that one event has occurred changes the probability that the second event occurs, the events are called **dependent**. Therefore, if knowing that one event has occurred does *not* change the chance that the second event occurs, the events are called **independent**.

    Independence check: Events A and B are independent if $P(B|A) = P(B)$.

Example: Are the events "girl" and "sophomore" independent?

Answer: $P(\text{girl}) = \dfrac{32}{60} \approx 0.533$ and $P(\text{girl}|\text{sophomore}) = \dfrac{8/60}{15/60} = \dfrac{8}{15} \approx 0.533$.

Since $P(\text{girl}) = P(\text{girl}|\text{sophomore})$, the events "girl" and "sophomore" are independent.

Example: Are the events "girl" and "junior" independent?

Answer: $P(\text{girl}) = \dfrac{32}{60} \approx 0.533$ and $P(\text{girl} \mid \text{junior}) = \dfrac{7/60}{12/60} = \dfrac{7}{12} \approx 0.583$.

Since $P(\text{girl}) \neq P(\text{girl} \mid \text{junior})$, the events "girl" and "junior" are *not* independent.

When we are interested in the probability of two events occurring simultaneously, or in successive trials, we use the **multiplication rule**.

Multiplication rule: $P(A \cap B) = P(A) \cdot P(B|A)$

Example: Two students are selected at random from the school without replacement. What is the probability that they are both boys?

	Freshmen	Sophomores	Juniors	Seniors	Total
Boys	9	7	5	7	28
Girls	7	8	7	10	32
Total	16	15	12	17	60

Answer:

$P(\text{first is boy} \cap \text{second is boy}) = P(\text{first is boy}) \cdot P(\text{second is boy}|\text{first is boy})$.

$P(\text{first is boy}) = \dfrac{28}{60}$ and $P(\text{second is boy} \mid \text{first is boy}) = \dfrac{27}{59}$, because the first boy is not replaced leaving 27 boys out of 59 students.

$P(\text{first is boy} \cap \text{second is boy}) = \dfrac{28}{60} \cdot \dfrac{27}{59} = \dfrac{756}{3{,}540} \approx 0.214$.

If events are **independent**, then $P(B|A) = P(B)$, so the **multiplication rule** becomes $P(A \cap B) = P(A) \cdot P(B)$.

Example: Two fair six-sided dice are rolled. What is the probability that the first die shows an odd number and the second die shows a number greater than 4?

Answer: Since the first die's outcome does not influence the second's, the two events are independent. Thus,

$$P(\text{first die odd} \cap \text{second die} > 4) = P(\text{first die odd}) \cdot P(\text{second die} > 4)$$

$$= \frac{3}{6} \cdot \frac{2}{6} = \frac{6}{36} \approx 0.167.$$

A tree diagram is a helpful way to picture the probabilities of successive or compound events, particularly when there are conditional probabilities to consider. A tree diagram for two events, A and B, is shown below. Probabilities for each outcome are listed on the branches. The probability of the final result is the product of the probabilities along the branches.

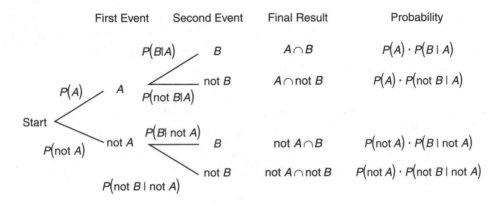

Example: At a particular school 47% of the students are boys and 53% are girls. Of the boys, 25% are seniors. Of the girls, 31% are seniors. If a randomly selected student is a senior, what is the probability that it is a girl?

Answer: Making a tree diagram, let event G represent a girl and event S represent a senior.

First Event	Second Event	Final Result	Probability
0.53 — G	0.31 — S	$G \cap S$	$(0.53)(0.31) = 0.1643$
	0.69 — not S	$G \cap \text{not } S$	$(0.53)(0.69) = 0.3657$
0.47 — not G	0.25 — S	not $G \cap S$	$(0.47)(0.25) = 0.1175$
	0.75 — not S	not $G \cap \text{not } S$	$(0.47)(0.75) = 0.3525$

The question asks, what is $P(G|S)$?

$$P(G \mid S) = \frac{P(G \cap S)}{P(S)} = \frac{0.1643}{0.1643 + 0.1175} = \frac{0.1643}{0.2818} \approx 0.5830.$$

Discrete Random Variables

A **random variable** is a *numerical* outcome of a random phenomenon. It could be the number of heads seen in 10 flips of a coin, the number of pets in an animal shelter on any given day, the heights of high school volleyball players, or the amount of gasoline purchased at the most recent fill-up.

Random variables can be either **discrete** or **continuous**. Discrete random variables are those usually obtained by counting, such as counting heads of coin flips or pets in a shelter. Continuous random variables are those typically found by measuring, such as heights of volleyball players or amount of gasoline.

The **probability distribution** of a discrete random variable X is a function matching all n possible outcomes of the random variable (x_i) and their associated probabilities $P(x_i)$. For a probability distribution to be valid, it must meet two characteristics:

(1)   For each value of x_i, where $i = 1, 2, \ldots, n$, $0 \leq P(x_i) \leq 1$.

(2) $\sum_{i=1}^{n} P(x_i) = 1$.

Example: The number of cars X owned by the families of students at a small high school can be given by the probability distribution:

Number of cars, x	0	1	2	3	4
Probability, $P(x)$	0.05	0.15	0.35	0.30	?

What is the probability that a randomly selected student's family owns four cars?

Answer: Since the total of the probabilities must equal 1, the probability that student's family owns four cars is $1 - (0.05 + 0.15 + 0.35 + 0.30) = 1 - 0.85 = 0.15$.

Example: The number of cars X owned by the families of students at a small high school can be given by the probability distribution:

Number of cars, x	0	1	2	3	4
Probability, $P(x)$	0.05	0.15	0.35	0.30	0.15

Create a probability histogram for the random variable X.

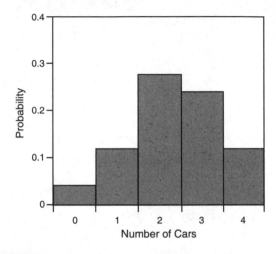

Answer: Measures of center and spread can be computed for discrete random variables just like data. The most common of these measures are mean, median, standard deviation, and variance.

Mean of a discrete random variable X: $\mu_X = \sum_{i=1}^{n} x_i \cdot P(x_i)$. The mean μ_X of random variable X is also referred to as the **expected value of X**, and symbolized $E(X)$.

Median of a discrete random variable X: The value of X such that $P(X \le x) \ge 0.5$ and $P(X \ge x) \ge 0.5$.

Variance of a discrete random variable X: $\sigma_X^2 = \sum_{i=1}^{n} (x_i - \mu_x)^2 \cdot P(x_i)$.

Standard deviation of a discrete random variable X: $\sigma_X = \sqrt{\sigma_X^2}$.

Example: The number of cars X owned by the families of students at a large high school can be given by the probability distribution:

Number of cars, x	0	1	2	3	4
Probability, $P(x)$	0.05	0.15	0.35	0.30	0.15

Find the mean, median, variance, and standard deviation of the probability distribution.

Answer: The mean of the probability distribution is

$$\mu_X = \sum_{i=1}^{n} x_i \cdot P(x_i)$$
$$= (0)(0.05) + (1)(0.15) + (2)(0.35) + (3)(0.3) + (4)(0.15)$$
$$= 2.35 \text{ cars.}$$

This can also be written as $E(X) = 2.35$ cars.

The median is the value of X where $P(X \le x) \ge 0.5$ and $P(X \ge x) \ge 0.5$. This occurs at $X = 2$ cars, since $P(X \le 2) = 0.55$ and $P(X \ge 2) = 0.8$.

The variance of the probability distribution is

$$\sigma_X^2 = \sum_{i=1}^{n} (x_i - \mu_X)^2 \cdot P(x_i)$$
$$= (0-2.35)^2(0.05) + (1-2.35)^2(0.15) + (2-2.35)^2(0.35) + (3-2.35)^2$$
$$(3-2.35)^2(0.3) + (4-2.35)^2(0.15)$$
$$= 1.1275 \text{ cars}^2.$$

The standard deviation of the probability distribution is

$$\sigma_X = \sqrt{\sigma_X^2} = \sqrt{1.1275} \approx 1.0618 \text{ cars.}$$

Calculator Tip:

The mean and standard deviation of a probability distribution can be calculated with the graphing calculator. Consider the previous example.

From the home screen, go to the list editor by pressing $\boxed{\text{STAT}}$; then from the EDIT menu choose 1:Edit.... Enter the values of the random variable x_i in list L1 and enter the corresponding probabilities $p(x_i)$ in list L2.

L1	L2	L3	2
0	.05	------	
1	.15		
2	.35		
3	.3		
4	.15		
------	------		
L2(5) =.15			

Return to the home screen and press $\boxed{\text{STAT}}$, scroll right to the CALC menu, and then choose 1: 1–Var Stats. Press $\boxed{\text{L1}}$, $\boxed{\text{L2}}$, and then press $\boxed{\text{ENTER}}$.

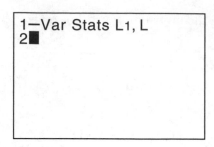

```
1—Var Stats L1, L
2█
```

The mean of the probability distribution will be listed as $\bar{x}$ (even though the correct symbol for it would be μ), and the standard deviation will be listed as σx. Note that the value of n should be 1, as the sum of the frequencies (probabilities) is 1.

```
1—Var Stats
x̄=2.35
Σx=2.35
Σx²=6.65
Sx=
σx=1.061838029
↓n=1
```

Binomial Random Variables

A random variable X is called a **binomial random variable** if it meets the following conditions:

(1)   There are a fixed number of trials, n, of a random phenomenon.

(2)   There are only two possible outcomes on each trial, often called *success* and *failure*.

(3)   The probability of success, p, is constant for each trial.

(4)   Each trial is independent of the other trials.

The random variable X is the count of the number of successes in the n trials.

The probability that exactly k successes are obtained in n trials of a binomial random variable is $P(X = k) = \binom{n}{k} p^k (1-p)^{n-k}$, where $\binom{n}{k}$ is called the *binomial coefficient* and has a value $\binom{n}{k} = \dfrac{n!}{k!(n-k)!}$.

Example: The probability of a thumbtack landing "point up" when tossed is 0.42. If a thumbtack is tossed eight times, what is the probability that it lands "point up" exactly twice?

Answer: The count of the number of "point up" landings of a tossed tack is a binomial random variable because the four conditions listed above are satisfied. The probability of exactly two tosses of eight "point up" landings is

$$
\begin{aligned}
P(X=2) &= \binom{8}{2}(0.42)^2(1-0.42)^{8-2} \\
&= \frac{8!}{2!\,6!}(0.42)^2(0.58)^6 \\
&= 28\,(0.42)^2(0.58)^6 \\
&\approx 0.188.
\end{aligned}
$$

Calculator Tip:

Binomial probabilities can be calculated with the graphing calculator. Consider the previous example.

From the home screen, press $\boxed{\text{DISTR}}$ (which is $\boxed{\text{2nd}}\ \boxed{\text{VARS}}$), and then choose A: binompdf(. This is the binomial probability density function command and is used for computing binomial probabilities for a particular number of successes.

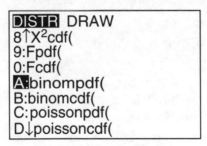

The syntax for the binompdf command is binompdf (number of trials, probability of success, number of successes). Key in 8, .42, 2) and then press $\boxed{\text{ENTER}}$.

The binomial probability for getting exactly two successes in eight trials with the probability of success of 0.42 is about 0.188.

Example: The probability of a thumbtack landing "point up" when tossed is 0.42. If a thumbtack is tossed eight times, what is the probability that it lands "point up" at most twice?

Answer: The probability of at most two of eight "point up" landings is

$$P(X \le 2) = P(X = 0) + P(X = 1) + P(X = 2).$$

From the previous example $P(X = 2) \approx 0.188$.

$$
\begin{aligned}
P(X = 1) &= \binom{8}{1}(0.42)^1(1 - 0.42)^{8-1} \\
&= 8(0.42)^1(0.58)^7 \\
&\approx 0.074.
\end{aligned}
$$

$$
\begin{aligned}
P(X = 0) &= \binom{8}{0}(0.42)^0(1 - 0.42)^{8-0} \\
&= 1(0.42)^0(0.58)^8 \\
&\approx 0.013.
\end{aligned}
$$

So, $P(X \le 2) \approx 0.188 + 0.074 + 0.013 \approx 0.275.$

Calculator Tip:

Cumulative binomial probabilities can be calculated with the graphing calculator. Consider the previous example.

From the home screen, press $\boxed{\text{DISTR}}$, and then choose B: binomcdf(. This is the binomial cumulative density function command and is used for computing binomial probabilities of a given number of successes or less.

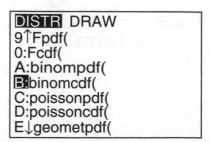

The syntax for the binomcdf command is binomcdf(number of trials, probability of success, number of successes or less). Key in 8, .42, 2) and then press ENTER .

```
binomcdf (8, .42, 2)
        .2750234624
```

The binomial probability for getting two or fewer successes in eight trials with the probability of success of 0.42 is about 0.275.

The **binomial distribution** is the probability distribution of a binomial random variable, that is, all possible outcomes of X in n trials and their associated probabilities.

Example: Give the binomial distribution of a thumbtack landing "point up" when it is tossed eight times and the probability of success is 0.42.

Number of "point up"	0	1	2	3	4	5	6	7	8
Probability	0.013	0.074	0.188	0.272	0.246	0.143	0.052	0.011	0.0001

Answer: Using the calculator's binompdf function, we get

Example: Create a probability histogram for the binomial distribution of a thumbtack landing "point up" when it is tossed four times and the probability of success is 0.42.

Number of "point up"	0	1	2	3	4
Probability	0.113	0.328	0.356	0.172	0.031

Answer: The probability distribution is

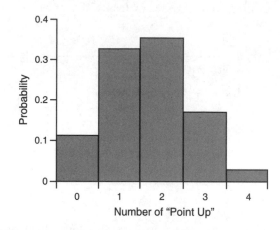

The corresponding histogram is

The mean and variance of a binomial random variable can be easily calculated. When the formulas $\mu_X = \sum_{i=1}^{n} x_i \cdot P(x_i)$ and $\sigma_X^2 = \sum_{i=1}^{n} (x_i - \mu_X)^2 \cdot P(x_i)$ are applied to a binomial random variable, the following result:

Mean of a binomial random variable X: $\mu_X = E(X) = np$.

Variance of a binomial random variable X: $\sigma_X^2 = np(1-p)$.

Standard deviation of a binomial random variable X: $\sigma_X = \sqrt{np(1-p)}$.

Example: A thumbtack that lands "point up" with probability 0.42 is tossed eight times. What are the mean, variance, and standard deviation of the number of times it lands "point up"?

Answer:

The mean is $\mu_X = np = (8)(0.42) = 3.36$ times,

$\sigma_X^2 = (8)(0.42)(0.58) = 1.9488$ times^2,

$\sigma_X = \sqrt{(8)(0.42)(0.58)} \approx 1.396$ times. (Note: The mean number of times the tack lands "point up" in eight tosses is 3.36. Even though the tack itself cannot land "point up" 3.36 times, it can on average.)

Geometric Random Variables

A random variable X is called a **geometric random variable** if it meets the following conditions:

(1)   There are only two possible outcomes on each trial, often called *success* and *failure*.

(2)   The probability of success, p, is constant for each trial.

(3)   Each trial is independent of the other trials.

The random variable X is the count of the number of trials until the first success is obtained. A geometric random variable results from what is often called a "wait time" situation.

The probability that exactly k trials occur before the first success of a geometric random variable is obtained is $P(X = k) = p(1-p)^{k-1}$.

Example: The probability of a thumbtack landing "point up" when tossed is 0.42. What is the probability that the tack is tossed exactly four times before it lands "point up"?

Answer: The number of trials before a tossed tack lands "point up" is a geometric random variable because the three conditions listed above are satisfied. The tprobability of exactly four tosses before landing "point up" is

$$
\begin{aligned}
P(X = 4) &= (0.42)(1-0.42)^{4-1} \\
&= (0.42)(0.58)^3 \\
&\approx 0.082.
\end{aligned}
$$

Calculator Tip:

Geometric probabilities can be calculated with the graphing calculator. Consider the previous example.

From the home screen, press $\boxed{\text{DISTR}}$, and then choose E: geometpdf(. This is the geometric probability density function command and is used for computing geometric probabilities for a particular number of trials.

```
DISTR DRAW
0↑Fcdf(
A:binompdf(
B:binomcdf(
C:poissonpdf(
D:poissoncdf(
E:geometpdf(
F:geometcdf(
```

The syntax for the geometpdf command is geometpdf(probability of success, number of trials). Key in .42,4) and then press $\boxed{\text{ENTER}}$.

$$\boxed{\begin{array}{l} \text{geometpdf}(.42, 4) \\ \qquad\qquad\qquad .08194704 \end{array}}$$

The geometric probability for getting the first success on the fourth trial with the probability of success of 0.42 is about 0.082.

Example: The probability of a thumbtack landing "point up" when tossed is 0.42. What is the probability that the tack is tossed at most four times before it lands "point up"?

Answer: The probability of at most four trials before landing "point up" is

$P(X \leq 4) = P(X = 1) + P(X = 2) + P(X = 3) + P(X = 4)$.
From the previous example, $P(X = 4) \approx 0.082$.

$$
\begin{aligned}
P(X = 1) &= (0.42)(1 - 0.42)^{1-1} \\
&= (0.42)(0.58)^0 \\
&= 0.42.
\end{aligned}
$$

$$
\begin{aligned}
P(X = 2) &= (0.42)(1 - 0.42)^{2-1} \\
&= (0.42)(0.58)^1 \\
&\approx 0.244.
\end{aligned}
$$

$$
\begin{aligned}
P(X = 3) &= (0.42)(1 - 0.42)^{3-1} \\
&= (0.42)(0.58)^2 \\
&\approx 0.141.
\end{aligned}
$$

So, $P(X \leq 4) \approx 0.42 + 0.244 + 0.141 + 0.082 \approx 0.887$.

Calculator Tip:

Cumulative geometric probabilities can be calculated with the graphing calculator. Consider the previous example.

From the home screen, press $\boxed{\text{DISTR}}$, and then choose F: geometcdf(. This is the geometric cumulative density function command and is used for computing geometric probabilities of a given number of trials or less.

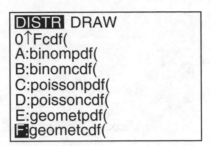

The syntax for the geometcdf command is geometcdf(probability of success, number of trials). Key in .42,4) and then press $\boxed{\text{ENTER}}$.

```
geometcdf(.42, 4)
                    .88683504
```

The geometric probability for getting the first success in four or fewer trials with the probability of success of 0.42 is about 0.887.

The **geometric distribution** is the probability distribution of a geometric random variable, that is, all possible outcomes of *X* before the first success is seen and their associated probabilities.

Example: Give the geometric distribution of a thumbtack landing "point up" if the probability of success is 0.42. Create the corresponding probability histogram.

Answer: Using the calculator's geometpdf function, we get

Number of trials	1	2	3	4	5	6	7	8	...
Probability	0.42	0.244	0.141	0.082	0.048	0.028	0.016	0.009	...

The corresponding histogram is

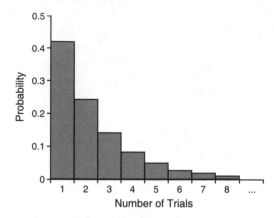

Note: that the geometric distribution goes on to infinity, but there will come a point where the number of trials before seeing the first success is practically zero.

The mean and variance of a geometric random variable can be easily calculated. When the formulas $\mu_X = \sum_{i=1}^{n} x_i \cdot P(x_i)$ and $\sigma_X^2 = \sum_{i=1}^{n} (x_i - \mu_X)^2 \cdot P(x_i)$ are applied to a geometric random variable, the following result (in spite of the number of possibilities being infinite):

Mean of a geometric random variable X: $\mu_X = E(X) = \dfrac{1}{p}$.

Variance of a geometric random variable X: $\sigma_X^2 = \dfrac{1-p}{p^2}$.

Standard deviation of a geometric random variable X: $\sigma_X = \sqrt{\dfrac{1-p}{p^2}}$.

Example: A thumbtack which lands "point up" with probability 0.42 is tossed. What are the mean, variance, and standard deviation of the number of trials before it lands "point up"?

Answer: The mean is $\mu_X = \dfrac{1}{0.42} \approx 2.381$ times, $\sigma_X^2 = \dfrac{1-0.42}{0.42^2} \approx 3.288$ times^2,

$\sigma_X = \sqrt{\dfrac{1-0.42}{0.42^2}} \approx 1.813$ times.

Simulations of Random Phenomena

Sometimes one is interested in finding the probability distribution of a random phenomenon, but the situation is too complex to use the methods outlined in this chapter thus far. Perhaps the scenario does not generate a binomial or geometric distribution. Computing the probabilities algebraically or with diagrams may be very time consuming. In these cases, **simulation** is a tool to answer the question.

Simulation is a method to model chance behavior that accurately mimics the situation being considered. The mechanism used to determine outcomes is called a **chance device**. A chance device could be a coin, a handful of dice, a random digit table, or computer/calculator code that generates random values. In this book, a **random digit table** will be used, as that is the chance device that will likely appear on the examination.

To conduct a simulation, follow these five steps:

(1)   Describe the situation and its possible outcomes.

(2)   Identify how a chance device used will model the outcomes of the situation.

(3)   Describe what one trial of the experiment will be and what response variable will be recorded.

(4)   Conduct several trials of the experiment.

(5)   Analyze the distribution of the response variable and draw a conclusion.

Example: Boxes of a cereal contain collector cards of characters from a movie. Some cards are more common than others. The distribution of the character cards in the boxes is given by the following:

Alfred the Agile: 20%
Brian the Brave: 30%
Craig the Crafty: 50%

What is the mean number of cereal boxes one would have to buy in order to get all three cards? Use the random digit table below to conduct a simulation. Do five trials of your simulation.

0 0 2 3 3	5 4 8 3 0	3 9 1 0 8
0 8 9 9 6	1 4 2 2 3	3 9 2 8 0
7 1 4 0 5	4 9 9 5 3	3 0 3 2 4

Answer: Conduct the simulation following the five-step process:

(1)   Simulate the opening of a box of cereal and determine which of the three cards (A, B, C) is in the box.

(2) Random digits will be taken one at a time from the table, each representing one box of cereal. The value of the digit corresponds to the card in the box as follows: 0–1 = A, 2–4 = B, 5–9 = C.

(3) One trial will consist of selecting random digits until at least one result of each of "A," "B," and "C" is obtained. The response variable is the number of boxes of cereal opened.

(4)

```
        0  0  2  3  3    5 | 4  8  3  0 | 3  9  1 | 0  8
Card    A  A  B  B  B    C | B  C  B  A | B  C  A | A  C
No. of
boxes              6 boxes |   4 boxes  | 3 boxes |


        0  8  9  9  6    1  4 | 2  2  3 | 3  9  2  8  0
Card    A  C  C  C  C    A  B | B  B  B | B  C  B  C  A
No. of
boxes             10 boxes   |         |      7 boxes

        7  1  4  0  5    4  9    9  5  3    3  0  3  2  4
```

(Note: When the end of the first line was reached, the trial was continued on the second line.)

(5) The numbers of boxes needed to get all three cards were 3, 4, 6, 7, and 10. The mean number of boxes is $\bar{x} = 6$.

Example: Fifteen students from a large high school have been selected to attend a meeting across town. Parents from the school have been asked to provide transportation to the event in their private cars and are to phone the school if interested. The school will accept calls until enough vehicles are obtained to transport the 15 students. The probability distribution below shows the number of passengers a car can hold, not including the driver, and the percentage of parents who own cars of that capacity.

Number of passengers	1	3	4	6
Percentage of cars	0.05	0.50	0.35	0.10

What is the average number of parents that will need to call to have enough transportation for 20 students? Use the random digit table below to conduct a simulation. Do five trials of your simulation, starting each trial on a new line.

0 1 4 0 5	4 9 9 5 3	3 0 3 2 4
9 6 0 8 0	5 1 2 9 0	3 3 8 4 3
9 5 9 4 5	0 4 8 3 4	3 7 5 2 0
9 3 0 1 5	9 3 6 1 5	0 3 4 1 3
3 6 3 7 0	1 0 3 5 6	0 3 7 6 8

Answer: Conduct the simulation following the five-step process:

(1) Simulate the phone call of a parent and determine how many passengers the parent's car will hold.

(2) Random digits will be taken two at a time from the table, each representing one parent's car. The value of the digits corresponds to the number of passengers the car will hold: 01–05 = 1 passenger, 06–55 = 3 passengers, 56–90 = 4 passengers, 91–99 and 00 = 6 passengers.

(3) One trial will consist of selecting pairs of random digits and recording the number of passengers the car holds until a total of 15 or more passengers are obtained. The response variable is the number of parents that called.

(4)

	0 1	4 0	5 4	9 9	5 3	3 0 3 2 4
No. of passengers	1	3	3	6	3	
Total passengers	1	4	8	14	17	
No. of calls			5			

	9 6	0 8	0 5	1 2	9 0	3 3 8 4 3
No. of passengers	6	3	1	3	4	
Total passengers	6	9	10	13	17	
No. of calls			5			

	9 5	9 4	5		0	4 8 3 4		3 7 5 2 0
No. of passengers	6	6	3					
Total passengers	6	12	15					
No. of calls			3					

	9 3	0 1	5		9	3 6	1 5		0 3 4 1 3
No. of passengers	6	1	4			3	3		
Total passengers	6	7	11			14	17		
No. of calls			5						

	3 6	3 7	0		1	0 3	5 6		0 3	7 6	8
No. of passengers	3	3	1		1	4			1	4	
Total passengers	3	6	7		8	12			13	17	
No. of calls					7						

(Note: It is alright to create a two-digit number by using adjacent ends of five-digit groups, as in "54" in the first row of the simulation.)

(5) The numbers of parents that called before we had the required passenger space were 3, 5, 5, 5, and 7. The mean is $\bar{x} = 5$ parents.

Linear Transformations of Random Variables

It is sometimes necessary to change or transform a random variable X by adding (or subtracting) a constant, multiplying (or dividing) by a constant, or both. Doing so affects measures of center and spread in a predicable manner.

If a random variable X is transformed by multiplying by the constant b, and/or adding the constant a, then

the mean of the transformed variable is $\mu_{a+bX} = a + b\mu_X$;

the variance of the transformed variable is $\sigma^2_{a+bX} = b^2\sigma^2_X$.

Example: Boxes of a cereal contain collector cards of characters from a movie. Some cards are more common than others. The distribution of the character cards in the boxes is given by the following:

Alfred the Agile: 20%

Brian the Brave: 30%

Craig the Crafty: 50%

The mean number of cereal boxes one would have to buy in order to get all three cards is approximately 6.7 with a standard deviation of 4.1. This was determined by running the earlier simulation 10,000 times! (On a computer, of course.)

Boxes of cereal currently cost $3.72 each. The cereal company also sells a special frame to hold the collectors cards for $5.99. What are the mean and standard deviation of the cost to complete the collection of three cards and put them in the special frame?

Answer: The random variable X is the number of boxes purchased to complete the three-card collection. It is given that $\mu_X = 6.7$ boxes and $\sigma_X = 4.1$ boxes. The variance of the number of boxes purchased would be $\sigma_X^2 = (\sigma_X)^2 = 4.1^2 = 16.81$.

For every box purchased, $3.72 is paid. When the set is complete, an additional $5.99 is spent regardless of the number of boxes purchased. The mean and standard deviation of the cost of completing the collection are

$$
\begin{aligned}
\mu_{a+bX} &= a + b\mu_X \\
\mu_{5.99+3.72X} &= 5.99 + 3.72\,(6.7) \\
&= 30.914
\end{aligned}
$$

and

$$
\begin{aligned}
\sigma_{a+bX}^2 &= b^2 \sigma_X^2 \\
\sigma_{5.99+3.72X}^2 &= 3.72^2\,(16.81). \\
&\approx 232.624
\end{aligned}
$$

The standard deviation is $\sigma_{a+bX} = \sqrt{\sigma_{a+bX}^2} = \sqrt{232.623504} = 15.252$.

Thus, the mean cost of completing the collection is about $30.91 with a standard deviation of $15.25.

Trial Run

1. Among a group of boys, 70% like chocolate ice cream, 40% like strawberry ice cream, and 30% like both. If a boy is randomly selected from the

group, what is the probability that he likes either chocolate or strawberry ice cream, but NOT both?

(A) 10%

(B) 20%

(C) 30%

(D) 50%

(E) 80%

2. Marketing managers at various department stores that are housed at malls are studying the types of people that might be shopping in their store. Their hopes are to make sure that they are catering to the clientele coming to their store. Vehicles parked within 200 feet of various "anchor" stores at a mall were categorized as shown in the table below as well as the type of store. The data were collected on a Saturday in May.

		Classification of Vehicle				
		Compact	Family/SUV	Luxury	Sport	Total
Store Class	Discount	130	198	12	32	372
	Mid-range	108	210	42	64	424
	High-end	64	178	53	73	368
	Total	302	586	107	169	1,164

If a vehicle is randomly selected, what is the probability that the vehicle is Compact given that it is parked within 200 feet of a Mid-range store?

(A) $\dfrac{108}{1,164}$

(B) $\dfrac{108}{302}$

(C) $\dfrac{108}{424}$

(D) $\dfrac{302}{1,164}$

(E) $\dfrac{302}{1,164}$

3. Events A and B are independent. If $P(A) = \dfrac{1}{3}$, which of the following statements is true?

(A) If $P(B) = \dfrac{4}{5}$, then $P(A \cap B) = \dfrac{7}{15}$.

(B) If $P(B) = \dfrac{1}{2}$, then $P(B \mid A) = \dfrac{1}{6}$.

(C) If $P(B) = \dfrac{2}{3}$, then $P(A \cup B) = \dfrac{2}{9}$.

(D) If $P(B) = \dfrac{1}{4}$, then $P(A \cap B) = \dfrac{1}{12}$.

(E) If $P(B) = \dfrac{1}{5}$, then $P(A \mid B) = \dfrac{8}{15}$.

4. A pair of fair four-sided dice, with faces numbered 1, 2, 3, and 4, is rolled. The maximum, M, of the two dice is recorded after each roll. Which of the following describes the probability distribution of M?

(A)

M	1	2	3	4
Probability	$\dfrac{1}{4}$	$\dfrac{1}{4}$	$\dfrac{1}{4}$	$\dfrac{1}{4}$

(B)

M	1	2	3	4
Probability	$\dfrac{3}{16}$	$\dfrac{5}{16}$	$\dfrac{5}{16}$	$\dfrac{3}{16}$

(C)

M	1	2	3	4
Probability	$\dfrac{1}{16}$	$\dfrac{3}{16}$	$\dfrac{5}{16}$	$\dfrac{7}{16}$

(D)

M	1	2	3	4
Probability	1	0	0	0

(E)

M	1	2	3	4
Probability	0	0	0	1

5. A baseball player has a batting average of 0.350, that is, he has a 0.350 probability of getting a hit any time he comes to bat. If the player comes to bat four times in a game, what is the probability that the first hit occurs on the fourth at bat?

(A) $\dfrac{1!}{4!}$

(B) $\dfrac{4!}{3! \cdot 1!} (0.35)^1 (0.65)^3$

(C) $\dfrac{0.35}{(0.65)^3}$

(D) $3(0.65)(0.35)$

(E) $(0.65)^3 (0.35)$

6. There are 13,000 students at a certain university, 55% of whom are women. Of the women, 58% live on campus while only 38% of the men do. If a random sample of 500 students is taken, what is the expected number of students in the sample who live on campus?

    (A) 190

    (B) 240

    (C) 245

    (D) 290

    (E) 480

7. Which of the pairs of events below are mutually exclusive when rolling a die once containing the numbers 1, 2, 3, 4, 5, and 6?

    (A) The probability of rolling a 5 and an odd number

    (B) The probability of rolling a 4 and an even number

    (C) The probability of rolling a number less than 4 and a multiple of 3

    (D) The probability of rolling a number greater than 5 and an odd number

    (E) The probability of rolling a perfect square and a number that is not odd

8. It has been shown that a certain medication alleviates arthritis symptoms in 26% of all cases.

    (a) If 40 randomly selected arthritis sufferers are given the medication, what are the mean and standard deviation of the number that will experience relief?

(b) What is the probability that exactly 10 of the 40 will experience relief? Show all work.

9. In a game of chance at a school carnival, a player rolls a dodecahedral die—a die with 12 faces. The faces are numbered from 1 through 12. On the basis of the roll of the die, the player wins a prize. In the table below, the monetary values of the prizes are listed with their corresponding die rolls.

Die Roll	1, 2, 3, 4, or 5	6, 7, 8, or 9	10 or 11	12
Prize Value	$0.50	$1.00	$2.00	$4.50

(a) What are the mean and standard deviation of the value of prizes won by a player who plays this game?

(b) It costs $1.00 to play the game. What is the net gain/loss in monetary value from the player's perspective?

10. A game is played by two players named "A" and "B." In the game, each of the players rolls a fair die with faces numbered 1 through 6. If the product of the rolls is even, A scores a point. If the product of the rolls is odd, B scores a point. The rolls are repeated until one player has five points, in which case that player wins the game.

Create a simulation to estimate the probability of Player A winning the game. Do three runs of your simulation to make your estimate. Use the random digit table below to conduct the simulation.

01405	49953	30324	90338
96080	51390	33843	01599
95945	04834	37520	13363
93015	93615	03413	14054
36370	10356	03768	97531

Trial Run Solutions

1. D. A Venn diagram of the situation makes this easy to solve. Seventy percent of the boys reside in the chocolate oval (*C*), 40% in the strawberry oval (*S*), and 30% in the intersection. Those who like either chocolate or strawberry but not both amount to 40% + 10% = 50%.

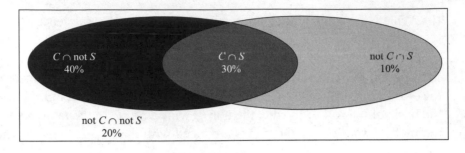

2. C.

$$P(\text{compact} \mid \text{mid–range}) = \frac{P(\text{compact} \cap \text{mid–range})}{P(\text{mid–range})} = \frac{108/1164}{424/1164} = \frac{108}{424}.$$

3. D. If events A and B are independent, then $P(A \cap B) = P(A) \cdot P(B)$; thus $P(A \cap B) = \frac{1}{3} \cdot \frac{1}{4} = \frac{1}{12}$. In choice A, $P(A \cap B) = \frac{1}{3} \cdot \frac{4}{5} = \frac{4}{15}$. In choices B and E, $P(B|A) = P(B)$ and $P(A|B) = P(A)$, since A and B are independent. In choice C,

$$P(A \cup B) = P(A) + P(B) - P(A \cap B) = \frac{1}{3} + \frac{2}{3} - \left(\frac{1}{3}\right)\left(\frac{2}{3}\right) = \frac{7}{9}.$$

4. C. There are 16 pairs that can be rolled: (1, 1), (1, 2), (1, 3), (1, 4), (2, 1), (2, 2), (2, 3), (2, 4), (3, 1), (3, 2), (3, 3), (3, 4), (4, 1), (4, 2), (4, 3), and (4, 4). The maximum M occurs in the following frequencies: 1—one time; 2—three times; 3—five times; and 4—seven times.

5. E. This is a "waiting time" situation with independent trials, so the number of times at bat until a hit occurs is a geometric random variable with $p = 0.35$. The probability that the first hit occurs on the fourth at bat is

$$P(X = 4) = 0.35\,(1 - 0.35)^{4-1} = 0.35\,(0.65)^3.$$

6. C. Fifty-five percent of students are women and 58% of them live on campus, so $(0.55)(0.58) = 0.319$ or 31.9% of the students are women who live on campus. Similarly, 45% of the students are men and 38% of them live on campus, so $(0.45)(0.38) = 0.171$ or 17.1% of the students are men who live on campus. Thus, 31.9% + 17.1% = 49% of the students live on campus. In a sample of 500 students, we would expect 49% of them, or 245, to live on campus.

7. D. Mutually exclusive means that events cannot occur at the same time. Only D satisfies this, as all numbers greater than 5—which is only 6—are even.

8. (a) The number of people getting relief is a binomial random variable. There are only two outcomes, relief or no relief; there are a fixed number of trials, $n = 40$; the probability of a success (pain relief) is constant, $p = 0.26$; and the trials should be independent—a person should be no more or less likely to experience relief if another person has.

   The mean and standard deviation of this binomial random variable are $\mu_X = np = 40\,(0.26) = 10.4$ people and

   $$\sigma_X = \sqrt{np\,(1-p)} = \sqrt{40\,(0.26)\,(1-0.26)} \approx 2.77 \text{ people, respectively.}$$

   (b) For a binomial random variable, the probability of exactly 10 of the 40 experiencing relief is

   $$P(X = 10) = \binom{40}{10} (0.26)^{10}\,(1 - 0.26)^{40-10} \approx 0.143.$$

9. (a) The mean of the probability distribution is

   $$
   \begin{aligned}
   \mu_X &= \sum_{i=1}^{n} x_i \cdot P(x_i) \\
   &= (0.50)\left(\frac{5}{12}\right) + (1.00)\left(\frac{4}{12}\right) + (2.00)\left(\frac{2}{12}\right) + (4.50)\left(\frac{1}{12}\right). \\
   &= \$1.25.
   \end{aligned}
   $$

   The standard deviation is

   $$
   \begin{aligned}
   \sigma_X^2 &= \sum_{i=1}^{n} (x_i - \mu_X)^2 \cdot P(x_i) \\
   &= (0.50 - 1.25)^2 \left(\frac{5}{12}\right) + (1.00 - 1.25)^2 \left(\frac{4}{12}\right) \\
   &\quad + (2.00 - 1.25)^2 \left(\frac{2}{12}\right) + (4.50 - 1.25)^2 \left(\frac{1}{12}\right) \\
   &\approx \$1.109.
   \end{aligned}
   $$

   (b) If the player can expect to win a prize worth $1.25 on each play, and the player must pay $1.00 to play the game, then the net gain/loss from the player's perspective is a gain of $0.25 per game.

10. To conduct the simulation, follow the five-step process:

(1) Describe the situation and its possible outcomes.
Simulate the rolling of two dice, find the product of the rolls, and label it odd or even. Keep track of odds and evens until five of one or the other occurs, at which time a winner is established.

(2) Identify how a chance device used will model the outcomes of the situation.
Read single digits from the random digit table. Let the digits 1–6 represent a corresponding roll of 1–6; ignore results of 7, 8, 9, or 0.

(3) Describe what one trial of the experiment will be and what response variable will be recorded.
One trial will consist of selecting two random digits, finding their product, and recording if the product is even or odd. This is repeated until either five even or five odd results have occurred, the former indicating a win for *A*, the latter a win for *B*.

(4) Conduct three trials of the experiment.

```
0 1 4 0 5      4 9 9 5 3      3 0 3 2 4      9 0 3 3 8
   E              E              O      O  E     O

9 6 0 8 0      5 1 3 9 0      3 3 | 8 4 3      0 1 5 9 9
     E            O             O |  E            O
         trial 1, B wins 5–4 |

9 5 9 4 5      0 4 8 3 4      3 7 5 2 0      1 | 3 3 6 3
   E              E     E        O      E      | O  E
                    trial 2, A wins 5–3 |

9 3 0 1 5      9 3 6 1 5      0 3 4 1 3         | 4 0 0 4
   O              O     E        O     E     O  |
                    trial 3, B wins 5–3 |

3 6 3 7 0      1 0 3 5 6      0 3 7 6 8      9 7 5 3 1
```

(5) Analyze the distribution of the response variable and draw a conclusion.
Player *A* won one of the three games, so the estimated probability of *A* winning is one-third.

B. COMBINING INDEPENDENT RANDOM VARIABLES

Recall that a random variable is a numerical outcome of a random phenomenon. The heights of American male and female adults are random variables. So are math and verbal scores on college entrance exams. Sometimes, a new random variable is desired by combining or finding the difference between these random variables . When sums and differences of random variables are considered, their measures of center behave in predictable ways.

If a random variable X has mean μ_X and a random variable Y has mean μ_Y, then

the mean of the sum of the variables is $\mu_{X+Y} = \mu_X + \mu_Y$;

the mean of the difference of the variables is $\mu_{X-Y} = \mu_X - \mu_Y$.

The mean of the sum is the sum of the means. The mean of the difference is the difference of the means.

Example: A particular college entrance exam has two parts: math and verbal. The distribution of math scores M has a mean of 500 and a standard deviation of 100. The distribution of verbal scores V also has a mean of 500 and a standard deviation of 100. What is the average combined score (math + verbal) on the exam?

Answer: It is given that $\mu_M = 500$ and that $\mu_V = 500$, so the mean of the combined score is $\mu_{M+V} = \mu_M + \mu_V = 500 + 500 = 1,000$.

Example: American adult males have heights that are distributed with a mean of 173 cm and a standard deviation of 7.5 cm. American adult females have heights that are distributed with a mean of 161 cm and a standard deviation of 6.5 cm. If one male and one female are randomly selected from the population, what is the average difference in their heights?

Answer: It is given that $\mu_{male} = 173$ cm and that $\mu_{female} = 161$ cm, so the mean difference in heights is $\mu_{male-female} = \mu_{male} - \mu_{female} = 173 - 161 = 12$ cm.

Knowing only the mean of the combined random variables is usually insufficient. A measure of spread is also needed. The variance and standard deviation of a combination of random variables can be determined if the variables themselves are **independent**. Random variables are independent if there is no correlation between them. If variables are not independent—that is, they are correlated in some way—they are called **dependent**.

The college entrance exam referenced earlier has math and verbal scores. Are these random variables independent? No, they are not. It is likely that students with high math scores will tend to have higher verbal scores, and vice versa. That is, verbal and math scores will tend to be positively correlated.

If a male and a female are randomly selected from the adult population, would the heights of the pair be correlated? It is unlikely. It is safe to say that the heights of randomly selected males and females from the population are independent random variables. However, if we compare male and female adult heights by randomly selecting a married *couple*, those heights probably are not independent. Taller men may tend to marry taller women and vice versa.

If a random variable X has variance σ_X^2 and a random variable Y has variance σ_Y^2, then

the variance of the sum of the variables is $\sigma_{X+Y}^2 = \sigma_X^2 + \sigma_Y^2$;

the variance of the difference of the variables is $\sigma_{X-Y}^2 = \sigma_X^2 + \sigma_Y^2$.

The variance of the sum is the sum of the variances. The variance of the difference is also the *sum* of the variances.

Example: American adult males have heights that are distributed with a mean of 173 cm and a standard deviation of 7.5 cm. American adult females have heights that are distributed with a mean of 161 cm and a standard deviation of 6.5 cm. If one male and one female are randomly selected from the population, what is the standard deviation of the difference in their heights?

Answer: It is given that $\sigma_{\text{male}} = 7.5$ cm and that $\sigma_{\text{female}} = 6.5$ cm, so the variances are $\sigma_{\text{male}}^2 = 56.25$ and $\sigma_{\text{female}}^2 = 42.25$. The variance of the difference in heights is $\sigma_{\text{male}-\text{female}}^2 = \sigma_{\text{male}}^2 + \sigma_{\text{female}}^2 = 56.25 + 42.25 = 98.5$ cm². The standard deviation of the difference is therefore $\sigma_{\text{male}-\text{female}} = \sqrt{98.5} \approx 9.9$ cm.

Example: A particular college entrance exam has two parts: math and verbal. The distribution of math scores M has a mean of 500 and a standard deviation of 100. The distribution of verbal scores V also has a mean of 500 and a standard deviation of 100. What is the standard deviation of the combined score (math + verbal) on the exam?

Answer: Since the random variables, math score and verbal score, are not independent, one cannot calculate the standard deviation of the combined score.

(Note: Actually one can calculate it, but it requires information about the correlation between the variables. It is not a topic on the *AP Statistics* exam.)

Trial Run

1. A brand of model rocket kit, when finished, produces rockets with a mean mass of 134 grams and a standard deviation of 4.0 grams. The model rocket engine required to fly the rocket is purchased separately and has a mass with mean 36 grams and standard deviation 2.0 grams. If a randomly selected engine is inserted into a randomly selected rocket, what are the mean and standard deviation of the total mass?

   (A) mean = 85 grams, standard deviation = 3.0 grams

   (B) mean = 85 grams, standard deviation = 3.2 grams

   (C) mean = 170 grams, standard deviation = 4.5 grams

   (D) mean = 170 grams, standard deviation = 6.0 grams

   (E) The mean = 170 grams, but the standard deviation cannot be determined from the information given.

Trial Run Solutions

1. C. Since the rocket and engine are both randomly selected, their weights are independent of each other.

   $$\mu_{Rocket+Engine} = \mu_{Rocket} + \mu_{Motor} = 134 + 36 = 170 \text{ grams}$$

   $$\sigma^2_{Rocket+Engine} = \sigma^2_{Rocket} + \sigma^2_{Engine} = 4.0^2 + 2.0^2 = 20, \quad \text{so}$$

   $$\sigma_{Rocket+Engine} = \sqrt{20} \approx 4.47 \text{ grams}.$$

C. THE NORMAL DISTRIBUTION

Probability Distributions of Continuous Random Variables

Probability distributions of discrete random variables consist of a function that matches all possible outcomes of a random phenomenon with their associated probabilities. Continuous random variables have probability distributions as well, but because there are an infinite number of outcomes, a definite probability cannot be matched with any particular outcome.

Probability distributions for continuous random variables are usually defined with a mathematical formula or **density curve**. Probabilities are determined for ranges of outcomes by finding the area under the curve. Probability distributions defined for continuous random variables using density curves must meet the same criteria as discrete random variables. The key is that the sum of all probabilities must be 1. With continuous random variables the total area under the curve is 1.

The probability that the continuous random variable X lies between any two values is equal to the area under the curve between the two values. In the two continuous probability density functions below, $P(5 \leq X \leq 10)$ equals 0.5 and 0.75, respectively.

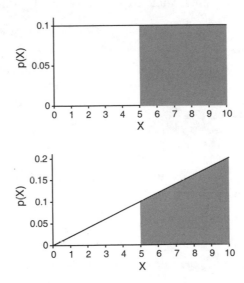

Properties of the Normal Distribution

The **normal distribution** is a continuous probability distribution that appears in many situations, both natural and man-made. It is also, as will be described later, the basis for many of the statistical inference procedures covered by the AP Statistics curriculum. The normal distribution has several important properties:

(1) It is perfectly symmetric, unimodal, and bell-shaped. In fact, it is where the term "bell curve" comes from.

(2) The curve continues infinitely in both directions, and is asymptotic to the horizontal axis as it approaches $\pm\infty$.

(3) It is defined by only two parameters: mean μ and standard deviation σ.

(4) The distribution is centered at the mean μ.

(5) The "points of inflection," where the curve changes from curving downward to curving upward, occur at exactly $\pm 1\sigma$.

(6) The total area under the curve equals 1.

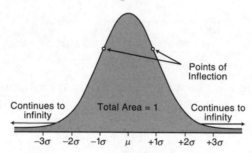

Probabilities of outcomes from random phenomena that have a normal distribution are computed by finding the area under the curve. These areas are determined by first determining how many standard deviations a point lies from the mean. Regardless of the value of the mean and standard deviation, all normal distributions have the same area between the given points. The **68-95-99.7 rule** (sometimes called the **empirical rule**) gives some benchmarks for understanding how probability is distributed under a normal curve.

If a continuous random variable has a normal distribution, approximately 68% of all outcomes will be within 1 standard deviation of the mean. About 95% of all outcomes are within 2 standard deviations of the mean and 99.7% are within 3 standard deviations of the mean. Therefore, only 0.3%—about one outcome in 330—will be more than 3 standard deviations from the mean.

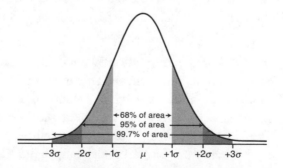

Many phenomena are normally distributed, or at least are very close to being so. For instance, American adult males have heights that are approximately normally distributed with a mean of $\mu = 173$ cm and a standard deviation of $\sigma = 7.5$ cm.

The probability distribution for males would look like this:

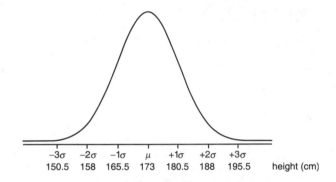

-3σ	-2σ	-1σ	μ	$+1\sigma$	$+2\sigma$	$+3\sigma$	
150.5	158	165.5	173	180.5	188	195.5	height (cm)

If an adult male were randomly selected from the population, it would not be surprising to find one of height 173 cm or even 180 cm. However, finding a male with a height of 188 cm or more looks unlikely.

Example: American adult males have heights that are approximately distributed with a mean of $\mu = 173$ cm and a standard deviation of $\sigma = 7.5$ cm. What percent of males have heights between 165.5 cm and 180.5 cm?

Answer: Using the 68-95-99.7 rule, about 68% of all outcomes lie within 1 standard deviation of the mean. Since 165.5 cm is 1 standard deviation below the mean of 173 cm and 180.5 cm is 1 standard deviation above, about 68% of all males have heights between 165.5 cm and 180.5 cm.

Example: American adult males have heights that are approximately distributed with a mean of $\mu = 173$ cm and a standard deviation of $\sigma = 7.5$ cm. What percent of males have heights over 188 cm?

Answer. Using the 68-95-99.7 rule, about 95% of all outcomes lie within 2 standard deviations of the mean. This means that about 5% fall below 2 standard deviations and above 2 standard deviations combined. Thus, about 2.5% would be above 2 standard deviations from the mean. The height 188 cm is 2 standard deviations above the mean of 173 cm, so roughly 2.5% of all males have heights above 188 cm.

Example: A particular college entrance exam has two parts: math and verbal. The distribution of math scores is normal with a mean of 500 and a standard deviation of 100. Between which two values will the middle 99.7% of all test scores roughly lie?

Answer: Using the 68-95-99.7 rule, about 99.7% of all outcomes lie within 3 standard deviations of the mean. The standard deviation of the distribution is 100, so 3 standard deviations is 300. The middle 99.7% of all scores will lie within 300 of the mean, or between 200 and 800.

The 68-95-99.7 rule only gives benchmark values for the area under the normal distribution at whole numbers of standard deviations from the mean. If locations other than whole standard deviations are desired, then **Table A: Standard Normal Probabilities** is required.

Determining probabilities from Table A requires one to compute a **standard** score or **z-score**. The z-score is simply the number of standard deviations an observation lies from the mean. The z-score is computed by $z = \dfrac{x - \mu}{\sigma}$, where x is the value of the observed outcome.

Example: American adult males have heights that are approximately normally distributed with a mean of $\mu = 173$ cm and a standard deviation of $\sigma = 7.5$ cm. What is the z-score for a male of height 183 cm?

Answer: The z-score for a male of height 183 cm is

$$z = \frac{x - \mu}{\sigma} = \frac{183 - 173}{7.5} = \frac{10}{7.5} \approx 1.33.$$

The table of standard normal probabilities gives the probability of observing an outcome below the given z-score. The table is read by cross-referencing the row of the table containing the whole number and tenths place of the z-score with the column holding the hundredths place.

Example: What is the value of the standard normal probability table (Table A) for a z-score of 1.33?

Answer: Cross-reference the 1.3 row of the table with the 0.03 column.

z	0.00	0.01	0.02	0.03	0.04	...
0.0	0.5000	0.5040	0.5080	0.5120	0.5199	...
.	.	.	.	.	.	...
.	.	.	.	.	.	...
.	.	.	.	.	.	...
1.1	0.8643	0.8665	0.8686	0.8708	0.8729	...
1.2	0.8849	0.8869	0.8888	0.8907	0.8925	...
1.3	0.9032	0.9049	0.9066	**0.9082**	0.9099	...
1.4	0.9192	0.9207	0.9222	0.9236	0.9251	...
1.5	0.9332	0.9345	0.9357	0.9370	0.9382	...
.	.	.	.	.	.	...
.	.	.	.	.	.	...
.	.	.	.	.	.	...

The value of the standard normal probability table (Table A) for a z-score of 1.33 is 0.9082.

Calculator Tip:

Cumulative normal probabilities can be calculated with the graphing calculator. Consider the previous example.

From the home screen, press $\boxed{\text{DISTR}}$, and then choose 2:normalcdf(. This is the normal cumulative density function command and is used for computing normal probabilities (areas under the normal curve) between two values.

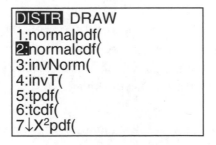

The syntax for the normalcdf command is normalcdf(left bound, right bound, mean, standard deviation). For standard normal distributions (mean = 0 and standard deviation = 1), no mean or standard deviation needs to be entered—the calculator defaults to the values 0 and 1, respectively.

The normal distribution continues to infinity in both the positive and negative directions. When the area in a tail is required and one of the bounds is at infinity, use of an extreme value is needed. In most cases, –1,000 or 1,000 will suffice.

Key in -1000,1.33) and then press ENTER .

normalcdf(–1000,
1.33)

.9082408019

The area under the normal curve below $z = 1.33$ is about 0.9082.

Example: American adult males have heights that are approximately normally distributed with a mean of $\mu = 173$ cm and a standard deviation of $\sigma = 7.5$ cm. What percent of adult males have heights less than 183 cm?

Answer: Since Table A gives the gives the probability of observing an outcome below the given z-score, and the z-score for 183 cm is $z = 1.33$, about 90.82% of adult males have heights less than 183 cm.

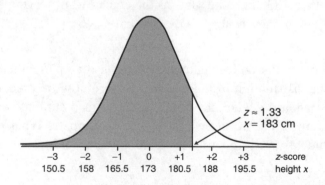

Note: Using probability notation, the above solution would be written as

$$P(x < 183\,\text{cm}) \approx P(z < 1.33) \approx 0.9082.$$

Calculator Tip:

From the home screen, press DISTR , and then choose 2:normalcdf(.
The syntax for the normalcdf command is normalcdf(left bound, right bound, mean, standard deviation). For nonstandard normal distributions (those not having mean = 0 and standard deviation = 1), mean and standard deviation need to be entered.
Key in -1000,183,173,7.5) and then press ENTER .

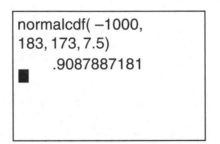

normalcdf(−1000,
183, 173, 7.5)
            .9087887181
■

The area under the normal curve, with mean = 173 and standard deviation = 7.5, below x = 183 is about 0.9088.

Note: The difference between the previous example's area of 0.9082 and the current area of 0.9088 is due to the fact that the z-score used earlier is not exactly 1.33. A rounded value was used for z, which was, in fact, a little higher than 1.33.

Note: Because a definite probability cannot be matched with any particular outcome, only a range of outcomes, the chance of observing a male with a height of less than 183 cm is the same as the chance of observing a male with a height of 183 cm or less. That is $P(x < 183 \text{ cm}) = P(x \le 183 \text{ cm})$.

Example: A particular college entrance exam has two parts: math and verbal. The distribution of math scores is normal with a mean of 500 and a standard deviation of 100. An advanced summer math program requires a score of at least 625 to participate. What proportion of students is eligible to participate in the program?

Answer: First, the z-score must be computed. $z = \dfrac{x-\mu}{\sigma} = \dfrac{625-500}{100} = 1.25$.
Cross-indexing row 1.2 with column 0.05 in Table A, the result is 0.8944. The table gives the proportion below a score of 625, so the proportion of students with scores of at least 625 is $1 - 0.8944 = 0.1056$.

Example: American adult females have heights that are normally distributed with a mean of 161 cm and a standard deviation of 6.5 cm. A company is seeking women of a certain height to operate a particular vehicle. Women should not be shorter than 146 cm (because they will not be able to reach the controls) or taller than 173 cm (because they hit their heads on the roof). What percent of women could hold this job?

Answer: The z-scores for 146 cm and 173 cm are $z = \dfrac{146 - 161}{6.5} \approx -2.31$ and $z = \dfrac{173 - 161}{6.5} \approx 1.85$, respectively. Table A shows that 0.0104 of females are below 146 cm and 0.9678 of females are below 173 cm. Therefore, the proportion of females between 146 cm and 173 cm is 0.9678 – 0.0104 = 0.9574. Almost 96% of women could operate this vehicle.

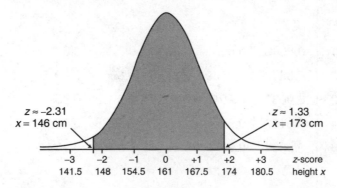

Calculator Tip:

From the home screen, press $\boxed{\text{DISTR}}$, and then choose 2:normalcdf(. Key in 146,173,161,6.5) and then press $\boxed{\text{ENTER}}$.

```
normalcdf(146, 17
3, 161, 6.5)
        .9570570251
```

The area under the normal curve, with mean = 161 and standard deviation = 6.5, between $x = 146$ and $x = 173$ is about 0.9571.

Note: The difference between the table-calculated area of 0.9574 and the calculator result of 0.9571 is, again, due to the round-off error in the by-hand calculations.

It is possible to determine outcomes (or mean or standard deviation) given a probability. To do this, one first has to read Table A in "reverse." That is, find the probability in the center of the table and read horizontally and vertically to the margins.

Example: What z-score corresponds to a Table A value of 0.8907?

z	0.00	0.01	0.02	**0.03**	0.04	...
0.0	0.5000	0.5040	0.5080	0.5120	0.5199	...
.	.	.	.	.	.	...
.	.	.	.	.	.	...
.	.	.	.	.	.	...
1.1	0.8643	0.8665	0.8686	0.8708	0.8729	...
1.2	0.8849	0.8869	0.8888	0.8907	0.8925	...
1.3	0.9032	0.9049	0.9066	0.9082	0.9099	...
1.4	0.9192	0.9207	0.9222	0.9236	0.9251	...
1.5	0.9332	0.9345	0.9357	0.9370	0.9382	...
.	.	.	.	.	.	...
.	.	.	.	.	.	...
.	.	.	.	.	.	...

Answer: Since the probability is greater than 0.5, the z-score must be positive. Locating 0.8869 and reading "backward" gives a z-value of 1.23.

Calculator Tip:

Inverse cumulative normal probabilities can be calculated with the graphing calculator. Consider the previous example.

From the home screen, press ⟦DISTR⟧, and then choose 3:invNorm(. This is the inverse normal cumulative density function command and is used for finding z-scores or nonstandard normal scores given the area in the left tail of a normal distribution.

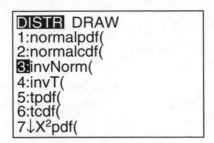

The syntax for the invNorm command is invNorm(area, mean, standard deviation). For standard normal distributions (mean = 0 and standard deviation = 1), no mean or standard deviation need to be entered—the calculator defaults to the values 0 and 1, respectively.

Key in .89) and then press ENTER .

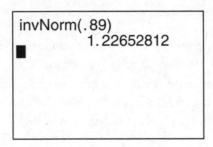

The z-score that corresponds to an area under the normal curve in the left tail of 0.89 is about $z = 1.23$.

Note: The calculator can use the value 0.89 rather than the closest value of 0.8907 from the table.

Once a z-score is determined, the unknown values in the equation $z = \dfrac{x - \mu}{\sigma}$ can be determined.

Example: A particular college entrance exam has two parts: math and verbal. The distribution of verbal scores is normal with a mean of 500 and a standard deviation of 100. What is the verbal score of a student who scores in the 89th percentile?

Answer. The 89th percentile is the point where 89% of outcomes are at or below that point. The probability in the table that is closest to 0.89 is 0.8907, which corresponds to a z-score of 1.23. Solving $z = \dfrac{x - \mu}{\sigma}$ for the unknown x, $x = \mu + z\sigma = 500 + 1.23(100) = 623$. Thus, a score of 623 corresponds to the 89th percentile.

Calculator Tip:

From the home screen, press $\boxed{\text{DISTR}}$, and then choose 3:invNorm(.

The syntax for the invNorm command is invNorm(area, mean, standard deviation). For nonstandard normal distributions (those not having mean = 0 and standard deviation = 1), mean and standard deviation need to be entered.

Key in .89,500,100) and then press $\boxed{\text{ENTER}}$.

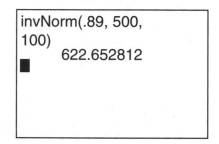

```
invNorm(.89, 500,
100)
■        622.652812
```

The test score that corresponds to an area under the normal curve in the left tail of 0.89, with mean 500 and standard deviation 100, is about $x = 622.6$.

(Note: The difference between the hand-and-table-calculated value of 623 and the calculator result of 622.6 is due to using the closest value in the table to the 89th percentile, 0.8907. The calculator uses 0.89.)

Example: American adult males have heights that are approximately normally distributed with a mean of $\mu = 173$ cm and a standard deviation of $\sigma = 7.5$ cm. Between which two values are the middle 90% of all male heights?

Answer: Considering the middle 90% of males leaves 10% of the males in the two tails of the distribution, or 5% in each distribution. Finding the area in Table A closest to 0.0500 and reading its corresponding z-score gives $z = -1.645$. This is the z-score that cuts off the lowest 5% of the distribution. By symmetry, the top 5% will be cut off by $z = 1.645$.

Solving $-1.645 = \dfrac{x - 173}{7.5}$ and $1.645 = \dfrac{x - 173}{7.5}$ for x, gives values of $x = 160.7$ cm and $x = 185.3$ cm, respectively. The middle 90% of male heights are between these two values.

Normal Approximation of the Binomial Distribution

Under certain conditions, a binomial distribution can be approximated by a normal distribution. The key word is *approximated*, as the binomial distribution is a particular discrete random variable and the normal distribution models continuous random variables.

For a binomial distribution with parameters n and p, it is well approximated by a normal distribution if $np \geq 10$ and $n(1-p) \geq 10$. Another way to look at this is that np is the mean number of successes and $n(1-p)$ is the mean number of failures.

Example: A tossed tack lands "point up" with a probability of 0.42. If it is tossed 50 times, can the distribution of successes be approximated with a normal distribution?

Answer: The situation stated is binomial with $n = 50$ and $p = 0.42$, so $np = (50)(0.42) = 21$ and $n(1-p) = (50)(0.58) = 29$. Yes, this binomial situation can be approximated with a normal distribution, since $np \geq 10$ and $n(1-p) \geq 10$.

Recall that the mean of a binomial distribution is $\mu_X = np$ and the standard deviation is $\sigma_X = \sqrt{np(1-p)}$.

Example: A tossed tack lands "point up" with a probability of 0.42. If it is tossed 50 times, what is the probability that it will land "point up" at least 25 times?

Answer: The mean number of tacks landing "point up" is

$\mu_X = np = 50(0.42) = 21$ and the standard deviation is

$\sigma_X = \sqrt{np(1-p)} = \sqrt{50(0.42)(0.58)} \approx 3.49$. The z-score for 25 successes is $z = \dfrac{x-\mu}{\sigma} = \dfrac{25-21}{3.49} \approx 1.15$. The value of Table A that

corresponds to $z = 1.15$ is 0.8749. Thus, the probability of at least 25 successes is $1 - 0.8749 = 0.1251$.

Trial Run

1. The diameters of a certain type of ball bearing are approximately normally distributed with a mean of 2.20 cm and a standard deviation of 0.02 cm. The largest 1% of all ball bearings will have diameters greater than

(A) 2.15 cm

(B) 2.20 cm

(C) 2.22 cm

(D) 2.25 cm

(E) 2.29 cm

2.   A standardized test has scores that are normally distributed with a mean of 680 and a standard deviation of 25. Approximately what proportion of scores is between 650 and 720?

(A) 0.11

(B) 0.17

(C) 0.38

(D) 0.83

(E) 0.95

3.   The distribution of heights of students at 20 high schools in a Midwestern city follows an approximate normal distribution. Twenty percent of the students are less than 55 inches and 10% of the students are more than 62 inches. What are the mean and standard deviation of the distribution of heights of high school students in this Midwestern city?

(A) mean = 57.8, standard deviation = 3.30

(B) mean = 58.0, standard deviation = 3.57

(C) mean = 58.0, standard deviation = 4.76

(D) mean = 59.0, standard deviation = 2.34

(E) mean = 59.0, standard deviation = 3.13

4.   Railroad freight cars filled with coal have weights that are approximately normally distributed with a mean of 72 tons and a standard deviation of 9 tons. A train of 50 coal cars is compiled. The engine assigned to pull the trail can pull a maximum weight of 3,750 tons.

(a) What percentage of all coal cars weigh less than 74 tons?

(b) Assuming the weights of the cars are independent, what are the mean and standard deviation of the weight of the entire train, not including engine?

(c) Compute the probability that the engine will be able to pull the train.

5. It has been shown that a certain medication alleviates arthritis symptoms in 26% of all cases. If 40 people are given the medication, what is the probability that at least 10 of them will experience relief? Show all work.

Trial Run Solutions

1. D. The z-value that cuts off an area of 0.01 in the right tail of a normal distribution, using Table A, is 2.33. Given $z = \frac{x - \mu}{\sigma}$, solve $2.33 = \frac{x - 2.20}{0.02}$ for x; $x = 2.2466$.

2. D. The z-scores for 650 and 720 are $z = \frac{650 - 680}{25} = -1.20$ and $z = \frac{720 - 680}{25} = 1.60$, respectively. The area of the normal distribution to the left of $z = -1.20$ is 0.1151 and the area of the normal distribution to the left of $z = 1.60$ is 0.9452. The area between the two z-values is $0.9452 - 0.1151 = 0.8301$.

3. A. The lowest 20% of the normal distribution is cut off by $z = -0.84$; thus $-0.84 = \frac{55 - \mu}{\sigma}$. The highest 10% is cut off by $z = 1.28$; thus $1.28 = \frac{62 - \mu}{\sigma}$. Solving each for μ gives $\mu = 55 + 0.84\sigma$ and $\mu = 62 - 1.28\sigma$. Setting them equal to each other and solving for σ gives

$$55 + 0.84\sigma = 62 - 1.28\sigma$$
$$2.12\sigma = 7$$
$$\sigma \approx 3.30.$$

4. (a) The z-score for a 74 ton car is $z = \frac{74 - 72}{9} \approx 0.22$. The area under the normal curve below $z = 0.22$ is 0.5871. About 58.7% of cars weigh less than 74 tons.

   (b) If the mean and standard deviation of the weights of individual cars are $\mu_X = 72$ and $\sigma_X = 9$, respectively, the mean weight of 50 cars is

   $$\underbrace{\mu_X + \mu_X + \cdots + \mu_X}_{(50 \text{ times})} = 50(72) = 3,600 \text{ tons.}$$ The variance of the weight

of 50 cars is $\underset{\text{(50 times)}}{\underline{\sigma_X^2 + \sigma_X^2 + \cdots + \sigma_X^2}} = 50(81) = 4{,}050 \text{ tons}^2$, so the standard

deviation is $\sqrt{4{,}050} \approx 63.64$ tons.

(c) The probability that the engine can pull the train is the probability that the total weight is less than 3,750 tons. This is equivalent to

$$P\left(z < \frac{3{,}750 - 3{,}600}{63.64}\right) = P(z < 2.36) \approx 0.9909.$$

5. For a binomial random variable, the probability of at least 10 of 40 experiencing relief can be obtained by applying the binomial probability formula for all values of X between 10 and 40 inclusive. Or, one may use the normal approximation of the binomial since the conditions $np \geq 10$ and $n(1-p) \geq 10$ are both met: $np = 10.4$ and $n(1-p) = 29.6$. The mean is $(40)(0.26) = 1.04$, and the standard deviation is $\sqrt{np(1-p)} = \sqrt{10(0.26)(0.74)} \approx 2.77$. So, using the normal *approximation* of the binomial,

$$P(X \geq 10) \approx P\left(z > \frac{10 - 10.4}{2.77}\right) \approx P(z > -0.14) = 0.5557.$$

Note: The exact binomial probability from the graphing calculator is $1 - \text{binomcdf}(40, 0.26, 9) = 0.617$.

D. SAMPLING DISTRIBUTIONS

A **sampling distribution** is the probability distribution of a sample statistic when a sample is drawn from a population. Recall that a probability distribution is all possible outcomes of a random variable and their associated probabilities. A sample statistic is also a random variable. Thus, a sampling distribution is simply a function describing all possible statistics and their corresponding probabilities from all possible samples of a given size.

Sample statistics are random variables. In most cases, the mean and standard deviation of the sampling distribution of the statistic can be calculated from the characteristics of the population. The mean of a sample statistic is the mean of the statistics from all possible samples of a given size. The standard deviation of a sample statistic is the standard deviation of the statistics from all possible samples of a given size.

The Sampling Distribution of a Sample Proportion

The **sampling distribution of a sample proportion** $\hat{p}$ is described when all possible simple random samples of size n are taken from a population where the probability of an individual success is p. The value of the sample proportion $\hat{p}$ is $\hat{p} = \dfrac{X}{n} = \dfrac{\text{number of } \textit{successes} \text{ in the sample}}{n}$. It has the following characteristics:

the mean of the sample proportion $\hat{p}$ is $\mu_{\hat{p}} = p$;

the standard deviation of the sample proportion $\hat{p}$ is $\sigma_{\hat{p}} = \sqrt{\dfrac{p(1-p)}{n}}$.

Example: In a large high school of 2,500 students, 21% of them are seniors. A simple random sample of 150 students is taken and the proportion of seniors calculated. What are the mean and standard deviation of the sample proportion, $\hat{p}$?

Answer: In this case, the population proportion is $p = 0.21$ and the sample size is $n = 150$. The mean of the sample proportion $\hat{p}$ is $\mu_{\hat{p}} = p = 0.21$ and the standard deviation is $\sigma_{\hat{p}} = \sqrt{\dfrac{p(1-p)}{n}} = \sqrt{\dfrac{0.21(0.79)}{36}} \approx 0.033$.

Note: The value of $\sigma_{\hat{p}}$ assumes that the probability of a success remains constant throughout the sampling process. When sampling from a population without replacement, this is not the case, but the formula is reasonably accurate when the sample size is no more than 10% of the population size. In the previous example, the sample size of 150 is clearly less than 10% of 2,500.

Example: A tossed tack lands "point up" with probability 0.42. If the tack is tossed 50 times, what are the mean and standard deviation of $\hat{p}$, the proportion of times the tack lands "point up"?

Answer: The probability of landing "point up" is 0.42; this is considered the population proportion $p = 0.42$. The number of tosses is the sample size $n = 50$. The mean of the sample proportion $\hat{p}$ is $\mu_{\hat{p}} = p = 0.42$ and

the standard deviation is $\sigma_{\hat{p}} = \sqrt{\dfrac{p(1-p)}{n}} = \sqrt{\dfrac{0.42(0.58)}{50}} \approx 0.070$.

The distribution of sample proportions is closely related to the binomial distribution. In fact, the mean and standard deviation of the sample proportion $\hat{p}$ are simply the mean and standard deviation of the binomial random variable X when divided by the sample size n. Because of this, the sampling distribution of sample proportions can be modeled with a normal distribution like the binomial distribution if $np \geq 10$ and $n(1-p) \geq 10$.

Example: In a large high school of 2,500 students, 21% of them are seniors. A simple random sample of 150 students is taken and the proportion of seniors calculated. What is the probability that the sample will contain less than 15% seniors?

Answer: Since the binomial conditions $np \geq 10$ and $n(1-p) \geq 10$ are met—$np = 150(0.21) = 31.5$ and $n(1-p) = 150(0.79) = 118.5$—the sampling distribution of $\hat{p}$ can be approximated by a normal distribution with mean $\mu_{\hat{p}} = 0.21$ and standard deviation $\sigma_{\hat{p}} \approx 0.033$.

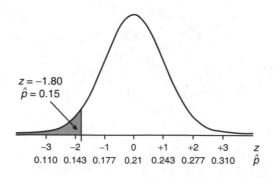

$z = -1.80$
$\hat{p} = 0.15$

| | -3 | -2 | -1 | 0 | +1 | +2 | +3 | z |
| | 0.110 | 0.143 | 0.177 | 0.21 | 0.243 | 0.277 | 0.310 | $\hat{p}$ |

The z-score for 15% is $z = \dfrac{0.15 - 0.21}{\sqrt{\frac{0.21(0.79)}{150}}} \approx -1.80$. From Table A, the probability of z being less than -1.80 is 0.0359. Thus, the chance of obtaining a sample with less than 15% seniors is about 3.6%—not very likely.

Example: A tossed tack lands "point up" with probability 0.42. If the tack is tossed 50 times, what proportions of successes correspond to the highest 10% of all possible outcomes?

Answer: From the previous example, the mean of the sample proportion $\hat{p}$ is $\mu_{\hat{p}} = 0.42$ and the standard deviation is $\sigma_{\hat{p}} \approx 0.070$. Because np and $n(1 - p)$ are both at least 10—21 and 29, respectively—we can approximate the distribution of $\hat{p}$ with a normal distribution.

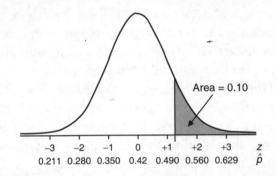

The 90th percentile on the table of standard normal probabilities corresponds to a z-score of about 1.28. Thus, $\hat{p} = \mu + z\sigma = 0.42 + 1.28\,(0.070) \approx 0.51$. A success rate of $\hat{p} = 0.51$ corresponds to the 90th percentile, so the highest 10% of all possible outcomes are 51% or more.

The Sampling Distribution of a Sample Mean

The **sampling distribution of a sample mean** $\bar{x}$ is described when all possible simple random samples of size n are taken from a population with mean μ and standard deviation σ. It has the following characteristics:

the mean of the sample mean $\bar{x}$ is $\mu_{\bar{x}} = \mu$;

the standard deviation of the sample mean is $\bar{x}$ is $\sigma_{\bar{x}} = \dfrac{\sigma}{\sqrt{n}}$.

Example: In a large high school of 2,500 students, the mean number of cars owned by students' families is 2.35 with a standard deviation of 1.06. A simple random sample of 36 students is taken and the mean number of cars owned is calculated. What are the mean and standard deviation of the sample mean, $\bar{x}$?

Answer: The population mean is $\mu = 2.35$ cars, the standard deviation is $\sigma = 1.06$ cars, and the sample size is $n = 36$. The mean of the sample mean x is $\mu_{\bar{x}} = \mu = 2.35$ cars and the standard deviation is

$$\sigma_{\bar{x}} = \frac{\sigma}{\sqrt{n}} = \frac{1.06}{\sqrt{36}} \approx 0.177 \text{ cars.}$$

Note: The value of $\sigma_{\bar{x}}$ assumes sampling with replacement, which is unlikely in practice. When sampling from a population without replacement, the formula for $\sigma_{\bar{x}}$ is reasonably accurate when the sample size is no more than 10% of the population size, or data come from a randomized experiment. In the previous example, the sample size of 36 is clearly less than 10% of 2,500.

The shape of the sampling distribution of the sample mean $\bar{x}$ is dependent on the shape of the original population. If the population is normally distributed, the sampling distribution of $\bar{x}$ will always be normally distributed. If the population distribution is skewed, the sampling distribution of $\bar{x}$ will also *tend* to be skewed in the same way. However, as the sample size n increases, the shape of the distribution of $\bar{x}$ looks less like the population and more like a normal distribution. This characteristic of the sampling distribution of $\bar{x}$ is so important that it has a special name: the **central limit theorem**.

Central limit theorem: As the size n of a simple random sample increases, the shape of the sampling distribution of $\bar{x}$ tends toward being normally distributed.

The consequence of the central limit theorem is that if the sample size n is sufficiently "large," the sampling distribution of $\bar{x}$ can be approximated by a normal distribution.

Example: In a large high school of 2,500 students, the mean number of cars owned by students' families is 2.35 with a standard deviation of 1.06. A histogram of the population is shown.

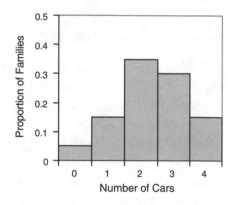

A simple random sample of 36 students is taken and the mean number of cars owned is calculated. What is the probability that the sample mean is greater than 2.5 cars?

Answer: The population mean is $\mu = 2.35$ cars, the standard deviation is $\sigma = 1.06$ cars, and the sample size is $n = 36$. The mean of the sample mean $\bar{x}$ is $\mu_{\bar{x}} = \mu = 2.35$ cars and the standard deviation is

$$\sigma_{\bar{x}} = \frac{\sigma}{\sqrt{n}} = \frac{1.06}{\sqrt{36}} \approx 0.177 \text{ cars.}$$ Since the population distribution is

fairly symmetric, a sample size of 36 should be sufficiently large enough to allow the sampling distribution of $\bar{x}$ to be approximated by a normal distribution.

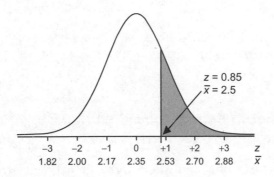

The z-score for a sample mean of 2.5 cars is $z = \dfrac{2.5 - 2.35}{1.06 / \sqrt{36}} \approx 0.85$. From

Table A, the probability of z being less than 0.85 is 0.8023. The chance of obtaining a sample with a mean of more than 2.5 cars is $1 - 0.8023 = 0.1977$, or about 19%.

How "large" is large enough? That depends on how far from normal the population distribution is. A rule of thumb is that a little skewness can be tolerated for samples up to about size 15, moderate skewness up to about size 40, and heavy skewness for samples over size 40.

As with proportions, one may also determine the value of a particular percentile rank in a sampling distribution of the sample mean.

Example: In a large high school of 2,500 students, the mean number of cars owned by students' families is 2.35 with a standard deviation of 1.06. A simple random sample of 36 students is taken. Below what value is the lowest 5% of all possible sample means?

Answer: From the previous examples, the mean of the sample mean $\bar{x}$ is $\mu_{\bar{x}} = \mu = 2.35$ cars and the standard deviation is

$$\sigma_{\bar{x}} = \frac{\sigma}{\sqrt{n}} = \frac{1.06}{\sqrt{36}} \approx 0.177 \text{ cars.}$$

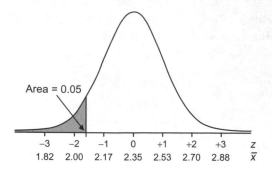

The 5th percentile in Table A corresponds to a z-score of -1.65. Therefore, $\bar{x} = \mu + z\sigma = 2.35 + (-1.65)(0.177) \approx 2.958$. The lowest 5% of all sample means will be below 2.958 cars.

The Sampling Distribution of the Difference Between Two Independent Sample Proportions

The **sampling distribution of the difference between two independent sample proportions** $\hat{p}_1 - \hat{p}_2$ is described when all possible simple random samples of size n_1 are taken from one population and of size n_2 from a second population, and the probabilities of an individual success in each population are p_1 and p_2. The samples must be independent, that is, there should not be a correlation between individuals of the two populations. The value of the difference in sample proportions $\hat{p}_1 - \hat{p}_2$ is $\hat{p}_1 - \hat{p}_2 = \dfrac{X_1}{n_1} - \dfrac{X_2}{n_2}$. It has the following characteristics:

the mean of the difference between sample proportions $\hat{p}_1 - \hat{p}_2$ is
$$\mu_{\hat{p}_1 - \hat{p}_2} = p_1 - p_2;$$
the standard deviation of the difference between sample proportions

$\hat{p}_1 - \hat{p}_2$ is $\sigma_{\hat{p}_1 - \hat{p}_2} = \sqrt{\dfrac{p_1(1-p_1)}{n_1} + \dfrac{p_2(1-p_2)}{n_2}}.$

As with a single sample for a proportion, the value of $\sigma_{\hat{p}_1 - \hat{p}_2}$ assumes that the probabilities of a success in each population remain constant throughout the sampling process. When sampling from a population without replacement the formula is reasonably accurate when both sample sizes are no more than 10% of their respective population sizes. Also, the sampling distribution of the difference in sample proportions can be modeled with a normal distribution if all of $n_1 p_1 \geq 10$, $n_1(1 - p_1) \geq 10$, $n_2 p_2 \geq 10$, and $n_2(1 - p_2) \geq 10$ are satisfied.

Example: In a large high school with 525 seniors, 23% of them own a car. A second high school has 510 seniors, 21% of whom own cars. Simple random samples of 50 seniors are taken from each school, and the proportion of seniors owning cars in each is calculated. What is the likelihood that the survey will indicate that more seniors in the second school own cars than the first school?

Answer: Since both samples are no more than 10% of the population, the formula for the standard deviation of $\hat{p}_1 - \hat{p}_2$ will work. Since $n_1 p_1 = (50)(0.23) = 11.5$, $n_1(1 - p_1) = (50)(0.77) = 38.5$, $n_2 p_2 = (50)(0.21) = 10.5$, and $n_2(1 - p_2) = (50)(0.79) = 39.5$ are all at least 10, the difference $\hat{p}_1 - \hat{p}_2$ can be approximated by the normal distribution.

The mean of the difference in sample proportions $\hat{p}_1 - \hat{p}_2$ is
$\mu_{\hat{p}_1 - \hat{p}_2} = p_1 - p_2 = 0.23 - 0.21 = 0.02$ and the standard deviation is

$$\sigma_{\hat{p}_1 - \hat{p}_2} = \sqrt{\frac{0.23\,(0.77)}{50} + \frac{0.21\,(0.79)}{50}} \approx 0.083.$$

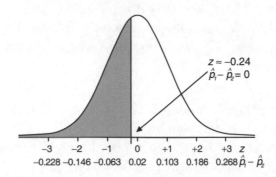

The question asks the probability that $\hat{p}_1 < \hat{p}_2$, or $\hat{p}_1 - \hat{p}_2 < 0$. The value of $\hat{p}_1 - \hat{p}_2 = 0$ has a z-score of $z = \dfrac{0 - 0.02}{0.083} \approx -0.24$. From Table A, the probability of a z-score being -0.24 or less is 0.4052. Thus, the chance that the survey would show a greater proportion of seniors owning cars in the second school than the first is about 41%, a very likely occurrence.

The Sampling Distribution of the Difference Between Two Independent Sample Means

The **sampling distribution of the difference between two independent sample means** $\bar{x}_1 - \bar{x}_2$ is described when all possible simple random samples of size n_1 are taken from one population and of size n_2 from a second population, and the parameters of the populations are μ_1, σ_1, μ_2, and σ_2. The samples must be independent, that is, there should not be a correlation between individuals of the two populations. The value of the difference in sample means $\bar{x}_1 - \bar{x}_2$ has the following characteristics:

the mean of the difference between sample means $\bar{x}_1 - \bar{x}_2$ is

$$\mu_{\bar{x}_1 - \bar{x}_2} = \mu_1 - \mu_2;$$

the standard deviation of the difference between sample means $\bar{x}_1 - \bar{x}_2$ is

$$\sigma_{\bar{x}_1 - \bar{x}_2} = \sqrt{\frac{\sigma_1^2}{n_1} + \frac{\sigma_2^2}{n_2}}.$$

As with single samples, the value of $\sigma_{\bar{x}_1 - \bar{x}_2}$ assumes sampling with replacement. When sampling from populations without replacement, the formula for $\sigma_{\bar{x}_1 - \bar{x}_2}$ is reasonably accurate when the sample sizes are no more than 10% of the population size or the data come from a completely randomized experiment.

The shape of the sampling distribution of the difference in sample means $\bar{x}_1 - \bar{x}_2$ is also subject to the central limit theorem. As the sizes of the two independent simple random samples increase, the shape of the sampling distribution of $\bar{x}_1 - \bar{x}_2$ tends toward being normally distributed. Skewness or non-normality in the population distributions is less of a factor with two independent samples and the distribution of $\bar{x}_1 - \bar{x}_2$ can be modeled well by the normal distribution for even small samples.

Example: In a large high school of 2,500 students, the mean number of cars owned by students' families is 2.35 with a standard deviation of 1.06. A second large high school has 2,350 students. The mean number of cars owned by students' families is 2.01 with standard deviation of 1.19.

Simple random samples of 36 students are taken from each school, and the mean number of cars per family is calculated for each. What is the likelihood that the survey will indicate that the average number of cars owned by families in the second school is greater than the first?

Answer: Since both samples are no more than 10% of the population, the formula for the standard deviation of $\bar{x}_1 - \bar{x}_2$ will work. Unless either or both of the populations are extremely skewed, the sample sizes of 36 are sufficiently large to allow the normal distribution to model the sampling distribution of $\bar{x}_1 - \bar{x}_2$.

The mean of the difference in sample means $\bar{x}_1 - \bar{x}_2$ is

$$\mu_{\bar{x}_1 - \bar{x}_2} = \mu_1 - \mu_2 = 2.35 - 2.01 = 0.34 \text{ cars, and the standard deviation is}$$

$$\sigma_{\bar{x}_1 - \bar{x}_2} = \sqrt{\frac{1.06^2}{36} + \frac{1.19^2}{36}} \approx 0.266 \text{ cars.}$$

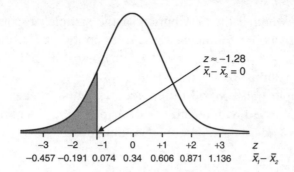

The question asks the probability that $\bar{x}_1 < \bar{x}_2$ or $\bar{x}_1 - \bar{x}_2 < 0$. The value of $\bar{x}_1 - \bar{x}_2 = 0$ has a z-score of $z = \dfrac{0 - 0.34}{0.266} \approx -1.28$. From Table A, the probability of a z-score being -1.28 or less is 0.1003. Thus, the chance that the survey would show a greater average number of cars per family in the second school than the first is about 10%.

Standard Error

It is a rare occasion that one knows the parameter(s) of population(s); after all, part of statistics is determining what those parameters are. When one does not know the parameters necessary to calculate the standard deviation of the sample statistic, then one estimates them with the **standard error**.

In the case of proportions, if p is unknown, the sample proportion $\hat{p}$ will be used to estimate it. In the case of means, if σ is unknown, the sample standard deviation s will be used to estimate it.

Sample Statistic	Standard Deviation	Standard Error
$\hat{p}$	$\sigma_{\hat{p}} = \sqrt{\dfrac{p(1-p)}{n}}$	$SE_{\hat{p}} = \sqrt{\dfrac{\hat{p}(1-\hat{p})}{n}}$
$\bar{x}$	$\sigma_{\bar{x}} = \dfrac{\sigma}{\sqrt{n}}$	$SE_{\bar{x}} = \dfrac{s}{\sqrt{n}}$
$\hat{p}_1 - \hat{p}_2$	$\sigma_{\hat{p}_1-\hat{p}_2} = \sqrt{\dfrac{p_1(1-p_1)}{n_1} + \dfrac{p_2(1-p_2)}{n_2}}$	$SE_{\hat{p}_1-\hat{p}_2} = \sqrt{\dfrac{\hat{p}_1(1-p_1)}{n_1} + \dfrac{\hat{p}_2(1-p_2)}{n_2}}$
$\bar{x}_1 - \bar{x}_2$	$\sigma_{\bar{x}_1-\bar{x}_2} = \sqrt{\dfrac{\sigma_1^2}{n_1} + \dfrac{\sigma_2^2}{n_2}}$	$SE_{\bar{x}_1-\bar{x}_2} = \sqrt{\dfrac{s_1^2}{n_1} + \dfrac{s_2^2}{n_2}}$

In assessing whether the distribution of the sample proportion $\hat{p}$ can be modeled by a normal distribution, the same rules apply for $\hat{p}$ as they did with p. Both of $n\hat{p}$ and $n(1-\hat{p})$ must be at least 10. For $\hat{p}_1 - \hat{p}_2$, all of $n_1\hat{p}_1$, $n_1(1-\hat{p}_1)$, $n_2\hat{p}_2$, and $n_2(1-\hat{p}_2)$ must be at least 10.

For the sample mean $\bar{x}$ and difference of sample means $\bar{x}_1 - \bar{x}_2$, other issues must be addressed with regard to the shape of the sampling distribution if the population standard deviation(s) is/are unknown.

t-distributions

When the sample standard deviation s is used as an estimate of the population standard deviation σ, the distribution of the standardized score $\dfrac{\bar{x} - \mu}{s/\sqrt{n}}$ is not well approximated by the normal distribution for small and moderate sample sizes. Even if the population itself is normally distributed, the sampling distribution of $\dfrac{\bar{x} - \mu}{s/\sqrt{n}}$ will not be. In this case, a new distribution is required: the *t*-**distribution**.

The *t*-distribution, sometimes known as Student's *t*, is actually a family of curves that have the following characteristics:

(1) They are symmetric and unimodal, and have a mean equal to zero, like the normal distribution.

(2) The height of the *t*-distribution is shorter at the mean than that of the normal distribution and thicker in the tails.

(3) Each curve in the family is defined by its **degrees of freedom**.

(4) As the number of degrees of freedom increases, the curve approaches a normal distribution.

(5) The standard deviation of the distribution is greater than 1, and approaches 1 as the number of degrees of freedom increases.

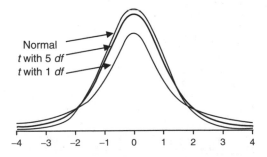

Table B is the table of **t-distribution critical values**. The values in the table give *t*-critical values, labeled *t**, that cut off a certain percentage of the curve area in the right tail.

The table can be used in three ways. The first is by cross-referencing the row containing the number of degrees of freedom *df* and the probability that a *t*-score will be above a certain critical value, *t**. The result is that value.

Example: What value of the *t*-score cuts off the highest 10% of a *t*-distribution with 9 degrees of freedom?

Answer: Cross-reference the 9 *df* row of the table with the 0.10 column.

df	Tail probability p					
	0.25	0.20	0.15	0.10	0.05	...
1	1.000	1.376	1.963	3.078	6.314	...
.	.	.	.	.	.	...
.	.	.	.	.	.	...
.	.	.	.	.	.	...
7	0.711	0.896	1.119	1.415	1.895	...
8	0.706	0.889	1.108	1.397	1.860	...
9	0.703	0.883	1.100	**1.383**	1.833	...
10	0.700	0.879	1.093	1.372	1.812	...
11	0.697	0.876	1.088	1.363	1.796	...
.	.	.	.	.	.	...
.	.	.	.	.	.	...
.	.	.	.	.	.	...

The value of the *t*-score that cuts off the highest 10% of a *t*-distribution with 9 degrees of freedom is *t** = 1.383. Another way to interpret this is that the 90th percentile of a *t*-distribution with 9 *df* is 1.383 standard errors above the mean.

Calculator Tip:

Inverse cumulative *t*-distribution probabilities can be calculated with the graphing calculator. Consider the previous example.

From the home screen, press DISTR, and then choose 4:invT(. This is the inverse *t*-distribution cumulative density function command and is used for finding *t*-scores given the area in the left tail of a *t*-distribution given the number of degrees of freedom.

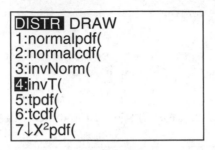

The syntax for the invT command is invT(area, df).
Key in .9,9) and then press ENTER.

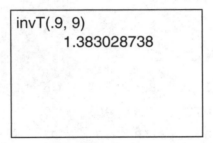

The *t*-score that corresponds to an area of 0.1 in the right tail (0.9 in the left tail) of the *t*-distribution with 9 *df* is about $t = 1.383$.
(Note: Not all calculators come programmed with the invT function.)

Note that Table B contains no negative values for t^*. Since the *t*-distribution is symmetric, the opposite of t^*, $-t^*$, will cut off an equal area in the left tail as t^*.

Example: What value of the *t*-score cuts off the lowest 5% of a *t*-distribution with 10 degrees of freedom?

Answer: Cross-reference the 10 *df* row of the table with the 0.05 column. The table reads 1.812. Since the area under consideration is the *lowest* 5%, $t^* = -1.812$.

df	Tail probability *p*					
	0.25	0.20	0.15	0.10	0.05	...
1	1.000	1.376	1.963	3.078	6.314	...
.	.	.	.	.	.	...
.	.	.	.	.	.	...
.	.	.	.	.	.	...
7	0.711	0.896	1.119	1.415	1.895	...
8	0.706	0.889	1.108	1.397	1.860	...
9	0.703	0.883	1.100	1.383	1.833	...
10	0.700	0.879	1.093	1.372	**1.812**	...
11	0.697	0.876	1.088	1.363	1.796	...
.	.	.	.	.	.	...
.	.	.	.	.	.	...
.	.	.	.	.	.	...
	50%	60%	70%	80%	90%	...

Confidence level *C*

The second way that the table can be used is to find the probability that a *t*-score will be above a certain critical value, t^*.

Example: What is the probability that a *t*-score will be larger than $t^* = 1.110$ with 9 degrees of freedom?

Answer: Read across the 9 *df* row of the table until 1.110 is found. Then read the tail probability for that column. The tail probability is 0.15; thus, the probability that a *t*-score will be larger than $t^* = 1.110$ with 9 *df* is 0.15. Another way to interpret this is that a score 1.100 standard errors above the mean, with 9 *df*, is the 85th percentile.

Remember that the *t*-distribution is symmetric and that Table B contains no negative values for t^*. The probability that a t-score will be larger than $t^* = 1.110$ with 9 df is 0.15. Correspondingly, the probability that a *t*-score will be smaller than $t^* = -1.110$ with 9 *df* is also 0.15. This means that with 9 *df*, $t^* = -1.110$ is the 15th percentile.

df	Tail probability p					
	0.25	0.20	0.15	0.10	0.05	...
1	1.000	1.376	1.963	3.078	6.314	...
.	.	.	.	.	.	...
.	.	.	.	.	.	...
.	.	.	.	.	.	...
7	0.711	0.896	1.119	1.415	1.895	...
8	0.706	0.889	1.108	1.397	1.860	...
9	0.703	0.883	1.100	1.383	1.833	...
10	0.700	0.879	1.093	1.372	1.812	...
11	0.697	0.876	1.088	1.363	1.796	...
.	.	.	.	.	.	...
.	.	.	.	.	.	...
.	.	.	.	.	.	...
	50%	60%	70%	80%	90%	...

Confidence level C

Calculator Tip:

Cumulative t-distribution probabilities can be calculated with the graphing calculator. Consider the previous example.

From the home screen, press $\boxed{\text{DISTR}}$, and then choose 6:tcdf(. This is the t-distribution cumulative density function command and is used for computing t-distribution probabilities (areas under the t-curve) between two values for a number of degrees of freedom.

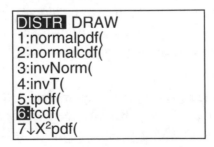

The protocol for the tcdf command is tcdf(left bound, right bound, df).

The *t*-distribution continues to infinity in both the positive and negative directions. When the area in a tail is required and one of the bounds is at infinity, use of an extreme value is needed. In most cases, −1,000 or 1,000 will suffice. Key in 1.100,1000,9) and then press ENTER .

```
tcdf(1.100, 1000,
9)
        .149941381
```

The area under the *t*-curve above $t^* = 1.100$ is about 0.15.

A third way to read the table is to find the values of $\pm t^*$ given the central area of a *t*-distribution, or vice versa.

Example: What values of the *t*-score bound the middle 80% of a *t*-distribution with 9 degrees of freedom?

Answer: The area under consideration is the middle 80%, so there must be 20% left in the tails. Since the *t*-distribution is symmetric, an equal proportion of the area must exist in each tail. The tail probability is therefore 0.10. Cross-reference the 9 *df* row of the table with the 0.10 column.

	Tail probability *p*					
df	0.25	0.20	0.15	0.10	0.05	...
1	1.000	1.376	1.963	3.078	6.314	...
.	.	.	.	.	.	...
.	.	.	.	.	.	...
.	.	.	.	.	.	...
7	0.711	0.896	1.119	1.415	1.895	...
8	0.706	0.889	1.108	1.397	1.860	...
9	0.703	0.883	1.100	**1.383**	1.833	...
10	0.700	0.879	1.093	1.372	1.812	...
11	0.697	0.876	1.088	1.363	1.796	...
.	.	.	.	.	.	...
.	.	.	.	.	.	...
.	.	.	.	.	.	...
	50%	60%	70%	80%	90%	...

Confidence level *C*

The values of *t*-scores that bound the middle 80% of a *t*-distribution with 9 degrees of freedom are $t^* = \pm 1.383$.

Note that the value at the bottom of the table above the line "Confidence level *C*" when 9 *df* and $t^* = 1.383$ are cross-referenced is also 80%. This "confidence level" will be discussed later, but corresponds to central area. Twice the tail probability is equal to the complement of the confidence level, or $1 - 2p = C$.

Calculator Tip:

From the home screen, press DISTR , and then choose 4:invT(.

Key in .1,9) and then press ENTER .

```
invT(.1, 9)
        -1.383028738
```

The *t*-scores that correspond to a central area of 0.8 (0.1 in the left tail) of a *t*-distribution with 9 *df* is about $t = \pm 1.383$.

Example: What is the probability that an observation lies within 1.812 standard errors of the mean in a *t*-distribution with 10 degrees of freedom?

Answer: Read across the 10 *df* row until 1.812 is found; then read the confidence level (or tail probability) for that column. The confidence level is 90%; thus, the probability of an observation lying within 1.812 standard errors of the mean in the *t*-distribution with 10 *df* is 0.90. (Note: The tail probability is 0.05. The combined probability of both the left and right tails is 0.10, leaving 0.90 in the central area.)

df	Tail probability *p*					
	0.25	0.20	0.15	0.10	0.05	...
1	1.000	1.376	1.963	3.078	6.314	...
.	.	.	.	.	.	...
.	.	.	.	.	.	...
.	.	.	.	.	.	...

7	0.711	0.896	1.119	1.415	1.895	...
8	0.706	0.889	1.108	1.397	1.860	...
9	0.703	0.883	1.100	1.383	1.833	...
10	0.700	0.879	1.093	1.372	**1.812**	...
11	0.697	0.876	1.088	1.363	1.796	...
.	.	.	.	.	.	...
.	.	.	.	.	.	...
.	.	.	.	.	.	...
	50%	60%	70%	80%	90%	...

Confidence level *C*

Calculator Tip:

From the home screen, press $\boxed{\text{DISTR}}$, and then choose 6:tcdf(. Key in -1.812,1.812,10) and then press $\boxed{\text{ENTER}}$.

```
tcdf(−1.812, 1.81
2, 10)
        .8999247413
```

The area under the *t*-curve between $t^* = \pm 1.812$ is about 0.9.

There are times when Table B does not provide exact information. Note that the t^*-values are only for tail probabilities with round numbers: 0.05, 0.025, 0.02, 0.01, etc. It is likely that a computed t^*-value will not be among those in the table. In this case, the table can only provide a range of values for the tail probability *p*, or confidence level (central area) *C*.

Example: What is the probability that a *t*-score will be larger than $t^* = 1.5$ with 9 degrees of freedom?

Answer: Read across the 9 *df* row of the table until 1.5 is found. The value of 1.5 is not shown in the table, but would be located between 1.383 and 1.833, which correspond to the tail probabilities $p = 0.10$ and $p = 0.05$, respectively. The probability that a *t*-score will be larger than $t^* = 1.5$ with 9 *df* is between 0.05 and 0.10. Thus, $0.05 < p < 0.10$. This is the best information that the table can provide.

df	0.25	0.20	0.15	0.10	0.05	...
	Tail probability *p*					
1	1.000	1.376	1.963	3.078	6.314	...
.	.	.	.	.	.	...
.	.	.	.	.	.	...
.	.	.	.	.	.	...
7	0.711	0.896	1.119	1.415	1.895	...
8	0.706	0.889	1.108	1.397	1.860	...
9	0.703	0.883	1.100	**1.383**	**1.833**	...
10	0.700	0.879	1.093	1.372	1.812	...
11	0.697	0.876	1.088	1.363	1.796	...
.	.	.	.	.	.	...
.	.	.	.	.	.	...
.	.	.	.	.	.	...
	50%	60%	70%	80%	90%	...
	Confidence level *C*					

To get more precise answers, one would need technology, like a computer or graphing calculator.

Calculator Tip:

From the home screen, press $\boxed{\text{DISTR}}$, and then choose 6:tcdf(.

Key in 1.5,1000,9) and then press $\boxed{\text{ENTER}}$.

```
tcdf(1.5, 1000, 9)
            .083925328
```

The area under the *t*-curve above $t^* = 1.5$ is about 0.084.

Table B has lines for only certain numbers of degrees of freedom. There are lines for 30 and 40 *df*, but not for values between 30 and 40. When the number of degrees of freedom is between two rows in the table, it is recommended that one use the line with the smaller number of degrees of freedom. (For example, for 38 *df*, use 30.) However, technology will be able to give precise values for any number of degrees of freedom.

Finally, the last line of Table B has the symbol ∞ (infinity). Recall that as the number degrees of freedom increases, the *t*-curve approaches a normal curve. A *t*-distribution with an infinite number of degrees of freedom is a normal distribution. Thus, the ∞ line of Table B can be used for normal distributions.

χ^2 (Chi-Square) Distributions

The chi-square distribution is another form of probability distribution, like the normal and *t*-distributions. The distribution is used to model how far the counts of an observed set of categorical data, with several categories, are from what one would expect given a random sample.

The χ^2-distribution is a family of curves that have the following characteristics:

(1) They are right-skewed, unimodal, and have only non-negative values.

(2) Each curve in the family is defined by its **degrees of freedom, *df***.

(3) As the number degrees of freedom increases, the curve approaches a normal distribution.

(4) The mean of the distribution is equal to the number of degrees of freedom.

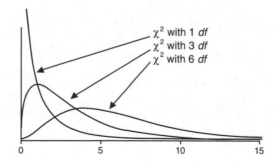

Table C is the table of χ^2 **critical values**. The values in the table give χ^2 critical values that cut off a certain percentage of the curve's area in the right tail.

Example: What value of χ^2 cuts off the highest 10% of a χ^2-distribution with 3 degrees of freedom?

Answer: Cross-reference the 3 *df* row of the table with the 0.10 column.

df	Tail probability p					
	0.25	0.20	0.15	0.10	0.05	...
1	1.32	1.64	2.07	2.71	3.84	...
2	2.77	3.22	3.79	4.61	5.99	...
3	4.11	4.64	5.32	**6.25**	7.81	...
4	5.39	5.99	6.74	7.78	9.49	...
5	6.63	7.29	8.12	9.24	11.07	...
.	.	.	.	.	.	...
.	.	.	.	.	.	...
.	.	.	.	.	.	...

The value of χ^2 that cuts off the highest 10% of a χ^2-distribution with 3 degrees of freedom is 6.25. Another way to interpret this is that the 90th percentile of a χ^2-distribution with 3 *df* is a χ^2-statistic of 6.25.

Example: What is the area of the right tail of a χ^2-distribution with 1 degree of freedom cut off by a χ^2-statistic of 2.71?

Answer: Read across the 1 *df* row until 2.71 is found; then read the tail probability for that column. The right-tail probability is 0.10.

df	Tail probability p					
	0.25	0.20	0.15	0.10	0.05	...
1	1.32	1.64	2.07	**2.71**	3.84	...
2	2.77	3.22	3.79	4.61	5.99	...
3	4.11	4.64	5.32	6.25	7.81	...
4	5.39	5.99	6.74	7.78	9.49	...
5	6.63	7.29	8.12	9.24	11.07	...
.	.	.	.	.	.	...
.	.	.	.	.	.	...
.	.	.	.	.	.	...

Calculator Tip

Cumulative χ^2-distribution probabilities can be calculated with the graphing calculator. Consider the previous example.

From the home screen, press $\boxed{\text{DISTR}}$, and then choose 8: X2cdf(. This is the χ^2-distribution cumulative density function command and is used for computing χ^2-distribution probabilities (areas under the χ^2-curve) between two values for a number of degrees of freedom.

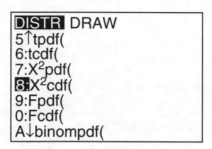

```
DISTR DRAW
5↑tpdf(
6:tcdf(
7:X²pdf(
8:X²cdf(
9:Fpdf(
0:Fcdf(
A↓binompdf(
```

The syntax for the X^2cdf command is X^2cdf(left bound, right bound, df).

The χ^2-distribution continues to infinity in the positive direction. When the area in the tail is required, use of an extreme value is needed. In most cases, 1,000 will suffice.

Key in 2.71,1000,1) and then press $\boxed{\text{ENTER}}$.

```
X²cdf(2.71, 1000,
1)
      .0997209906
```

The area under the χ^2-curve above $\chi^2 = 2.81$ is about 0.10.

There are times when Table C does not provide exact information. Note that the χ^2-statistics are only for tail probabilities with round numbers: 0.05, 0.025, 0.02, 0.01, etc. It is likely that a computed χ^2-statistic will not be among those in the table. In this case, the table can only provide a range of values for the tail probability p.

Example: What is the probability that a χ^2-statistic will be larger than $\chi^2 = 4$ with 2 degrees of freedom?

Answer: Read across the 2 *df* row of the table until 4 is found. The value of 4 is not in the table, but would be located between 3.79 and 4.61, which correspond to the tail probabilities $p = 0.15$ and $p = 0.10$, respectively. The probability that a χ^2-statistic will be larger than $\chi^2 = 4$ with 2 *df* is between 0.10 and 0.15. Thus, $0.10 < p < 0.15$. This is the best information that the table can provide.

To get more precise answers, one would need technology, like a computer or graphing calculator.

Calculator Tip:

From the home screen, press $\boxed{\text{DISTR}}$, and then choose 8: *X2cdf*(.

Key in 4,1000,2) and then press $\boxed{\text{ENTER}}$.

X²cdf(4, 1000, 2)
              .1353352832

The area under the χ^2-curve above $\chi^2 = 4$ is about 0.135.

The **sampling distribution of the χ^2-statistic** is described when all possible simple random samples of size n are taken from a population where one or two categorical variables, each with two or more categories, are under consideration. The value of the χ^2-statistic is

$$\chi^2 = \sum_{\substack{\text{all} \\ \text{cells}}} \frac{(\text{observed} - \text{expected})^2}{\text{expected}}.$$

The χ^2-statistic is essentially an aggregate of the relative differences between the observed counts of categories in a sample and the expected counts of those categories based on population characteristics.

Note: The distribution of this χ^2-statistic assumes sampling with replacement, which is unlikely in practice. When sampling from a population without replacement, the χ^2 model is reasonable if the sample size is no more than 10% of the population size. Also, expected counts for all categories should be at least 5.

The number of degrees of freedom for the distribution and the method of computing expected cell counts are dependent on how many populations and how many variables are under study. These issues will be addressed in detail in Chapter 4.

Trial Run

1. Which of the following statements is always true about the sampling distribution of sample statistics?

   (A) The sampling distribution of the mean $\bar{x}$ is normal if $n \geq 30$.

   (B) The sampling distribution of $\hat{p}$ is normal if $p = 0.5$.

   (C) The sampling distribution of the χ^2-statistic is right-skewed.

   (D) The standard deviation of the sampling distribution of $\bar{x}_1 - \bar{x}_2$ is zero.

   (E) The mean of the sampling distribution of the χ^2-statistic is 1.

2. Two fair dice are rolled 200 times. Which of the following graphs is the most likely to represent the distribution of the sum of the 200 pairs of die rolls?

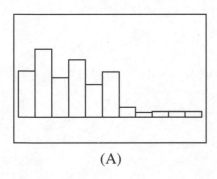

(A)

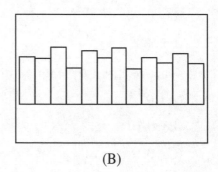

(B)

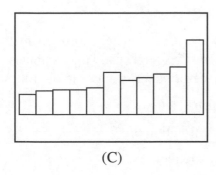

(C)

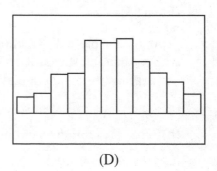

(D)

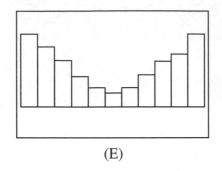

(E)

3. A large population has a mean of 16 and a standard deviation of 8. Consider all possible samples of size 100. What is the value of the standard deviation of the sample means?

    (A) 0.08

    (B) 0.16

    (C) 0.24

    (D) 0.50

    (E) 0.80

4. What is $P(t < 1.018)$ for a t-distribution with 8 degrees of freedom?

    (A) 0.05

    (B) 0.10

    (C) 0.15

    (D) 0.075

    (E) 0.85

5. A population has a distribution that is approximately normally distributed with mean μ and standard deviation σ. As larger and larger samples of size n are drawn from the population, describe the changes in the following:

    (a) The center of the sampling distribution of $\bar{x}$

    (b) The spread of the sampling distribution of $\bar{x}$

    (c) The shape of the sampling distribution of $\bar{x}$

Trial Run Solutions

1.   C. The χ^2-distribution is always right-skewed. Choice A is a common misconception. Some texts suggest using the normal distribution as a model for the sampling distribution of $\bar{x}$ if the sample size is greater than 30 (these authors do not), but it does NOT mean that the sampling distribution IS normal. The sampling distribution of $\hat{p}$ is symmetric if $p = 0.5$, but it is NOT normal. The standard deviation of the sampling distribution of $\bar{x}_1 - \bar{x}_2$ could only be zero if $\sigma_1^2 = 0$ and $\tau_2^2 = 0$. The mean of the sampling distribution of the χ^2-distribution is equal to the number of degrees of freedom.

2.   D. The distribution of the results of each die is uniform, but the sum will be distributed in a mound-shaped distribution. More sums will be near the center than near the extremes.

3.   E. The standard deviation of the sample means is $\sigma_{\bar{x}} = \dfrac{\sigma}{\sqrt{n}} = \dfrac{8}{\sqrt{100}} = 0.8$.

4.   E. Reading across Table B on the line for 8 degrees of freedom, 1.108 is located in the column corresponding to a tail probability of 0.15. That is the upper tail, so the area below $t = 1.018$ is 0.85.

5.   (a) The mean of the sampling distribution of $\bar{x}$, $\mu_{\bar{x}}$, is equal to μ for any sample size. It does not "approach" μ; it is μ.

   (b) The spread of the sampling distribution decreases. Specifically, the standard deviation of the sample mean, $\sigma_{\bar{x}}$, is equal to $\dfrac{\sigma}{\sqrt{n}}$. As n increases, the standard deviation decreases.

   (c) Since the population was approximately normally distributed, the sampling distribution for any sample size n will also be approximately normally distributed. Any deviations of the population from true normality will decrease as n increases, and the sampling distribution's shape will approach normal (but will never *be* normal).

CHAPTER 4
Statistical Inference

Chapter 4

STATISTICAL INFERENCE

A. ESTIMATION (POINT ESTIMATORS AND CONFIDENCE INTERVALS)

Estimation is the process of determining the value of a population **parameter** from information provided by a sample **statistic**. Sometimes, this will be a single value; other times, it will be a range of values.

Point and Interval Estimates

A **point estimate** is a single value that has been calculated to estimate the unknown parameter. The point estimates used in inference are sample statistics. The table below shows which statistics are used as point estimates for parameters.

Parameter	Statistic
Population proportion, p	Sample proportion, $\hat{p}$
Population mean, μ	Sample mean, $\bar{x}$
Difference in population proportions, $p_1 - p_2$	Difference in sample proportions, $\hat{p}_1 - \hat{p}_2$
Difference in population means, $\mu_1 - \mu_2$	Difference in sample means, $\bar{x}_1 - \bar{x}_2$
Population mean difference, μ_d (matched pairs)	Sample mean difference, $\bar{x}_d$
Slope of a population linear model, β_1	Slope of a sample least-squares line, b_1

A **confidence interval** gives us a range of plausible values that is likely to contain the unknown population parameter. This range of values is generated using a set of sample data. The center of a confidence interval for a population parameter is the sample statistic. Confidence intervals are always constructed as *statistic ± margin of error*.

The **margin of error** is the range of values to the left and right of the point estimate in which the parameter likely lies. For example, suppose you read in the school newspaper that 70% of students surveyed said they want more soda machines in the school building. The student who wrote the story reports that the survey has a 10% margin of error. This means it is likely that between 60% and 80% of the entire student body wants more soda machines. We could write this as 70% ± 10%.

Interpreting Confidence Level and Confidence Intervals

We can never be totally certain about what the unknown parameter is, but do have a level of certainty whether or not it is in our interval. This is known as the **confidence level**. The most commonly used confidence levels are 90%, 95%, and 99%. The graph below is an example of a series of 90% confidence intervals created by taking random samples from a population.

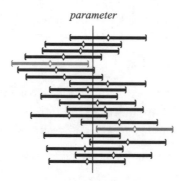

The vertical line represents the value of the parameter. Each of these intervals shows the form *statistic ± margin of error*. The diamonds in the center of each interval are point estimates of the parameter (statistics), and the bars extend out equal to the margin of error on both sides of the point estimate. Eighteen of the 20 intervals, or 90% of the intervals, intersect the vertical line. This illustrates what 90% confidence means. If we collect repeated samples and construct 90% confidence intervals for the parameter, on average 90% of the intervals generated would contain or "capture" the population parameter.

When we generate a sample and construct a confidence interval, an interpretation of that interval should follow. That interpretation reflects our confidence that the population parameter is within a given range. This is not the same as confidence level.

Example: You are interested in finding out what the true proportion of yellow candies is in a very large bag without counting them all. After taking a sample and determining its proportion of yellow, the 95% confidence interval for the true proportion of yellow candies is

0.2 ± 0.1 or (0.1, 0.3). Interpret the interval and describe what is meant by 95% confidence.

Answer: I am 95% confident that the true population proportion of yellow candies is between 0.1 and 0.3.

Note: This is not a probability statement about the "chance" that there is a certain proportion of yellow candies in the bag or the chance that the true proportion is actually in our interval. It may be or it may not be—we will never know. It is about how confident we are that our interval has captured the true proportion.

Ninety-five percent confidence means if we collected more samples using the same sampling method and generated confidence intervals, 95% of the intervals would contain the population parameter.

General Formula for Confidence Intervals

Recall that all confidence intervals are in the same format: *statistic ± margin of error*. The margin of error is the product of two numbers: the **critical value** and the **standard deviation of the statistic**. Thus, a confidence interval can be thought of as *statistic ± (critical value)(standard deviation of the statistic)*. If the standard deviation of the statistic cannot be computed, then the **standard error** is used. (See Chapter 3, Section D.)

The critical value is found from **Table B: *t*-distribution critical values**, by cross-referencing the confidence level *C* and the number of degrees of freedom *df*. In cases where the *z*-distribution is used to find the critical value—inference for sample proportions or when the population standard deviation is known in inference for means—the last line (∞) is used.

General Procedure for Inference with Confidence Intervals

To do any inference problem, the four-step procedure for inference is used.

Step 1: State the parameter of interest. The parameter of interest is a characteristic of the population under study. It will be a population proportion, a difference of population means, and so on. This should be defined in words and symbols. (In the next section, *Tests of Significance*, another element will be added to this step.)

Step 2: Name the inference procedure and check assumptions/conditions. The procedure is named by giving the level of confidence and what parameter it is estimating.

There are assumptions/conditions that must be *checked* in order to proceed with various inference procedures. It is not enough to merely state them—you must verify that they apply.

Step 3: Calculate the confidence interval. Confidence intervals are always of the form *statistic* ± (*critical value*)(*standard deviation of the statistic*). Write the appropriate formula for the type of confidence interval being computed, substitute in the values in the formula, and compute the interval.

Step 4: Interpret the results in context. Describe in the context of the situation what the confidence interval means. Refer back to step 1, as this is where the parameter of interest was defined.

Confidence Intervals for Proportions

The formula to compute a confidence interval for a population proportion p is $\hat{p} \pm z^* \sqrt{\dfrac{\hat{p}(1-\hat{p})}{n}}$, where $\hat{p}$ is the sample proportion, n is the sample size, and z^* is the z-critical value.

The assumptions/conditions for inference for a population proportion are as follows:

(1)   The sample must be an SRS from the population of interest.

(2)   The population is at least 10 times as large as the sample size.

(3)   The number of successes and failures are both at least 10. That is, $n\hat{p} \geq 10$ and $n(1-\hat{p}) \geq 10$.

Example: A random sample of 100 candies has 25 that are yellow. Construct the 95% confidence interval for the true proportion of yellow candies.

Answer: Follow the four-step procedure for inference.

Step 1: State the parameter of interest. The parameter of interest is p, the true proportion of yellow candies in the population of all candies.

Step 2: Name the inference procedure and check assumptions/conditions. The procedure is a 95% confidence interval for p, as defined above.

(1)   The sample must be an SRS from the population of interest. OK—the problem states that we have a random sample.

(2)   The population is at least 10 times as large as the sample size. OK—it is a good bet that there are more than 1,000 candies in the population.

(3) The number of successes and failures are both at least 10. OK—there are 25 yellow candies (successes) and 75 of other colors (failures).

Step 3: Calculate the confidence interval. In our sample $\hat{p} = \dfrac{25}{100} = 0.25$, and the z-critical value for 95% confidence is 1.960. Substituting into the formula $\hat{p} \pm z^* \sqrt{\dfrac{\hat{p}(1-\hat{p})}{n}}$, we get

$$\hat{p} \pm z^* \sqrt{\tfrac{\hat{p}(1-\hat{p})}{n}}$$
$$0.25 \pm 1.960\sqrt{\tfrac{(0.25)(0.75)}{100}}$$
$$0.25 \pm 0.08487$$
$$(0.16513, 0.33487).$$

Step 4: Interpret the results in context. We are 95% confident that the true proportion of yellow candies in the population is between about 0.165 and 0.335.

Calculator Tip:

Confidence intervals for proportions can be calculated with the graphing calculator.

From the home screen, press $\boxed{\text{STAT}}$, arrow right to TESTS, and then choose A:1-PropZInt....

```
EDIT  CALC  TESTS
8↑ TInterval...
9 : 2-SampZInt...
0 : 2-SampTInt...
A: 1-PropZInt...
B : 2-PropZInt...
C : χ²-Test...
D↓ χ² GOF-Test...
```

Enter the values of yellow candies found in the sample, total number of candies in the sample, and the confidence level.

```
1-PropZInt
 X : 25
 n : 100
 C-Level : 95
 Calculate
```

Arrow down to Calculate, and then press $\boxed{\text{ENTER}}$. The interval is shown along with the sample proportion and sample size.

```
1-PropZInt
 ( .16513, .33487)
p̂ = .25
n = 100
```

Changing the confidence level affects the width of the interval. As the confidence level increases, so does the critical value used to construct the interval. Thus, the higher the confidence level, the larger the margin of error and the wider the interval.

Example: A random sample of 100 candies has 25 that are yellow. Construct the 90% and 99% confidence intervals for the true proportion of yellow candies.

Answer: $90\% : 0.25 \pm 1.645\sqrt{\frac{(0.25)(0.75)}{100}} = (0.17878,\ 0.32122)$

$99\% : 0.25 \pm 2.576\sqrt{\frac{(0.25)(0.75)}{100}} = (0.13846,\ 0.36154)$.

The 95% confidence interval from the previous example is $(0.16513, 0.33487)$.

Note: The interval becomes wider as you increase the confidence level. The widest interval comes from the highest confidence level.

Sometimes, you are asked to find the minimum sample size required to produce a confidence interval with a particular margin of error. Recall, that the margin of error for a one-sample confidence interval for proportion is $ME = z^*\sqrt{\dfrac{\hat{p}(1-\hat{p})}{n}}$. Solving for n, we get $n = \dfrac{(z^*)^2\,\hat{p}(1-\hat{p})}{ME^2}$.

Example: What is the minimum number of candies needed in a sample to estimate the true proportion of green candies with a 4% margin of error at 95% confidence? Assume that previous information estimated the proportion of green to be 30%.

Answer: The margin of error is $ME = z^*\sqrt{\dfrac{\hat{p}(1-\hat{p})}{n}}$. In this case, the maximum allowable margin of error is 0.04. So, $0.04 \geq 1.960\sqrt{\dfrac{0.3(1-0.3)}{n}}$. Solving for n, $n \geq \dfrac{(z^*)^2\,\hat{p}(1-\hat{p})}{ME^2} \Rightarrow n \geq \dfrac{(1.960)^2\,0.3(0.7)}{0.04^2} \Rightarrow n \geq 504.21$.

The calculations lead to a sample size of at least 504.21, so we round up to the next integer; 505 candies are needed.

Note: When you do not have information about the population proportion on which to base your sample size calculations, use $\hat{p} = 0.5$ as the estimate. This will ensure an appropriate sample size.

In the previous example, if we wanted the margin of error to be 2%, we would find that the sample size becomes 2,017, roughly four times that before. To cut the margin of error in half, and therefore the width of the interval, you must quadruple the sample size.

Confidence Intervals for the Difference Between Two Proportions

The formula to compute a confidence interval for the difference of two population proportions

$$p_1 - p_2 \text{ is } (\hat{p}_1 - \hat{p}_2) \pm z^* \sqrt{\frac{\hat{p}_1(1 - \hat{p}_1)}{n_1} + \frac{\hat{p}_2(1 - \hat{p}_2)}{n_2}}, \text{ where } \hat{p}_1 \text{ and } \hat{p}_2 \text{ are}$$

the respective sample proportions, n_1 and n_2 are the respective sample sizes, and z^* is the z-critical value.

The assumptions/conditions for inference for a difference between two proportions change slightly from the one-sample procedure:

(1) Both samples must be independent SRSs from the populations of interest.

(2) The population sizes are both at least 10 times as large as the respective sample sizes.

(3) The number of successes and failures in both samples are both at least 10. That is, $n_1\hat{p}_1 \geq 10$, $n_1(1 - \hat{p}_1) \geq 10$, $n_2\hat{p}_2 \geq 10$, and $n_2(1 - \hat{p}_2) \geq 10$.

Example: We are interested in finding the difference in the proportions of high school seniors taking AP Statistics between rural and urban areas of a populous state. An SRS of 250 rural high school seniors was taken and 82 are taking AP Statistics. In urban areas, an SRS of 280 seniors produced 56 taking AP Statistics. Compute a 90% confidence interval for the true difference between the proportions of high school seniors taking AP Statistics in rural and urban areas.

Answer: Follow the four-step procedure for inference.

Step 1: State the parameter of interest. The parameter of interest is the difference in proportions $p_1 - p_2$, where p_1 = the proportion of all rural seniors taking AP Statistics in the state and p_2 = the true proportion of all urban seniors taking AP Statistics in the state.

Step 2: Name the inference procedure and check assumptions/conditions.
The procedure is a 95% confidence interval for $p_1 - p_2$, as defined above.

(1) The samples must be independent SRSs from the populations of interest. OK—the problem states that we have two independent random samples.

(2) The populations are at least 10 times as large as the sample sizes. OK as long as there are 2,500 rural and 2,800 urban seniors in the state. Since the state is "populous," this is reasonable.

(3) The number of successes and failures in each sample are both at least 10. OK—there are 82 successes and 168 failures in the rural sample; there are 56 successes and 224 failures in the urban sample.

Step 3: Calculate the confidence interval. In our sample $\hat{p}_1 = \dfrac{82}{250} = 0.328$, $\hat{p}_2 = \dfrac{56}{180} = 0.2$, and the z-critical value for 90% confidence is 1.645. Substituting into the formula $(\hat{p}_1 - \hat{p}_2) \pm z^* \sqrt{\dfrac{\hat{p}_1(1-\hat{p}_1)}{n_1} + \dfrac{\hat{p}_2(1-\hat{p}_2)}{n_2}}$, we get

$$(0.328 - 0.2) \pm 1.645 \sqrt{\tfrac{0.328(0.672)}{250} + \tfrac{0.2(0.8)}{280}}$$
$$0.128 \pm 0.0627$$
$$(0.0653, \ 0.1907).$$

Step 4: Interpret the results in context. We are 90% confident that the difference between the true proportions of high school seniors who take AP Statistics in rural and urban areas is between 7% and 19%. We could alternately say that the proportion of rural seniors taking AP Statistics is between 7% and 19% higher than the proportion of urban seniors.

Calculator Tip:

Confidence intervals for difference in proportions can be calculated with the graphing calculator.

From the home screen, press $\boxed{\text{STAT}}$, arrow right to TESTS, and then choose B: 2-PropZInt....

```
EDIT  CALC  TESTS
9↑ 2-SampZInt...
0 : 2-SampTInt...
A : 1-PropZInt...
B: 2-PropZInt...
C : χ²-Tes t...
D : χ² GOF-Test...
E↓ 2 -SampFTest...
```

Input the number of rural seniors taking AP Statistics found in the sample, the rural sample size, the number of total urban seniors taking AP Statistics, the urban sample size, and the confidence level.

```
2-PropZInt
  x1 : 82
  n1 : 250
  x2 : 56
  n2 : 280
  C-Level : 90
  Calculate
```

Arrow down to Calculate, and then press ENTER. The interval is shown along with the sample proportions and sample sizes.

```
2-PropZInt
  (.0653, .1907)
  p̂1=.328
  p̂2=.2
  n1=250
  n2=280
```

Confidence Intervals for Means

Confidence intervals for population means can be calculated and interpreted as easily as those for proportions. Since we usually do not know the population standard deviation σ, the sample standard deviation s is used to compute standard error. A t-distribution is appropriate to use for the critical value instead of the standard normal when σ is unknown. The value of t^* will depend on degrees of freedom and the confidence level chosen.

The formula to compute a confidence interval for a population mean μ is $\bar{x} \pm t^* \dfrac{s}{\sqrt{n}}$, where $\bar{x}$ is the sample mean, s is the sample standard deviation, n is the sample size, and t^* is the t-critical value. The number of degrees of freedom is $n - 1$. (If the population standard deviation is known, use σ and z^*.)

The assumptions/conditions for inference for a population mean are as follows:

(1) The sample must be an SRS from the population of interest.

(2) The data come from a normally distributed population. This is rarely ever going to be the case. But, we can satisfy this condition if the following criteria are met:

- For small samples (up to size 15), a plot of the data is generally symmetric, unimodal, and has no outliers.

- For sample sizes between 15 and 40, the plot should be unimodal and have no outliers. Moderate skewness can be tolerated.

- For large samples (over size 40), the procedures are useful even in the presence of extreme skewness. Outliers are still a concern.

Example: A popular weight loss plan claims that most people will lose an average of 6 pounds per month if they follow the plan exactly as prescribed and exercise 30 minutes each day. A random sample of 45 people who have been on the plan for 1 month produced a mean weight loss of 5.6 pounds and the standard deviation was 1.32 pounds. A dotplot of the data is shown below.

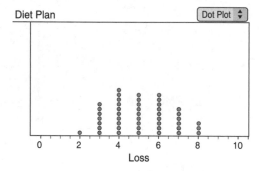

Construct a 95% confidence interval for the true mean weight loss after 1 month on this plan.

Answer: Follow the four-step inference procedure.

Step 1: State the parameter of interest. The parameter of interest is μ, the true mean weight loss after 1 month on this diet plan.

Step 2: Name the inference procedure and check assumptions/conditions. The procedure is a 95% confidence interval for μ, as defined above.

(1)   The sample must be an SRS from the population of interest. OK— the problem states that we have a random sample.

(2)   The data come from a normally distributed population. OK—the dotplot of the data is unimodal and symmetric, with no outliers.

Step 3: Calculate the confidence interval. In our sample $\bar{x} = 5.6$, $s = 1.32$, and the *t*-critical value for 95% confidence and $n - 1 = 44$ degrees of freedom is

2.021. (Note: If the number of degrees of freedom is not shown in Table B, use the next *lower* value.) Substituting into the formula $\bar{x} \pm t^* \dfrac{s}{\sqrt{n}}$, we get

$$\bar{x} \pm t^* \tfrac{s}{\sqrt{n}}$$
$$5.6 \pm 2.021 \tfrac{1.32}{\sqrt{45}}$$
$$5.6 \pm 0.3966$$
$$(5.2034,\ 5.9966).$$

Step 4: Interpret the results in context. We are 95% confident that the true mean weight loss per month for people on this plan is between 5.2 and 6.0 pounds.

Calculator Tip:

Confidence intervals for means can be calculated with the graphing calculator.

From the home screen, press $\boxed{\text{STAT}}$, arrow right to TESTS, and then choose 8:TInterval....

```
EDIT  CALC  TESTS
5↑1-PropZTest...
6 : 2-PropZTest...
7 : ZInterval...
8 : TInterval...
9 : 2-SampZInt...
0 : 2-SampTInt...
A↓ 1-PropZInt...
```

Input the mean and standard deviation of the sample, the sample size, and the confidence level.

```
TInterval
 Inpt : Data  Stats
 x̄ : 5.6
 Sx : 1.32
 n : 45
 C-Level : 95
 Calculate
```

Arrow down to Calculate, and then press $\boxed{\text{ENTER}}$. The interval is shown along with the sample mean, sample standard deviation, and sample size.

```
TInterval
(5.2034, 5.9966)
x̄=5.6
Sx=1.32
n=45
```

Confidence Intervals for Means with Paired Data

The same formula can be used to estimate mean difference in a paired situation. The matched-pairs design uses a one-sample procedure. Remember that you are using the differences in the two sets of data to find the confidence interval for the mean difference. You do not have to worry about the condition of independence, which we will find is true of two-sample procedures, since the data are paired and not independent of each other.

Example: A baseball bat manufacturer makes two different types of bats, aluminum and ceramic. The company wants to know which type of bat provides better performance for little leaguers as measured by number of balls hit into the outfield. Twenty-three boys who play little league baseball participated in the study. Each player was randomly assigned one type of bat with which he took 20 swings, followed by 20 swings with the other bat. The number of hits into the outfield was recorded for each bat. The number of hits into the outfield for each type of bat is shown in the table below.

Aluminum	4	2	3	3	6	3	5	7	5	9	6	3
Ceramic	5	5	3	6	8	6	6	12	8	15	8	2
Difference $(C - A)$	1	3	0	3	2	3	1	5	3	6	2	-1
Aluminum	1	2	4	8	8	3	2	2	6	5	4	
Ceramic	3	5	8	7	8	6	5	4	11	9	6	
Difference $(C - A)$	2	3	4	-1	0	3	3	2	5	4	2	

Find the 90% confidence interval for the mean difference in the number of hits into the outfield between the two types of bats.

Answer: Follow the four-step inference procedure.

Step 1: State the parameter of interest. The parameter of interest is μ_d, the true mean difference in hits into the outfield between ceramic and aluminum bats.

Step 2: Name the inference procedure and check assumptions/conditions.
The procedure is a 90% confidence interval for μ_d, as defined above.

(1)   The sample must be an SRS from the population of interest. OK—
the players may not be a random sample, but the data come from a
randomized comparative experiment, so the randomization condition
is satisfied.

(2)   The data come from a normally distributed population. OK—the histogram of differences is unimodal and symmetric, with no outliers.

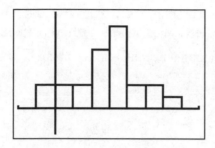

Step 3: Calculate the confidence interval. In our sample $\bar{x}_d = 2.3913$, $s = 1.827$, and the *t*-critical value for 90% confidence and $n - 1 = 22$ degrees of
freedom is 1.717.

Substituting into the formula $\bar{x}_d \pm t^* \dfrac{s_d}{\sqrt{n}}$, we get

$$\bar{x}_d \pm t^* \frac{s_d}{\sqrt{n}}$$
$$2.3913 \pm 1.717 \frac{1.828}{\sqrt{23}}$$
$$2.3913 \pm 0.6544$$
$$(1.7369, \ 3.0457).$$

Step 4: Interpret the results in context. We are 90% confident that for little
league players, the ceramic bat produces, on average, between 1.7 and 3.0 more
hits to the outfield (per 20 swings) than the aluminum bat.

Below is an example of a computer printout that you might see. In this case
the interval has been calculated by the software and is circled.

Variable	N	Mean	StDev	SE Mean	90.0 % CI
Difference	23	2.391	1.828	0.381	1.737, 3.046

Sometimes you might be given the information with the confidence interval
information missing, like that below.

Variable	N	Mean	StDev	SE Mean
Difference	23	2.391	1.828	0.381 $\dfrac{s}{\sqrt{n}}$

You would be expected to generate an interval from this information. In this case you need the critical value, the sample mean, and the standard deviation of the sample in order to compute a confidence interval. The "SE Mean" on the printout (circled) is the standard error—the standard deviation from the sample divided by the square root of the sample size. The interval would be $2.391 \pm 1.717(0.381)$.

Just as we saw with proportions, we can also determine a minimum sample size needed for a predetermined margin of error. Recall, that the margin of error for a one-sample confidence interval for mean is $ME = z^* \dfrac{\sigma}{\sqrt{n}}$. Solving for n, we get

$$n = \frac{(z^*)^2 \sigma^2}{ME^2}.$$

Example: Ball bearings must be manufactured to strict tolerances or they will not function properly. If a quality control inspector randomly samples ball bearings from a production process, what is the minimum sample size required to be 99% confident that the mean diameter is within 0.04 mm? Past data indicate that the standard deviation of bearing diameters is 0.10 mm.

Answer: The margin of error is $ME = z^* \dfrac{\sigma}{\sqrt{n}}$. In this case, the maximum allowable margin of error is 0.04 mm. So, So, $0.04 \geq 2.576 \dfrac{0.10}{\sqrt{n}}$. Solving for n,

$$n \geq \frac{(z^*)^2 \sigma^2}{ME^2} \Rightarrow n \geq \frac{(2.576)^2 (0.1)^2}{0.04^2} \Rightarrow n \geq 41.4736.$$

Round up to next integer; we need to sample 42 ball bearings for the required margin of error.

Confidence Intervals for the Difference Between Two Means

A two-sample confidence interval for the difference between population means is used when you have two independent random samples. The formula to compute the interval for $\mu_1 - \mu_2$ is $(\bar{x}_1 - \bar{x}_2) \pm t^* \sqrt{\dfrac{s_1^2}{n_1} + \dfrac{s_2^2}{n_2}}$, where $\bar{x}_1$ and $\bar{x}_2$ are the sample means, s_1 and s_2 are the sample standard deviations, n_1 and n_2 are the sample sizes, and t^* is the t-critical value.

The number of degrees of freedom is computed by a complex formula not presented here. If technology is used, this exact number of degrees of freedom will be provided. If by-hand calculations are performed, a conservative interval can be constructed using the smaller of $n_1 - 1$ and $n_2 - 1$.

If the population standard deviations are known, use σ_1, σ_2, and z^*.

The assumptions/conditions for inference for the difference in population means are as follows:

(1)   The samples must be SRSs from the populations of interest.

(2)   The data come from normally distributed populations. This is rarely ever going to be the case. But, we can satisfy this condition if the following criteria are met:

- For small samples (up to size 15), plots of the data are generally symmetric, unimodal, and have no outliers.

- For sample sizes between 15 and 40, the plots should be unimodal and have no outliers. Moderate skewness can be tolerated.

- For large samples (over size 40), the procedures are useful even in the presence of extreme skewness. Outliers are still a concern.

Example: A cruise line is trying to determine if there is a difference in the mean amount of money passengers spend on board their ships during a 1-week cruise to Alaska and a 1-week cruise to the Caribbean. This includes food, beverages, gift shops, and the spa. Some items are the same on both ships and there are regional souvenirs that are different. Random samples of 35 passengers from each ship are taken. The mean amount of money spent on board the ship in Alaska is $\bar{x}_1 = \$582.16$ with a standard deviation of $s_1 = \$32.65$. The mean amount of money spent on board the ship in the Caribbean is $\bar{x}_2 = \$493.62$ with a standard deviation of $s_2 = \$28.73$. Find the 95% confidence interval for the difference in the mean amounts of money spent on board the ships. Histograms of the data are shown below.

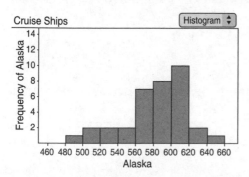

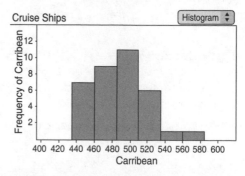

Answer: Follow the four-step inference procedure.

Step 1: State the parameter of interest. The parameter of interest is $\mu_1 - \mu_2$, the true difference in the mean amounts spent by passengers on Alaska and Caribbean ships, where μ_1 is the true mean amount spent by Alaskan passengers and μ_2 is the true mean amount spent by Caribbean passengers.

Step 2: Name the inference procedure and check assumptions/conditions. The procedure is a 95% confidence interval for $\mu_1 - \mu_2$, as defined above.

(1)   The samples must be SRSs from the populations of interest. OK—the problem states that the samples were random.

(2)   The data come from normally distributed populations. OK—the histogram of Caribbean passenger spending is symmetric and unimodal; the histogram of the Alaskan passengers' expenditures is skewed left, but the sample size of 35 is large enough to tolerate it.

Step 3: Calculate the confidence interval. In our samples $\bar{x}_1 = \$582.16$, $s_1 = \$32.65$, $\bar{x}_2 = \$493.62$, $s_2 = \$28.73$, and the t-critical value for 95% confidence and 30 degrees of freedom is 2.042. ($df = 34$ is not in the table.)

Substituting into the formula $(\bar{x}_1 - \bar{x}_2) \pm t^* \sqrt{\dfrac{s_1^2}{n_1} + \dfrac{s_2^2}{n_2}}$, we get

$$(\bar{x}_1 - \bar{x}_2) \pm t^* \sqrt{\tfrac{s_1^2}{n_1} + \tfrac{s_2^2}{n_2}}$$
$$(582.16 - 493.62) \pm 2.042 \sqrt{\tfrac{32.65^2}{35} + \tfrac{28.73^2}{35}}$$
$$88.54 \pm 15.01$$
$$(73.53,\ 103.55).$$

Step 4: Interpret the results in context. We are 95% confident that the difference in the mean amount of money spent by passengers on board the two ships is between \$73.53 and \$103.55. Another way to interpret this is that passengers on Alaskan cruises spend on average between \$73.53 and \$103.55 more than passengers on Caribbean cruises.

Calculator Tip:

Confidence intervals for the difference in means can be calculated with the graphing calculator.

From the home screen, press STAT, arrow right to TESTS, and then choose 0:2-SampTInt....

```
EDIT  CALC  TESTS
7↑ ZInterval...
8 : TInterval...
9 : 2-SampZInt...
0 : 2-SampTInt...
A : 1-PropZInt...
B : 2-PropZInt...
C↓ χ²-Test...
```

Input the means and standard deviations of the samples, and the sample sizes.

```
2-SampTInt
 Inpt : Data  Stats
 x̄1 : 582.16
 Sx1 : 32.65
 n1 : 35
 x̄2 : 493.62
 Sx2 : 28.73
↓n2 : 35
```

Arrow down to input the confidence level. When you reach the **Pooled** line, choose **No**. We only use a pooled *t*-test if we know the two populations have equal standard deviations, that is, $\sigma_1 = \sigma_2$. This is unlikely to occur.

```
2-SampTInt
↑n1 : 35
 x̄2 : 493.62
 Sx2 : 28.73
 n2 : 35
 C-Level : 95
 Pooled :No Yes
 Calculate
```

Arrow down to **Calculate**, and then press ENTER . The interval is shown along with the sample means, sample standard deviations, and the exact number of degrees of freedom.

```
2-SampTInt
 (73.866, 103.21)
 df=66.91712053
 x̄1=582.16
 x̄2= 493.62
 Sx1=32.65
↓Sx2=28.73
```

Note: The degrees of freedom used from the table was 30. Calculators and software packages will use the exact degrees of freedom, in this case about 67. The calculator's interval is a bit narrower than the one done by hand.

Confidence Intervals for the Slope of the Regression Line

As we can never truly know the parameters for the true regression line, these being the slope and intercept, we can estimate what these values are. In AP Statistics, we only concern ourselves with the more important of the two: slope. The slope of the regression line is the mean rate of change of the response variable when the explanatory variable increases by one unit. We can estimate the slope of the population model with a confidence interval.

The formula to compute a confidence interval for a population slope β_1 is $b_1 \pm t^* SE_{b_1}$, where b_1 is the slope of the sample regression line, SE_{b_1} is the standard error of the slope, and t^* is the t-critical value. The number of degrees of freedom is $n - 2$.

The assumptions/conditions for inference for the slope of a population model are as follows:

(1)   The mean y values for all the fixed x values are related linearly by the equation $\mu_y = \beta_0 + \beta_{yx}$ We check this by verifying that our scatterplot is linear and that a residual plot has no "U"-shaped pattern.

(2)   For any fixed value of x, the value of each y is independent. We check this by looking for grouping patterns in the residual plot.

(3)   For any fixed value of x, the value of y is normally distributed. We check this by looking at a histogram of the residuals. The plot should be symmetric and unimodal, although skewness can be tolerated for larger samples.

(4)   For all fixed values of x, the standard deviation of y is equal. We check this by verifying that the variability of the residuals is relatively constant across the explanatory variable.

Often, a computer printout will be given to you to calculate the confidence interval for the slope of the true regression model.

Example: The heights (in inches) x, and shoe sizes y, of 15 women are shown in the table below.

x	63	62	62	63	68	65	68	69	70	62	60	60	61	63	64
y	7.5	7	7.5	6.5	8	7.5	9	9	10	6	5	5.5	6	7	7.5

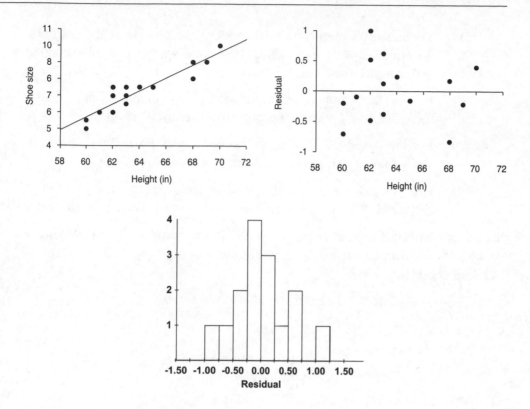

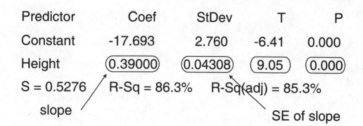

The regression equation is
Shoe Size = - 17.7 + 0.390 Height

Predictor	Coef	StDev	T	P
Constant	-17.693	2.760	-6.41	0.000
Height	(0.39000)	(0.04308)	(9.05)	(0.000)

S = 0.5276   R-Sq = 86.3%   R-Sq(adj) = 85.3%

slope   SE of slope

Computer output of the regression analysis, a scatterplot, a residual plot, and a histogram of the residuals are provided. Calculate the 95% confidence interval for the slope of the true regression line.

Answer: Follow the four-step inference procedure.

Step 1: State the parameter of interest. The parameter of interest is β_1, the slope of the population regression model.

Step 2: Name the inference procedure and check assumptions/conditions. The procedure is a 95% confidence interval for β_1, as defined above.

(1) The mean y values for all the fixed x values are related linearly by the equation $\mu_y = \beta_0 + \beta_{1x}$. OK—the scatterplot is linear and the residual plot shows no U-shaped pattern.

(2) For any fixed value of x, the value of each y is independent. OK—there does not appear to be any clustering in the residual plot.

(3) For any fixed value of x, the value of y is normally distributed. OK—the histogram of the residuals is symmetric and unimodal.

(4) For all fixed values of x, the standard deviation of y is equal. OK—the variability of the residuals across the values of x is consistent.

Step 3: Calculate the confidence interval. In our sample $b_1 = 0.39$, $SE_{b1} = 0.043$ and the t-critical value for 95% confidence and $n - 2 = 13$ degrees of freedom is 2.160.

Substituting into the formula $b_1 \pm t^* SE_{b_1}$, we get

$$b_1 \pm t^* SE_{b_1}$$
$$0.39 \pm 2.160\,(0.04308)$$
$$0.39 \pm 0.093$$
$$(0.297,\ 0.483).$$

Step 4: Interpret the results in context. We are 95% confident that the slope of the true regression line for height and shoe size is between 0.2969 and 0.4831. That is, for each additional inch of height, a woman's shoe size is between about 0.3 and 0.5 sizes larger.

Calculator Tip:

Confidence intervals for the slope of the population model can be calculated with the graphing calculator. You must, however, have the raw data in lists.

In this case, the women's heights are in list L1 and shoe sizes are in list L2. From the home screen, press STAT, arrow right to TESTS, and then choose G:LinRegTInt….

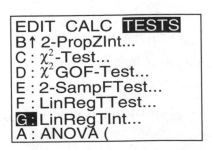

Input the data lists, the confidence level, and where the regression equation is to be stored.

```
LinRegTInt
   Xlist : L₁
   Ylist : L₂
   Freq : 1
   C-Level : 95
   RegEQ : Y1
   Calculate
```

Arrow down to Calculate, and then press ENTER . The interval is shown along with the sample slope, degrees of freedom, standard error about the regression line, and intercept. Scrolling down will give r and r^2.

```
LinRegTInt
  y = a+bx
  ( .29694, .48306)
  b = .39
  df = 13
  s = .5275730597
↓ a = −17.69333333
```

Trial Run

1. A survey was conducted to determine the percentage of cat owners who vaccinate their pets on a yearly basis. A random sample of 200 cat owners showed that 126 of them vaccinate their pets yearly. A 90% confidence interval for the true percentage of cat owners that vaccinate their pets yearly is

    (A) $0.63 \pm 2.576 \sqrt{\dfrac{(0.63)(0.37)}{200}}$

    (B) $0.63 \pm 1.960 \sqrt{\dfrac{(0.63)(0.37)}{200}}$

    (C) $0.63 \pm 1.645 \sqrt{\dfrac{(0.63)(0.37)}{200}}$

(D) $0.63 \pm 1.645\sqrt{\dfrac{(0.63)(0.37)}{126}}$

(E) $0.63 \pm 1.960\sqrt{\dfrac{(0.63)(0.37)}{126}}$

2. A random sample of the actual weight of 5 pound bags of Barks-A-Lot Dog Food produces a mean of 4.963 pounds and a standard deviation of 0.067 pound. If the sample size is 50, which of the following will approximate a 95% confidence interval for the mean weight of dog food from this company?

   (A) 4.963 ± 0.009

   (B) 4.963 ± 0.016

   (C) 4.963 ± 0.019

   (D) 4.963 ± 0.067

   (E) 4.963 ± 50

3. A television news station wants to make sure that election polls have a margin of error of $\pm 3\%$. What is the minimum number of voters that must be polled using 95% confidence and an estimate of 0.5 for p?

   (A) 17

   (B) 544

   (C) 752

   (D) 1,068

   (E) 3,000

4. An SRS yields a sample mean, $\bar{x}$, of 8.6. A 90% confidence interval from the same data is 8.6 ± 2.4. Which of the following statements is true about the situation?

   (A) If the population mean were 5.2, the sample mean of 8.6 would be highly likely.

   (B) If the population mean were 5.2, the sample mean of 8.6 would be highly unlikely.

   (C) There is a 90% chance that the population mean lies between 6.2 and 11.0.

    (D)   If this procedure were repeated many times, 90% of the sample means would fall between 6.2 and 11.

    (E)   90% of the sample data lie between 6.2 and 11.

5.   In which of the following confidence intervals is the critical value derived from the z-distribution?

    I.   Confidence interval for population proportion.

    II.   Confidence interval for population mean where population standard deviation is known, sample size is small.

    III.   Two-sample confidence interval for the difference in population means where population standard deviations are unknown, sample sizes are large.

    (A)   I only

    (B)   I and II only

    (C)   I and III only

    (D)   II and III only

    (E)   I, II, and III

6.   A random sample of Illinois high school seniors was taken to determine what proportion will attend college out of state. The SRS produced 239 out of 950 seniors that they are going to attend college out of state.

    (a)   Calculate and interpret a 95% confidence interval for the true proportion of Illinois high school seniors that attend college out of state.

    (b)   What does 95% confidence mean?

7.   An entomologist is studying a newly discovered species of an insect. He wants to determine the mean lifespan of the insect. Similar species of insects have lifespans with a standard deviation of $\sigma = 2$ days.

    (a)   How many insects would the entomologist have to study so that the margin of error for his estimate of the mean lifespan is at most 1 day? He will use a 95% confidence interval.

    (b)   The entomologist actually uses a sample of 10 insects. Will his margin of error likely be larger or smaller than 1 day? Explain.

    (c)   The entomologist's 10 insects have a mean lifespan of 11.8 days with a standard deviation of 1.6 days. Compute and interpret the

95% confidence interval for the mean lifetime. Assume that the conditions/assumptions for inference are satisfied.

Trial Run Solutions

1. C. $0.63 \pm 1.645\sqrt{\dfrac{(0.63)(0.37)}{200}}$. There were two choices with 1.645 as the correct critical value. The other choice had a sample size of 126, which is incorrect, as there were 200.

2. C. 4.963 ± 0.019. All of the choices had the correct estimate for the mean. The margin of error is calculated as $2.021 \left(\dfrac{0.067}{\sqrt{50}} \right) = 0.019$.

3. D. 1068. Solving for the sample size $1.96\sqrt{\dfrac{0.25(0.75)}{n}} \leq 0.03$. From this calculation $n \geq 1067.11$, we round up to the next integer, which is 1068. Rounding up guarantees that the margin of error will be less than or equal to 0.03.

4. B. The interval estimates the population mean to be between 6.2 and 9.0. The value 5.2 falls outside of the interval. If the population mean really were 5.2, it is unlikely that a sample mean of 8.6 would result.

5. B. I and II only. Choice I is true because the confidence interval for a proportion is always calculated using a z-critical value. Choice II is true because you know the population standard deviation σ and can use the z-critical value. If the population standard deviation(s) are unknown, the t-distribution must be used.

6. (a) The calculation for the interval is
    $$\dfrac{239}{950} \pm 1.96\sqrt{\dfrac{(239/950)(711/950)}{950}} = (0.22399, 0.27917).$$ You can use the one-proportion z-interval on the graphing calculator to obtain the same result.

    (b) 95% confidence means that if we generate many intervals using the same method, 95 out of 100 intervals would contain the true population parameter.

7.   (a)   Using the formula for sample size from the margin of error:

$$n \geq \frac{(z^*)^2 \sigma^2}{ME^2} \Rightarrow n \geq \frac{(1.960)^2 (2)^2}{1^2} \Rightarrow n \geq 15.3664.$$

The calculation yields 15.3664. Round up to the next integer, so 16 would be the minimum sample size of insects needed.

(b)   With a smaller sample size, the margin of error will become larger, since $\frac{\sigma}{\sqrt{n}}$ will be larger. As n decreases, $\frac{\sigma}{\sqrt{n}}$.

(c)   The 95% confidence interval for μ, the mean lifetime of the insects,

$$\text{is } 11.8 \pm 2.262 \left(\frac{1.6}{\sqrt{10}} \right) = (10.655, \ 12.945).$$

Note that we used the *t*-critical value of 2.262 with 9 degrees of freedom since we did not know the population standard deviation, σ, in this case. We are 95% confident that the true mean lifespan for the newly discovered species of insect is between 10.655 and 12.945 days.

B: TESTS OF SIGNIFICANCE

Significance tests are performed to determine whether the observed value of a sample **statistic** differs significantly from the **hypothesized value** of a population **parameter**. A significance test evaluates evidence with respect to two competing hypotheses: the null hypothesis and the alternative hypothesis. These are both decided before data are collected.

The Two Hypotheses

A **null hypothesis** is written as the claim about the population parameter that is initially thought to be true. It is the hypothesis of no difference, of no change, of no association, or of the status quo. It is a statement of equality. It is always written in the form

H_0: *parameter* = hypothesized value.

The **alternative hypothesis** is tested *against* the null hypothesis, and is based on what the researcher is seeking evidence of. It is a statement of inequality. It can be written looking for the difference or change in one direction from the null hypothesis or both. It is written in one of three forms:

H_a: *parameter* < hypothesized value (one-sided test),
H_a: *parameter* > hypothesized value (one-sided test), or
H_a: *parameter* ≠ hypothesized value (two-sided test).

Example: A high school junior running for student body president claims that 80% of the student body favors her in the school election. If her opponent believes this percentage to be lower, write the appropriate null and alternative hypotheses.

Answer: The null hypothesis is the statement of no difference and is H_0: $p = 0.80$. The opponent seeks evidence of a lower proportion of votes, so the alternative hypothesis is H_a: $p < 0.80$.

Example: In the year 1976, the mean beef consumption of U.S. residents was 89 pounds per person. A health studies researcher wishes to know if this has changed and will do a study. Write the appropriate null and alternative hypotheses to test whether mean beef consumption has changed.

Answer: The null hypothesis is the statement of no difference and is H_0: $\mu = 89$ pounds. The researcher seeks evidence of a change in consumption, so the alternative hypothesis is H_a: $\mu \neq 89$ pounds.

Statistical Significance and *P*-Values

When the sample statistic is shown to be far from the hypothesized parameter, the difference is said to be **statistically significant** and we have evidence to **reject** the null hypothesis in favor of the alternative hypothesis. If the statistic is not far, the lack of evidence means we **fail to reject** (*not* accept) the null hypothesis.

We measure the *strength* of the evidence with the **P-value**. The *P*-value tells us how likely it would be to observe a statistic as far as it is, or farther, from the hypothesized value in the direction of the alternative hypothesis, if the null hypothesis were indeed true. The *P*-value is therefore a probability. The smaller the *P*-value, the greater the evidence is *against* the null hypothesis.

Example: A high school junior running for student body president claims that 80% of the student body favors her in the school election. Her opponent believes this percentage to be lower and conducts a random sample of likely voters. The opponent tests H_0: $p = 0.80$ versus H_a: $p < 0.80$, where p is the true proportion of voters that favor the first student. The sample results in 72% favoring the first student and the test produces a *P*-value of 0.02. Interpret the *P*-value.

Answer: The *P*-value of 0.02 means that if the first candidate really were favored by 80% of the voters, a sample proportion of 72% or less would occur about 2% of the time by chance alone. That is, if H_0 were true, and repeated samples were taken, only 2% of the sample proportions would be 72% or less. This is not very likely and would lead us toward *rejecting* the null hypothesis.

Sometimes, *P*-values are compared against a predetermined benchmark, known as the **significance level** or **alpha level**. Three common alpha levels in testing are $\alpha = 0.10$, $\alpha = 0.05$, and $\alpha = 0.01$. If the *P*-value is less than alpha ($P < \alpha$), we consider the result to be statistically significant and reject the null hypothesis. In the previous example, the results of the survey were statistically significant for $\alpha = 0.10$ and $\alpha = 0.05$, since the *P*-value is 0.02, but not for $\alpha = 0.01$.

As stated, the *P*-value is computed by determining the probability of observing a **test statistic** as extreme as or more extreme than we observed if the null hypothesis is true. The test statistic is the number of standard deviations (or standard errors) our sample statistic lies from the population parameter. The *P*-value's probability is always calculated by finding the area in the tails of the appropriate distribution in the direction(s) of the alternative hypothesis.

Example: In 1976, the mean beef consumption of U.S. residents was 89 pounds per person. A health studies research wishes to know if this has decreased and does a study to test $H_0: \mu = 89$ pounds versus $H_a: \mu < 89$ pounds. The test statistic is $t = -2.147$ with 30 degrees of freedom. Compute the *P*-value for this test.

Answer: The test statistic is a *t*-statistic, so consult Table B: *t*-distribution critical values. We see that on the $df = 30$ line, $t = 2.147$ corresponds to a tail probability of 0.02. The *P*-value is 0.02.

Note: If this were a two-sided test, using $H_a: \mu \neq 89$ pounds, we would be interested in the chance of getting a test statistic of -2.147 or less, or $+2.147$ or more. In that case, the *P*-value would be twice as large, or 0.04.

Decision Errors in Hypothesis Tests

Decision errors can be made when rejecting or failing to reject the null hypothesis. If one sets the significance level to be 0.05, then 5% of the time the null hypothesis is true one will still reject it. Rejecting the null hypothesis when in fact it is true is a **Type I error**. The significance level α is the probability of committing a Type I error. If we fail to reject the null hypothesis in favor of the alternative when in fact the null hypothesis was false, we have committed a **Type II error**. The probability of committing the Type II error is given by the value β. The table below is a summary of decisions that can be made in a hypothesis test.

	What is true about the population parameter	
	H_0 is true	H_a is true
Reject H_0	Type I error probability = α	Decision is correct
Fail to reject H_0	Decision is correct	Type II error probability = β

Decision made based on the sample

It is important to be able to describe Type I and Type II errors in the context of a situation.

Example: A manufacturer of computer monitors receives shipments of LCD panels from a supplier overseas. It is not cost effective to inspect each LCD panel for defects, so a sample is taken from each shipment. A significance test is conducted to determine whether the proportion of defective LCD panels is greater than the acceptable limit of 1%. If it is, the shipment will be returned to the supplier. Essentially, this is a test of H_0: $p = 0.01$ vs. H_a: $p > 0.01$, where p is the true proportion of defective panels in the shipment.

    (a) Describe the Type I and Type II errors in the context of the situation.

    (b) If you were the supplier of the LCD panels, which error would be more serious and why?

    (c) If you were the computer monitor manufacturer, which error would be more serious and why?

Answer: (a) If a Type I error were committed, we would conclude that there are more than 1% defective panels when there really were not. The shipment would be returned when it was not warranted. If a Type II error were committed, we would conclude that there are no more than 1% of defective panels when there really were. Faulty LCD panels would be accepted from the supplier.

    (b) The supplier would think that the Type I error is more serious because they would be receiving LCD panels back that work fine.

    (c) The computer monitor manufacturer would think that the Type II error is more serious because they would be receiving panels of poor quality.

Power

The **power** of a test is defined as the probability that you will correctly reject the null hypothesis when it is false. Given β is the probability that you fail to reject the null hypothesis when it is actually false, the power is simply $1 - \beta$. We want the value of the power to be high since that gives us the confidence we made the correct decision concerning the null hypothesis.

You will not be asked to compute power on the AP Statistics Examination, but you must know what factors increase or decrease the power of a test.

1. Sample size. As the sample size increases, the power of a test increases.

2. Significance level α. Higher levels of α increase power, as it is more likely that one will reject the null hypothesis.

3. The value of an alternative parameter. If the alternative hypothesis is true, then the value of the parameter must be something other than what is stated in the null hypothesis. The farther an alternative parameter from the hypothesized value *in the direction of the alternative hypothesis,* the greater the power. This is because a greater difference is easier to detect.

General Procedure for Inference with Hypothesis Tests

To do any inference problem, the same four-step procedure for inference is used. Differences from the confidence interval procedures are shown in *italics*.

Step 1: State the parameter of interest *and a correct pair of hypotheses.* The parameter of interest is from the population under study. It will be a population proportion, a difference of population means, and so on. This should be defined in words and symbols.

The null and alternative hypotheses for the test are written. These may be in the form of words and/or symbols, but if in symbols, those symbols should be defined.

Step 2: Name the inference procedure and check assumptions/conditions. The procedure is named by giving the name of the test and what parameter is being tested.

There are assumptions/conditions that must be checked in order to proceed with various inference procedures. It is not enough to merely state them—you must verify that they apply.

Step 3: Calculate the *test statistic and P-value.* With the exception of chi-square tests (which will be covered later in this chapter), test statistics are always computed as

$$\text{test statistic} = \frac{\text{statistic} - \text{parameter}}{\text{standard deviation of statistic}}.$$

Write the appropriate formula for the type of test statistic being computed, substitute the values into the formula, and compute the test statistic.

Once the test statistic is computed, compute the P-value using the direction dictated by the alternative hypothesis and appropriate distribution (z, t, or χ^2).

Step 4: Interpret the results in context. Describe in the context of the situation what the P-value means and whether the decision is to reject or fail to reject the null hypothesis. Refer back to step 1, as this is where the parameter of interest and hypotheses were defined.

Hypothesis Tests for Proportions

The formula to compute the test statistic for the population proportion p, with the null hypothesis $H_0 : p = p_0$, is $z = \dfrac{\hat{p} - p_0}{\sqrt{\frac{p_0(1-p_0)}{n}}}$, where $\hat{p}$ is the sample proportion, p_0 is the hypothesized parameter, n is the sample size, and z is the z-test statistic. The P-value will be computed using the normal (z) distribution.

The assumptions/conditions for a hypothesis test for a population proportion are the same as for confidence intervals with one exception: The number of successes and failures based on the hypothesized parameter are both at least 10. That is, $np_0 \geq 10$ and $n(1 - p_0) \geq 10$.

Example: A high school junior running for student body president claims that 80% of the student body will vote for her in the school election. Her opponent believes this to be lower and surveys an SRS of 95 likely voters in student body. The opponent finds that 68 out of 95 students surveyed say they will vote for the junior running for student body president. The school has 3,500 students. Perform a hypothesis test and write a conclusion in the context of the situation.

Answer: Follow the four-step inference procedure.

Step 1: State the parameter of interest and a correct pair of hypotheses. Let p be the true proportion of students that will vote for the junior candidate.

H_0: $p = 0.80$
H_a: $p < 0.80$.

Alternately, the parameter of interest and the hypotheses statements can be stated together as shown below.

H_0: $p = 0.80$. The true proportion of students that will vote for the junior candidate is 0.80.

H_a: $p < 0.80$. The true proportion of students that will vote for the junior candidate is less than 0.80.

Step 2: Name the inference procedure and check assumptions/conditions. The procedure is a one-sample test for the true proportion of students that will vote for the junior candidate.

(1) The sample must be an SRS from the population of interest. OK—the problem states that we have an SRS.

(2) The population is at least 10 times as large as the sample size. OK—there are more than 950 students in the school. (This may pose a problem if there are *not* 950 likely voters, but we will continue.)

(3) The number of successes and failures based on the hypothesized parameter are both at least 10. OK—since $np_0 = (95)(0.8) = 76$ and $n(1 - p_0) = (95)(0.2) = 19$.

Note: It is required that you show the actual calculations for condition (3). Just restating the formulas will not give credit on the exam.

Step 3: Calculate the test statistic and *P*-value. In our sample $\hat{p} = \dfrac{68}{95}$.

Substituting into the formula $z = \dfrac{\hat{p} - p_0}{\sqrt{\dfrac{p_0(1-p_0)}{n}}}$, we get

$$z = \frac{\hat{p} - p_0}{\sqrt{\frac{p_0(1-p_0)}{n}}} = \frac{\frac{68}{95} - 0.8}{\sqrt{\frac{0.8(0.2)}{95}}} \approx -2.05.$$

The *P*-value is the probability of seeing a *z*-test statistic of –2.05 or less, or $P(z \le -2.05)$. From Table A, this is 0.0202. Thus, *P-value* = 0.0202.

A sketch of the *P*-value is shown below, and is a good idea to show on the exam.

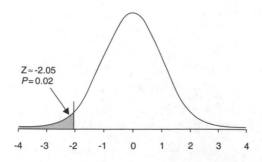

Step 4: Interpret the results in context. The test statistic produced a *P*-value very small (0.02), which means that if 80% of students actually did favor the junior candidate, there is only a 2% chance of getting a test statistic this small or smaller. We have sufficient evidence to reject the null hypothesis in favor of the alternative hypothesis; the true proportion of students who will vote for the junior candidate is less than 0.80.

Calculator Tip:

Hypothesis tests for proportions can be performed with the graphing calculator.

From the home screen, press $\boxed{\text{STAT}}$, arrow right to TESTS, and then choose 5:1-PropZTest....

```
EDIT  CALC  TESTS
1 : Z-Test...
2 : T-Test...
3 : 2-SampZTest...
4 : 2-SampTTest...
5 : 1-PropZTest...
6 : 2-PropZTest...
7↓ ZInterval...
```

Enter the values of the hypothesized parameter, number of students answering yes (successes), sample size, and highlight the appropriate direction of the alternative hypothesis.

```
1-PropZTest
 p▯ : .8
 x : 68
 n : 95
 prop ≠ p ▯  <p ▯  >p ▯
 Calculate Draw
```

Arrow down to Calculate, and then press $\boxed{\text{ENTER}}$. The alternate hypothesis, test statistic, *P*-value, sample proportion, and sample size are shown.

```
1-PropZTest
 prop< .8
 z= −2.051956704
 p= .0200868676
 p̂= .7157894737
 n=95
```

If you had chosen **Draw** instead of **Calculate**, a sketch of the appropriate distribution is shown with the test statistic, *P*-value, and the area that corresponds to the *P*-value is shaded in.

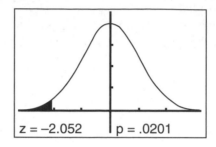

z = −2.052   p = .0201

Hypothesis Tests for the Difference Between Two Proportions

The two-proportion *z*-test is used when you want to know if there is a significant difference between two population proportions. In this case the null hypothesis states that there is no difference between the two population proportions, or $p_1 = p_2$. This can be written alternatively as the difference $p_1 - p_2 = 0$.

The formula to compute the test statistic for the difference of two population proportions $p_1 - p_2$, with the null hypothesis H_0: $p_1 - p_2 = 0$, is

$$z = \frac{\hat{p}_1 - \hat{p}_2}{\sqrt{\hat{p}(1 - \hat{p})\left(\frac{1}{n_1} + \frac{1}{n_2}\right)}},$$

where $\hat{p}_1$ and $\hat{p}_2$ are the respective sample proportions, n_1 and n_2 are the respective sample sizes, $\hat{p}$ is the *pooled* sample proportion, and *z* is the *z*-test statistic. The pooled sample proportion $\hat{p}$ is calculated as $\hat{p} = \frac{x_1 + x_2}{n_1 + n_2}$; we "pool" our individual samples and treat them as one big sample. The *P*-value will be computed using the *z*-distribution. The assumptions/conditions for a hypothesis test for a difference in population proportions are the same as for confidence intervals.

Example: An airline wants to know if there is a difference in the proportion of business travelers on the 4:00 PM flight between Chicago and New York and the 6:00 PM flight between the same two cities. These flights operate 7 days a week. Random samples of 40 passengers were taken from flight manifests of each flight for the past month. There were 12 business travelers on 4:00 PM flights and 18 on 6:00 PM flights. Is there a significant difference in the proportion of business travelers at these different times?

Answer: Follow the four-step inference procedure.

Step 1: State the parameter of interest and a correct pair of hypotheses. Let p_1 be the true proportion of 4:00 PM business travelers between New York and Chicago. Let p_2 be the true proportion of 6:00 PM business travelers between New York and Chicago. The parameter of interest is $p_1 - p_2$, the true difference in proportion between the two groups.

$$H_0: p_1 - p_2 = 0 \quad \text{or} \quad H_0: p_1 = p_2$$
$$H_a: p_1 - p_2 \neq 0 \qquad\qquad H_a: p_1 \neq p_2$$

Step 2: Name the inference procedure and check assumptions/conditions. This is a two-proportion z-test for $p_1 - p_2$, the true difference in the proportion of business travelers between 4:00 PM and 6:00 PM flights.

(1) The samples must be independent SRSs from the populations of interest. OK—the problem states that we have two independent random samples.

(2) The populations are at least 10 times as large as the sample sizes. OK—it is reasonable to assume that there were at least 400 total passengers on each flight over the course of the month.

(3) The number of successes and failures in each sample are both at least 10. OK—there were 12 successes and 28 failures in the 4:00 PM sample and 18 successes and 22 failures in the 6:00 PM sample.

Step 3: Calculate the test statistic and *P*-value. In our sample

$$\hat{p}_1 = \frac{12}{40} = 0.3, \ \hat{p}_2 = \frac{18}{40} = 0.45, \text{ and } \hat{p} = \frac{12+18}{40+40} = 0.375.$$

Substituting into the formula $z = \dfrac{\hat{p}_1 - \hat{p}_2}{\sqrt{\hat{p}(1-\hat{p})\left(\frac{1}{n_1}+\frac{1}{n_2}\right)}}$, we get

$$z = \frac{\hat{p}_1 - \hat{p}_2}{\sqrt{\hat{p}(1-\hat{p})\left(\frac{1}{n_1}+\frac{1}{n_2}\right)}} = \frac{0.3 - 0.45}{\sqrt{0.375\,(0.625)\left(\frac{1}{40}+\frac{1}{40}\right)}} \approx -1.39.$$

Since the alternative hypothesis is two-sided, the *P*-value is the probability of seeing a z-test statistic of -1.39 or less, or $+1.39$ or more. From Table A, $P(z \leq -1.39) = 0.0838$, so the *P*-value $= 2 \times 0.0838 = 0.1676$.

Step 4: Interpret the results in context. The *P*-value found is large—there is about a 17% chance of seeing a test statistic as extreme as or more extreme than the one we observed, if the null hypothesis were true. We fail to reject the null hypothesis. There is not enough evidence to say that there is a difference in the proportion of business travelers between the 4:00 PM and 6:00 PM flights between New York and Chicago.

Calculator Tip:

Hypothesis tests for differences in proportions can be performed with the graphing calculator.

From the home screen, press $\boxed{\text{STAT}}$, arrow right to TESTS, and then choose 6:2-PropZTest....

```
EDIT  CALC  TESTS
3↑ 2-SampZTest...
4 : 2-SampTTest...
5 : 1-PropZTest...
6 : 2-PropZTest...
7 : ZInterval...
8 : TInterval...
9↓ 2-SampZInt...
```

Input the number of business travelers in the 4:00 PM sample, the 4:00 PM sample size, the number of business travelers in the 6:00 PM sample, the 6:00 PM sample size, and the correct alternative hypothesis that relates p_1 and p_2.

```
2-PropZTest
   x1 : 12
   n1 : 40
   x2 : 18
   n2 : 40
   p1 : ≠ p2  <p2  >p2
   Calculate  Draw
```

Arrow down to **Calculate**, and then press $\boxed{\text{ENTER}}$. The alternate hypothesis, test statistic, P-value, sample proportions, and pooled proportion are shown. Scrolling down shows the sample sizes.

```
2-PropZTest
   p1 ≠ p2
   z = −1.385640646
   p = .1658567696
   p̂1 = .3
   p̂2 = .45
↓ p̂ = .375
```

Note that the P-value on the calculator screen is very close to what was found by doubling the value from the table. The calculator automatically doubles the table value.

Using the **Draw** feature, we can see that a sketch of the appropriate distribution is shown with the test statistic, *P*-value, and the area that corresponds to the *P*-value is shaded in.

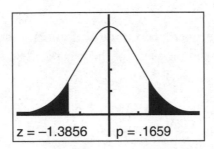

| z = −1.3856 | p = .1659 |

Hypothesis Tests for Means

Hypothesis tests for means have the same issues as confidence intervals. Since we usually do not know the population standard deviation σ, the sample standard deviation s is used to compute standard error.

The formula to compute the test statistic for the population mean μ, with the null hypothesis $H_0 : \mu = \mu_0$, is $t = \dfrac{\overline{x} - \mu_0}{\frac{s}{\sqrt{n}}}$, where $\overline{X}$ is the sample mean, μ_0 is the hypothesized parameter, s is the sample standard deviation, n is the sample size, and t is the t-test statistic. The number of degrees of freedom is $n - 1$. The *P*-value will be computed using the t-distribution. (If the population standard deviation is known, use s and the z-distribution.)

The assumptions/conditions for a hypothesis for a population mean are the same as for confidence intervals.

Example: At North High School the average number of cars owned by a family is 2.35. South High School is in a more affluent area of the town and students claim they have on average more cars per family. An SRS of 36 students was selected and they were asked how many cars are in each of their families. The number of cars is shown below.

| 1 | 3 | 3 | 4 | 3 | 4 | 5 | 3 | 2 | 3 | 2 | 2 | 3 | 3 | 4 | 4 | 4 | 5 |
| 2 | 1 | 3 | 3 | 2 | 2 | 3 | 3 | 4 | 3 | 4 | 3 | 2 | 2 | 2 | 1 | 1 | 3 |

The mean number of cars from this sample is 2.833 with a standard deviation of 1.056. Is there statistical evidence that there are more cars per family on average at South High School than North High School?

Answer: Follow the four-step inference procedure.

Step 1: State the parameter of interest and a correct pair of hypotheses.
H_0: $\mu = 2.35$—The mean number of cars per family at South High School is 2.35. H_0: $\mu > 2.35$—The mean number of cars per family at South High School is greater than 2.35.

Step 2: Name the inference procedure and check assumptions/conditions.
The procedure is a one-sample t-test for the true mean number of cars per family at South High School.

(1)   The sample must be an SRS from the population of interest. OK—the problem states that we have a random sample.

(2)   The data come from a normally distributed population. OK—a histogram of the data (shown below) is unimodal and symmetric, with no outliers.

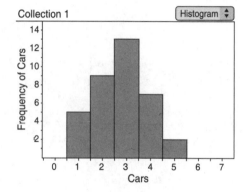

Step 3: Calculate the test statistic and *P*-value. In our sample $\bar{x} = 2.833$ and $s = 1.056$. Substituting into the formula $t = \dfrac{\bar{x} - \mu_0}{\frac{s}{\sqrt{n}}}$ we get

$$t = \frac{\bar{x} - \mu_0}{\frac{s}{\sqrt{n}}} = \frac{2.833 - 2.35}{\frac{1.056}{\sqrt{36}}} \approx 2.74,$$ with $n - 1 = 35$ degrees of freedom.

Using the t-distribution table with 30 degrees of freedom (since 35 is not in the table, use the next *lower* value), the probability that the test statistic is 2.74 or more is just a little less than 0.005.

Step 4: Interpret the results in context. This extremely small *P*-value is significant for any of the commonly used alpha levels. It means that if the null hypothesis were true—that the mean number of cars owned by families of students at South High School were indeed 2.35—we would see a test statistic *at least* this large about 0.5% of the time, that is about one chance in 200. Thus, we have sufficient evidence to reject the null hypothesis in favor of the alternative one, and we conclude that the true mean number of cars per family at South High School is more than 2.35.

Hypothesis tests for means can be performed with the graphing calculator. From the home screen, press $\boxed{\text{STAT}}$, arrow right to TESTS, and then choose 2:TTest....

```
EDIT  CALC  TESTS
1↑ Z-Test...
2 : T-Test...
3 : 2-SampZTest...
4 : 2-SampTTest...
5 : 1-PropZTest...
6 : 2-PropZTest...
7↓ ZInterval...
```

Input the hypothesized parameter, the mean and standard deviation of the sample, the sample size, and highlight the appropriate direction of the alternative hypothesis.

```
T-Test
  Inpt : Data   Stats
  μ □ : 2.35
  x̄ : 2.833
  Sx : 1.056
  n : 36
  μ : ≠μ □   <μ □   >μ □
  Calculate Draw
```

Arrow down to Calculate, and then press $\boxed{\text{ENTER}}$. The alternative hypothesis, *t*-test statistic, *P*-value, sample mean, sample standard deviation, and sample size are shown.

```
T-Test
  μ>2.35
  t =2.744318182
  p= .0047507285
  x̄=2.833
  Sx=1.056
  n=36
```

Using the Draw feature, we can see that a sketch of the appropriate distribution is shown with the test statistic and *P*-value, and the area that corresponds to the *P*-value is shaded in (but is so small that it cannot be distinguished from the curve and axis).

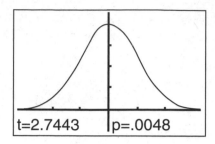

You may also be expected to interpret hypothesis test results from a computer printout. The following is a printout from statistics software for the previous example.

T-Test of the Mean

Test of mu = 2.350 vs mu > 2.350

Variable	N	Mean	StDev	SE Mean	T	P-Value
Cars	36	2.833	1.056	0.176	2.75	0.0047

$$\frac{s}{\sqrt{n}} \qquad \text{test statistic}$$

The printout shows the null and alternative hypotheses, the sample information, the standard error of the sample mean $\frac{s}{\sqrt{n}}$, the t-test statistic, and the test's P-value.

Hypothesis Tests for Means with Paired Data

Another use of the one-sample t-procedure is looking at paired differences. Often called a **matched-pairs t-test**, it tests to see if there is a significant mean difference between two groups that are paired in some way. The assumptions/conditions for this test and formula for the test statistic are the same as the one-sample t-test; however, the null hypothesis is that there is no mean difference, μ_d.

Example: A baseball bat manufacturer makes two different types of bats, aluminum and ceramic. The company wants to know which type of bat provides better performance for little leaguers as measured by the number of balls hit into the outfield. Twenty-three boys who play little league baseball participated in the study. Each player was randomly assigned one type of bat with which he took 20 swings, followed by 20 swings with the other bat. The number of hits into the outfield was recorded for each bat. (The raw data are provided in a table in the previous section on confidence intervals.) Is there statistical evidence that ceramic bats produce more hits into the outfield than aluminum bats?

Answer: Follow the four-step inference procedure.

Step 1: State the parameter of interest and a correct pair of hypotheses.

H_0: $\mu_d = 0$—The mean difference (ceramic − aluminum) in the number of hits into the outfield is 0.

H_0: $\mu_d > 0$—The mean difference (ceramic − aluminum) in the number of hits into the outfield is greater than 0. (We believe they will get more hits, on average, with the ceramic bat)

Step 2: Name the inference procedure and check assumptions/conditions. A one-sample paired *t*-test for the true mean difference in hits into the outfield between ceramic and aluminum bats.

(1)   The sample must be an SRS from the population of interest. OK—the players may not be a random sample, but the data come from a randomized comparative experiment, so the randomization condition is satisfied.

(2)   The data come from a normally distributed population. OK—the histogram of differences is unimodal and symmetric, with no outliers.

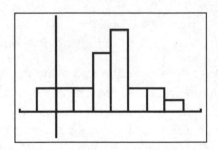

Step 3: Calculate the test statistic and *P*-value. In our sample $\overline{x}_d = 2.3913$ and $s_d = 1.827$. Substituting into the formula $t = \dfrac{\overline{x} - \mu_0}{\frac{s}{\sqrt{n}}}$, we get

$$t = \frac{\overline{x}_d - \mu_0}{\frac{s_d}{\sqrt{n}}} = \frac{2.3913 - 0}{\frac{1.8275}{\sqrt{25}}} \approx 6.28, \text{ , with } n - 1 = 24 \text{ degrees of freedom.}$$

Using the *t*-distribution table with 24 degrees of freedom, the probability that the test statistic is 6.28 or more is smaller than 0.0005, the last column in the table. We know that $P < 0.0005$.

A calculator output for the test reveals that the *P*-value is 1.37×10^{-6}, or 0.00000137. That is about one chance in 730,000!

```
T-Test
 μ>0
 t=6.249145612
 p=1.3679192E−6
 x̄=2.3813
 Sx=1.8275
 n=23
```

Step 4: Interpret the results in context. The test statistic produced an extremely small *P*-value. There is overwhelming evidence to reject the null hypothesis, and it is concluded that the ceramic bats will produce a higher average number of hits into the outfield than the aluminum bats.

Hypothesis Tests for the Difference Between Two Means

We use a two-sample *t*-test when we are interested in the difference in the means of two independent populations. In this case the null hypothesis states that there is no difference between the two population means, or $\mu_1 = \mu_2$. This can be written alternatively as the difference $\mu_1 - \mu_2 = 0$.

The formula to compute the test statistic for the difference of the two population means $\mu_1 - \mu_2$, with the null hypothesis H$_0$: $\mu_1 - \mu_2 = 0$, is

$$t = \frac{\overline{x}_1 - \overline{x}_2}{\sqrt{\frac{s_1^2}{n_1} + \frac{s_2^2}{n_2}}},$$

where $\overline{x}_1$ and $\overline{x}_2$ are the sample means, s_1 and s_2 are the sample standard deviations, and n_1 and n_2 are the sample sizes. The *P*-value will be computed using the *t*-distribution.

As with confidence intervals, the number of degrees of freedom is computed by a complex formula not presented here. If technology is used, the exact number of degrees of freedom will be obtained. If by-hand calculations are performed, use the smaller of $n_1 - 1$ and $n_2 - 1$.

If the population standard deviations are known, use σ_1, σ_2, and the *z*-distribution.

The assumptions/conditions for a hypothesis test for a difference in population means are the same as for confidence intervals.

Example: A cruise line is trying to determine if there is a difference in the mean amount of money passengers spend on board their ships during a 1-week cruise to Alaska and a 1-week cruise to Mexico.

A random sample of 35 passengers is taken from the Alaskan cruise; a random sample of 30 passengers is taken from the Mexican cruise. The mean amount of money spent on board the ship in Alaska is $\bar{x}_1 =$ \$582.16 with a standard deviation of $s_1 =$ \$32.65. The mean amount of money spent on board the ship in Mexico is $\bar{x}_2 =$ \$563.22 with a standard deviation of $s_2 =$ \$35.23. Is there a significant difference between the mean amounts spent by passengers on the two cruise ships? Histograms of the data are shown below.

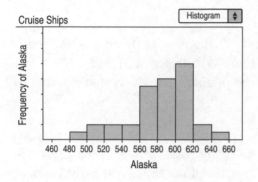
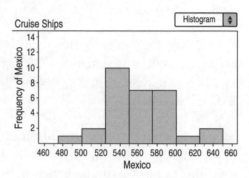

Answer: Follow the four-step inference procedure.

Step 1: State the parameter of interest and a correct pair of hypotheses.

$H_0: \mu_1 = \mu_2$ The mean amount of money spent by passengers on board the cruise to Alaska (μ_1) is the same as the mean amount of money spent by passengers on board the cruise to the Mexico (μ_2).

$H_0: \mu_1 \neq \mu_2$ The mean amount of money spent by passengers on board the cruise to Alaska is *not* the same as the mean amount of money spent by passengers on board the cruise to the Mexico.

Step 2: Name the inference procedure and check assumptions/conditions. A two-sample *t*-test of means for the true difference in the mean amount of money spent by passengers on board the two different cruises.

(1) The samples must be SRSs from the populations of interest. OK—the problem states that the samples were random.

(2) The data come from a normally distributed population. OK—the histogram of Mexican passenger spending is symmetric and unimodal; the histogram of the Alaskan passengers' expenditures is skewed left, but the sample size of 35 is large enough to tolerate it.

Step 3: Calculate the test statistic and *P*-value. In our sample $\bar{x}_1 =$ \$582.16, $s_1 =$ \$32.65, $\bar{x}_2 =$ \$563.22, and $s_2 =$ \$35.23. Substituting into the formula

$$t = \frac{\overline{x}_1 - \overline{x}_2}{\sqrt{\frac{s_1^2}{n_1} + \frac{s_2^2}{n_2}}} \quad \text{we get } t = \frac{\overline{x}_1 - \overline{x}_2}{\sqrt{\frac{s_1^2}{n_1} + \frac{s_2^2}{n_2}}}$$

$$= \frac{582.16 - 563.22}{\sqrt{\frac{32.65^2}{35} + \frac{35.23^2}{30}}} \approx 2.23, \text{ with } n_2 - 1 = 29$$

degrees of freedom.

Using the t-distribution table with 29 degrees of freedom, the probability that the test statistic is 2.23 or more is between 0.01 and 0.02. Since this is a two-sided test, the P-value is the double of what the table gives, so $0.02 < P < 0.04$.

Step 4: Interpret the results in context. The P-value is between 0.02 and 0.04, indicating that if the null hypothesis were really true, we would see a test statistic this or more extreme between 2% and 4% of the time. This is fairly small and gives evidence to reject the null hypothesis.

There is evidence that the mean amount of money spent by passengers on board each cruise ship is different.

Calculator Tip:

Hypothesis tests for the difference in means can be performed with the graphing calculator.

From the home screen, press $\boxed{\text{STAT}}$, arrow right to TESTS, and then choose 4:2-SampTTest....

```
EDIT  CALC  TESTS
1 : Z-Test...
2 : T-Test...
3 : 2-SampZTest...
4 : 2-SampTTest...
5 : 1-PropZTest...
6 : 2-PropZTest...
7↓ ZInterval...
```

Input the means and standard deviations of the samples, and the sample sizes.

```
2-SampTTest
 Inpt : Data  Stats
 x̄1 : 582.16
 Sx1 : 32.65
 n1 : 35
 x̄2 : 563.22
 Sx2 : 35.23
↓ n2 : 30
```

Arrow down to select the appropriate alternative hypothesis. When you reach the **Pooled** line, choose **No**. We only use a pooled *t*-test if we know the two populations have equal standard deviations, that is, $\sigma_1 = \sigma_2$.

```
2-SampTTest
↑n1 : 35
 x̄2 : 563.22
 Sx2 : 35 : 23
 n2 : 30
 μ1 :  ≠μ2  <μ2  >μ2
 Pooled :  No  Yes
 Calculate Draw
```

Arrow down to **Calculate**, and then press $\boxed{\text{ENTER}}$. The alternative hypothesis, test statistic, *P*-value, exact number of degrees of freedom, and sample means are shown. Scrolling down gives the sample standard deviations and sample sizes.

```
2-SampTTest
 μ₁ ≠ μ₂
 t = 2.234747215
 p = .0291836162
 df = 59 78123227
 x̄₁ = 582.16
↓ x̄₂ = 563.22
```

Note: The degrees of freedom used from the table was 29. Calculators and software packages will use the exact degrees of freedom, in this case about 60. The corresponding *P*-value is about 0.03.

Using the **Draw** feature, we can see that a sketch of the appropriate distribution is shown with the test statistic and *P*-value, and the area that corresponds to the *P*-value is shaded.

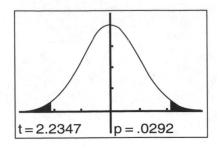

t = 2.2347   p = .0292

Duality of Confidence Intervals and Hypothesis Tests

Hypotheses can also be evaluated with confidence intervals, provided that the alternative hypothesis is two-sided. If the hypothesized parameter is within a $C\%$ confidence interval, then there is not statistically significant evidence of a difference at the $\alpha = 1 - C$ significance level. We would fail to reject the null hypothesis in this case. The opposite is true if the hypothesized parameter is not in the interval.

Example: An airline wants to know if there is a difference in the proportion of business travelers on the 4:00 PM flight between Chicago and New York and the 6:00 PM flight between the same two cities. The null and alternative hypotheses for a two-sample test of proportions are H_0: $p_1 - p_2 = 0$ and H_a: $p_1 - p_2 \neq 0$, where p_1 is the true proportion of 4:00 PM business travelers between New York and Chicago and p_2 is the true proportion of 6:00 PM business travelers between New York and Chicago. The 95% confidence interval for the true difference in proportions, $p_1 - p_2$, is (–0.360, 0.060). Is there evidence of a significant difference between the two proportions of business travelers?

Answer: No, there is insignificant evidence of a difference in the proportion of business travelers on the two flights at the $\alpha = 0.05$ level of significance. The interval contains zero, so it is plausible that there is no difference in the proportion of business flyers. Note that this is consistent with the results of the hypothesis test earlier in the section.

Example: Consider the cruise line example from a few pages back. The question asked if there was a significant difference between the mean amount spent by passengers on Alaskan and Mexican cruises. We tested H_0: $\mu_1 = \mu_2$ vs. H_a: $\mu_1 \neq \mu_2$, where μ_1 and μ_2 are the mean amounts of money spent by passengers on board Alaskan and Mexican cruises, respectively. The *P*-value for the two-sample *t*-test was 0.03. For which of the common confidence levels, 90%, 95%, and 99%, would the confidence interval for $\mu_1 - \mu_2$ contain zero?

Answer: The test is significant at the common significance levels $\alpha = 0.05$ and $\alpha = 0.10$. These correspond to the 95% and 90% confidence intervals, respectively. Therefore, zero would not be in those intervals, and would not be a plausible value for the difference. The test is not significant at the $\alpha = 0.01$ level, so the 99% confidence interval would contain zero. The intervals are provided below as a point of reference.
90% CI: (4.78, 33.10)
95% CI: (1.99, 35.89)
99% CI: (−3.61, 41.49)

One-sided alternatives can also be addressed with confidence intervals, but one-sided intervals are not part of the AP Statistics curriculum.

Inference for Categorical/Count Data

There are several procedures to compare the distribution of categorical data to a hypothesized distribution. Two have already been discussed in this book: the one-sample and two-sample proportion *z*-tests. These tests work for categorical data of a single variable that is binomial—there are only two outcomes—for inference on one and two populations, respectively.

When a categorical variable has multiple categories, when there are two categorical variables under consideration, or when there are multiple populations under study, a new type of test is required: the chi-square test. The chi-square test is used to compare count data from categorical variables to a hypothesized distribution. There are three forms of chi-square tests, each used in a particular situation.

Chi-square test of goodness of fit: One categorical variable with multiple categories from one population. The test compares the distribution of sample counts with the hypothesized distribution of the population.

Chi-square test of homogeneity: One categorical variable with multiple categories from two or more populations. The test compares the distribution of sample counts with the hypothesized distribution of the population assuming the populations have identical distributions.

Chi-square test of independence: Two categorical variables with multiple categories from one population. The test compares the distribution of sample counts with the hypothesized distribution of the population assuming the two variables are independent.

Chi-Square Test of Goodness of Fit

The chi-square test of goodness of fit is used to compare the distribution of sample counts of one categorical variable from one population with a hypothesized distribution of the population. For instance, a certain brand of bite-sized candies comes in four colors: red, green, blue, and yellow. The manufacturer claims that all colors are made in equal proportion. One particular bag of 60 candies contains 8 red, 16 green, 15 blue, and 21 yellow—certainly not 25% of each color. There is certainly random variability in the process of mixing and packaging the candies, but are these results so far off from 15 of each that the manufacturer's claim can be called into question?

The previous question calls for a chi-square test of goodness of fit. There is one variable (color) with multiple categories (red, green, blue, yellow) and a single population under consideration (all candies of this type by the manufacturer). One will compare the counts of each category observed in the sample to what one would expect to see.

To perform a chi-square test of goodness of fit, the same four-step procedure for inference is used.

Step 1: State the parameter of interest and a correct pair of hypotheses. The null hypothesis is that all proportions of the categories of the variable are not different from what one would expect—the status quo.

H_0: $p_{category\ 1}$ = hypothesized proportion of category 1
 $p_{category\ 2}$ = hypothesized proportion of category 2
 $p_{category\ 3}$ = hypothesized proportion of category 3
 etc.

The alternative hypothesis is that *any one of* the proportions of the categories of the variable is different from what one would expect.

H_a: at least one of the statements in H_0 is not true.

There is no "parameter" of interest. One wants to know about the distribution of proportions over the categories of the variable.

Step 2: Name the inference procedure and check assumptions/conditions. The procedure is the chi-square test of goodness of fit.

There are three assumptions/conditions that must be checked in order to proceed with the chi-square test for goodness of fit.

(1)   The data come from a simple random sample.

(2)   The size of the sample is no more than 10% of the population size.

(3)   All expected cell counts are at least 5.

The expected cell counts for each category of the variable are equal to the product of the sample size and the hypothesized proportion. That is, the expected count of category one = np_1, the expected count of category two = np_2, and so on.

Step 3: Calculate the test statistic and *P*-value. The chi-square test statistic is computed as

$$\chi^2 = \sum_{\substack{\text{all} \\ \text{cells}}} \frac{(\text{observed} - \text{expected})^2}{\text{expected}}.$$

The number of degrees of freedom for the chi-square test for goodness of fit is equal to one less than the number of categories of the variable.

The *P*-value for the test would be the probability of obtaining a χ^2-statistic at least as large as that computed above if the null hypothesis were true. It is determined by consulting Table C, the table of χ^2 critical values, or by using technology.

Step 4: Interpret the results in context. Make a conclusion as to whether to reject, or fail to reject, the null hypothesis, based on the meaning of the *P*-value. Describe in the context of the situation what the conclusion means.

Example: A certain brand of bite-sized candies comes in four colors: red, green, blue, and yellow. The manufacturer claims that all colors are made in equal proportion. One particular bag of 60 candies contains 8 red, 16 green, 15 blue, and 21 yellow. Is there evidence that the proportions of the candy colors differ from the manufacturer's claim?

Answer:

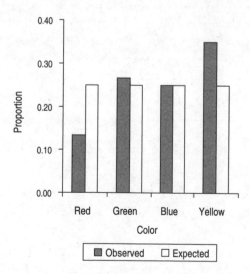

The graph suggests that there may be a difference between the observed proportions of each color and the manufacturer's claimed proportions. Because this difference may be due to sampling variability, an inference procedure is performed to assess the chance of this.

Step 1: State the parameter of interest and a correct pair of hypotheses.

H_0: p_{red} $= 0.25$
p_{green} $= 0.25$
p_{blue} $= 0.25$
$p_{yellow} = 0.25$

H_a: at least one of the statements in H_0 is not true.

There is no parameter of interest in a chi-square test.

Step 2: Name the inference procedure and check assumptions/conditions. Chi-square test of goodness of fit to determine if the distribution of the proportions of the candy colors matches the manufacturer's claim of equal proportions.

(1) The data come from a simple random sample: OK—the bag of candies is likely a random sample of candies produced.

(2) The size of the sample is no more than 10% of the population size: OK—there are 60 candies in the sample. It is likely that the manufacturer has produced more than 600 candies.

(3) All expected cell counts are at least 5. OK—expected cell counts are given below and all are at least 5.

Actual Counts

Color				
Red	Green	Blue	Yellow	Total
8	16	15	21	60

Expected Counts

Color				
Red	Green	Blue	Yellow	Total
(60)(0.25) = 15	(60)(0.25) = 15	(60)(0.25) = 15	(60)(0.25) = 15	60

Step 3: Calculate the test statistic and *P*-value.

$$\chi^2 = \sum_{\substack{\text{all} \\ \text{cells}}} \frac{(\text{observed} - \text{expected})^2}{\text{expected}}$$

$$= \frac{(8-15)^2}{15} + \frac{(16-15)^2}{15} + \frac{(15-15)^2}{15} + \frac{(21-15)^2}{15}$$

$$\approx 3.266\ldots + 0.066\ldots + 0 + 2.4$$

$$\approx 5.733.$$

df = number of categories − 1 = 4 − 1 = 3.

P-value from Table C: the χ^2-statistic of 5.733 lies between 5.32 and 6.25 in the 3 *df* row, so $0.10 < p < 0.15$.

Step 4: Interpret the results in context. The *P*-value is between 0.10 and 0.15. If the colors were distributed as the manufacturer claims, a chi-square statistic of 5.733 or larger would occur somewhere between 10% and 15% of the time—between 1 chance in 7 and 1 chance in 10. This is fairly likely to occur by chance and leads one to fail to reject the null hypothesis. There is insufficient evidence that the distribution of candy colors differs from that of the manufacturer's claim.

Calculator Tip:

As shown in Chapter 3, the *X*2cdf(function can compute the *P*-value.

$$X^2cdf(5.733, 1000$$
$$, 3)$$
$$.1253481055$$

A corresponding sketch of the χ^2-distribution is shown below.

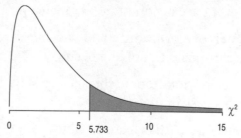

Note: Even though the null hypothesis is defined in terms of the *proportion* of each category, the chi-square test statistic is computed using *counts* of each category.

Chi-Square Test of Homogeneity

The chi-square test of homogeneity is used to compare the distributions of sample counts of one categorical variable from several populations to see if the distributions of the populations are identical. For instance, a certain brand of bite-sized candies comes in three varieties: smooth, crunchy, and chewy. The manufacturer is interested if preferences for the types of candies differ between three school-age groups: elementary, middle, and high school. Random samples of students at three local schools, one of each age group, are taken and the distribution of candy preferences is compared.

The previous situation calls for a chi-square test of homogeneity. There is one variable (preferred variety) with multiple categories (smooth, crunchy, and chewy) and multiple populations under consideration (elementary-, middle-, and high school-aged children). One will compare the counts of each category observed among the different samples to see if they are identically distributed.

To perform a chi-square test of homogeneity, the same four-step inference procedure is used.

Step 1: State the parameter of interest and a correct pair of hypotheses. The null hypothesis is that all proportions of the categories of the variable are the same for all populations (they are homogeneous).

H_0: $p_{\text{category 1 of population 1}} = p_{\text{category 1 of population 2}} = p_{\text{category 1 of population 3}} = \cdots$

$\quad\ p_{\text{category 2 of population 1}} = p_{\text{category 2 of population 2}} = p_{\text{category 2 of population 3}} = \cdots$

$\quad\ p_{\text{category 3 of population 1}} = p_{\text{category 3 of population 2}} = p_{\text{category 3 of population 3}} = \cdots$

etc.

The alternative hypothesis is that *any one* of the proportions of the categories of the variable is not the same for all populations under consideration.

H_a: at least one of the statements in H_0 is not true.

There is no parameter of interest. One wants to know about the distributions of proportions over the categories of the variable for each population.

Step 2: Name the inference procedure and check assumptions/conditions. The procedure is the chi-square test of homogeneity.

The assumptions/conditions for the chi-square test for homogeneity are the same as the test for goodness of fit.

The expected cell counts for each cell are equal to $\dfrac{(\text{row total})(\text{column total})}{\text{grand total}}$.

This is equivalent to the count that each category of the response variable would have if it were proportionally distributed among the samples.

Step 3: Calculate the test statistic and *P*-value. The chi-square test statistic is computed as

$$\chi^2 = \sum_{\substack{\text{all} \\ \text{cells}}} \frac{(\text{observed} - \text{expected})^2}{\text{expected}}$$

The number of degrees of freedom for the chi-square test for homogeneity is equal to (number of rows − 1)(number of columns − 1).

The P-value for the test would be the probability of obtaining a χ^2-statistic at least as large as that computed above, if the null hypothesis were true. It is determined by consulting Table C, the table of χ^2 critical values, or by using technology.

Step 4: Interpret the results in context. Make a conclusion as to whether to reject, or fail to reject, the null hypothesis, based on the meaning of the P-value. Describe in the context of the situation what the conclusion means.

Example: A certain brand of bite-sized candies comes in three varieties: creamy, crispy, and chewy. The manufacturer is interested if preferences for the types of candies differ between three school-age groups: elementary, middle, and high school. Random samples of students at three local schools, one of each age group, are taken and the sample data compiled in the table below.

		Variety		
		Creamy	Crispy	Chewy
	Elementary	33	14	19
Population	Middle	21	16	17
	High	16	12	32

Is there evidence that the proportion of students that prefer each variety of candy differs among the various age groups?

Answer:

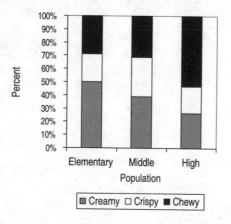

The graph suggests that there may be a difference in the proportions of each variety among the three populations. There seems to be an increase in the popularity of chewy candies and a corresponding decrease in the popularity of creamy candies as students get older. Because the observed difference may be due to sampling variability, an inference procedure is performed to assess the chance of this.

Step 1: State the parameter of interest and a correct pair of hypotheses.

H_0: $p_{\text{creamy in elementary}} = p_{\text{creamy in middle}} = p_{\text{creamy in high}}$

$p_{\text{crispy in elementary}} = p_{\text{crispy in middle}} = p_{\text{crispy in high}}$

$p_{\text{chewy in elementary}} = p_{\text{chewy in middle}} = p_{\text{chewy in high}}$

H_a: at least one of the statements in H_0 is not true.

Step 2: Name the inference procedure and check assumptions/conditions.
Chi-square test of homogeneity to determine if the distribution of proportions of preferred candy varieties is the same for all levels of students.

(1)   The data come from independent random samples: OK—each group of students was randomly selected from their respective schools.

(2)   The size of the samples is no more than 10% of the population sizes: OK so long as there are at least 660 elementary, 540 middle, and 600 high school students in the respective populations.

(3)   All expected cell counts are at least 5. OK—expected cell counts are given below and all are at least 5.

Actual Counts		Variety			
		Creamy	Crispy	Chewy	Total
	Elementary	33	14	19	66
	Middle	21	16	17	54
Population	High	16	12	32	60
	Total	70	42	68	180

Expected Counts		Variety			
		Creamy	Crispy	Chewy	Total
	Elementary	$\dfrac{(66)(70)}{180}$ ≈ 25.667	$\dfrac{(66)(42)}{180}$ $=15.4$	$\dfrac{(66)(68)}{180}$ ≈ 24.933	66
Population	Middle	$\dfrac{(54)(70)}{180}$ $=21$	$\dfrac{(54)(42)}{180}$ $=12.6$	$\dfrac{(54)(68)}{180}$ $=20.4$	54
	High	$\dfrac{(60)(70)}{180}$ ≈ 23.333	$\dfrac{(60)(42)}{180}$ $=14$	$\dfrac{(60)(68)}{180}$ ≈ 22.667	60
	Total	70	42	68	180

$$\text{Expected cell count} = \frac{(\text{row total})(\text{column total})}{\text{grand total}}.$$

Note: The row and column totals for the actual and expected cell counts are equal.

Step 3: Calculate the test statistic and *P*-value.

$$\chi^2 = \sum_{\substack{\text{all} \\ \text{cells}}} \frac{(\text{observed} - \text{expected})^2}{\text{expected}}$$

$$= \frac{(33 - 25.667)^2}{25.667} + \frac{(14 - 15.4)^2}{15.4} + \frac{(19 - 24.933)^2}{24.933}$$
$$+ \frac{(21 - 21)^2}{21} + \frac{(16 - 12.6)^2}{12.6} + \frac{(17 - 20.4)^2}{20.4}$$
$$+ \frac{(16 - 23.333)^2}{23.333} + \frac{(12 - 14)^2}{14} + \frac{(32 - 22.667)^2}{22.667}$$
$$\approx 2.095 + 0.127 + 1.412$$
$$+ 0 + 0.917 + 0.567$$
$$+ 2.305 + 0.286 + 3.843$$
$$\approx 11.552.$$

df = (number of rows – 1)(number of columns – 1) = (3 – 1)(3 – 1) = 4.

P-value from Table C: the χ^2-statistic of 11.552 lies between 11.14 and 11.67 in the 4 *df* row, so $0.02 < p < 0.025$.

Step 4: Interpret the results in context. The *P*-value is between 0.02 and 0.025. If the preferences for the different varieties of candies were distributed in the same proportions among all three age groups of students, a chi-square statistic of 11.552 or larger would occur somewhere between 2% and 2.5% of the time—between 1 chance in 40 and 1 chance in 50. This is very unlikely to occur by chance and leads one to reject the null hypothesis. There is strong evidence that the preferences for the different varieties of candies are different among the three age groups of students.

The differences in expected and observed counts of Elementary/Creamy, High/Creamy, and High/Chewy appear to be contributing most to the differences between the populations.

Calculator Tip:

The chi-square test of homogeneity can be computed with a graphing calculator. Consider the previous example.

First, the two-way table must be entered into a matrix. From the home screen, press $\boxed{2^{nd}}$ $\boxed{x^{-1}}$, which brings up the MATRIX screen.

```
NAMES MATH EDIT
1 : [A]
2 : [B]
3 : [C]
4 : [D]
5 : [E]
6 : [F]
7↓[G]
```

Scroll right to the EDIT column, and then press $\boxed{\text{ENTER}}$ to select matrix [A].

```
NAMES MATH EDIT
1 : [A]
2 : [B]
3 : [C]
4 : [D]
5 : [E]
6 : [F]
7↓[G]
```

At this point, the dimensions of the matrix are entered as rows × columns. In this example, there are three rows and three columns; key in $\boxed{3}$ $\boxed{\text{ENTER}}$ $\boxed{3}$ $\boxed{\text{ENTER}}$.

```
MATRIX[A]      3 x 3
[0      0      0        ]
[0      0      0        ]
[0      0      0        ]
```

Enter the values from the two-way table going across each row, column by column, pressing $\boxed{\text{ENTER}}$ after each entry.

```
MATRIX[A]  3 x3
[33     14     19       ]
[21     16     17       ]
[16     12     32       ]

3, 3 = 32
```

Return to the home screen, press STAT , scroll right arrow to the TEST menu, and then choose C: χ^2-Test....

```
EDIT  CALC  TESTS
7↑ ZInterval...
8 : TInterval...
9 : 2-SampZInt...
0 : 2-SampTInt...
A : 1-PropZInt...
B : 2-PropZInt...
C : χ²-Test...
```

This is the chi-square test command for two-way tables. The matrix containing the observed counts is named on the first line.

```
χ²-Test
  Observed : [A]
  Expected : [B]
  Calculate Draw
```

If the correct matrix is not named, key in 2nd x⁻¹ , which brings up the MATRIX screen, and select the correct matrix from the NAMES menu. The expected count matrix will be calculated when the test is executed. From the NAMES menu in the MATRIX screen, select which matrix will hold the expected counts.

Scroll down to Calculate and press ENTER .

```
χ²-Test
  χ² = 11.55219421
  p = .0210112805
  df = 4
```

The chi-square test statistic is about 11.552 and the corresponding P-value, for a χ^2-curve with 4 degrees of freedom, is approximately 0.021.

To access the expected counts, go to the MATRIX screen and select the matrix in which the expected cell counts were stored.

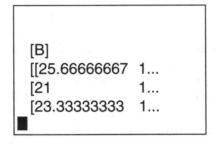

Press ENTER twice.

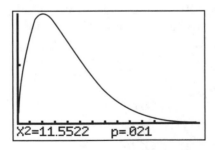

The expected cell counts are displayed on the screen. You may have to scroll right if the numbers run off the screen.

Repeating the above steps, but choosing **Draw** from the *X2-Test* function instead of **Calculate** displays the χ^2-curve with the appropriate shaded area, the test statistic, and the *P-value*.

X2=11.5522   p=.021

The chi-square test can also be performed on a computer. It is important to be able to read and interpret the computer output. Given below is a computer printout of the previous example.

Chi-Square Test

Expected counts are printed below observed counts

	Creamy	Crispy	Chewy	Total	
Elemen	33	14	19	66	
	25.67	15.40	24.93		← observed counts
Middle	21	16	17	54	← expected counts
	21.00	12.60	20.40		
High	16	12	32	60	
	23.33	14.00	22.67		
Total	70	42	68	180	

Chi-Sq = 2.095 + 0.127 + 1.412 +
0.000 + 0.917 + 0.567 +   Chi-square
2.305 + 0.286 + 3.843 = (11.552)   test statistic

(DF = 4), (P-value = 0.021)

degrees of   *P*-value
freedom

The observed and expected counts are given one above the other; the individual components, $\dfrac{(\text{observed} - \text{expected})^2}{\text{expected}}$, of the chi-square test statistic are provided and summed; and the *P*-value along with the appropriate number of degrees of freedom is provided.

Chi-Square Test of Independence

The chi-square test of independence is used to compare the distributions of sample counts of two categorical variables from a single population to see if there is an association between the variables. For instance, parents of incoming freshmen in a large school district were asked if they supported school uniforms. Parents were classified by whether or not they favored uniforms, and by the type of uniform policy at their child's previous school: uniform mandatory, uniform optional, or no uniform.

The previous situation calls for a chi-square test of independence. There are two variables (uniform preference and previous school policy) with multiple categories (favorable/unfavorable for preference and mandatory/optional/no policy for previous policy) and one population under consideration (parents of incoming freshmen). One will compare the counts of the intersection of the categories of each variable to what would be expected if the variables were independent.

To perform a chi-square test of independence, use the same four-step inference procedure.

Step 1: State the parameter of interest and a correct pair of hypotheses. The null hypothesis is that the variables under consideration are independent. That is, knowing what category of one variable an individual respondent or subject falls into does not affect the probability that the individual will fall into any category of the second variable.

H_0: Variable A and Variable B are independent.

The alternative hypothesis is that knowing what category of one variable an individual respondent or subject falls into changes the probability that the individual will fall into any category of the second variable.

H_a: Variable A and Variable B are not independent.

There is no parameter of interest. One wants to know if there is an association between the two categorical variables.

Step 2: Name the inference procedure and check assumptions/conditions. The procedure is the chi-square test of independence.

The assumptions/conditions for the chi-square test for independence are the same as the other two χ^2-tests.

The expected cell counts for each cell are equal to $\dfrac{(\text{row total})\,(\text{column total})}{\text{grand total}}$.

This is equivalent to the count of the total sample that would occur given independence between variables A and B, that is, $P(A) \times P(B) = P(A \text{ and } B)$

Step 3: Calculate the test statistic and *P*-value. The chi-square test statistic is computed as

$$\chi^2 = \sum_{\substack{\text{all}\\ \text{cells}}} \frac{(\text{observed} - \text{expected})^2}{\text{expected}}.$$

The number of degrees of freedom for the chi-square test for independence is equal to (number of rows $-$ 1)(number of columns $-$ 1).

The *P*-value for the test would be the probability of obtaining a χ^2-statistic at least as large as that computed above if the null hypothesis were true. It is determined by consulting Table C, the table of χ^2-critical values, or by using technology.

Step 4: Interpret the results in context. Make a conclusion as to whether to reject, or fail to reject, the null hypothesis, based on the meaning of the *P*-value. Describe in the context of the situation what the conclusion means.

Example: A random sample of parents of incoming freshmen in a large school district were asked if they supported school uniforms. Parents were classified by whether or not they favored uniforms, and by the type of uniform policy at their child's previous school: uniform mandatory, uniform optional, or no uniform. The results of the survey are shown in the table below.

		Favor Uniforms		
		Yes	No	Total
Previous Policy	Mandatory	28	7	35
	Optional	12	8	20
	No Policy	38	27	65
	Total	78	42	120

Is there evidence of a relationship between a parent's favoring uniforms and the uniform policy at the child's previous school?

Answer:

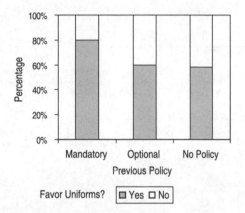

The graph suggests that there may be an association between the uniform policy at an incoming freshman's previous school and a parent's favoring uniforms. Parents of children who come from uniform-mandatory schools appear to be more favorable toward uniforms than parents of children who attended uniform-optional or no policy schools. Because the observed difference may be due to sampling variability, an inference procedure is performed to assess the chance of this.

Step 1: State the parameter of interest and a correct pair of hypotheses.

H_0: A parent's uniform favorability is independent of the uniform policy at the child's previous school.

H_a: A parent's uniform favorability is not independent of the uniform policy at the child's previous school.

Step 2: Name the inference procedure and check assumptions/conditions.
Chi-square test of independence to determine if parents' favorability toward uniforms is independent of the uniform policy at the child's previous school.

(1)   The data come from a simple random sample: OK—the question states that the parents were randomly selected.

(2)   The size of the sample is no more than 10% of the population size: OK so long as there are at least 1,200 parents of incoming freshman in this school district. This would seem reasonable for large districts.

(3)   All expected cell counts are at least 5. OK—expected cell counts are given below and all are at least 5.

Actual Counts		Favor Uniforms		
		Yes	No	Total
Previous Policy	Mandatory	28	7	35
	Optional	12	8	20
	No Policy	38	27	65
	Total	78	42	120

Expected Counts		Favor Uniforms		
		Yes	No	Total
Previous Policy	Mandatory	$\dfrac{(35)(78)}{120}$ $=22.75$	$\dfrac{(35)(42)}{120}$ $=12.25$	35
	Optional	$\dfrac{(20)(78)}{120}$ $=13$	$\dfrac{(20)(42)}{120}$ $=7$	20
	No Policy	$\dfrac{(65)(78)}{120}$ $=42.25$	$\dfrac{(65)(42)}{120}$ $=22.75$	65
	Total	78	42	120

$$\text{Expected cell count} = \frac{(\text{row total})(\text{column total})}{\text{grand total}}.$$

Note: The row and column totals for the actual and expected cell counts are equal.

Step 3: Calculate the test statistic and *P*-value.

$$\chi^2 = \sum_{\substack{\text{all} \\ \text{cells}}} \frac{(\text{observed} - \text{expected})^2}{\text{expected}}$$

$$\approx \frac{(28 - 22.75)^2}{22.75} + \frac{(7 - 12.25)^2}{12.25} + \frac{(12 - 13)^2}{13}$$

$$+ \frac{(8 - 7)^2}{7} + \frac{(38 - 42.25)^2}{42.25} + \frac{(27 - 22.75)^2}{22.75}$$

$$\approx 1.212 + 2.25 + 0.077 + 0.143 + 0.428 + 0.798$$

$$\approx 4.903.$$

df = (number of rows − 1)(number of columns − 1) = (3 − 1)(2 − 1) = 2.

P-value from Table C: the χ^2-statistic of 4.903 lies between 4.61 and 5.99 in the 2 *df* row, so $0.05 < p < 0.10$.

Step 4: Interpret the results in context. The *P*-value is between 0.10 and 0.05. If a parent's favorability toward uniforms were indeed independent of the uniform policy at a child's previous school, a chi-square statistic of 4.903 or larger would occur somewhere between 5% and 10% of the time—between 1 chance in 10 and 1 chance in 20. This is fairly likely to occur by chance and leads one to fail to reject the null hypothesis. There is insufficient evidence that a parent's favorability toward uniforms is dependent on the uniform policy at a child's previous school.

Calculator screens are shown below for the observed counts, χ^2-test, and expected counts.

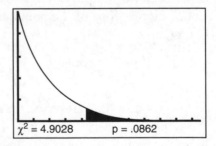

MATRIX [A] 3 x2	
[28	7]
[12	8]
[38	27]

3, 2 = 27

$\chi^2 = 4.9028$ p = .0862

[B]
[[22.75 12 25]
  [13   7   ]
  [42.25 22 75]]

Hypothesis Tests for the Slope of the Regression Line

The hypothesis test for slope allows us to determine if there is a useful linear relationship between x and y in the population. That is, does the slope of the population model differ from zero—does y tend to change linearly with changes in x? If there is a linear relationship between the two variables, the slope should not equal zero. The null hypothesis will state that the slope of the true regression line is equal to zero. The alternative hypothesis will be either greater than, less than, or not equal zero depending on the direction in which the researcher is seeking evidence.

The formula to compute the test statistic for the population slope β_1, with the null hypothesis H_0: $\beta_1 = 0$, is $t = \dfrac{b_1}{SE_{b_1}}$, where b_1 is the slope of the sample regression line and SE_{b_1} is the standard error of the slope. The number of degrees of freedom is $n - 2$. The P-value will be computed using the t-distribution.

The assumptions/conditions for a hypothesis for a population slope are the same as for confidence intervals.

Example: Let us revisit the height and shoe size problem from Section A. You will find the raw data there, along with a scatterplot, residual plot, and residual histogram. Is there a significant straight-line relationship between the heights of women and their shoe sizes?

Answer: Follow the four-step inference procedure.

Step 1: State the parameter of interest and a correct pair of hypotheses.
Let β_1 be the slope of the population regression line of women's shoe sizes on height.

H_0: $\beta_1 = 0$
H_a: $\beta_1 \neq 0$.

Step 2: Name the inference procedure and check assumptions/conditions.
We will use a linear regression t-test for the slope of the population regression line of women's shoe sizes on height.

(1) The mean y values for all the fixed x values are related linearly by the equation $\mu_y = \beta_0 + \beta_1 x$. OK—the scatterplot is linear and the residual plot shows no U-shaped pattern.

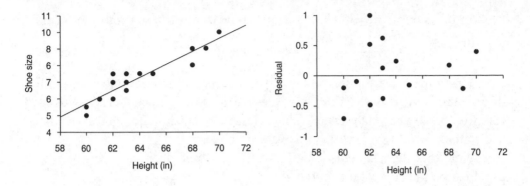

(2) For any fixed value of *x*, the value of each *y* is independent. OK—there does not appear to be any clustering in the residual plot.

(3) For any fixed value of *x*, the value of *y* is normally distributed. OK—the histogram of the residuals is symmetric and unimodal.

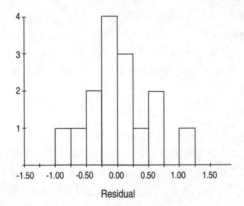

(4) For all fixed values of *x*, the standard deviation of *y* is equal. OK—the variability of the residuals across the values of *x* is consistent.

Step 3: Calculate the test statistic and *P*-value. Most of the time you will be given a computer printout of the regression information.

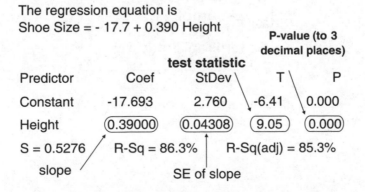

In our sample $b_1 = 0.39$ and $SE_{b_1} = 0.043$. Substituting into the formula $t = \dfrac{b_1}{SE_{b_1}}$, we get $t = \dfrac{b_1}{SE_{b_1}} = \dfrac{0.39}{0.043} \approx 9.053$, with $n - 2 = 13$ degrees of freedom.

Using the t-distribution table with 13 degrees of freedom, the probability that the test statistic is 9.053 or more is less than 0.0005. Since this is a two-sided test, we double that value. The P-value is less than 0.001, although the very large test statistic would suggest that it is very much less.

Note that the test statistic and P-value (to three decimal places) are also provided on the computer printout.

Step 4: Interpret the results in context. The P-value calculated is very small, far less than 0.001. We have strong evidence to reject the null hypothesis in favor of the alternative, and we determine that there is a linear (or straight-line) relationship between the heights of women and their shoe sizes.

Note: Returning to the concept of duality of hypothesis tests and confidence intervals, recall that in the corresponding example in Section A we were 95% confident that the slope of the true regression line for height and shoe size was between 0.2969 and 0.4831. Zero is not in the interval, so we could conclude, at least at the $\alpha = 0.05$ level of significance, that the slope is not equal to 0.

Calculator Tip:

Hypothesis tests for the slope of the population model can be performed with the graphing calculator. You must, however, have the raw data in lists.

In this case, the women's heights are in list L1 and shoe sizes are in list L2. From the home screen, press $\boxed{\text{STAT}}$, arrow right to TESTS, and then choose F:LinRegTTest....

```
EDIT  CALC  TESTS
B↑ 2-PropZInt...
C : χ²-Test...
D : χ²GOF-Test...
E : 2-SampFTest...
F : LinRegTTest...
G : LinRegTInt...
A : ANOVA (
```

Input the data lists, the appropriate alternative hypothesis, and where the regression equation is to be stored.

```
LinRegTTest
  Xlist : L1
  Ylist : L2
  Freq : 1
  β & ρ : ≠0  <0 >0
  ReqEQ : Y1
  Calculate
```

Arrow down to Calculate, and then press ENTER . The alternative hypothesis is shown along with the test statistic, *P*-value, degrees of freedom, and intercept. Scrolling down will give the slope, standard error about the regression line, *r*, and r^2.

```
LinRegTTest
  y=a+bx
  β≠0 and ρ≠0
  t=9.053731821
  p = 5.628817 E-7
  df = 13
↓a = −17.69333333
```

```
LinRegTTest
  y=a+bx
  β≠0 and ρ≠0
↑b = .39
  s = .5275730597
  r² = .8631147541
  r = .9290396946
```

Note the very small *P*-value of 0.000000563. Also, the alternative hypothesis is given in two forms. The second is $\rho \neq 0$. Rho (ρ) is the population correlation coefficient. If the slope is zero, so must be the correlation coefficient.

Trial Run

1. A beekeeper conducting experiments reported results from significance tests on the mean number of bees that return to various hives after time has passed. The *P*-value for one particular test was 0.04. What is one conclusion the beekeeper can make from this value?

    (A) If the null hypothesis were true, we would expect results at least as extreme as those observed 4% of the time.

    (B) If the alternative hypothesis were true, we would expect results this extreme as those observed 4% of the time.

    (C) 4% of the bees return to the hive.

    (D) 4% of the bees did not return to the hive.

(E)   There is a 4% chance that if he rejects the null hypothesis, he will have made a Type I error.

2.   One reason a researcher would conduct a one-sample z-test of means instead of a one-sample t-test of means is that

(A)   he has a sample size greater than 30

(B)   he knows the population standard deviation

(C)   the sample data has three extreme outliers

(D)   the sample size is 18 with no skewness or outliers

(E)   the population mean is known

3.   Which of the following is a correct set of hypotheses to test whether the mean number of room cancellations at a downtown hotel has increased from 7?

(A) $H_0: \bar{x} = 7$ $H_a: \bar{x} > 7$

(B) $H_0: \mu = 7$ $H_a: \mu > 7$

(C) $H_0: p = 7$ $H_a: p > 7$

(D) $H_0: \hat{p} = 7$ $H_a: \hat{p} > 7$

(E) $H_0: \sigma = 7$ $H_a: \sigma > 7$

4.   A golf instructor is interested in how much improvement individual beginner golf class students make during the course of the 4-week clinic she teaches each summer. Before the clinic began, each golfer played all 18 holes of the course and the score for each round was recorded. The same was done when the players completed the clinic. Which is the correct hypothesis test for this situation?

(A)   Two-sample t-test of means

(B)   Two-sample z-test of proportions

(C)   One-sample paired t-test of means

(D)   Chi-square test of independence

(E)   Linear regression t-test for the slope of the regression line.

5.   A science-fiction club was debating if there is an association between politicians' party affiliation and their preference between *Star Voyages*, a television show focusing on exploration and the human condition, and

Star Conflict, a movie series about political struggle and redemption. They surveyed 100 randomly selected public office holders in their area, and asked each their political party and their preference of *Star Voyages* or *Star Conflict*. What type inference procedure should be used to resolve their debate?

(A)   Chi-square test of goodness of fit test

(B)   Chi-square test of homogeneity test

(C)   Chi-square test of independence test

(D)   Two-sample *z*-test for proportions

(E)   Linear regression *t*-test for slope

6.   Marketing managers at various department stores that are housed at malls are studying the types of people that might be shopping in their store. Their hopes are to make sure that they are catering to the clientele coming to their store. Vehicles parked within 200 feet of various "anchor" stores at a mall were categorized as shown in the table below as well as the type of store. The data were collected on a Saturday in May.

		Classification of Vehicle				
		Compact	Family/SUV	Luxury	Sport	Total
Store Class	Discount	130	198	12	32	372
	Mid-range	108	210	42	64	424
	High-end	64	178	53	73	368
	Total	302	586	107	169	1164

If a chi-square test of independence is performed, what is the approximate expected cell count for drivers of Luxury cars that shop at High-end stores?

(A)   14

(B)   34

(C)   53

(D)   107

(E)   743

7.   In the previous question, how many degrees of freedom are needed for the chi-square test of independence?

(A)   5

(B)   6

(C)   11

(D)   12

(E)   1,163

8.   For each situation below,

(1)   define the parameter of interest

(2)   write an appropriate pair of hypothesis statements

(3)   name an appropriate inference procedure to be used

(a)   A school district in a large suburban area is trying to determine if student absences are distributed equally throughout the days of the week.

(b)   Mrs. Smith and Mr. Jones both teach statistics at the local community college. The dean was receiving some complaints that Mrs. Smith was grading too strictly. The dean used the school's computer system and randomly selected 25 students from each teacher's class to determine if, in fact, Mrs. Smith's grades were lower than Mr. Jones'.

(c)   One hundred participants were randomly selected to participate in a medical study to investigate the effects of a low-fat diet on lowering cholesterol level. Cholesterol levels for each individual were recorded before the diet began and then again 6 months later.

9.   A local chamber of commerce has received reports that the cost of renting an apartment has dropped significantly from the previous year. If this were true, the chamber would want to immediately advertise that fact in its promotional literature. Such literature is used to encourage people to move to the community and to attract new businesses.

Last year, the average rental price of a one-bedroom apartment was $650 per month. The chamber of commerce randomly samples nine apartment buildings in the community and records the rental price of a one-bedroom apartment. The apartment rents are as follows:

$565 $600 $590 $645 $625 $580 $695 $680 $575

Is there significant statistical evidence that the average one-bedroom price has decreased from the last year?

10. A school district in a large suburban area is trying to determine if student absences are distributed equally throughout the school week. A researcher randomly selects 150 student absences during the past month and records the day of the absence. The absences were distributed as follows: 37 on Mondays, 29 on Tuesdays, 20 on Wednesdays, 30 on Thursdays, and 34 on Fridays.

    Is there sufficient evidence to conclude that the absences are not distributed equally throughout the school week? Support your answer with appropriate statistical evidence.

Trial Run Solutions

1. A. This is the explanation of the *P*-value. If the null hypothesis were indeed true, we would see results as extreme as or more extreme than what we observed in 4% of all samples.

2. B. A *z*-test of means is only used when the population standard deviation is known. The sample size is not an issue. Neither test should be performed with small sample sizes if there is extreme skewness in the sample distribution, or if outliers are present.

3. B. This is the only set that uses the parameter, μ, in the hypotheses statements. Since this is a test of means we are interested in μ, not p, which is used for proportions. The sample statistics $\bar{x}$ or $\hat{p}$ are never used in a statement of hypotheses.

4. C. We are interested in the improvement of each golfer so the scores are *matched* or *paired* for each golfer. This is not a two-sample test since we are not comparing the means of each round of scores for different samples of golfers.

5. C. The data collected are of two categorical variables—political affiliation and preferred show—therefore, if inference is performed a chi-square test is necessary. The club is considering if there is an *association* between the two variables. One sample was taken from a single population. A chi-square test of independence is in order. Recall that a test of homogeneity is appropriate for comparing one variable across two or more populations, and the test of goodness of fit is required for a single variable with multiple categories from a single population.

6.   B. Expected cell count =

$$\frac{(\text{row total})(\text{column total})}{\text{grand total}} = \frac{(368)(107)}{1,164} = 33.83.$$

7.   B. The number of degrees of freedom for the chi-square test for independence is equal to (number of rows $- 1$)(number of columns $- 1$) = $(3 - 1)(4 - 1) = 6$.

8.   (a)   This is a chi-square goodness of fit test.

H_0: $p_{\text{Monday}} = p_{\text{Tuesday}} = p_{\text{Wednesday}} = p_{\text{Thursday}} = p_{\text{Friday}} = 0.2$

H_a: at least one of the proportions in H_0 is not equal to 0.2

There is no parameter of interest in a chi-square test.

(b)   This is a two-sample test of means. We are comparing means of two samples from two independent populations.

Let μ_1 = the mean grades for Mrs. Smith's class.

Let μ_2 = the mean grades for Mr. Jones' class.

$$H_0\text{: } \mu_1 = \mu_2$$
$$H_a\text{: } \mu_1 < \mu_2.$$

(c)   This is a paired t-test of means as we are comparing cholesterol levels for individual participants. This can be thought of as a before–after scheme.

Let μ_d = mean difference between in cholesterol levels before and after the low-fat diet.

$$H_0\text{: } \mu_d = 0$$
$$H_a\text{: } \mu_d < 0.$$

9. **Step 1: State the parameter of interest and a correct pair of hypotheses.** The parameter of interest, μ, is the mean rent for a one-bedroom apartment in a community.

$$H_0\text{: } \mu = 650 \qquad\qquad H_a\text{: } \mu < 650.$$

Step 2: Name the inference procedure and check assumptions/conditions. This is a one-sample t-test for the mean rent for a one-bedroom apartment in a community.

(1)   The sample must be an SRS from the population of interest. OK—the problem states that we have a random sample.

(2)   The data come from a normally distributed population. OK—a dotplot

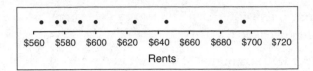

of the data (shown below) is fairly symmetric, with no extreme values.

Step 3: Calculate the test statistic and *P*-value.

$$t = \frac{\bar{x} - \mu_0}{\frac{s}{\sqrt{n}}} = \frac{617.222 - 650}{\left(\frac{47.11}{\sqrt{9}}\right)} = -2.0873.$$

Using Table B with 8 degrees of freedom, find the corresponding *t*-value. (Keep in mind that this table only uses positive values so we are looking for 2.0873.) It shows that the *P*-value will be between 0.05 and 0.025.

```
T-Test
  μ<650
  t=-2.087269956
  p=.0351579678
  x̄=617.222222
  Sx=47.11098008
  n=9
```

(The calculator produces an exact *P*-value of 0.03516.)

Step 4: Interpret the results in context. The test statistic is –2.087, which produced a *P*-value of 0.035. If the null hypothesis were true, the probability of getting a test statistic this small or smaller would be 0.035. This is unlikely to have happened by chance. We reject the null hypothesis in favor of the alternative one and conclude that the mean rent for one-bedroom apartments in this community has decreased significantly from the last year's mean of $650.

10. First, a quick bar chart gives reason to believe that the distribution of the absences may not be equal throughout the week.

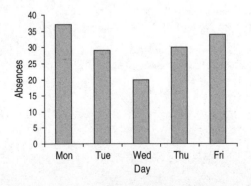

An inference procedure can be used to determine if the differences are merely due to chance.

Step 1: State the parameter of interest and a correct pair of hypotheses.

H_0: $p_{\text{Monday}} = p_{\text{Tuesday}} = p_{\text{Wednesday}} = p_{\text{Thursday}} = p_{\text{Friday}} = 0.2$

H_a: at least one of the proportions in H0 is not equal to 0.2

(There is no parameter of interest for chi-square tests.)

Step 2: Name the inference procedure and check assumptions/conditions.
Chi-square test of goodness of fit to determine if the distribution of the absences is equal for each day of the week.

(1)   The data come from a simple random sample: OK—the absences were randomly selected.

(2)   The size of the sample is no more than 10% of the population size: OK if there were at least 1,500 student absences last month. Since the school district is "large," this is certainly plausible.

(3)   All expected cell counts are at least 5. OK—expected cell counts are given below and all are at least 5.

Day	Mon	Tue	Wed	Thu	Fri	Total
Actual Count	37	29	20	30	34	150
Expected Count	30	30	30	30	30	150

Step 3: Calculate the test statistic and *P*-value.

$$\chi^2 = \sum_{\substack{all \\ cells}} \frac{(\text{observed} - \text{expected})^2}{\text{expected}}$$

$$= \frac{(37-30)^2}{30} + \frac{(29-30)^2}{30} + \frac{(20-30)^2}{30} + \frac{(30-30)^2}{30} + \frac{(34-30)^2}{15}$$

$$= 1.633\ldots + 0.033\ldots + 3.333\ldots + 0 + 0.533\ldots$$

$$\approx 5.533.$$

df = number of categories − 1 = 5 − 1 = 4.

P-value from Table C: the χ^2-statistic of 5.533 is between 5.39 and 5.99 on the 4 *df* row, so $0.20 < P < 0.25$. (The actual value as given by a graphing calculator is 0.237.)

Step 4: Interpret the results in context. The *P*-value is between 0.20 and 0.25. If the absences were distributed evenly, a chi-square statistic of 5.533 or larger would occur between 20% and 25% of the time—between 1 chance in 4 and 1 chance in 5. This is very likely to occur by chance and leads one to fail to reject the null hypothesis. There is insufficient evidence that the distribution of the absences is not evenly distributed across the week.

OR (with actual *P*-value)

The *P*-value is about 0.237. If the absences were distributed evenly, a chi-square statistic of 5.533 or larger would occur 24% of the time—about 1 chance in 4. This is very likely to occur by chance and leads one to fail to reject the null hypothesis. There is insufficient evidence that the distribution of the absences is not even across the week.

▼

PRACTICE EXAM 1
AP Statistics

This test is also on CD-ROM in our special interactive AP Statistics TEST*ware*®. It is highly recommended that you first take this exam on computer. You will then have the additional study features and benefits of timed conditions and instantaneous, accurate scoring. See page xx for guidance on how to get the most out of our AP Statistics software.

AP STATISTICS

PRACTICE EXAM 1

SECTION I

Time—1 hour and 30 minutes
Number of Questions—40
Percent of Total Grade—50

(Answer sheets appear in the back of this book)

DIRECTIONS: Solve each of the following problems using the available space for scratchwork. Decide which is the best of the choices given and fill in the corresponding oval on the answer sheet. No credit will be given for anything written in the test book. Do not spend too much time on any one problem.

1. An occupational safety administrator is interested in reducing repetitive motion injuries for office workers who use computers. The administrator divides 48 volunteers at random into two groups. The first group will use a standard keyboard for 12 months. The second group will use a new keyboard design for the same period of time. At the end of the study the frequencies of volunteers experiencing repetitive motion injuries with their respective keyboards will be compared. What would be the appropriate method of inference in this situation?

    (A) One-sample t-test

    (B) Paired t-test

    (C) Two-sample t-test

    (D) One-proportion z-test

    (E) Two-proportion z-test

2. A simple random sample of size n is taken from a large population whose distribution of the variable under consideration is extremely right-skewed. Which of the following statements is true?

(A) As *n* increases, the sample mean is more likely to be within a given distance of the population mean.

(B) When $n > 30$, the distribution of the sample mean is normal.

(C) As *n* increases, the sample standard deviation decreases.

(D) As *n* increases, the distribution of the sample data becomes more normal.

(E) The sample standard deviation is equal to

$$\frac{\text{population standard deviation}}{\sqrt{n}}.$$

3. The power of a significance test for a particular value of the parameter is computed to be 0.93. Which statement below is true?

(A) The probability of committing a Type I error is 0.07.

(B) The probability of committing a Type I error is 0.93.

(C) The probability of committing a Type II error is 0.07.

(D) The probability of committing a Type II error is 0.93.

(E) The probability of committing a Type II error is the same as the alpha level.

4. John recently scored 113 on a particular standardized achievement test. The scores on the test are distributed with a mean of 100 and a standard deviation of 10. His cousin, Brandon, took a different standardized test and scored 263. The scores on Brandon's test have a mean of 250 and a standard deviation of 25. Which student did relatively better on his particular test?

(A) John did better on his test.

(B) Brandon did better on his test.

(C) They both performed equally as well on their respective tests.

(D) It is impossible to tell since they did not take the same test.

(E) It is impossible to tell since the number of students taking the test is unknown.

5. Who makes more mistakes on their income tax forms: accountants or tax-payers who prepare the forms themselves? A random sample of income tax forms that were prepared by accountants was drawn from IRS records.

An equal number of forms that were self-prepared by taxpayers was also drawn. The average number of errors per form was compared to determine if one group tends to make more mistakes than the other. What type of study is this?

(A) Census

(B) Experiment

(C) Voluntary response survey

(D) Observational study

(E) Matched-pairs study

6. A study was conducted to estimate the proportion of American families who owned a video tape player (VCR) and/or a digital video disc player (DVD). A random sample of a large group of Americans was taken. The 95% confidence interval created from the data produced the interval (0.784, 0.844). Which of the following is the correct interpretation of 95% confidence?

(A) We are 95% confident that the true proportion of American families that own a VCR or DVD player is between 0.784 and 0.844.

(B) Ninety-five percent of the time, a sample such as this one will produce a sample proportion between 0.784 and 0.844.

(C) There is a 95% chance that the sample proportion from the data is between 0.784 and 0.844.

(D) Ninety-five percent of all intervals created like this one will contain the true population proportion.

(E) There is a 95% chance that the population proportion is between 0.784 and 0.844.

7. The baggage handling services of On-Time Airlines is interested in how many baggage handlers they need on duty at various times of the day to ensure that passengers do not wait an unreasonable amount of time for their baggage. An airport executive performed a study and found that there is a correlation between the number of passengers arriving at given times and the number of baggage handlers needed. She sampled various times during the day and different days of the week including weekend. She recorded the number of passengers arriving within any 1-hour time block.

The computer output from the regression equation analysis is shown below.

Predicted Baggage Handlers = 2.86 + 0.00408
(number of passengers)

Predictor	Coef	StDev	T	P
Constant	2.860	1.324	2.16	0.083
Passengers	0.004081	0.001168	3.49	0.017
S = 1.562	R-sq = 70.9%		R-Sq(adj) = 65.1%	

What is the value of the correlation coefficient for the number of baggage handlers and number of arriving passengers?

(A) −0.842

(B) 0.651

(C) 0.709

(D) 0.842

(E) 1.562

8. A dance club holds a raffle at the end of each dance. Five dancers are selected at random to each draw one numbered tag from a hat without replacement. There are 50 tags in the hat numbered from 1 to 50. Drawing a tag from 1 through 5 wins $20, tags from 6 through 25 wins $10, and tags from 26 through 50 wins $5. In order to determine the average amount of money paid out, a simulation will be conducted using a random number table. Which of the following assignments of random numbers to tag values is most appropriate for the simulation?

(A) Using single-digit numbers, assign 0 to represent a $20 prize, 1–4 to represent a $10 prize, and 5–9 to represent a $5 prize.

(B) Using single-digit numbers, assign 0 to represent a $20 prize, 1 to represent a $10 prize, and 2 to represent a $5 prize. Numbers 3–9 are ignored.

(C) Using two-digit numbers, assign 20 to represent a $20 prize, 10 to represent a $10 prize, and 05 to represent a $5 prize. Numbers 00–04, 06–09, 11–19, 21–99 are ignored.

(D) Using two-digit numbers, assign 01–05 to represent a $20 prize, 06–25 to represent a $10 prize, and 26–50 to represent a $5 prize. Numbers 51–99 and 00 are ignored.

(E) Using two-digit numbers, assign 01–10 to represent a $20 prize, 11–40 to represent a $10 prize, and 41–99 and 00 to represent a $5 prize.

9. The student council wants to survey students at the school to see what brands of soda pop they want in the school machines. They randomly sampled 30 freshmen, 30 sophomores, 30 juniors, and 30 seniors. The sampling method they used is a

(A) simple random sample

(B) stratified random sample

(C) cluster sample

(D) systematic random sample

(E) convenience sample

10. Which of the following is a legitimate probability distribution?

(A)

x	3	4	5	6
$P(x)$	0.1	0.1	0.1	0.1

(B)

x	0	1	2	3	4	5
$P(x)$	0.2	0.1	0.1	0.2	0.2	0.3

(C)

x	−5	0	5	10	15
$P(x)$	0.6	0.1	0.2	0.1	0

(D)

x	1	3	5	7
$P(x)$	0.3	0.2	0.2	0.4

(E)

x	1	1.5	2	2.5	3	3.5	4	4.5
$P(x)$	0.05	0.08	0.07	0.20	0.30	0.10	0.21	−0.01

11. A 95% confidence interval is to be calculated in order to find an estimate for a population proportion. What is the smallest sample size that will guarantee a margin of error of at most 5%?

(A) 225

(B) 350

(C)   400

(D)   575

(E)   800

12.   Some AP Statistics students were interested in finding out if there was a relationship between the number of hours of study for a chapter test and the score on that test. On the basis of the number of hours their classmates studied for the chapter 3 test and the scores on the test (out of 100%), the least-squares regression line calculated was $\hat{y} = 72.53 + 5.88x$, where x is the number of hours studied and $\hat{y}$ is the predicted score on the test. Which statement correctly interprets the meaning of the slope of this regression line?

(A)   For each additional hour studied, the predicted score on the test increases by approximately 73%.

(B)   For each additional hour studied, the predicted score on the test increases by approximately 6%.

(C)   For each additional percent of increase on the test, the predicted score on the test increases approximately 73%.

(D)   For each additional percent of increase on the test, the predicted score on the test increases approximately 6%.

(E)   We cannot use this regression equation, since cause–effect has not been proven.

13.   A group of statistics students want to know if there is a difference in how well their classmates like two of a beverage producer's latest juice blends. Ten students were randomly selected from the class to be taste testers. Each taste tester was randomly given one of the two juices, recorded how well it was liked on a scale of 1 to 10, and then given the other juice to evaluate. The scores given by the tasters are shown below.

Taste tester No.	1	2	3	4	5	6	7	8	9	10
Lemon-Grape	7.8	8.6	9.5	9.6	9.8	9.9	8.5	9.3	8.0	9.8
Cran-Pineapple	6.6	9.9	7.2	9.0	9.7	8.8	8.9	7.5	6.2	8.6

The statistics students want to use confidence intervals to determine if there is a difference in taste preference between the two juices. They think of three possible ways to do this.

I. Do a two-sample 95% *t*-confidence interval for the true difference between the mean ratings of Lemon-Grape and Cran-Pineapple juices. The result is

$$-0.18 < \mu_{\text{LemonGrape}} - \mu_{\text{CranPineapple}} < 1.86.$$

II. Do a paired 95% *t*-confidence interval for the true mean difference between the ratings of Lemon-Grape and Cran-Pineapple juices. The result is

$$0.05 < \mu_{\text{LemonGrape}-\text{CranPineapple}} < 1.63.$$

III. Do a one-sample 95% *t*-confidence interval for the true mean rating of each juice and see if the intervals overlap. The results are

$$8.52 < \mu_{\text{LemonGrape}} < 9.64 \text{ and } 7.32 < \mu_{\text{CranPineapple}} < 9.16.$$

Which of the methods listed above is/are appropriate to answer the students' original question?

(A) I only

(B) II only

(C) III only

(D) I and III only

(E) None of the methods are appropriate. A hypothesis test is required to draw any sort of conclusion from these data.

14. A doll-making company has been able to streamline their production process by having three jobs: assembling the doll, putting clothing on the doll, and putting the doll in the box. The table below illustrates the mean times (in seconds) and standard deviations for each task.

	Mean	Standard Deviation
Assembly	36	2.5
Clothing	22	1.8
Boxing	8	0.75

The distributions of times for each step are approximately normal and independent. What are the mean and standard deviation of the total time (in seconds) to complete all three tasks?

(A) $\mu_x = 60.6$ $\sigma_x = 3.17$

(B) $\mu_x = 60.6$ $\sigma_x = 5.05$

(C) $\mu_x = 66$ $\sigma_x = 0.88$

(D) $\mu_x = 66$ $\sigma_x = 3.17$

(E) $\mu_x = 66$ $\sigma_x = 5.05$

15. When is a linear regression *t*-test used?

   (A) To find the value of a residual

   (B) To find the value of the slope of the true regression line

   (C) To find the confidence interval for the intercept of the true regression line

   (D) To find the value of the intercept of the true regression line

   (E) To find out if there is a meaningful linear relationship between two variables

16. A baseball coach wants to compare the number of hits by two groups of batters each using a different type of bat. Which type of graphical display would NOT be appropriate?

   (A) Parallel boxplots

   (B) Dotplots drawn on the same scale

   (C) Back-to-back stemplots

   (D) Histograms drawn on the same scale

   (E) Scatterplot

17. A distribution of scores has a mean of 60 and a standard deviation of 18. If each score is doubled, and then 5 is subtracted from that result, what will be the mean and standard deviation of the new scores?

   (A) mean = 115, standard deviation = 31

   (B) mean = 115, standard deviation = 36

   (C) mean = 120, standard deviation = 6

   (D) mean = 120, standard deviation = 31

   (E) mean = 120, standard deviation = 36

18. A hypothesis test is conducted with respect to the mean weight (in ounces) of potato chip bags from a certain manufacturer. The test's hypotheses are H_0: $\mu = 0.8$ and H_a: $\mu \neq 0.8$. Which confidence interval below would support the conclusion that there is insufficient evidence to reject the null hypothesis at the $\alpha = 0.03$ level of significance?

    (A) The 97% confidence interval for the mean weight in ounces of potato chips is (0.765, 0.823).

    (B) The 94% confidence interval for the mean weight in ounces of potato chips is (0.765, 0.823).

    (C) The 97% confidence interval for the mean weight in ounces of potato chips is (0.725, 0.783).

    (D) The 94% confidence interval for the mean weight in ounces of potato chips is (0.725, 0.783).

    (E) We cannot conclude anything with a confidence interval unless we have the actual data set to construct the interval.

19. A new medication has been developed to cure a certain disease. The disease progresses in three stages, stages I, II, and III, each progressively worse than the one before it. Ninety volunteers are gathered to test the new medication, 30 in each of the three stages of the disease. The medication will be administered to subjects daily in one of three dosages: 100 mg for each subject in stage I of the disease, 200 mg to each subject in stage II, and 400 mg to each subject in stage III. After 8 weeks, the proportion of subjects cured of the disease will be recorded. Why is this NOT a good experimental design?

    I. Because experiments of this type should only use one dosage level of medication.

    II. Because disease stage is potentially confounded with dosage level.

    III. Because the experiment lacks a control group.

    (A) I only

    (B) II only

    (C) I and II only

    (D) II and III only

    (E) I, II, and III

20. Sparkles, a small tart candy, comes in four colors. Their website states that there are twice as many red as each of the other three colors. A random sample of 80 candies was taken and the colors were distributed as follows:

Red	Yellow	Green	Blue
37	15	18	10

The χ^2 test statistic for the goodness of fit test is

(A) $\chi^2 < 1$

(B) $1 \le \chi^2 < 4$

(C) $4 \le \chi^2 < 15$

(D) $15 \le \chi^2 < 75$

(E) $75 < \chi^2$

21. A certain variety of table grapes has fruit diameters that are distributed normally with mean 13 mm and standard deviation 2 mm. Approximately what proportion of grapes have diameters between 12 mm and 16 mm?

(A) 0.134

(B) 0.378

(C) 0.500

(D) 0.625

(E) 0.683

22. A tire manufacturer is testing a new tread design for its light-truck tires. The previous design had a mean tread life of 47,500 miles. Tires with the new design are manufactured and tested on a variety of light trucks. Which of the following is the correct pair of hypotheses to test the assertion that the new tread design has a longer life than the old design?

(A) $H_0: \mu < 47,500$, $H_a: \mu = 47,500$

(B) $H_0: \mu = 47,500$, $H_a: \mu \ne 47,500$

(C) $H_0: \mu = 47,500$, $H_a: \mu < 47,500$

(D) $H_0: \mu = 47,500$, $H_a: \mu > 47,500$

(E) $H_0: \mu > 47,500$, $H_a: \mu \le 47,500$

23. A study was done to explore a link between a particular medication prescribed to pregnant women and the incidence of a certain medical condition in newborns. Records of 952 recent newborns and their mothers were examined. The following table shows the results of the study.

		Mother took medication?		
		Yes	No	Total
Newborn has condition?	Yes	21	245	266
	No	57	629	686
	Total	78	874	952

Which of the following best describes the association between mothers-to-be taking the medication and the presence of the condition in newborns?

(A) There appears to be no association since the condition was present in newborns of mothers that either took or did not take the medication.

(B) There appears to be no association since the condition was present in about the same proportion of newborns of mothers that either took or did not take the medication.

(C) There appears to be no association because more newborns of mothers who did not take the medication had the condition than newborns of mothers who did take the medication.

(D) There appears to be no association because more newborns did not have the condition than those who did.

(E) There appears to be an association because the condition was present in newborns of mothers who took the drug.

24. The Sunday edition of the newspaper has 585,320 readers. Sixty-three percent of the readers are men. It is known that about 12% of the women and 23% of the men that read this newspaper will read the book review section. If a random sample of 200 readers is taken, what is the expected number of people that will read the book review section?

(A) 23

(B) 24

(C) 38

(D) 46

(E) 70

25. A restaurant recognizes customers who go there on their birthdays with a free piece of cake and the singing of a song. On one particular day, a server noticed that 10 out of the 187 customers at the restaurant celebrated birthdays that day. Having taken statistics, the server did a significance test to determine if the true proportion of people with birthdays on that day is significantly different from what is expected. In a test of H_0: $p = \dfrac{1}{365}$ versus $H_A : p \neq \dfrac{1}{365}$, the test statistic was 13.27 and the *P*-value was 3.43×10^{-40}. Which of the following statements is true?

    (A) There is a significantly different proportion of people born on that day than one would expect.

    (B) The test is invalid; a sample size of 187 is far too small to do inference for a proportion.

    (C) The test is inappropriate; a confidence interval should have been done instead.

    (D) The test was incorrectly performed. The alternative hypothesis should have been $H_A : p > \dfrac{1}{365}$.

    (E) Any inference is invalid. The sample of restaurant customers is not representative of the population.

26. A baseball pitcher has a history of throwing only 40% of his pitches for strikes. The coach has suspended the player until he improves his strike-throwing percentage to at least 55%. If a practice session of 40 pitches is scheduled, and the player has not actually improved, what is the probability that the player will throw at least 55% of his pitches for strikes?

    (A) $P\left(z > \dfrac{0.55 - 0.40}{\sqrt{\frac{(0.40)(0.60)}{40}}} \right)$

    (B) $P\left(z > \dfrac{0.50 - 0.40}{\sqrt{\frac{(0.50)(0.50)}{40}}} \right)$

    (C) $P\left(z > \dfrac{0.55 - 0.50}{\sqrt{\frac{(0.55)(0.45)}{40}}} \right)$

(D) $\dbinom{40}{22} (0.40)^{22} (0.60)^{18}$

(E) $\dbinom{40}{22} (0.55)^{22} (0.45)^{18}$

27. In a recent high school basketball tournament where over 750 games were played, the mean team score was 68 points and the standard deviation was 13 points. The scores were approximately normally distributed. A coach was overheard saying that his team scored 95 points in one game. About what proportion of teams' scores during the tournament were more than 95 points?

   (A) 0.0035

   (B) 0.0190

   (C) 0.05

   (D) 0.9810

   (E) 2.07

28. The traffic safety officer of a local police force was trying to see if there was an association between the number of cars that did not use a main intersection in town because of the traffic light and the number of tickets written for speeding on the alternate route. The correlation between these two variables was found to be 0.58. Which of the following statements is true?

   (A) About 58% of the variation in the number of speeding tickets can be explained by the linear relationship between the number of speeding tickets issued and the number of cars that did not use the main intersection in town.

   (B) Any potential linear relationship between the number of cars not using the main intersection in town and the number of speeding tickets written on an alternate route would be positive.

   (C) If one uses the main intersection through town, one is 58% more likely to receive a ticket than using the alternate route.

   (D) Since the correlation is not close to 1, there cannot be a linear relationship between the number of cars not using the main intersection in town and the number of speeding tickets written on an alternate route.

(E)   Getting a speeding ticket is a direct cause of taking the alternate route.

29.   A major automobile manufacturer is trying to improve its customer service at its dealerships across the United States. A survey of 200 customers in Arizona who recently purchased a vehicle from this manufacturer were asked if they were satisfied with the customer service at the dealership. Is it reasonable to generalize the conclusion to the population of all customers in the United States that purchased from this manufacturer?

(A)   No, because customers were only sampled in one state.

(B)   No, because 200 is not a large enough sample.

(C)   No, because only one sample was taken.

(D)   Yes, because the sample size is more than 30.

(E)   Yes, because the population of all new vehicle owners by this manufacturer is more than 2,000.

30.   A politician is considering running for public office. He wants to measure his name recognition by doing a survey of voters in his district. Which of the following survey methods would produce unbiased results?

(A)   The politician stands in front of a grocery store in his district on Saturday morning and asking each person entering the store if he or she recognizes the politician's name.

(B)   Placing pollsters in front of every grocery store in his district on Saturday morning and asking each person entering the store if he or she recognizes the politician's name.

(C)   Sending a survey card to all registered voters in the district asking them to call a phone number to state whether or not they recognize the politician's name.

(D)   Calling people from his district listed in the phone book and asking each if he or she recognizes the politician's name.

(E)   None of these methods would produce unbiased results.

31.   A ski resort rental shop wants to make sure that they have enough of the three different types of skis on hand for all of their customers. A random sample of skiers was taken to determine if males or females tend to prefer one type of ski versus another. The three types of skis they offer for rental are high performance, parabolic, and beginner (short skis). Which is a correct pair of hypotheses for the ski resort shop to test?

(A) H_0: Gender and type of ski rented are independent.
     H_a: Gender and type of ski rented are not independent.

(B) H_0: Gender and type of ski rented are not independent.
     H_a: Gender and type of ski rented are independent.

(C) H_0: The proportions of types of skis rented are the same.
     H_a: The proportions of types of skis rented are not the same.

(D) H_0: There is an association between gender and type of ski rented.
     H_a: There is no association between gender and type of ski rented.

(E) H_0: The proportions of genders renting skis are the same.
     H_a: The proportions of genders renting skis are not the same.

32. A garage door manufacturer has developed a new type of door for houses
     in the Southeast part of the United States. Doors in this area of the coun-
     try are particularly susceptible to damage from salty ocean spray and the
     sun's rays, which tend to shine mainly on the north side of the house. An
     experiment will test the new type of garage door against the existing type
     of door on eight houses in a particular residential area. An overhead view
     of the area is shown below. The location of the garage door on each home
     is marked with an "X."

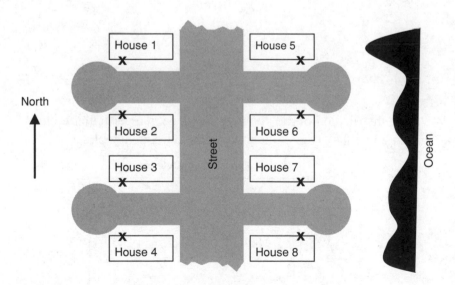

Which of the following blocking schemes is most appropriate to account
for variables in this study other than the type of door?

(A) Form the houses into two blocks: {1, 2, 3, 4} and {5, 6, 7, 8}.

(B) Form the houses into two blocks: {1, 3, 5, 7} and {2, 4, 6, 8}.

(C) Form the houses into four blocks: {1, 5}, {2, 6}, {3, 7}, and {4, 8}.

(D) Form the houses into four blocks: {1, 3}, {2, 4}, {5, 7}, and {6, 8}.

(E) No blocking is necessary in this experiment.

33. What is the approximate residual of the data point "A" on the scatterplot with the least-squares regression line shown below?

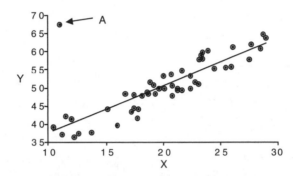

(A) 11

(B) 29

(C) 39

(D) 58

(E) 68

34. The distribution of the population by age in a particular country is represented by the given cumulative relative frequency plot.

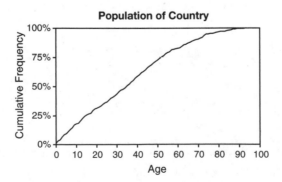

Which of the following statements about the population is true?

(A) The median age is about 46 years.

(B) The interquartile range of ages is about 27 years.

(C) The mean age is greater than the median age.

(D) There are more people younger than 65 years of age than those older than 30 years of age.

(E) Seventy-five percent of people are older than 50 years of age.

35. A significance test was performed with hypotheses of H_0: $\mu = 15$ and H_a: $\mu < 15$. The *P*-value for the test was 0.026. Which of the following conclusions is most appropriate for this test?

(A) 2.6% of the time the mean will be exactly 15.

(B) 97.4% of the time the mean will be less than 15.

(C) There is a 2.6% chance of making a Type II error.

(D) There is reason to believe that the mean μ is less than 15.

(E) The true mean is approximately 2.6% of 15.

36. A consumer is considering the purchase of a new appliance and has narrowed the selection down to two brands: Brand M and Brand S. The consumer found the following information about the repair history of the appliances as done by a nonprofit product-testing group.

Cost of Brand		Percentage needing repairs within 5 years			
		0 repair	1 repair	2 repairs	3 repairs
M	$350	50%	25%	15%	10%
S	$325	40%	30%	20%	10%

The consumer can purchase an extended warranty for either brand at a cost of $300. The extended warranty provides free repairs for a 5-year period. For which of the brands under consideration is the cost of the extended warranty less than the expected cost of repairing the appliance over a 5-year period?

(A) Brand M only

(B) Brand S only

(C) Both Brand M and Brand S

(D)   Neither Brand M nor Brand S

(E)   It cannot be determined without knowing the purchase price of the appliance.

37.   A class consists of 10 male and 10 female students. If four students are selected at random, without replacement, what is the probability that all four are male?

(A) $\dfrac{20!}{4!16!}(0.5)^4(0.5)^{16}$

(B) $\dfrac{10!}{4!6!}(0.5)^4(0.5)^6$

(C) $(0.5)^4$

(D) $\dfrac{\left(\frac{10!}{6!}\right)}{\left(\frac{20!}{16!}\right)}$

(E) $P(z > 2)$

38.   A light bulb manufacturer wishes to estimate the mean lifetime (in hours) of its new "long-life" bulb. Thirty bulbs were tested and the lifetime was recorded for each. The mean of the sample was 1,450 hours and the standard deviation of the sample was 150 hours. Assuming all conditions for inference are satisfied, what is the 99% confidence interval for μ, the mean lifetime of the new "long-life" bulb?

(A) $1450 \pm 2.750\dfrac{150}{\sqrt{30}}$

(B) $1450 \pm 2.756\dfrac{150}{\sqrt{30}}$

(C) $1450 \pm 2.750\dfrac{150}{\sqrt{29}}$

(D) $1450 \pm 2.756\dfrac{150}{\sqrt{29}}$

(E) $1450 \pm 0.8389\dfrac{150}{\sqrt{29}}$

39. A statistics class randomly surveyed 200 boys and 200 girls at their school and asked each respondent how many movies they saw in theaters over summer break. The results are shown in the frequency table below. (Example: 15 boys saw no movies.)

Number of Movies	Frequency of Boys	Frequency of Girls
0	15	6
1	31	8
2	32	15
3	37	18
4	20	23
5	18	30
6	17	37
7	13	30
8	11	23
9	3	8
10	3	2

Which of the following graphs is appropriate to compare the number of movies seen by boys and girls over summer break?

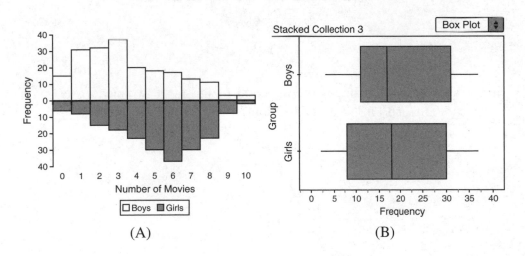

(A)　　　　　　　　　　　　　(B)

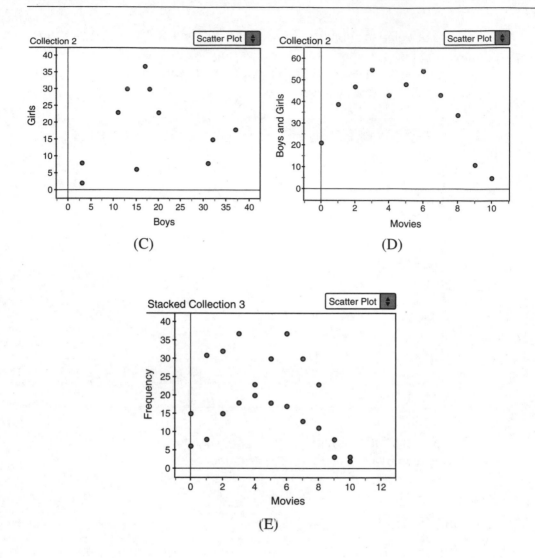

(C)

(D)

(E)

40. Which graph illustrates the rejection region for a two-sided t-test with $\alpha = 0.05$ and 11 degrees of freedom?

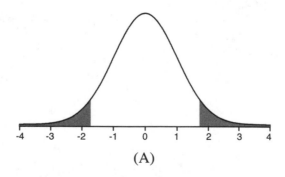

(A)

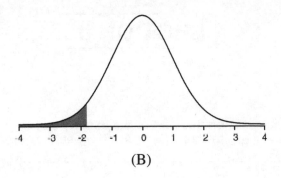

(B)

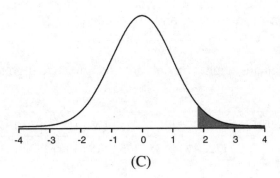

(C)

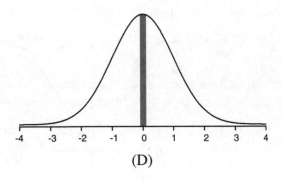

(D)

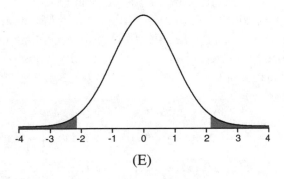

(E)

SECTION II

Part A
Questions 1–5
Spend about 65 minutes on this part of the exam.
Percent of Section II grade—75

> **DIRECTIONS:** Show all your work. Indicate clearly the methods you use, because you will be graded on the correctness of your methods as well as on the accuracy of your results and explanation.

1. Male and female heights (in cm) arc given for two high school basketball teams.

Male	169	170	170	173	174	175	178	180	183	185	185	191	185
Female	163	168	172	173	175	175	178	180	180	183	187	188	

    (a) Construct parallel box-and-whisker plots of the data.

    (b) Construct back-to-back stem-and-leaf plots of the data.

    (c) Compare the distribution of the heights of male and female basketball players.

    (d) What information is more readily available to you using the box-and-whisker plot that is not with the stem-and-leaf plot?

    (e) What information is more readily available to you using the stem-and-leaf plot that is not with the box-and-whisker plot?

2. The physical condition of an SRS of 12 people is tested after 1 year's membership in a health club and is compared to their condition before they joined the club. The trainer at the health club claims that the membership has improved the health of the 12 people. One measure of health is resting pulse rate, with a lower rate generally being better. The data are given in the table below.

Member	Pulse Rate Before Membership	Pulse Rate After One Year Membership
1	78	72
2	89	74

3	92	86
4	80	93
5	103	84
6	77	84
7	83	81
8	81	80
9	113	104
10	96	98
11	100	86
12	88	79

(a) Is there significant improvement in the health condition of a person who has been a member of the health club for 1 year? Give appropriate statistical justification.

(b) Comment on the design of selecting the subjects at the end of the year rather than the beginning.

3. Robin the Hood is competing in an archery tournament. He can score by hitting the target in three different areas: the "bullseye," the "eight" ring, and the "six" ring. Any arrow not striking in those three areas is classified as a "miss." The table below shows Robin's probability of hitting the various target areas and the number of points scored for each area.

Target Area	Bullseye	Eight Ring	Six Ring	Miss
Points Scored	10	8	6	0
Probability	0.20	0.40	0.30	0.10

(a) What are the mean and standard deviation of the number of points Robin scores on any given shot?

(b) A tournament match consists of 25 shots. Assume that each shot Robin takes is independent of the others. What are the mean and standard deviation of Robin's scores for a particular match?

(c) To win the tournament, Robin estimates that he will need to put at least one-fourth of his arrows in the bullseye. Over the course of the tournament, Robin will shoot 400 arrows. What are Robin's chances of winning the tournament?

4.   A dentist has just returned from a dental convention where a new formula of toothpaste with additional fluoride was announced. The maker of the toothpaste claims a reduction in cavities over the existing formula. Before recommending this new toothpaste to her patients, the dentist decides to conduct and experiment of her own. She asks 80 patients to volunteer to be part of the experiment. The experiment will last for 1 year.

(a)   Design the experiment that will allow the dentist to determine if the new formula reduces cavities as compared to the old formula.

(b)   Explain "blinding" in the context of this situation and why it is important for the experiment.

5.   A new housing development is being built where the houses are required to be painted one of two different colors: beige or gray. The developer is interested in finding the true proportion of prospective homeowners that prefer each color, as he wishes to provide house colors corresponding to consumer preference. As prospective customers tour the development, they complete a survey that includes a question on their preferred house color.

Several thousand prospective customers were surveyed; 520 completed the survey. Of those, 286 preferred beige and 234 preferred gray. Assume that the 520 customers are a representative sample of all potential home buyers.

(a)   Is there statistical evidence that prospective customers prefer beige-colored houses to gray-colored houses?

(b)   The prices of paint for the two colors are different. The developer wants to spend the least amount on paint possible. Beige paint costs more than gray paint. What proportion of houses would you recommend be painted beige? Justify your answer.

Part B
Questions 6
Spend about 25 minutes on this part of the exam.
Percent of Section II grade—25

> **DIRECTIONS:** Show all your work. Indicate clearly the methods you use, because you will be graded on the correctness of your methods as well as on the accuracy of your results and explanation.

6. The summary statistics for the number of strikeouts per year for Major League pitcher Roger Clemens are displayed below (through the 2004 season).

N	Min.	Q_1	Median	Q_3	Max	Mean	Standard Deviation
21	74	165.5	209	248.5	292	205.571	55.88

(a) How would you determine if there are any outliers in the data?

(b) If in the next year, Roger Clemens' number of strikeouts is an outlier, how many strikeouts would be considered an outlier in the data? Show statistical methods used to compute the outlier.

(c) Would a year with 240 strikeouts be considered an unusually great year? Give statistical support for your conclusion.

Because of the wide range of strikeout totals, there is interest about whether strikeout totals are related to the number of innings pitched in a season. Below is a scatterplot and least-squares regression model for strikeouts versus innings pitched.

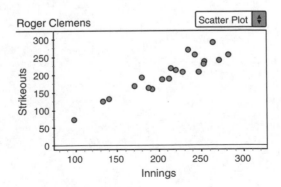

The regression equation is

Strikeouts = – 19.5 + 1.05 Innings

Predictor	Coef	Stdev	t-ratio	p
Constant	−19.51	21.63	−0.90	0.378
Innings	1.05202	0.09863	10.67	0.000

s = 21.69   R-sq = 85.7%   R-sq(adj) = 84.9%

(d) Interpret the slope of the least-squares regression line in the context of this situation.

(e) Interpret the value of r^2 in the context of this situation.

(f) If Clemens's three lowest strikeout years were removed, would the strength of the linear relationship increase or decrease? Justify your answer.

AP STATISTICS

PRACTICE EXAM 1

Answer Key

1.	(E)	21.	(D)
2.	(A)	22.	(D)
3.	(C)	23.	(B)
4.	(A)	24.	(C)
5.	(D)	25.	(E)
6.	(D)	26.	(A)
7.	(D)	27.	(B)
8.	(D)	28.	(B)
9.	(B)	29.	(A)
10.	(C)	30.	(E)
11.	(C)	31.	(A)
12.	(B)	32.	(D)
13.	(B)	33.	(B)
14.	(D)	34.	(C)
15.	(E)	35.	(D)
16.	(E)	36.	(B)
17.	(B)	37.	(D)
18.	(A)	38.	(B)
19.	(D)	39.	(A)
20.	(B)	40.	(E)

DETAILED EXPLANATIONS OF ANSWERS

PRACTICE EXAM 1

SECTION I

1. (E)

The subjects were randomly divided into two groups. The groups can therefore be considered independent of each other. There is no natural matching or pairing between them. The variable of interest is just the number of volunteers in each group that experience the injuries, from which a proportion is easily obtained. So, the experiment will compare two proportions.

2. (A)

Choice A is the law of large numbers. As the sample size increases, the sample statistic will approach the true value of the parameter. Choice B is wrong because the distribution of $\bar{x}$ approaches normal, but never actually *is* normal. Choices C, D, and E are referring to sample data and not the distribution of the sample mean—do not confuse a distribution of a variable with a sampling distribution of a statistic.

3. (C)

The power of a test is $1 - \beta$, where β is the probability of a Type II error. So, $\beta = 1 - \text{power} = 1 - 0.93 = 0.07$.

4. (A)

To compare individuals from different populations, we can compare z-scores. Since $z = \dfrac{x - \mu}{\sigma}$, we have $z_{\text{John}} = \dfrac{113 - 100}{10} = 1.3$ and $z_{\text{Brandon}} = \dfrac{263 - 250}{25} = 0.52$. Since John's z-score is higher, he did better relative to his test.

5. (D)

This is an observational study because we are comparing data between two groups, but is not an experiment because no treatments were imposed on those two groups. The returns are not matched in any way and are a random sample of all forms.

6.   **(D)**

Choice A is a decent interpretation of the interval itself, but it does not tell us what is meant by 95% confidence. Keep in mind that confidence intervals are for the unknown population parameter, not sample statistics, so choices B and C are incorrect. Choice E is a common misconception. Remember that the population proportion is a value already determined, even if we do not know it. It is either in the interval or it isn't. We do not assign a probability to that question.

7.   **(D)**

The given value of R-squared is 70.9%. We know the correlation will be positive because the slope of the line is positive (0.004081), so we take the positive square root of 0.709. This gives us $r = 0.842$.

8.   **(D)**

Choice A has a random digit assignment that gives the correct proportions of each type of ticket, but the choice will not work because the tags are drawn without replacement. So, the proportions of each type of prize change with each pick. Choices D and E are the only ones that allow for this. Choice D is better, since there are 50 tags and 50 numbers. A setup like choice E would require one to remember to throw away two numbers each time one is drawn.

9.   **(B)**

A stratified sample allows the sampler to select a fixed number of people from different subgroups of the population.

10.   **(C)**

The sum of all the individual probabilities must equal 1, and any individual probability must be a number between 0 and 1.

11.   **(C)**

The margin of error for a 95% confidence interval for a proportion is given by $1.96\sqrt{\dfrac{p(1-p)}{n}}$. Since we do not know what p will be before the sample, we use a conservative estimate of 0.5. This value gives the widest possible interval. So,

$$1.96\sqrt{\frac{(0.5)(0.5)}{n}} \leq 0.05 \Rightarrow \sqrt{n} \geq 1.96\frac{0.5}{0.05} \Rightarrow n \geq 384.16.$$ The smallest choice that is greater than this value is 400.

12.   **(B)**

The slope of the regression line is 5.88. Since $\hat{y}$ is measured in percent and x is measured in hours, the units on the slope is percent per hour. Thus, for every additional hour, the score will go up by about 6%. Cause and effect is not a requirement to use a regression equation.

13.   **(B)**

Choice I gives a two-sample t-interval for the difference in means. Choice II gives a matched pairs interval for the mean difference in ratings. Since each student tester actually tasted and rated both drinks, the data are paired. So, the inference procedures in choice I are inappropriate. Choice III is also inappropriate. Seeing if two individual one-sample confidence intervals overlap is akin to adding standard deviations of two variables. The two-sample intervals do the correct procedure of adding variances instead.

14.   **(D)**

When we add independent random variables to form a new one, we add the means and the variances. Do not make the mistake of simply adding standard deviations. The mean of the total time is $36 + 22 + 8 = 66$ seconds. The variance of the total time is $2.5^2 + 1.8^2 + 0.75^2 = 10.0525$. The standard deviation is the square root of the variance, or 3.17 seconds.

15.   **(E)**

A linear regression t-test tests the null hypothesis that the slope of the regression line and the correlation between the two variables are both zero. It is not for calculating an actual value for the slope, but rather to see if the slope might be significantly different from zero. If it is, we can say that some linear relationship exists between the two variables.

16.   **(E)**

Since we have two separate groups of batters, the data are not paired. Scatterplots are only used with paired data.

17.   **(B)**

Doubling every data point changes both the center and the spread of the distribution. The mean and standard deviation are both doubled. Subtracting 5 from each value moves the center of the distribution again, but does not affect how spread out the data are. So, the original mean will be first doubled, and then lowered by 5. The original standard deviation will just be doubled.

18.   **(A)**

If you reject a null hypothesis in favor of a two-sided alternative at some α level, then the value of the parameter in the null will not be in a $(1 - \alpha)$ confidence interval. There is a duality between hypothesis tests and confidence intervals, where a confidence interval represents a set of values that would not be rejected. If the alternative hypothesis were only one-sided, then the test would go hand-in-hand with a 94% confidence interval (so as to have the 3% α on both sides of the interval).

19.   **(D)**

Choice I is wrong—experiments should always be comparing at least two groups. Choice II points out a clear problem with the design—without random assignment of patients to the drugs, we would not know if a difference in proportions among the dosages was due to the stage of the disease or the dosage itself. Choice III shows that while comparing dosages will tell you if there are differences among them, we would not know if the drug was better than nothing at all or some existing drug.

20.   **(B)**

If the claim is that there are twice as many red as each of the other colors, we can use some simple algebra to find the expected count of each color. Let $2x =$ the number of red colors, and $x =$ the number of each of the other three colors. So, $2x + x + x + x = 80$, or $x = 16$. We calculate the chi-squared statistic in the following table:

Color	Observed	Expected	$\dfrac{(O-E)^2}{E}$
Red	37	32	0.78125
Yellow	15	16	0.0625
Green	18	16	0.25
Blue	10	16	2.25
		Total	3.34375

21.   **(D)**

If we change the diameters to z-scores, we can use normal probability calculations.

$$P(12 < x < 16) = P\left(\frac{12-13}{2} < z < \frac{16-13}{2}\right) = P(-0.5 < z < 1.5) = 0.625$$

On your calculator, use the command normalcdf(−0.5,1.5).

22.   **(D)**

The null hypothesis should be an equation using the pre-existing mean. The alternative should be an inequality that tests the new assertion. Since the purpose is to see if the new tread design has a longer life than the old, the direction of the alternative hypothesis is greater than (right-tailed).

23.   **(B)**

The variables would have no association if the proportions of newborns with the condition is nearly the same for mothers that took medication and mothers that did not take the medication. Note that the overall proportion of newborns with the condition is $266/952 = 0.279$. The proportion of newborns with the condition of mothers who took the medication is $21/78 = 0.269$. The proportion of newborns with the condition of mothers who did not take the medication is $245/874 = 0.280$. The key is that the proportions are similar. We cannot look at raw numbers since the number of mothers who took the medication is much different than the number of mothers who did not.

24.   **(C)**

If 63% of the readers are men, then 37% are women. The proportion of readers that will read the book review section is $(0.63)(0.23) + (0.37)(0.12) = 0.1449 + 0.0444 = 0.1893$. Out of the 200 readers, we expect $(0.1893)(200) = 38$ to read the book review. Note that the total number of readers really does not matter.

25.   **(E)**

An inference test on a proportion requires a sample that is representative of the population. People are more likely to go out to dinner on their birthdays, so we have a confounding variable. Any inference procedure is meaningless if conditions are not met.

26.   **(A)**

Using the normal approximation of the binomial, if the player is really still a 40% pitcher, the probability that he will throw 55% of pitches (or more) for strikes is choice A. Choice D is the binomial probability of throwing *exactly* 55% (22 pitches) for strikes if the player is still a 40% thrower.

27.   **(B)**

Since scores were approximately normally distributed, we can change to z-scores and use normal probabilities.

$$P(X > 95) = P\left(z > \frac{95 - 68}{13}\right) = P(z > 2.077) = 0.0190.$$

On the calculator, we use the command normalcdf(2.077, 1000).

28.   **(B)**

We do not know if there is a linear relationship without a scatterplot, but a positive correlation indicates that any linear association between the variables would be positive. Choice A is an interpretation of R-squared and would be true if the value were $(0.58)^2 = 34\%$. The correlation is not a probability as in choice C. A linear relationship can exist for correlations much different than 1. A cause–effect relationship cannot be inferred from an observational study, even if a positive association is indicated.

29.   **(A)**

We can generalize the results of a study to the population if our sample is representative of that population. Two hundred customers in Arizona cannot be representative of all customers in the United States. The sampling frame should have included customers from all states.

30.   **(E)**

Choices A and B are convenience samples. Those who go to grocery stores on Saturday are not representative of the whole district, so those are not good plans. Choice C is a voluntary response sample, which is never a good idea. Choice D involves selection bias or undercoverage, since those without listings in the phone book cannot be picked.

31.   **(A)**

The null hypothesis is always the assumption that there is no significant change. In a chi-square test for independence, the null hypothesis should therefore always be that the variables are independent of each other, or that there is no association between the two.

32.   **(D)**

We are told in the problem that doors are susceptible to damage from the sun's rays and from salty ocean spray. So, the extraneous variables to be taken into account in our blocking scheme are proximity to the ocean, and the side of the house on which the door is made. Blocking scheme D pairs up houses that have both the same proximity to the ocean and the door on the same side of the house.

33. **(B)**

Point A has an actual y-value of around 68. A vertical line through that point shows a predicted y-value on the regression line of around 39. Residuals are calculated as actual value − predicted value = 68 − 39 = 29.

34. **(C)**

We can show that choice A is false by tracing a horizontal line from the 50% marker. This shows that the median is around 38 years. By tracing from the 25% and 75% markers, we see that the quartiles are about 15 and 53 years, so the IQR is about 38. Choice C is true since the distribution would be skewed right. We know this since for higher ages the graph does not rise much—this means there are fewer people at those age levels. Choice D is false—about 40% of people are younger than 30 as compared with about 15% older than 65. Choice E is also false—almost 75% of people are at ages LESS than or equal to 50.

35. **(D)**

A P-value of 0.026 provides significant evidence against the null hypothesis, giving reason to believe that the alternative is true. This P-value would represent the probability of observing data at least as extreme as this sample, if the null hypothesis were true. So, we have sufficient evidence to show the mean to be less than 15. The P-value is not the probability of a Type II error. It is wrong to assign a probability to the mean of being a certain value. The true mean does not change!

36. **(B)**

We need to calculate the expected cost of repairs over the next 5 years for each brand of appliance, and then compare those expected costs to the cost of the extended warranty. The expected cost of repairs from brand M is $350[(0)(0.50) + (1)(0.25) + (2)(0.15) + (3)(0.10)] = \$297.50$. The expected cost of repairs for brand S is $325[(0)(0.40) + (1)(0.30) + (2)(0.20) + (3)(0.10)] = \$325$. Note that only brand S has the warranty costing less than the expected cost of its repairs.

37. **(D)**

The probability that the first selection is a male is $\frac{10}{20}$. The probability that each subsequent selection is male is conditional on the previous selections being male. The probability of the second selection being male is $\frac{9}{19}$, the third is $\frac{8}{18}$, and the fourth is $\frac{7}{17}$. The probability of all four being male is $\frac{10}{20} \cdot \frac{9}{19} \cdot \frac{8}{18} \cdot \frac{7}{17}$.

This can be written as $\dfrac{(10!/6!)}{(20!/16!)}$.

38. **(B)**

A 99% confidence interval for μ with a sample size of 30 is given by $\bar{x} \pm t^*_{29df} \dfrac{s}{\sqrt{n}} = 1450 \pm 2.756 \dfrac{150}{\sqrt{30}}$. Note that choices A and C use the t^*-value with 30 degrees of freedom, and the denominator for choice D uses a sample size of 29.

39. **(A)**

The histograms on the same scale show that girls tended to watch more movies than the boys. The boxplots in choice B used the frequencies as the data instead of the number of movies. Scatterplots are not appropriate since the data are not paired. We just have two separate frequency distributions to compare.

40. **(E)**

A two-sided t-test will have a two-sided rejection region. The t^* critical value for $\alpha = 0.05$ (0.025 in each tail) and 11 df will be 2.201. That is, we will reject the null hypothesis for any t-test statistics greater than 2.201 or less than -2.201.

Free-Response Solutions

1.

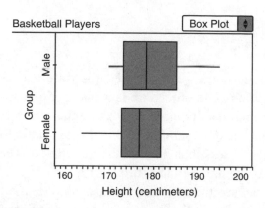

(a)

(b) Heights of basketball players (cm)

	Males		Females	
	9	|16|	38	
	854300	|17|	23558	
	5530	|18|	00378	
	51	|19|		

(c) For these teams, the median height for the male team is only slightly higher than the median height for the female team. The distribution of heights for the males is skewed to the right, while the female team's heights have a slight negative (left) skew. The range is similar for each gender, although the males show more spread among the middle 50% of players than the females do.

(d) Using the boxplots, we can easily see the medians of each data set. We can also quickly compare the range and interquartile range for two distributions. These values would all take some time to calculate with the stemplot.

(e) The stemplot has the advantage of showing us individual data points, and thus giving a more complete picture of the shape of a distribution.

2.   (a) Step 1: State the parameter of interest and a correct pair of hypotheses.If we define μ_d to be the mean difference in pulse rate after one year (after − before), then we want to test the hypotheses

H_0: $\mu_d = 0$
H_a: $\mu_d < 0$

Step 2: Name the inference procedure and check assumptions/conditions.The procedure is a matched pairs *t*-test.We are given 12 paired data points. We are told that these 12 individuals are a simple random sample, and it is reasonable to assume that they represent less than 10% of the population. The 12 differences in pulse rate are −6, −15, −6, 13, −19, −7, −2, −1, −9, 2, −14, and −9. We can see that it is not unreasonable to assume that they come from a normal distribution, since a stemplot of these differences is fairly symmetric and unimodal.

```
 1|  3

 0|  27

-0|  126699

-1|  459
```

Step 3: Calculate the test statistic and *P*-value.

Our test statistic is $t = \dfrac{\bar{x}_d}{s_d / \sqrt{n}} = \dfrac{-4.92}{9.31 / \sqrt{12}} = -1.83$. With 11 degrees of freedom, this gives a *P*-value of 0.047.

Step 4: Interpret the result in context.
Since our *P*-value is small (< 0.05) we have evidence that the true mean difference in pulse rate is less than zero, suggesting a significant improvement in the health condition of a person who has been a member of a health club for 1 year.

(b) Since we only sampled from those who had been with the health club a whole year, we are excluding those who dropped out within that first year. Certainly those dropouts were more likely to not have improved health. This confounding variable suggests that maybe it is not membership alone that leads to increased health.

3.　　　(a) If X is the number of points Robin scores on any given shot, then

$$\mu_x = E(X) = \sum x_i p_i = (10)(0.20) + (8)(0.40) + (6)(0.30) + (0)(0.10) = 7$$

$$\begin{aligned}
\sigma_X^2 &= \sum (x_i - \mu_x)^2 p_i \\
&= (10-7)^2 (0.20) + (8-7)^2 (0.40) + (6-7)^2 (0.30) + (0-7)^2 (0.10) \\
&= 7.4
\end{aligned}$$

$$\sigma_X = \sqrt{7.4} \approx 2.72.$$

(b) For 25 independent shots, we are interested in the sum of scores. We can add the means and variances of the 25 individual shots together to get the mean and variance of the total. We cannot add standard deviations.

$\mu_{total} = 25(7) = 175$ and $\sigma_{total}^2 = 25(7.4) = 185$, so $\sigma_{total} \approx 13.6$.

(c) We want $P(\hat{p} \geq 0.25)$, where $\hat{p}$ is the proportion of the 400 shots that result in a bullseye. We can assume that $\hat{p}$ is approximately normal since of the 400 shots, we have at least 10 expected successes and 10 expected failures. The mean of $\hat{p}$ is given as 0.20 and the standard deviation is $\sqrt{\dfrac{(0.20)(0.80)}{400}} = 0.02$. We can use this formula for standard deviation because the shots are independent of each other. So,

$$P(\hat{p} \geq 0.25) = P\left(z \geq \frac{0.25 - 0.20}{0.02}\right) = P(z \geq 2.50) = 0.006.$$

Robin's chances of winning do not look very good.

4.　　　(a) The dentist wants to determine if the new formula of toothpaste will show fewer cavities than the old formula. The 80 volunteers shall be randomly allocated into two groups of 40. One group will use the old toothpaste exclusively. The other group will only use the new toothpaste. After 1 year, the volunteers will be checked and new cavities will be counted. Then, the number of new cavities for each of the two groups will be compared. A schematic of the design would look like this:

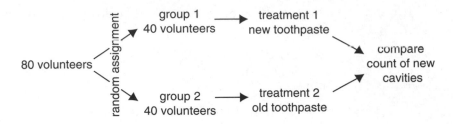

(b) This experiment can be blind if the volunteers do not know whether they are using the old formula of toothpaste or the new. Blinding can be important in eliminating potentially confounding variables. If the group using the new formula knew they had the new formula, they might eat healthier or brush more carefully to help show that the formula works. Then the researchers would not know if fewer cavities were caused by the toothpaste or by this other behavior. The experiment could be double-blind if the dentist also did not know which patients had which toothpaste during the experiment.

5.   (a) The parameter of interest is p, the true proportion of prospective home buyers that prefer beige paint to gray.

The procedure will be a 95% confidence interval for p. (Be sure not to perform a two-sample procedure, since the groups are not independent.) We are asking if the proportion of p is at least 50%.

A 95% confidence interval for the proportion of customer preferring beige is therefore

$$\hat{p} \pm 1.96\sqrt{\frac{\hat{p}(1-\hat{p})}{n}} = 0.55 \pm 1.96\sqrt{\frac{0.55\,(0.45)}{520}} = (0.51,\ 0.59).$$

Since this interval is entirely above 0.50, we can say that customers prefer beige to gray.

An alternate solution would be a test of H_0: $p = 0.50$ vs. H_a: $p > 0.50$. The test statistic for this procedure is

$$z = \frac{0.55 - 0.50}{\sqrt{\frac{0.50(0.50)}{520}}} = 2.28 \text{ and the } P\text{-alaue is } 0.0113.$$

The P-value tells us that if the proportion of buyers preferring beige really were only 50%, we would have seen a result of 55% or more in about 1% of all possible samples. Since this is not likely, we will reject the null hypothesis and conclude that more than half of prospective customers prefer beige to gray. (Note: if you drew the conclusion from a hypothesis test, you will still need an interval in part b.)

(b) By the confidence interval, the proportion of customers preferring beige may very well be as low as 0.51. Since the beige paint costs more, I would recommend only painting 51% of the houses beige. If this is done, we would be quite surprised if there were not enough demand for the beige.

6.   (a) I would determine any outliers by seeing if there are values that are more than 1.5 IQR from the nearest quartile. That is, the outliers are any values less than $Q_1 - 1.5 \times IQR$, or greater than $Q_3 + 1.5 \times IQR$.

(b) The *IQR* of this dataset is $248.5 - 165.5 = 83$. One-and-a-half times this value is $(1.5)(83) = 124.5$. Outliers would be any value above $Q_3 + 124.5 = 248.5 + 124.5 = 373$ and any value below $Q_1 - 124.5 = 165.5 - 124.5 = 41$.

(c) 240 strikeouts is below the third quartile of Roger Clemens's yearly totals. This means that in at least 25% of his seasons, he has had more than 240 strikeouts. There would be nothing unusually great about a year with 240.

(d) The slope is 1.05 strikeouts per inning. For each additional inning pitched, Roger will strike out *about* 1.05 additional batters. Remember, slope is an *average*, not an absolute.

(e) $r^2 = 85.7\%$ of the variability in strikeouts from year to year can be explained by its linear relationship with the number of innings he pitches.

(f) If the three lowest strikeout years were removed, the strength of the relationship would decrease. These three points, having the smallest innings, are the most influential on the correlation and regression line. The rest of the data points form an elliptical shape with less eccentricity.

PRACTICE EXAM 2
AP Statistics

This test is also on CD-ROM in our special interactive AP Statistics TEST*ware*®. It is highly recommended that you first take this exam on computer. You will then have the additional study features and benefits of timed conditions and instantaneous, accurate scoring. See page xx for guidance on how to get the most out of our AP Statistics software.

AP STATISTICS

PRACTICE EXAM 2

SECTION I

Time—1 hour and 30 minutes
Number of Questions—40
Percent of Total Grade—50

(Answer sheets appear in the back of this book)

DIRECTIONS: Solve each of the following problems, using the available space for scratchwork. Decide which is the best of the choices given and fill in the corresponding oval on the answer sheet. No credit will be given for anything written in the test book. Do not spend too much time on any one problem.

---

1. A study was conducted of the relationship between the number of *hours* of television a student watched in the 24-hour period before a statistics examination and the *score* on the exam. The following is a computer printout from a least-squares regression analysis.

Predictor	Coeff	StDev	T	P
Constant	93.052	3.426	27.16	0.000
Hours	–3.2319	0.7819	–4.13	0.001

$s = 7.843 \qquad R\text{–Sq} = 55.0\% \qquad R\text{–Sq(adj)} = 51.7\%$

Which of the following gives the correct value and interpretation of the correlation coefficient for the linear relationship between the test score and the number of hours of television watched?

(A) Correlation = –0.742. The linear relationship between the test score and the number of hours of TV watched is moderate and negative.

(B) Correlation = 0.550. Fifty-five percent of the variation in test scores is explained by the number of hours of TV watched.

(C) Correlation = 7.416. There is a relatively weak linear relationship between the test score and the number of hours of TV watched.

(D) Correlation = 0.742. About 74% of the data points lie on the least-squares regression line.

(E) Correlation = –0.742. For every additional hour of television watched, the average test score dropped by about three-fourths of a point.

2. Allison and her twin sister Brenda both take Advanced Placement European History. Allison is in the morning class while Brenda is in the afternoon class. On the final exam, Allison received a score of 89 where the scores had a mean of 87 and a standard deviation of 3. Brenda received a score of 90 on the same test except that her class scores had a mean of 89 with a standard deviation of 5. Which statement is true concerning the scores of the sisters relative to the scores on their own classes?

   (A) Brenda had a higher score on the test and therefore performed better relative to her own classmate's scores.

   (B) Allison performed better relative to her own classmate's scores.

   (C) Allison and Brenda performed equally as well relative to their own classmate's scores.

   (D) We cannot compare their scores since they are in different classes.

   (E) We do not know how many students are in each class, so any comparison may not be fair.

3. The maker of printer cartridges for laser printers wants to estimate the mean number of documents μ that can be printed on a new high-speed printer. The company decides to test the cartridge on two dozen different laser printers. Each document is identical in number of words and amount of graphics. A histogram of the number of pages printed for each printer shows no outliers and is fairly bell-shaped. The mean and standard deviation of the sample were 3,875 sheets, and 170 sheets, respectively. It can be assumed that the laser printers were a random sample of all laser printers on the market. Which of the following is the correct formula for a 90% confidence interval for the mean number of pages printed with the new type of cartridge?

   (A) $3,875 \pm 1.711 \times \dfrac{170}{\sqrt{24}}$

   (B) $3,875 \pm 1.714 \times \dfrac{170}{\sqrt{24}}$

   (C) $3,875 \pm 1.711 \times \dfrac{170}{\sqrt{23}}$

(D) $3,875 \pm 1.714 \times \dfrac{170}{\sqrt{23}}$

(E) The company should only compute a 95% confidence interval for these data.

4. The manager at an employment agency is interested in knowing if there is a significant difference in the mean ages of executives at two rival computer software companies. This information will help him to best place people in positions at these companies. He was allowed access to the ages of all of the executives. He found a 95% *t*-confidence interval for the difference in the mean ages of all the executives at both companies. There are 86 executives at one company and 79 at the other. Why is the information provided by this interval NOT useful for this situation?

(A) There is too much variation in the length of time the workers have been at their jobs.

(B) There is too much variation in the ages of the executives at both companies.

(C) Both populations of executive ages were used, so a confidence interval to estimate the difference in mean ages is not necessary.

(D) The sample sizes are not the same.

(E) The shapes of the distribution of ages are probably not normal.

5. The owner of a camera shop deals with on average 40 customers per day. Typically, 15% of these customers require repairs to camera equipment. If *X* is the number of customers the owner sees on a given day until one needs repairs, which of the following best describes the probability distribution of *X*?

(A) Binomial

(B) Chi-square

(C) Geometric

(D) Normal

(E) *t*

6. A well-known diet doctor has developed a new formula for a drug that will suppress appetites. The Food and Drug Administration (FDA) wants this doctor to submit research to show that there is a significant difference in weight loss for patients using the new drug versus the old drug. Which

of the following would be the best method to obtain results the FDA is requesting?

(A)   The doctor should randomly choose patients and allow them to select which drug they want to use.

(B)   The doctor should randomly choose patients to take the new drug and ask patients using the old drug how much weight they have lost.

(C)   The doctor should randomly assign patients to two groups: one group takes the new drug and the other group takes the old drug.

(D)   The doctor should randomly assign the patients to two groups: one group takes the new drug and the other group takes a placebo.

(E)   The doctor assigns the new drug to patients who have more than 10 pounds to lose and the old drug to patients with less than 10 pounds to lose.

7.   A least-squares regression model of y on x is $\hat{y} = -73.71 + 27.76x$. The residual graph is shown below.

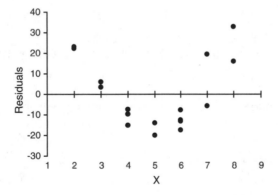

A transformation is made and the residual plot for the model $\widehat{\log y} = -0.1348 + 2.623\log x$ is shown.

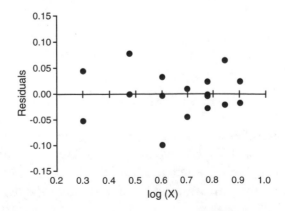

Which of the following is the correct conclusion given the graphs above?

(A) Neither model provides an appropriate relationship between the variables.

(B) There is a linear relationship between the two variables; the first model is more appropriate.

(C) There is a linear relationship between the two variables; the second model is more appropriate.

(D) There is a nonlinear relationship between the two variables; the first model is more appropriate.

(E) There is a nonlinear relationship between the two variables; the second model is more appropriate.

8. In a test of H_0: $\mu_1 = \mu_2$ versus H_A: $\mu_1 > \mu_2$, samples from approximately normal populations produce means of $\bar{x}_1 = 24.3$ and $\bar{x}_2 = 22.4$. The t-test statistic is 1.44 and the P-value is 0.085. Based upon these results, which of the following conclusions can be drawn?

(A) There is good reason to conclude that $\mu_1 > \mu_2$ because $\bar{x}_1 > \bar{x}_2$.

(B) About 8.5% of the time $\bar{x}_1 = \bar{x}_2$.

(C) About 8.5% of the time $\mu_1 > \mu_2$.

(D) The null hypothesis can be rejected since $\bar{x}_1 - \bar{x}_2$ is greater than the t-test statistic.

(E) The observed difference between $\bar{x}_1$ and $\bar{x}_2$ is significant at the $\alpha = 0.10$ level.

9. X and Y are independent random variables. X is normally distributed with mean 100 and standard deviation 8. Y is normally distributed with mean 96 and standard deviation 6. For randomly generated values of X and Y, what is the probability that X is greater than Y?

(A) 0.0401

(B) 0.6554

(C) 0.8273

(D) 0.9772

(E) 1

10. A student studying the commuting habits of students at a particular college wants to compare the mean commuting time for undergraduates with that of graduate students. The question is whether or not there is a significant difference between the mean travel time. Random samples of size 50 are taken from each group and their commuting times recorded. Which would be the appropriate test procedure to use in this situation?

    (A) One-sample z-test

    (B) Two-sample z-test

    (C) Paired t-test

    (D) Two-sample t-test

    (E) Chi-square test of homogeneity

11. The salaries for an electronics company were posted in their annual sales report for all stockholders. The president of the company makes the most money. His salary was mistakenly shown to be $25,000 less than it actually is. Even with the mistake, his salary is still higher than anyone else's. Which statistic did NOT change after the mistake was corrected?

    (A) Standard deviation

    (B) Mean

    (C) Median

    (D) Variance

    (E) Range

12. Which of the following allow inference about a population parameter?

    I. A randomized controlled experiment using volunteers

    II. An observational study using volunteers

    III. A survey of a random sample from the population

    (A) I only

    (B) II only

    (C) III only

    (D) I and II only

    (E) I and III only

13. The least-squares regression line has been computed to predict the yield of a certain variety of roses from the number of seeds planted. The equation is $\hat{y} = -1.05 + 0.385x$. What does the model predict the yield will be for 18 seeds planted?

    (A) About 6

    (B) About 18

    (C) About 50

    (D) About 690

    (E) There are not enough seeds to yield any plants

14. Baccarat is a casino card game between a "player" and a "dealer" where bettors wager on which will have the higher hand. Let Y represent the amount won or lost by the bettor on a single wager on the "dealer." The expected value of Y is –$1.06 and the standard deviation of Y is $92.72. If a bettor places 400 wagers on the "dealer" during the course of a gambling session, what is the approximate probability that the bettor ends up with a positive outcome, that is, makes money?

    (A) 0

    (B) 0.410

    (C) 0.495

    (D) 0.500

    (E) 0.590

15. There is presently a dispute about allocation of federal funds to schools in two regions of a large school district. The director of federal funds, whose spouse works in the West region, has been accused of providing more money to schools in the West region than the East region.

    Two sets of data are gathered by the school board: one listing the amount of money allocated per pupil in the 26 West region schools, the other listing the same for the 26 East region schools. The school board wants to make a graph showing a comparison of the spending between the regions. Which of the following graphs is *inappropriate* to make such a comparison?

    (A) A scatterplot

    (B) Parallel boxplots

    (C)   Back-to-back stemplots

    (D)   Parallel dotplots using the same scale

    (E)   Parallel histograms using the same scale

16.   The number of team flags the booster club will sell at a football game has the probability distribution as shown in the table below.

Number of team flags (X)	5	6	7	8	9	10
$P(X)$	0.20	0.15	0.10	0.25	0.18	0.12

If each team flag costs $8.00, what is the expected amount of money the booster club will take in at a football game?

    (A) $7.42

    (B) $8.00

    (C) $53.15

    (D) $59.36

    (E) $64.00

17.   In the computation of a confidence interval, if the sample size is not changed but the confidence level is changed from 99% to 95%, you can expect

    (A)   an interval with the same width since the mean has not changed

    (B)   an interval with the same width since the sample size has not changed

    (C)   an interval that is wider

    (D)   an interval that is narrower

    (E)   The change cannot be determined from the information given

18.   The makers of Save-More Showerheads claim that their showerhead will save water and therefore save money on water bills. They cite evidence from a recent study where sales records from a home improvement center were used to identify customers who purchased a Save-More Showerhead. Twenty of these customers were contacted and 19 of them indicated that they used less water in the month following the installation of the showerhead. Which of the following statements best describes the claim made by the makers of the showerheads?

(A)   It is valid. The evidence shows lower water use by nearly all customers

(B)   It is invalid because there were not enough customers in the study.

(C)   It is invalid because changes in water usage due to the showerhead are confounded with other variables.

(D)   It is invalid because Save-More should have sold more than one type of showerhead.

(E)   It is invalid because no other brands of showerheads were included in the study.

19.   A significance test is performed with a significance level of $\alpha = 0.05$. For a particular value of the population parameter, the probability of committing a Type II error is computed to be $\beta = 0.13$. What is the power of the test for this situation?

(A)   0.05

(B)   0.13

(C)   0.82

(D)   0.87

(E)   0.95

20.   Alex, Bryan, and Charlie are all playing tennis matches in a tournament against different opponents. Based on previous performances, there is a 0.4 probability that Alex will win his first match, a 0.3 probability that Bryan will win his first match, and a 0.2 probability that Charlie will win his first match. If the chance that each wins his match is independent of the others, what is the probability that none of them wins in their first matches?

(A)   0.024

(B)   0.304

(C)   0.336

(D)   0.700

(E)   0.900

21.   A study was conducted to determine if the proportion of cars in a given area that do not meet exhaust emission standards has changed from 10 years ago when it was 8%. A test of H_0: $p = 0.08$ against H_A: $p \neq 0.08$

was performed with a significance level of $\alpha = 0.05$. Given that the data showed that there was a significant difference in the proportion of cars not meeting emission standards now versus 10 years ago, which of the following statements is true?

(A) The researchers would have reached the same conclusion at $\alpha = 0.01$ and $\alpha = 0.10$.

(B) The researchers would have reached the same conclusion at $\alpha = 0.01$, but not at $\alpha = 0.10$.

(C) A 95% confidence interval for the population proportion p would contain 0.08.

(D) A 90% confidence interval for the population proportion p would contain 0.08.

(E) The correct statement cannot be determined without knowing the P-value.

22. An entomologist is studying fruit flies to determine if eye color is a sex-linked trait. The hypothesis is that a particular generation of flies will be evenly divided between males and females, with eye color—red or white—evenly divided within each gender. The actual results are shown below.

Male, red eyes	Male, white eyes	Female, red eyes	Female, white eyes
19	22	33	26

What is the value of the χ^2-statistic for a goodness-of-fit test on these data?

(A) 0

(B) 0.17

(C) 4.28

(D) 4.40

(E) 27.5

23. A pediatrician is looking over records of female patients, specifically girls aged 10 years. The tallest 10% of girls had heights of 146.0 cm or more, while the shortest 25% of girls had heights of 133.0 cm or less. If the heights of 10-year-old girls are approximately normally distributed, what are the mean and standard deviation of the heights?

(A)   Mean = 136.7 cm; standard deviation = 7.27 cm

(B)   Mean = 137.5 cm; standard deviation = 6.64 cm

(C)   Mean = 139.5 cm; standard deviation = 5.08 cm

(D)   Mean = 139.5 cm; standard deviation = 9.70 cm

(E)   Mean = 141.5 cm; standard deviation = 3.52 cm

24.   The display below shows the cumulative relative frequency histogram of scores from the 20-question math placement examination taken by 40 freshmen upon entering a high school.

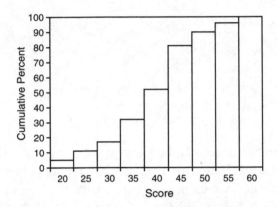

Which of the following is a correct statement based on the information in the display?

(A)   The median score is 30.

(B)   Most students scored above 50.

(C)   No one scored 35 on this test.

(D)   About four times as many students scored 30 than 20.

(E)   There were about equal numbers of students with scores between 50 and 60.

25.   What is the major difference between an experiment and an observational study?

(A)   A treatment is imposed in an experiment.

(B)   An observational study can establish cause–effect relationships.

(C)   There are two control groups instead on one in an experiment.

(D)   Observational studies use only one population.

(E)   Experiments are blinded.

26.   Five homes from a subdivision will be randomly selected to receive 1 month of free cable TV. There are 80 homes in the subdivision. The homes are assigned numbers 01–80 and the random number table below is used to select the five homes. No home may receive more than one free month of service. Which of the following is a correct selection of the five homes?

$$99154 \quad 70392 \quad 23889 \quad 92335$$
$$92210 \quad 70439 \quad 08629 \quad 73299$$

(A)   9, 1, 5, 4, 7

(B)   15, 47, 03, 23, 23

(C)   15, 47, 03, 23, 35

(D)   99, 70, 23, 92, 08

(E)   99, 15, 47, 03, 92

27.   A tire manufacturer claims that the average tire tread will last about 50,000 miles. An automobile magazine does not believe this claim; they believe the tire tread to wear out sooner. If μ represents the true number of miles the tread will last, which of the following pairs of hypotheses is correct to test the claim?

(A) $H_0 : \mu = 50,000$
      $H_a : \mu > 50,000$

(B) $H_0 : \mu = 50,000$
      $H_a : \mu < 50,000$

(C) $H_0 : \mu = 50,000$
      $H_a : \mu \neq 50,000$

(D) $H_0 : \mu < 50,000$
      $H_a : \mu \geq 50,000$

(E) $H_0 : \mu > 50,000$
      $H_a : \mu \leq 50,000$

28.   A fair six-sided die has four faces painted green and two faces painted red. The die is rolled 12 times; let X be the number of times a red face shows.

This procedure of 12 rolls is repeated 100 times. Which of the following plots is most likely to display the distribution of *X* from these 100 trials?

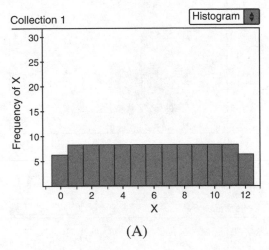

(A)

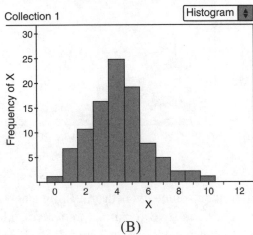

(B)

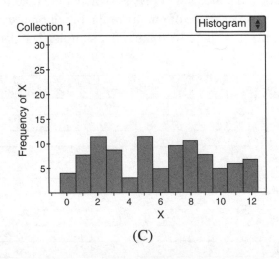

(C)

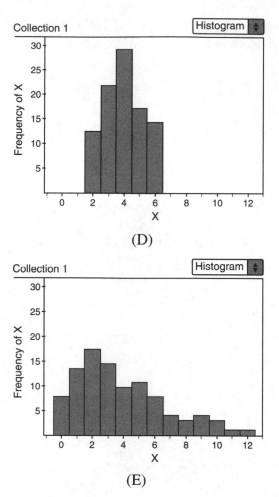

(D)

(E)

29. A group of 10 trained volunteers is taste-testing a new cola for a soft drink manufacturer. There are two formulas under consideration. One of the characteristics the tasters will rate is "spice." Each volunteer is randomly assigned to taste a sample of one formula, rate it on a scale of 1 to 10, and then repeat the procedure with the other sample. The data are given in the table below.

Tester	Spice for Formula A	Spice for Formula B
1	9	6
2	7	5
3	8	8
4	6	6
5	9	7
6	7	7
7	7	8
8	9	7
9	4	5
10	7	6

What is the number of degrees of freedom associated with the appropriate *t*-confidence interval to see which formula has a higher "spice" rating?

(A)   9

(B)   10

(C)   16

(D)   18

(E)   20

30.   The cafeteria manager at a university wants to conduct a survey of 100 students about the quality of food for students that live in the dorms. Which of the following will give the best representation of all dorm students?

(A)   Survey every eighth student that arrives in the cafeteria.

(B)   Survey the first 100 students that arrive at the cafeteria at dinner time.

(C)   Select a random sample of dorm students.

(D)   Hand out a survey to any student who will take the time to answer the questions.

(E)   Put surveys in the dormitory mailboxes.

31.   The parallel boxplots below represent the amount of money collected (in dollars) in a 1-day fundraiser from each of 16 boys and 16 girls in a certain neighborhood in town. Which of the following is known to be true about the data by looking at the plots?

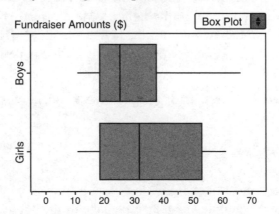

(A)   The boys collected more money than the girls.

(B)   The median of the amounts the girls collected is larger than the median of the amounts the boys collected.

(C) The distribution of the amounts the boys collected is fairly symmetric.

(D) The interquartile range of both distributions is the same.

(E) There is less variability in the amounts the girls collected than the boys.

32. In which of the following instances would the *t*-distribution be used to model the sampling distribution of a sample statistic instead of the *z*-distribution?

(A) Constructing a confidence interval for the population proportion; the population proportion, p, is unknown.

(B) Conducting a matched-pairs hypothesis test for the population mean difference; the population standard deviation of the difference, σ_d, is known.

(C) Constructing a confidence interval for the difference between two population means; the population standard deviations, σ_1 and σ_2, are unknown.

(D) Conducting a hypothesis test for the difference between two population proportions; the population proportions, p_1 and p_2, are unknown.

(E) Constructing a confidence interval for a population mean; the population standard deviation, σ, is known.

33. A poll was conducted to find out the percentage of town residents that would like an additional traffic light on Main Street. Of the 257 respondents, 61% said they would like the new traffic light. The poll had a margin of error of 3%. Which of the following correctly describes the margin of error?

(A) There are more than 3% of the town residents that want the traffic light.

(B) There are less than 3% of the town residents that want the traffic light.

(C) There is most likely more than 3% difference between the percentage in the sample and the percentage of the population.

(D) There is most likely less than 3% difference between the percentage in the sample and the percentage of the population.

(E) About 3% of the town residents did not respond to the poll.

34. A linear relationship exists between the amount of money spent (in thousands of dollars) on advertising and the amount (in thousands of dollars) of sales for a particular shoe manufacturer. The least-squares regression line was calculated to be $\hat{y} = 25.2 + 6.2x$, where x is the money spent on advertising and $\hat{y}$ is the amount in sales. What is the estimated increase in sales (in thousands of dollars) for every $3,000 spent on advertising?

   (A)   6.2

   (B)   18.6

   (C)   21.5

   (D)   25.2

   (E)   43.8

35. The manufacturer of an automobile battery claims that the battery provides at least 900 cold cranking amps (CCA) of current to a car's starter. To maintain this claim, a quality control inspector takes a random sample of 12 batteries each hour and measures the CCA put out by each battery. The inspector will shut down the assembly process if there is evidence that the mean CCA of the 12 batteries has dropped below 900.

   Explain the result of a Type I error in this situation.

   (A)   The manufacturer will decide that the mean battery CCA is greater than 900 CCA when in fact it is 900 CCA.

   (B)   The manufacturer will decide that the mean battery CCA is greater than 900 CCA when in fact it is less than 900 CCA.

   (C)   The manufacturer will decide that the mean battery CCA is greater than 900 CCA when in fact it is greater than 900 CCA.

   (D)   The manufacturer will decide that the mean battery CCA is 900 CCA when in fact it is greater than 900 CCA.

   (E)   The manufacturer will decide that the mean battery CCA is less than 900 CCA when in fact it is at least 900 CCA.

36. The school Parent–Teacher Association (PTA) wants to sample parents about the type of school lunches they prefer for their children. At a recent Open House parent night, the volunteer conducting the survey decided to hand the questions out to every 10th parent that came to the Open House. This sampling method is called a

   (A)   convenience sample

   (B)   multistage sample

(C)   cluster sample

(D)   stratified random sample

(E)   simple random sample

37.   Which of the following residual plots and corresponding residual histograms would indicate that the conditions for inference for the slope of the least-squares regression line have been satisfied?

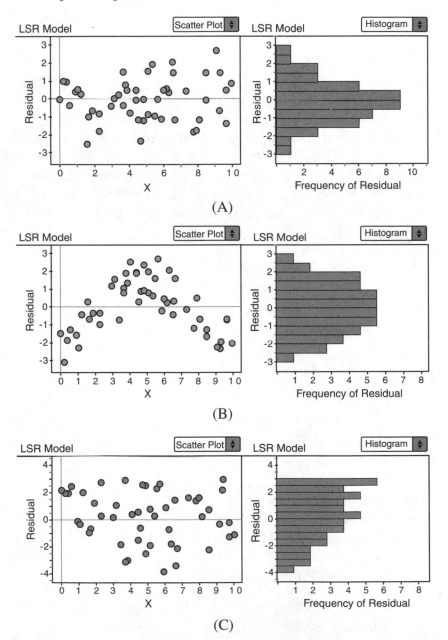

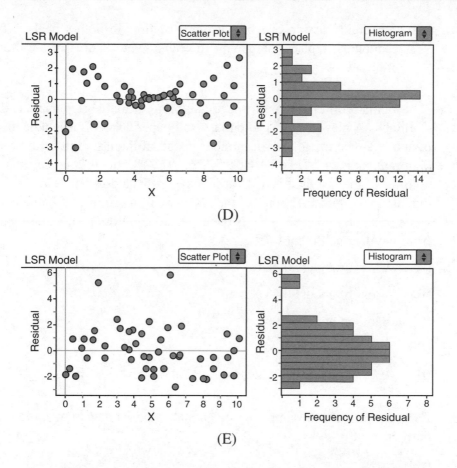

(D)

(E)

38. Researchers from a tire manufacturer want to conduct an experiment to compare tread wear of a new type of tires with the old design. They are going to secure 200 past customers as volunteers to participate in the experiment for 6 months. Tires will be placed on the front two wheels of the cars. The amount of tread wear will be measured after the tires are driven for a designated amount of time. The volunteers will not be able to distinguish between the types of tires on their vehicle. Of the following, which is the best design for this experiment?

(A) Since customers are volunteering their vehicles for the study, let each choose which type of tire they want on their car.

(B) Randomly assign the new type of tire to both wheels on 100 cars; the other 100 cars receive the old type of tire on both wheels.

(C) Put a new type of tire on the left wheel of each car and the old type of tire on the right wheel.

(D) Assign each car the new tire to both wheels. After 3 months, replace them with the old tire for another 3 months.

(E)   Randomly assign one of the types of tires to both wheels. After 3 months, replace them with the other type of tire for another 3 months.

39.   A particular golf club has a form of gambling available to players called "Pulltabs." A player pays $1 to pull a small paper ticket off a spindle, open it, and examine the four-digit number inside. If the last digit of the four-digit number is "1," "2," "3," "4," "5," "6," "7," "8," or "9," the player wins nothing. If the last digit is a "0," the player wins a golf ball. However, if the last two digits are both "0," the player wins a dozen golf balls. If the value of a golf ball is $2, what is the expected gain/loss in monetary value from buying one Pulltabs ticket?

(A)   A loss of about $0.48

(B)   A loss of about $0.58

(C)   A loss of about $0.99

(D)   A gain of about $0.42

(E)   Approximately break even—no gain or loss

40.   For a simple random sample of size n and standard deviation s, the standard error of $\bar{x}$ is

(A) $\dfrac{s}{\sqrt{n}}$

(B) $\dfrac{\sigma}{n}$

(C) s

(D) σ

(E) $\dfrac{s}{\sqrt{n-1}}$

SECTION II

Part A
Questions 1–5
Spend about 65 minutes on this part of the exam.
Percent of Section II grade—75

DIRECTIONS: Show all your work. Indicate clearly the methods you use, because you will be graded on the correctness of your methods as well as on the accuracy of your results and explanation.

---

1. The table below shows science test scores obtained by groups of fourth graders in different classrooms.
    Room A: 65 73 74 75 76 77 79 81 81 82 83 83 84 84 85 88 90 90 92 96
    Room B: 60 64 64 64 65 66 67 68 72 72 73 74 74 76 77 79 80 81 81 83
    Room C: 69 69 73 73 74 75 76 77 78 79 80 81 82 83 85 88 88 89 90 92

    (a) Create three parallel box-and-whisker plots using the same scale. Be sure to label the room letter for each plot.

    (b) Compare the three distributions.

2. The American Red Cross is responsible for collecting blood donations across the United States. The blood they collect can be divided into four types based on its antibodies: A, B, AB, and O. Blood can also be divided into two types by Rh-factor: positive and negative. The most sought-after blood type is O-negative, since it can be given to a person with any blood type or Rh-factor.
    Forty-five percent of Americans have O-type blood; 16% of Americans are Rh-negative.

    (a) If blood type and Rh-factor are independent, what percentage of Americans have O-negative blood?

    (b) The actual percentage of Americans with O-negative blood is 6%. If an American is selected at random, what is the probability that they are type O given that they are Rh-negative?

    (c) If Americans go to a blood bank to donate blood in a manner that is essentially random, what is the mean number of people that will donate blood before someone with O-negative is seen?

3.   In a study designed to investigate the relationship between mathematical reasoning of children aged 10 to 19, a single spatial reasoning test was administered to groups of 25 randomly selected children at each age level. The table below shows the mean scores of the 25 students in each group.

Relationship between Age and Spatial Reasoning Test Score

Group	1	2	3	4	5	6	7	8	9	10
Age	10	11	12	13	14	15	16	17	18	19
Mean Scores	65	63	70	73	81	79	81	80	83	85

Summary Statistics	Mean Age	SD Age	Mean Scores	SD Mean Scores	Correlation
	14.5	3.03	76	7.75	0.929

(a)   Find the equation of the least-squares regression line.

(b)   Calculate *and* interpret the value of r^2.

(c)   The plot of the residuals is shown below. Comment on the appropriateness of the linear model.

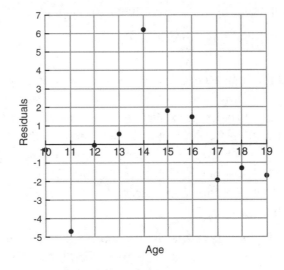

4.   Worldwide Airlines is studying the weights of passengers' carry-on bags. They are interested in how the weights of carry-on bags of pleasure travelers compare with those of business travelers.

Passengers with carry-on bags were randomly selected over a period of several weeks. Selected passengers were asked if their trip was for business or pleasure, and total weight of their carry-on bags measured. The summary statistics are shown in the table below.

Descriptive Statistics

Variable Type	N	Mean	Median	TrMean	StDev
Weights Business	31	33.68	35.00	33.82	4.62
Pleasure	59	8.92	6.00	8.62	7.42

Variable Type	SE Mean	Min	Max	Q1	Q3
Weights Business	0.830	25.0	41.0	30.0	38.0
Pleasure	0.966	0.00	23.0	2.00	15.0

(a)   Compute and interpret the 95% confidence interval for the true difference in average weights of carry-on bags between business and pleasure passengers.

(b)   Dotplots of the raw data are provided. Address whether all conditions for the inference procedure from part (a) have been met.

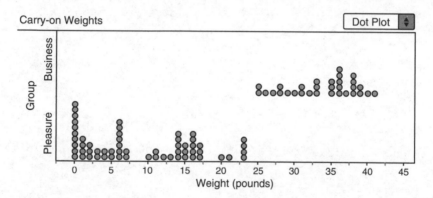

5.   The administrators in a high school are thinking of changing the school's parking policy effective about 3 weeks after school begins. The administration has asked the Student Council to conduct a survey during the first week of school to determine what students who own cars think about the proposal.

The student body has the following distribution. The number of students in each grade who own cars is also provided.

Grade	Freshmen	Sophomores	Juniors	Seniors
Population	500	550	500	450
Own cars	0	180	315	405

The Student Council has decided to survey 100 students. The student body president wants to conduct a simple random sample to obtain the names of the 100 students to be surveyed. The student body secretary wants to use a stratified sampling technique to obtain the names of the 100 students.

(a)   If the student body president's plan is chosen, describe the procedure used to select the 100 students.

(b)   If the student body secretary's plan is chosen, describe the procedure used to select the 100 students.

(c)   What are the advantages and disadvantages of each sampling method?

Part B
Questions 6
Spend about 25 minutes on this part of the exam.
Percent of Section II grade—25

DIRECTIONS: Show all your work. Indicate clearly the methods you use, because you will be graded on the correctness of your methods as well as on the accuracy of your results and explanation.

---

6. The championship series for professional baseball, basketball, and hockey involve two teams playing a series in which the first team to win four games wins the series. We are interested in studying the length of series. Consider two different championship series. In the first series, the two teams are evenly matched. That is, each has an equally likely chance of winning. In the second series, one team beats the other 70% of the time.

    (a) Explain how you would conduct a simulation using a random digit table to determine the length of a series if each team is evenly matched.

    (b) Explain how you would conduct a simulation using a random digit table to determine the length of a series if one team wins 70% of games between the teams.

    (c) Using the random digit table below, conduct your simulations described in parts (a) and (b) five times each. By marking directly on or above the table, make your procedure clear enough for someone to understand. Record the final number of games played in each series.

93015	93615	03413	72295	97291
36377	14756	03768	53840	55333
63186	77781	69103	43259	01660
23825	65704	49525	84121	44856
97187	05901	61053	04173	07717

(d) The results of two simulations of 100 trials each are shown below.

Length of Series	Number of Trials	
	Simulation 1	Simulation 2
4 games	12	25
5 games	25	30
6 games	33	27
7 games	30	18

Identify which simulation, 1 or 2, represents series in which the teams are evenly matched. Explain your reasoning.

(e) Use the distributions in part (d) to compute an estimate of the difference in length of series between two teams that are evenly matched versus a series where one team wins 70% of the time.

AP STATISTICS

PRACTICE EXAM 2

Answer Key

1. (A)		21. (E)	
2. (B)		22. (D)	
3. (B)		23. (B)	
4. (C)		24. (E)	
5. (C)		25. (A)	
6. (C)		26. (C)	
7. (E)		27. (B)	
8. (E)		28. (B)	
9. (B)		29. (A)	
10. (D)		30. (C)	
11. (C)		31. (B)	
12. (C)		32. (C)	
13. (A)		33. (D)	
14. (B)		34. (B)	
15. (A)		35. (E)	
16. (D)		36. (A)	
17. (D)		37. (A)	
18. (C)		38. (E)	
19. (D)		39. (B)	
20. (C)		40. (A)	

DETAILED EXPLANATIONS OF ANSWERS

PRACTICE EXAM 2

SECTION I

1. **(A)**

The output gives us a value of R-squared at 0.550. The correlation, r, is either the positive or negative square root of this value. Correlation has the same sign as the slope of the regression line. Since the regression line has a negative slope (–3.2319), the correlation must be $-\sqrt{0.550} = -0.742$. Correlation tells us the direction and strength of a linear relationship. Correlations between 0.5 and 0.8 (or –0.5 and –0.8) are usually considered "moderate."

2. **(B)**

We can see how one score compares to others in its distribution by looking at its z-score. Allison's z-score is $z = \dfrac{89 - 87}{3} = \dfrac{2}{3}$. Brenda's z-score is $z = \dfrac{90 - 89}{5} = \dfrac{1}{5}$. Since Allison's z-score is higher, she did better relative to the scores in her own class, even though Brenda's raw score was higher.

3. **(B)**

A 90% confidence interval for a mean is given by

$\bar{x} \pm t^*_{n-1}\dfrac{s}{\sqrt{n}} = 3875 \pm 1.714\dfrac{170}{\sqrt{24}}$. Note that 1.714 is the t-score for a 90% confidence interval with $24 - 1 = 23$ degrees of freedom.

4. **(C)**

The manager used the ages of ALL the executives at both companies, so he conducted a census. Inferential statistics use a sample to make generalizations about a population. Since we already have the entire population, there is no need for any inference!

5.　　**(C)**

The variable of interest in a geometric setting is the number of trials until the first success.

6.　　**(C)**

If the FDA wants to see if one of the drugs leads to more weight loss, a randomized experiment is necessary. Choices A, B, and E have no random assignment to groups. Choice D compares the new drug to a placebo, which is not the goal of the study.

7.　　**(E)**

The first residual plot clearly shows a curved pattern. This means that the linear model is not appropriate, and the relationship between the two variables is nonlinear. The second model has a residual plot with more random scatter, suggesting that the model is more appropriate.

8.　　**(E)**

With a *P*-value of 0.085, these results are significant at any alpha level greater than 0.085. Choices B and C are incorrect interpretations of a *P*-value. Choice D is nonsense—a difference in means and a *t*-test statistic measure completely different things. Choice A is wrong, because it takes more than $\bar{x}_1 > \bar{x}_2$ to conclude $\mu_1 > \mu_2$. The difference must be shown that it was unlikely to happen by chance alone.

9.　　**(B)**

Since *X* and *Y* are both distributed normally, $X - Y$ is distributed normally. We calculate $\mu_{X-Y} = \mu_X - \mu_Y = 100 - 96 = 4$ and

$$\sigma_{X-Y}^2 = \sigma_X^2 + \sigma_Y^2 = 36 + 64 = 100. \text{ So } \sigma_{X-Y} = 10. \text{ Now}$$

$$P(X > Y) = P(X - Y > 0) = P\left(z > \frac{0-4}{10}\right) = P(z > -0.40) = 0.6554.$$

10.　　**(D)**

We have two independent samples, so the one-sample tests are out. Scores on exams are numerical variables, so the chi-square test is out. Because we do not know the population standard deviations of the two groups, we use *t*-procedures instead of *z*-procedures.

11.　　**(C)**

The median is unaffected if the largest value of a data set is changed and remains the largest. Standard deviation, mean, and variance are all calculated using every value of the dataset, so they will change. The range is calculated from the largest and smallest values, so it will change.

12.   **(C)**

We can only make inferences about a population parameter if our sample is representative of that population. Using volunteers does not give us a representative sample. We can do inference with data from volunteers in a randomized comparative experiment, but we cannot generalize the results to the population.

13.   **(A)**

The question asks us for a predicted value, so we can substitute 18 for x. $\hat{y} = -1.05 + 0.385(18) = 5.88$. Note that we are asked for the yield. Other questions (like #34) ask for the change or increase in the response variable.

14.   **(B)**

The probability that the sum of all 400 wagers is greater than zero is equivalent to the probability that the average of all 400 wagers is greater than zero. Since we have a large sample size, $\bar{x}$ is approximately normally distributed with a mean of -1.06 and a standard deviation of $\dfrac{92.72}{\sqrt{400}}$. So,

$$P(\bar{x} > 0) = P\left(z > \frac{0 + 1.06}{92.72/\sqrt{400}} \right) = P(z > 0.2286) = 0.410.$$

15.   **(A)**

Scatterplots are only used with paired data. There is no pairing between individual schools in the West region and the East region. All of the other graphs can be used to compare two distributions.

16.   **(D)**

First, find the expected value of x.
$E(x) = 5(0.20) + 6(0.15) + 7(0.10) + 8(0.25) + 9(0.18) + 10(0.12) = 7.42$. The expected amount of revenue is (7.42 flags)($8/flag) = $59.36.

17.   **(D)**

A decrease in confidence level narrows the confidence interval. We gain confidence in capturing the parameter with wider intervals. Note that z^* for a 99% CI tells us it is 2.326 standard deviations wide, but for a 95% CI is only 1.960 standard deviations wide.

18.   **(C)**

The claim from this observational study is seriously flawed. This is because there are countless other confounding variables that come into play when considering reduction in water use. The most obvious one is that people who bought the showerheads were probably trying to save water to begin with, and it cannot be determined if their savings was due to the showerhead or the fact that they may be conserving water any place they can. The sample size is not too small—well-designed studies can be done with small sample sizes. Other types of showerheads, whether from the company in question or a competitor, are not the issue here.

19.   **(D)**

The power of the test is the probability of rejecting a false null hypothesis. A Type II error, β, is the probability of failing to reject a false null hypothesis. So power = $1 - \beta = 1 - 0.13 = 0.87$.

20.   **(C)**

Since their match outcomes are independent of each other, we can find the probability that all three lose by simply multiplying the three individual probabilities of losing. $P(\text{Alex loses}) = 1 - 0.4 = 0.6$. $P(\text{Bryan loses}) = 1 - 0.3 = 0.7$. $P(\text{Charlie loses}) = 1 - 0.2 = 0.8$. $P(\text{All 3 lose}) = (0.6)(0.7)(0.8) = 0.336$.

21.   **(E)**

Choices A and B are false. When you reject a null hypothesis, you would reject it at any significance level α greater than or equal to the one you used, but you cannot know if you would reject it at lower values of α without knowing the P-value. So rejecting at $\alpha = 0.05$ also means rejecting at $\alpha = 0.10$, but not necessarily $\alpha = 0.01$. Choice C is definitely false. A $(1 - \alpha)$ confidence interval represents a set of values for the parameter that would not have been rejected in a two-sided test of significance. Since the null hypothesis of $p = 0.08$ was rejected at $\alpha = 0.05$, then 0.08 would not be in the 95% confidence interval. Choice D is also false; if 0.08 is not in the 95% confidence interval, it cannot be in the narrower 90% confidence interval.

22.   **(D)**

Since the hypothesis is that colors and genders are equally divided, the expected values of each cell are all 25. We need to calculate

$$\sum \frac{(\text{observed} - \text{expected})^2}{\text{expected}}.$$

Observed O	Expected E	$\dfrac{(O-E)^2}{E}$
19	25	1.44
22	25	0.36
33	25	2.56
26	25	0.04
	TOTAL	4.40

23.   **(B)**

First, find the z-scores associated with the 90th and 25th percentiles. $z_{0.90} = 1.28$ and $z_{0.25} = -0.67$. Using these z-scores, we can write the equations $1.28 = \dfrac{146-\mu}{\sigma}$ and $-0.67 = \dfrac{133-\mu}{\sigma}$. We can then proceed to use algebra to solve this system:

$$\sigma = \tfrac{146-\mu}{1.28} \text{ and } \sigma = \tfrac{133-\mu}{-0.67}$$

$$\text{so } \tfrac{146-\mu}{1.28} = \tfrac{133-\mu}{-0.67}$$

$$-0.67(146-\mu) = 1.28(133-\mu)$$

$$-97.82 + 0.67\mu = 170.24 - 1.28\mu$$

$$1.95\mu = 268.06$$

$$\mu = 137.5.$$

24.   **(E)**

The change in cumulative percentage from 45 to 50 to 55 to 60 is fairly constant, indicating that about the same number of students scored 50, 55, and 60. Choice A is incorrect. To find the median in a cumulative graph, trace a horizontal line from 50 on the y-axis. We see that here the median is a score of 40. Choice B is incorrect. The height of the bar at score 50 is a cumulative percentage of about 90. This means 90% scored below or at 50. Choice C is wrong. The bars for scores 30 and 35 are not of the same height, so some students must have scored 35. Choice D is also wrong. It appears that about 5% of students scored 20. Looking at the difference in height between the bars for scores 25 and 30, it appears that about 5% of students also scored 30.

25.   **(A)**

This is the most important difference between experiments and observational studies. Experiments have a treatment imposed but are not always blinded. Observational studies can look at more than one population, but cannot establish cause–effect relationships.

26.   **(C)**

Since homes are assigned two-digit numbers, we will take digits two at a time off the table. If the two-digit number is greater than 80, or one that has already been selected, it will be ignored. So we ignore 99, select 15, select 47, select 03, ignore 92, select 23, ignore 99, 88, and 23 again, and select 35. There are other methods that will work, but all other choices either use one-digit instead of two (A), have repeated selections (B), and/or ignore the 01–80 assignment (D and E).

27.   **(B)**

The null hypothesis is the existing claim. We always look for it to be an equation. The alternative is what someone is trying to show, in this case, the magazine's claim.

28.   **(B)**

The random variable X has a binomial distribution in this problem. The mean of the distribution of X is $\mu_X = np = (12)\left(\dfrac{1}{3}\right) = 4$ and the standard deviation is

$\sigma_X = \sqrt{np(1-p)} = \sqrt{(12)\left(\dfrac{1}{3}\right)\left(\dfrac{2}{3}\right)} \approx 1.6$. The distribution distribution will be clustered near the expected value of 4, and tail off on both sides. Choices A and C are too uniform and choice E is centered too far left. Choice D has too little variability. The simulation from choice B is the best choice. Alternately, you could calculate a few of the binomial probabilities $P(X = 0) = 0.008$, $P(X = 1) = 0.046$, $P(X = 2) = 0.127$. You could get all of the theoretical probabilities at once with the command binompdf(12,1/3)$\Rightarrow$L$_1$.

29.   **(A)**

Since the volunteers tried each formula, the design is matched pairs. Using paired data, the confidence interval will use $n - 1 = 10 - 1 = 9$ degrees of freedom.

30.   **(C)**

The population of interest is students that live in the dorms. Surveying only students in the cafeteria causes selection bias or undercoverage. Choices D and E are guilty of nonresponse or voluntary response bias. A random sample from the population of interest is what is needed.

31.   **(B)**

The medians are clearly marked on boxplots. Choice A is wrong since we cannot know the total amount unless we knew individual data points. The skew on the boys' graph could put their mean above the girls', but we do not know for sure. The interquartile range is the width of the box—clearly more for the girls—so choice D is wrong. Choice E may be true, but we cannot know for sure unless we had the values of the data points.

32.   **(C)**

The *t*-distribution is used for inference on means when the population standard deviation is not known.

33.   **(D)**

The margin of error accounts for using sample data to estimate a population parameter. It has nothing to do with the population proportion itself, so choices A and B are wrong. We aim to be WITHIN a margin of error, not outside of it like choice C suggests. The margin of error is not a nonresponse rate, so choice E is wrong.

34.   **(B)**

We are asked for an estimate INCREASE in sales, not a total amount of sales. We simply need to multiply the slope by 3. Note that the unit of x is thousands of dollars.

35.   **(E)**

A Type I error is committed when rejecting a true null hypothesis. Hypotheses for this situation are H_0: $\mu = 900$ and H_a: $\mu < 900$. So, a Type I error is concluding that μ is less than 900 when it really is not.

36.   **(A)**

At first glance, this scenario may look like a systematic random sample, but it is unreasonable to think that the entire population of parents was present at the Open House. When you sample from the people at hand instead of the entire population of interest, you are doing a convenience sample.

37.   **(A)**

To meet the conditions for inference on slope, there must be no apparent pattern in the residuals plot, so choice B is incorrect. A histogram of residuals should look approximately unimodal and symmetric, with no outliers, so choices D and E are incorrect. Choice C is not good because the residuals plot does not have a consistent spread. The variability of the errors is not constant. Note that as the *x*-value increases, the spread of the residuals tends to decrease and then increases again.

38.   **(E)**

Random assignment must be present, so right away we can eliminate choices A, C, and D. Choice B is a nice design, but E is just better. A matched-pairs design allows for more powerful inference methods.

39.   **(B)**

If we let X = the gain/loss on one ticket, we can find the probability distribution of X. $P(X = -1) = 0.90$, since 9 out of 10 times the ticket will be a loser. $P(X = 23) = 0.01$, since the last two digits will both be "0" 1 out of 100 times. This leaves $P(X = 1) = 0.09$. Note that the possible values of X take into account the winnings and the \$1 for buying the ticket. We need to calculate the expected value of X. $E(X) = 0.90(-1) + 0.09(1) + 0.01(23) = -0.58$.

40.   **(A)**

This is the definition of the standard error of $\bar{x}$. Choice C is the sample standard deviation of x, not $\bar{x}$. Choice D is the population standard deviation of x.

Free-Response Solutions

1.

(a)

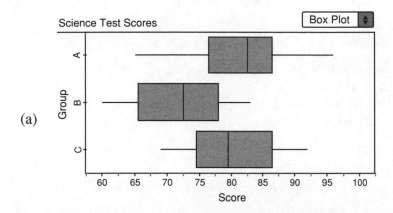

(b) The students from room A had a slightly higher median than the students in room C, 82.5 to 79.5. Room B's scores appear to be far lower than each of the other two, with a median 7 points lower than B, and more than half of its students scoring below the first quartile from each of the other rooms. All distributions are close to symmetric, with room A being slightly skewed left. The biggest difference among the rooms is the spread of scores. The scores in room A tended to spread out more than the scores in rooms B and C, with room A having a higher maximum and a lower minimum than room C.

2. (a) Let O = the event that a randomly selected American has O-type blood.
Let N = the event that a randomly selected American has Rh-negative blood.
If O and N are independent, then
$P(O \cap N) = P(O) \cdot P(N) = (0.45)(0.16) = 0.072$

(b) Given that $P(O \cap N) = 0.06$, we want to find $P(O \mid N)$.

$$P(O \mid N) = \frac{P(O \cap N)}{P(N)} = \frac{0.06}{0.16} = 0.375.$$

(c) Let X = the number of people that donate until someone with O-negative does. X has a geometric probability distribution, with parameter $p = 0.06$. In a geometric probability distribution,

$$E(X) = \frac{1}{p} = \frac{1}{0.06} \approx 16.7 \text{ people.}$$

3. (a) Let X = age level and Y = mean score. The slope of a least-squares regression line is given by $b_1 = r\frac{s_y}{s_x} = (0.929)\left(\frac{7.75}{3.03}\right) \approx 2.376$. To find the y-intercept of the line, we use the fact that the point $(\bar{x}, \bar{y})$ is always on the least-squares regression line.

$$\hat{y} = b_0 + b_1 x$$
$$\bar{y} = b_0 + (2.376)\bar{x}$$
$$76 = b_0 + (2.376)(14.5)$$
$$a = 41.546.$$

So, the equation of the least-squares regression line is $\hat{y} = 41.546 + 2.376x$, or better yet.
$$\widehat{meanscore} = 41.546 + 2.376 \cdot age$$

(b) If $r = 0.929$, then $r^2 = 0.863$. This means that 86.3% of the variation in mean scores can be explained by the regression with age level.

(c) The residuals plot shows a curved pattern. The first three residuals are all negative, followed by four positive ones, and three more negative ones. Such a pattern suggests that a linear model is not best for these data.

4. (a) If μ_B = true mean weight of business passenger bags, and μ_P = true mean weight of pleasure passenger bags, then a 95% confidence interval for $\mu_B - \mu_P$ is

$$(\bar{x}_B - \bar{x}_P) \pm t^*\sqrt{\frac{s_B^2}{n_B} + \frac{s_P^2}{n_P}}$$
$$= (33.68 - 8.92) \pm 2.042\sqrt{\frac{4.62^2}{31} + \frac{7.42^2}{59}}$$
$$= 24.76 \pm 2.60$$
$$= (22.16, \ 27.32).$$

This calculation uses the t-critical value for 95% and 30 degrees of freedom, one less than the smaller sample size.

If done with a graphing calculator, the interval is (22.228, 27.292), and the calculator uses the t-critical value for 85 degrees of freedom.

We are 95% confident that business travelers' carry-on bags are on average between about 22.2 and 27.3 pounds heavier than pleasure travelers' carry-on bags.

(b) We can assume that we have two independent random samples since the passengers were selected randomly over a period of several weeks.

Each sample size is less than 10% of a potentially infinite population, so individual observations are independent of each other. Although the dotplot for weights of bags of pleasure passengers is fairly right-skewed, having a sample size as large as 59 means that the sampling distribution for the sample mean of weights should be approximately normal. The dotplot for the weights of business passengers is skewed left somewhat, but again, the sample size is large enough that the sampling distribution of the sample mean will be approximately normal. Because of this, our conditions for inference, as described in part (a), have been met.

5. (a) The population of interest here is those students who own cars, not the entire student body. Therefore, the student body president should consider only those 900 students who own cars to be the sampling frame. Each of the 900 students should be assigned a three-digit number from 001 to 900; then three-digit numbers are taken from a random digit table (ignoring 901–999, 000, and repeats) until 100 students are chosen. This will yield an SRS of students who own cars.

(b) The sample should be divided proportionally between sophomores, juniors, and seniors. Sophomores are 180/900 = 20% of the students who own cars, juniors are 35%, and seniors are 45%. Therefore, a sample of 100 students should include 20 sophomores, 35 juniors, and 45 seniors. For the 180 sophomores with cars, assign each a number from 001 to 180 and then select 20 numbers at random without replacement. For the juniors, assign numbers 001–315 and select 35 numbers at random. For the seniors, assign the numbers 001–405 and select 45 numbers at random. Note how the stratified sample consists of three smaller simple random samples.

(c) Both methods will give good and unbiased results. The president's simple random sample is a little easier to implement, requiring only one assignment of numbers. The secretary's stratified random sample requires doing this three times. The advantage of the secretary's plan is that stratification will prevent a disproportionate number of one grade from being sampled. The simple random sample does not guarantee proportional representation.

6. (a) In the series where the two teams are evenly matched:

(1) Let the digits 0–4 represent a win for team A, and the digits 5–9 represent a win for team B.

(2) Choose digits one at a time moving across the table, until a team has won four games.

(3) Record the number of games the series lasted.

(4) Repeat this simulation five times.

(b) In the series where one team wins 70% of the time:

(1) Let the digits 0–6 will represent a win for team A, and 7–9 will represent a win for team B.
Steps (2)–(4) will be identical to part (a).

(c) For evenly matched teams,
$$9301593 = BAAABBA = 7 \text{ games}$$
$$615034 = BABAAA = 6 \text{ games}$$
$$13722 = AABAA = 5 \text{ games}$$
$$9597 = BBBB = 4 \text{ games}$$
$$291363 = ABAABA = 6 \text{ games}$$
For team A winning 70% of games,
$$7714756 = BBAABAA = 7 \text{ games}$$
$$037685 = AABABA = 6 \text{ games}$$
$$38405 = ABAAA = 5 \text{ games}$$
$$5333 = AAAA = 4 \text{ games}$$
$$63186 = AAABA = 5 \text{ games}$$

(d) If teams are evenly matched, more games will need to be played to find a winner than when one team wins a majority of games played between them. Simulation 1 has generally longer series than simulation 2; therefore, simulation 1 is of teams that are evenly matched.

(e) The expected number of games for an evenly matched series as determined by simulation 1 is
$(4)(0.12) + (5)(0.25) + (6)(0.33) + (7)(0.30) = 5.81$ games. The expected number of games for a series where one team wins 70% of the time as determined by simulation 2 is
$(4)(0.25) + (5)(0.30) + (6)(0.27) + (7)(0.18) = 5.38$ games. Evenly matched series last, on average, 0.43 games longer.

PRACTICE EXAM 3
AP Statistics

AP STATISTICS

PRACTICE EXAM 3

SECTION I

Time—1 hour and 30 minutes
Number of Questions—40
Percent of Total Grade—50

(Answer sheets appear in the back of this book)

> **DIRECTIONS:** Solve each of the following problems using the available space for scratchwork. Decide which is the best of the choices given and fill in the corresponding oval on the answer sheet. No credit will be given for anything written in the test book. Do not spend too much time on any one problem.

1. In which of the following distributions is the value (median–mean) likely to be the greatest?

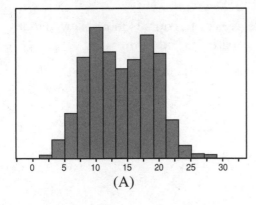

(A)

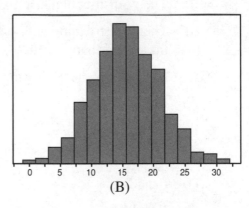

(B)

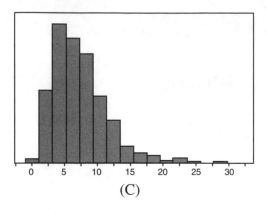

(C)

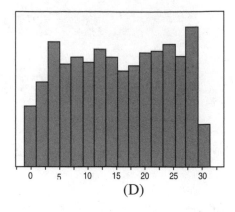

(D)

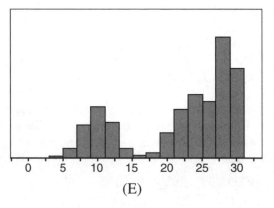

(E)

2. Which of the following statements is (are) true about the χ^2-distribution with k degrees of freedom?

    I.   The χ^2-distribution is left-skewed.

    II. The χ^2-distribution with k degrees of freedom is more skewed than the χ^2-distribution with $k + 1$ degrees of freedom.

    III. The mean of the χ^2-distribution with k degrees of freedom equals k.

    (A) I only

    (B) II only

    (C) III only

    (D) I and II

    (E) II and III

3. When a life insurance company sells a 1-year policy, the policyholder pays a *premium*, the amount of money to own the policy for 1 year. The insurance company promises to pay a *benefit* to the policyholder's survivors should the holder die during that year, but the company keeps the

premium. If the policyholder lives through the entire year, no benefit is paid and the company keeps the premium.

If a policyholder pays a premium of $120 for a 1-year policy with a benefit of $50,000, and the probability of the policyholder dying during the year is 0.0015, what is the expected monetary net loss/gain for the insurance company?

(A)   A gain of about $150

(B)   A gain of about $45

(C)   Break even—no net gain or loss

(D)   A loss of about $45

(E)   A loss of about $150

4.   A botanist is studying the killing of trees by pine beetles in a small square-shaped region of a national forest. Using an aerial photograph of the region, the botanist divides the area into a grid 20 units long by 20 units wide. Forty of the 400 squares on the grid are selected at random, and all trees within those squares are sampled. What type of sampling procedure is this?

(A)   Cluster sample

(B)   Convenience sample

(C)   Simple random sample

(D)   Stratified random sample

(E)   Systematic sample

5.   The segmented bar graphs shown below summarize a survey of high school students about their favorite genre of novel. Based on the graphs, which of the following statements CANNOT be justified?

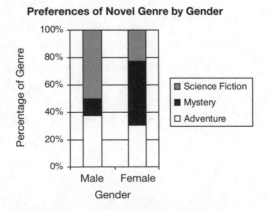

Preferences of Novel Genre by Gender

(A) For every male surveyed that preferred mystery, about four males preferred adventure.

(B) A greater proportion of males surveyed prefer adventure than females.

(C) Females surveyed prefer mystery to either adventure or science fiction.

(D) About half of males surveyed prefer science fiction.

(E) Approximately twice as many males as females surveyed prefer science fiction.

6. An economist has modeled the supply curve for a particular commodity on a supply–demand chart using least-squares regression. The data required transformation to achieve a good linear fit. The equation of the supply curve is $\log(price) = 0.46 + 0.15 \cdot quantity$, where *price* is in dollars per unit and *quantity* is in millions of units. Which of the following is the best estimate of the per unit price for a quantity of 10 million units?

(A) $0.29

(B) $1.96

(C) $3.60

(D) $34.51

(E) $91.20

7. Twenty-six randomly selected packages of multicolored candies were opened and the number of blue candies in each recorded. The sample mean number of blue candies was 7, and the standard deviation was 1. Which of the following is a 90% confidence interval for the mean number of blue candies per package?

(A) $7 \pm 1.706 \left(\dfrac{1}{\sqrt{26}} \right)$

(B) $7 \pm 1.708 \left(\dfrac{1}{\sqrt{25}} \right)$

(C) $7 \pm 1.708 \left(\dfrac{1}{\sqrt{26}} \right)$

(D) $7 \pm 2.060 \left(\dfrac{1}{\sqrt{26}} \right)$

(E) $7 \pm 2.060 \left(\dfrac{1}{\sqrt{25}} \right)$

8.   A media research firm regularly takes random samples of television viewers to determine their viewing habits. Data from last season indicate that the mean amount of time viewers spent watching network programming was 17 hours per week. The research firm wants to determine if the time viewers spend each week watching network programming has changed significantly from last season. It collects data for the first 3 weeks of the current season from a large sample of viewers. The 95% confidence interval for this season's mean weekly watching time μ (in hours) is (16.55, 17.05). Which of the following statements is valid?

(A)   Since more of the interval is below 17 hours than above it, the mean watching time has changed.

(B)   A test of H_0: $\mu = 17$ vs. H_a: $\mu \neq 17$ would be significant at the $\alpha = 0.01$ level, but not at the $\alpha = 0.05$ level.

(C)   It is likely that the sample mean viewing time is less than 15 minutes difference from the true mean viewing time.

(D)   An interval with a higher confidence level than 95% may indicate a change in mean viewing time.

(E)   There is a 95% chance that mean viewing time has not changed significantly.

9.   Doctors routinely use medical imaging for detecting certain physical conditions. One form of imaging detects a particular physical condition in 96% of male patients who have that condition. The scan also gives a negative result in 73% of male patients who do not have the condition. The condition is present in about 20% of males. What is the probability that a randomly selected male who tests positive for the condition does not have it? (Round to four decimal places)

(A)   0.0016

(B)   0.0064

(C)   0.0385

(D)   0.4705

(E)   0.5294

10.   Mary's best time for downhill skiing the challenging course has a z-score of 0.5 as compared to all skiers that are timed on the same course. Which statement best interprets her z-score?

(A)   Mary's time is 0.5 times faster than all skiers timed on the same course.

(B)   Mary's time is 0.5 seconds faster than all skiers timed on the same course.

(C)   Mary's time is 0.5 standard deviations below the mean time for all skiers timed on the same course.

(D)   Mary's time is 0.5 standard deviations above the mean time for all skiers timed on the same course.

(E)   Mary skis worse than the majority of the skiers timed on the same course.

11.   A local food store has cash registers that print red stars on the receipts. A receipt with a star entitles the holder to $5.00 on a future grocery order. The stars are randomly printed on the register receipts and the store claims that 10% of the receipts have a star.

Jane has not had a star printed on her receipts for the past 6 months. She doubts the validity of the store's claim and decides to stand outside the store and ask the next 100 customers if they have a star on their receipts. Seven of the 100 customers have stars. Assuming that the 100 customers' receipts are a random sample of all receipts, what conclusion should Jane reach?

(A)   There is evidence to dispute the store's claim because less than 10% of the sampled receipts had red stars.

(B)   There is evidence to dispute the store's claim at a significance level of 0.01.

(C)   There is evidence to dispute the store's claim at a significance level of 0.05.

(D)   There is evidence to dispute the store's claim at a significance level of 0.10.

(E)   There is insufficient evidence to dispute the store's claim at any commonly used significance level.

12. The maker of a popular pain reliever conducted an experiment to see if there were benefits from adding calcium to their formula. Five hundred people who experience regular headaches took part in the experiment. Two groups were randomly formed; one group took the pain reliever with the added calcium while the other group took the original formulation. The people in the group that took the new formula with calcium reported a shorter average waiting time for pain relief than the people with the original formulation. Which of the following is (are) true concerning the results of this experiment?

   I.   We cannot conclude a cause–effect relationship between the presence of calcium and waiting time for pain relief.

   II.   The addition of calcium to pain relievers may reduce the time to experience pain relief.

   III.   There were not enough subjects in the experiment to draw a conclusion.

   (A) I only

   (B) II only

   (C) III only

   (D) I and II only

   (E) I and III only

13. The weights of young-of-the-year moose are normally distributed with a mean of 430 pounds and a standard deviation of 42 pounds. Between what two values is the middle half of all young-of-the-year moose weights?

   (A) 304 pounds to 556 pounds

   (B) 346 pounds to 514 pounds

   (C) 388 pounds to 472 pounds

   (D) 402 pounds to 458 pounds

   (E) 409 pounds to 451 pounds

14. The equation of a least-squares regression line is $\hat{y} = 3.34x - 7.012$. One of the points in the scatter plot was (5, 10). Which is the residual for this x-value?

   (A) −10.388

   (B) −0.312

(C)   0.312

(D)   9.688

(E)   10.388

15. A study is conducted to estimate the mean family income in the eastern half of North Dakota by the construction of a 90% confidence interval. A pilot survey of 10 families and their income gives a sample standard deviation of $800. Assuming that the population standard deviation is also about $800, which of the following is the smallest sample size that will assure that the confidence interval's margin of error is at most $100?

(A)   15

(B)   55

(C)   175

(D)   250

(E)   425

16. The only way to ensure a cause–effect relationship between two variables is to

(A)   conduct an observational study

(B)   conduct a census

(C)   conduct a study with volunteers

(D)   conduct a survey

(E)   conduct an experiment

17. The Stroop Effect is a psychological phenomenon where in naming the physical color of a word, the word itself can "interfere" with the process of naming the color of the word. For example, the word "red" is colored blue and a person asked to describe the color of the word will often say "red." An experiment was done with 10 people comparing the time (in seconds) taken to say colors of words that were colored differently than the names of the words, and the time taken to say the colors of colored rectangles. What is the number of degrees of freedom that would be used for the significance test to see if there is a difference in the mean time it takes to read the cards?

Person	Rectangles	Words
1	5	6
2	3	5
3	3	7
4	4	6
5	6	11
6	5	9
7	3	6
8	4	5
9	5	12
10	6	9

(A)   8

(B)   9

(C)   10

(D)   16

(E)   20

18. It is thought that 40% of all students that take Physics also take Chemistry at some point in their high school careers. A simulation is designed to estimate the probability that 10 randomly selected students who take Physics will take Chemistry. The digits 0 through 9 will be used for the simulation. Which of the following assignments of digits would best model this simulation?

   (A)   Assign "1, 2, 3, and 4" as taking Chemistry and "5, 6, 7, 8, and 9" as not taking Chemistry.

   (B)   Assign "0, 1, 2, 3, and 4" as taking Chemistry and "5, 6, 7, 8, and 9" as not taking Chemistry.

   (C)   Assign "0, 1, 2, and 3" as taking Chemistry and "4, 5, 6, 7, 8, and 9" as not taking Chemistry.

   (D)   Assign "4" as taking Chemistry and "1, 2, and 3" as not taking Chemistry.

   (E)   Assign "4" as taking Chemistry and "0, 1, 2, 3, 5, 6, 7, 8, and 9" as not taking Chemistry.

19. A team of biologists has collected data for an experiment on caloric intake of 28 lab rats. They used a one-sample *t*-test with $\alpha = 0.05$ and chose to run a two-sided test. Which of the following is the smallest possible test statistic that would reject the null hypothesis in favor of the alternative hypothesis?

    (A) 1.253

    (B) 1.701

    (C) 1.703

    (D) 2.012

    (E) 2.301

20. The populations of two large private schools were studied, Hillside Academy and Franklin School. The graph below shows the cumulative percentage of students in the two schools, both of which offer grades kindergarten through 12th grade. (On the graph, kindergarten is noted as grade 0.)

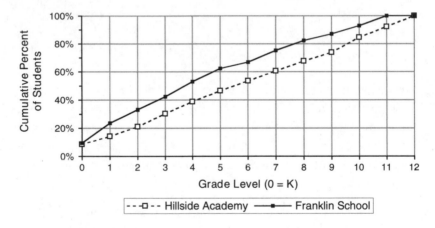

    Which of the following statements is a correct conclusion based on the graph?

    (A) More students attend Franklin School than Hillside Academy.

    (B) Franklin School has more 12th grade students than kindergarten students.

    (C) About half of the combined school population is at second grade and below.

    (D) Franklin School students are on average in earlier grades than students at Hillside Academy.

(E)   The number of students at Hillside Academy varies greatly from grade to grade.

21.   A telephone survey of households will be conducted to determine how many vehicles residents of each household own. Which is NOT a possible source of bias for this survey technique?

(A)   Households with unlisted phone numbers may not be called.

(B)   Households with a single resident most likely have only one car.

(C)   Households whose residents who have caller I.D. may not answer the phone.

(D)   Households without phones will not be called.

(E)   Households with residents who only have cell phones may not be called.

22.   A group of 416 kindergarten children was randomly selected from public schools in a large midwestern city. Each student was simultaneously presented with two different lollipops, one with a blue wrapper and one with a red wrapper, and chose which one they liked the best. The results are shown below.

Blue Wrapper	Red Wrapper
228	188

Which of the following is the 95% confidence interval for the proportion of kindergarten students in the population who prefer the Blue Wrapper lollipops?

(A) $\dfrac{188}{416} \pm 1.645\sqrt{\dfrac{\left(\frac{228}{416}\right)\left(\frac{188}{416}\right)}{416}}$

(B) $\dfrac{228}{416} \pm 1.645\sqrt{\dfrac{\left(\frac{228}{416}\right)\left(\frac{188}{416}\right)}{416}}$

(C) $\dfrac{188}{228} \pm 1.960\sqrt{\dfrac{\left(\frac{228}{416}\right)\left(\frac{188}{416}\right)}{416}}$

(D) $\dfrac{188}{416} \pm 1.960\sqrt{\dfrac{\left(\frac{228}{416}\right)\left(\frac{188}{416}\right)}{416}}$

(E) $\dfrac{228}{416} + 1.960\sqrt{\dfrac{\left(\frac{228}{416}\right)\left(\frac{188}{416}\right)}{416}}$

23. The cost of production of a product at a manufacturing plant can be modeled by the equation $\hat{C} = 7200 + 585n$, where n is the number of units of the product produced in a month and $\hat{C}$ is the estimated total cost of producing the product in dollars. What is the estimated increase in cost that corresponds to an increase in production of 100 units per month?

(A) $585

(B) $7,200

(C) $7,785

(D) $58,500

(E) $65,700

24. Suppose on any given day at school 0.15 of the English classes go to the computer lab, 0.10 of the Science classes go to the computer lab, and 0.04 of English and Science classes go to the computer lab. What is the probability on any given school day that either an English or Science class will go to the computer lab?

(A) 0.15

(B) 0.19

(C) 0.21

(D) 0.25

(E) 0.29

25. A hypothesis test for population proportion H_0: $p = 0.35$ versus H_a: $p > 0.35$ is conducted with a significance level of $\alpha = 0.05$. If the alternative hypothesis is true, for which of the following values of p will the power of the test be greatest?

(A) 0.25

(B) 0.32

(C) 0.35

(D) 0.40

(E) 0.42

26. Two independent random variables X and Y have standard deviations of $\sigma_x = 7$ and $\sigma_y = 10$. Compute σ_{X-Y}.

    (A) 17

    (B) 149

    (C) $\sqrt{3}$

    (D) $\sqrt{17}$

    (E) $\sqrt{149}$

27. A student recently took a standardized mathematics exam to measure academic knowledge. This exam is used to qualify candidates for admission to a college mathematics program. The student's exam results were given as follows:

Raw Score	Percentile
45	90

    Based on the test results shown, which of the following statements must be true?

    (A) There were 50 questions on the test.

    (B) The student answered 90% of the questions correctly.

    (C) The student scored higher than 90% of all those who took the test.

    (D) Each question was worth 2 points.

    (E) There is a 90% chance that the student will be accepted into the math program.

28. A popular women's magazine wants to survey its readers about some fashion ideas. Their questionnaire is included in the November issue of the magazine. Of the 622 respondents to the survey, 73% said they prefer to wear slacks to work. Before reporting back to their readers, they run a confidence interval on the true proportion of women that wear slacks to work. Which assumption/condition for confidence intervals is violated in this case?

    (A) There are no violations for this interval.

    (B) The population is at least 10 times the sample size is violated.

    (C) The data are from an SRS of the population of interest is violated.

    (D) $n\hat{p} \geq 10$ is violated.

    (E) $n(1 - \hat{p}) \geq 10$ is violated.

29. Which of the following statements is NOT true about the design of an experiment?

    (A) A purpose of blocking is to test the effect of outside variables.

    (B) A purpose of blocking is to reduce undesired variability.

    (C) A purpose of control groups is to provide a basis for comparison with other treatments.

    (D) A purpose of randomization is to even out variability due to lurking variables.

    (E) A purpose of randomization is to reduce bias due to confounding variables.

30. In a particular extended family, the correlation between the heights of mothers X and heights of their daughters Y when measured in inches is 0.7. The data are changed to centimeters by multiplying the heights in inches by 2.5. What is the correlation of the heights when measured in centimeters?

    (A) 0.112

    (B) 0.28

    (C) 0.7

    (D) 1.75

    (E) It cannot be determined from the information given.

31. A random sample of students was surveyed and each was asked to provide their grade level and in which location they eat lunch each day. The results are summarized in the table below.

	Large Cafeteria	Small Cafeteria	Student Center	Total
Freshman	22	87	16	125
Sophomore	30	75	25	130
Junior	75	10	42	127
Senior	110	0	36	146
Total	237	172	119	528

    If a chi-square test is performed to determine if grade level is independent of eating location, which of the following is the expected cell count for juniors that eat in the student center?

(A) $\dfrac{75 \times 119}{528}$

(B) $\dfrac{127 \times 75}{528}$

(C) $\dfrac{127 \times 119}{528}$

(D) $\dfrac{127 \times 172}{119}$

(E) $\dfrac{127 \times 172}{528}$

32. In each of the millions of boxes of Jolly Cereal there is a toy. There are five different kinds of toys of which Jimmy has four. Jimmy wants to know many more boxes he would expect to buy before he gets the fifth kind of toy.

    Why is this NOT a binomial calculation?

    (A) There are five types of toys.

    (B) The number of boxes he will buy is not fixed.

    (C) The probability of getting the fifth type of toy is not 0.5.

    (D) The probability of getting the fifth toy is effectively constant.

    (E) The five types of toys are not known to be equally distributed.

33. The student activity director at a local high school claims that the proportion p of seniors that attend basketball games is 0.35. The seniors claim more than 35% are coming to games. If the student activity director wants to conduct a test of significance to evaluate the seniors' claim, which of the following hypotheses would be used?

    (A) H_0: $p \neq 0.35$, H_a: $p = 0.35$

    (B) H_0: $p = 0.35$, H_a: $p \neq 0.35$

    (C) H_0: $p = 0.35$, H_a: $p > 0.35$

    (D) H_0: $p < 0.35$, H_a: $p = 0.35$

    (E) H_0: $p = 0.35$, H_a: $p < 0.35$

34. A random sample is taken from an infinite population whose distribution is highly skewed toward smaller values. If random sampling from the

population is conducted, which of the following is true about the sampling distribution of the sample mean?

I. As the sample size increases, the mean of the sampling distribution approaches the population mean.

II. The standard deviation of the sampling distribution will be larger than the standard deviation of the population.

III. The sampling distribution is skewed for small samples, but becomes more normal-shaped for larger samples.

(A) I only

(B) III only

(C) I and II only

(D) II and III only

(E) I, II, and III

35. A television advertisement is promoting a set of videotapes that will teach gamblers to win big money at the game Roulette. Calculations show that the probability of winning a certain bet in Roulette to be 0.474. The advertisement claims that a person using the program would win much more often than chance would dictate. If a group of interested gamblers tests this claim by making 100 independently placed bets, and 60 of those bets are won, which of the following represents the P-value for the appropriate test?

(A) $P\left(z > \dfrac{0.60 - 0.474}{\sqrt{\frac{(0.60)(0.40)}{100}}}\right)$

(B) $P\left(z > \dfrac{0.60 - 0.474}{\sqrt{\frac{(0.474)(0.526)}{100}}}\right)$

(C) $2 \cdot P\left(z > \dfrac{0.60 - 0.474}{\sqrt{\frac{(0.60)(0.40)}{100}}}\right)$

(D) $\dbinom{100}{60}(0.474)^{60}(0.526)^{40}$

(E) $\dbinom{100}{60}(0.60)^{60}(0.40)^{40}$

36. A set of residuals is created for a least-squares regression model. A negative residual indicates that the regression model

    (A) only predicts negative values

    (B) has overpredicted the explanatory variable

    (C) has overpredicted the response variable

    (D) has underpredicted the explanatory variable

    (E) has underpredicted the response variable

37. In a study of how fast students can write their names, 29 students recorded the length of each of their first names (in letters) and the time (in seconds) that it took to write 20 repetitions of their first name. A line satisfactorily represents the relationship between name length and writing time. The results of the regression analysis are given below.

    Regression Analysis

    The regression equation is

    Time = 29.3 + 5.42 NameLength

Predictor	Coef	Stdev	t-ratio	p
Constant	29.284	4.273	6.85	0.000
NameLength	5.4211	0.7573	7.16	0.000

    s = 5.219   R-sq = 64.7%   R-sq(adj) = 63.4%

    Which of the following should be used to compute a 95% confidence interval for the slope of the least-squares regression line?

    (A) $5.4211 \pm 2.052 \times 0.7573$

    (B) $5.4211 \pm 7.160 \times 5.219$

    (C) $5.4211 \pm 2.045 \times 0.7573$

    (D) $29.284 \pm 2.052 \times 4.273$

    (E) $29.284 \pm 1.703 \times 4.273$

38. The local scout troop is selling raffle tickets as a fundraiser. They have 500 tickets to sell and the scouts charge $5.00 for each ticket. The distribution of the prizes, X, is shown below.

X	$0	$10	$50	$100	$200
Number of winning tickets	461	30	6	2	1

If you purchase a ticket, what is the net expected gain/loss for your ticket?

(A) Gain of $2.00

(B) Gain of $3.00

(C) Loss of $2.00

(D) Loss of $3.00

(E) Loss of $5.00

39. An agricultural agency is studying ground squirrels and their effects on rangeland where cattle feed. The agency wants to know the mean number of squirrels per acre in a large area of rangeland. Several one-acre plots are randomly selected and the number of squirrels on each plot is determined through a variety of methods. A 95% confidence interval for the mean number of squirrels per acre is computed to be (3, 6).
Which of the following is the correct interpretation of the interval?

(A) In repeated sampling, 95% of the intervals constructed will capture the true mean number of squirrels per acre of rangeland.

(B) The agency is 95% confident that there are between 3 and 6 squirrels on each acre of rangeland.

(C) The agency is 95% confident that the mean number of squirrels per acre of rangeland is between 3 and 6.

(D) There is a 95% chance that the agency will find between 3 and 6 squirrels on any particular acre of rangeland.

(E) The agency is 95% confident that the mean number of squirrels per acre of rangeland in their sample is between 3 and 6.

40. A large telecommunications company wants to improve employee productivity. Studies have shown that exercise could help. The company decides to offer two different types of programs during the workday. One program is an aerobics class for 30 minutes; the other is a weight room session for 30 minutes. Employees can choose program in which they want to participants. If the company truly wants to find out if exercise during the day improves employee productivity, what else is needed in this study?

I. A third type of exercise group, as more treatments yield more reliable information.

II. A control group that does not exercise in order to determine if an increase in productivity was actually due to one of the treatments.

III. Random assignment of employees to treatment groups, instead of allowing employees to choose.

(A) I only

(B) II only

(C) III only

(D) I and III only

(E) II and III only

SECTION II

Part A
Questions 1–5
Spend about 65 minutes on this part of the exam.
Percent of Section II grade—75

DIRECTIONS: Show all your work. Indicate clearly the methods you use, because you will be graded on the correctness of your methods as well as on the accuracy of your results and explanation.

---

1. A computer software company employs a total of 25 persons. The following figures show their annual gross earnings:

One manager	$142,500
One senior analyst	$127,500
Four programmers	$45,000 each
Five salespersons	$31,500 each
Fourteen others	$27,000 each

   ("others" include dispatchers, secretaries, receptionists, etc.)

   (a) In a dispute between the company and the workers, which measure of center (mean or median) would the union representatives quote to support their claim that the company is "robbing" the workers? Use statistical support in your response.

   (b) Which measure of center (mean or median) would the company's attorney use to suggest that the company pays highly competitive salaries? Use statistical support in your response.

   (c) If the manager decided to increase the salaries for the other employees including him/herself by $3,000 each, how would the mean, median, and standard deviation of the salaries change?

2. A government watchdog group is studying the relationship between the open market selling price of houses in a rural area and the assessed value of those houses as determined by the county assessor. The table below shows the selling prices and assessed values of 10 homes recently sold in the area.

Selling Price (Thousands of dollars)	Assessed Value (Thousands of dollars)
66	56
115	84
98	73
124	81
84	64
97	59
108	77
52	47
86	62
145	94

(a)   Construct a scatterplot of the assessed value vs. selling price.

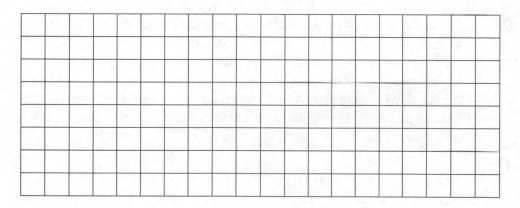

(b)   Describe the association between the assessed value of homes as determined by the county assessor and their selling price on the open market.

The computer printout below gives a summary of the least-squares regression model of the assessed value on the selling price.

Regression Analysis

Predictor	Coef	Stdev	T	P
Constant	20.354	5.601	3.63	0.007
Selling Price	0.50611	0.05551	9.12	0.000

s = 4.562   R–Sq = 91.2%   R–Sq(adj) = 90.1%

(c)   Write the equation of the least-squares regression line, and interpret the slope of the line in the context of the situation.

(d)   Interpret the value of r^2 in the context of the situation.

3.   A drug company has developed a new blood pressure medication that needs to go to clinical trials. The mean reduction in systolic blood pressure with the current medication is 10 points. The company wishes to determine if the mean reduction of systolic blood pressure with the new medication is greater than the current medication.

(a)   Define the parameter of interest.

(b)   Write the null and alternative hypotheses.

(c)   Explain the Type I error in the context of the situation and the consequences of committing this error.

(d)   Explain the Type II error in the context of the situation and the consequences of committing this error.

4.   A nursery grows rose bushes. A new fertilizer is on the market and the gardener in charge of the roses wants to determine if the roses will have more blooms than with the fertilizer he has been using. The rose bushes are planted in a rectangular plot along the east side of the nursery building; the south end of the plot receives more sunlight than the north end. Design an experiment using both brands of fertilizer that takes into account the variation in sunlight.

5.   It rains on Paradise Island on 40% of days. The chance of rain is independent from day to day. A travel agent is signing people up to go on a 5-day tour of the island. She wants to know the chances of getting at least two consecutive days of rain at any time during the 5 days. To determine this, you decide to do a simulation.

(a)   Describe how you would use a random digit table to simulate whether at least two consecutive days of rain occur over a 5-day period.

(b)   Conduct 10 trials of your simulation on the random digit table below. By marking directly on or above the table, make your procedure clear enough for someone to understand.

(c)   Use the results from part (b) to estimate the probability of at least two consecutive days of rain in a 5-day period.

```
00233   54830   39108   57935   28715
08996   19223   39280   22222   31405
71405   49953   30324   80154   39490
96080   51290   33843   62322   80262
95945   04834   37520   37866   11112
93015   93615   03413   72295   97291
36377   14756   03768   53840   55333
63186   77781   69103   43259   01660
```

Part B
Questions 6
Spend about 25 minutes on this part of the exam.
Percent of Section II grade—25

> **DIRECTIONS:** Show all your work. Indicate clearly the methods you use, because you will be graded on the correctness of your methods as well as on the accuracy of your results and explanation.

6. A pineapple grower has planted pineapple trees on a hillside. To minimize erosion, he carved the hillside into a terrace of 10 levels, like the seats in a stadium. (See the diagram below.) Each of the levels holds 50 trees, giving the grower a total of 500 pineapple trees. Each tree has produced at least one pineapple.

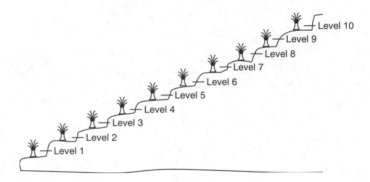

Because certain levels may get different amounts of water due to rainfall runoff, the size of pineapples may vary due to the level. The grower wants to determine if there is a relationship between the weights of pineapples and the terrace level. He will do this by taking a random sample of pineapples from the trees on the hillside. The grower wants to limit his sample to 50 pineapples, taking only one pineapple from each of the 50 selected trees.

(a) Describe an appropriate method for determining which trees will be sampled.

(b) If a particular selected tree has more than one pineapple, how should a pineapple be chosen?

The grower averages the weights of the pineapples from each level and plots the averages versus level number. The results are shown in the table below. A scatterplot and regression analysis are also provided.

Level	1	2	3	4	5	6	7	8	9	10
Mean Weight (g)	780	719	721	739	691	656	701	701	642	640

The regression equation is

Mean Weight = 767 − 12.4 Level

Predictor	Coef	StDev	T	P
Constant	767.27	17.05	44.99	0.000
Level	−12.412	2.749	−4.52	0.002

S = 24.96   R–Sq = 71.8%   R–Sq(adj) = 68.3%

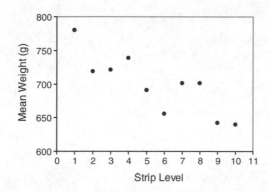

(c)   Interpret the slope of the least-squares regression line in context.

(d)   Compute and interpret a 95% confidence interval for the average change in mean pineapple weight per level.

(e)   The grower averaged the weights of the pineapples from each level before creating the least-squares model. If he had used the individual pineapple weights instead of the mean for each level, would the r^2 value be smaller or larger? Explain.

AP STATISTICS

PRACTICE EXAM 3

Answer Key

1. (E)	21. (B)
2. (E)	22. (E)
3. (B)	23. (D)
4. (A)	24. (C)
5. (E)	25. (E)
6. (E)	26. (E)
7. (C)	27. (C)
8. (C)	28. (C)
9. (E)	29. (A)
10. (D)	30. (C)
11. (E)	31. (C)
12. (B)	32. (B)
13. (D)	33. (C)
14. (C)	34. (B)
15. (C)	35. (B)
16. (E)	36. (C)
17. (B)	37. (A)
18. (C)	38. (D)
19. (E)	39. (C)
20. (D)	40. (E)

DETAILED EXPLANATIONS OF ANSWERS

PRACTICE EXAM 3

SECTION I

1.   **(E)**

The distributions for choices A, B, and D are roughly symmetric, so the mean and median will be near each other. The distribution for C is skewed right, so mean > median. Although the distribution for E is not truly left-skewed (skewed distributions are unimodal), the overall pattern has a leftward lean and the mean is less than the median for most distributions that are skewed left.

2.   **(E)**

Choice I is definitely false. The chi-square distribution is always skewed right. Choice II is true. Note that the critical values on the table decrease as the degrees of freedom increase. The distribution becomes closer to symmetric. The central limit theorem is at work. Choice III is also true.

3.   **(B)**

If the policyholder lives, the company gains $120. If the policyholder dies, the company loses a total of $49,880. Expected gain = $120(1 − 0.0015) − $49,880(0.0015) = $45.

4.   **(A)**

Sampling all the trees within a square tells us that clusters of trees are being selected.

5.   **(E)**

Without knowing how *many* males and how *many* females were surveyed, we can only make conclusions about proportions, not raw numbers.

6.   **(E)**

Substituting *quantity* = 10 into the equation, we get log(*price*) = 1.96. Thus, *price* = $10^{1.96} \approx 91.20$.

7.   **(C)**

Since the population standard deviation is unknown, the confidence interval is statistic ± (critical value)(standard *error* of statistic) or $\bar{x} \pm t^* \dfrac{s}{\sqrt{n}}$. We use the t-critical value with $n - 1 = 25$ degrees of freedom.

8.   **(C)**

The center of the confidence interval is 16.80 hours, and its margin of error is 0.25 hours, or 15 minutes. The confidence interval gives us a range of plausible values for the true mean watching time, which is 15 minutes on either side of 16.80 hours.

Choice A is a common misconception—for the interval to suggest watching time has changed, 17 should not be in the interval. Since the 95% confidence interval contains 17, a two-sided test like choice B would not be significant at the 0.05 level or lower. Choice D is wrong because intervals with higher levels are wider and will contain 17. Choice E is another common misinterpretation of what 95% confidence means.

9.   **(E)**

If you assume a population of 1,000 male patients, then 200 of them have the condition. 90% of those 200, or 192, will test positive. Of the 800 patients who do not have the condition, 27%, or 216, will test positive. So there would be 408 positive tests with only 192/408 actually having the condition. A tree diagram could also be helpful.

	Has Disease		Test Result	Final Outcome	Probability
		0.96	+	Y+	(0.2)(0.96) = 0.192
0.2	Y	0.04	−	Y−	(0.2)(0.04) = 0.008
Start					
0.8	N	0.27	+	N+	(0.8)(0.27) = 0.216
		0.73	−	N−	(0.8)(0.73) = 0.584

10.   **(D)**

z-scores do not have specific units. They measure the number of standard deviations from the mean.

11.   **(E)**

Essentially, Jane is testing $H_0: p = 0.10$ vs. $H_a: p < 0.10$. The associated test statistic and P-value are $z = \dfrac{0.07 - 0.10}{\sqrt{(0.10)(0.90)/100}} = -1$ and $P = 0.1587$. The most commonly used significance levels are 0.10, 0.05, and 0.01, and P is greater than all of them.

12.   (B)

In a well-designed experiment with random assignment, one can conclude a causal relationship between variables. Valid conclusions can be drawn in studies with sample sizes much smaller than 500.

13.   (D)

The middle half of a set of data falls between the first and third quartiles. The z-scores for the quartiles are approximately ± 0.67. $x = 430 \pm (0.67)(42)$.

14.   (C)

A residual is given by $y - \hat{y}$. The actual value $y = 10$; $\hat{y} = 3.34(5) - 7.012 = 9.688$. The residual equals $10 - 9.688$.

15.   (C)

Use the formula for the margin of error of a confidence interval, $z^* \dfrac{\sigma}{\sqrt{n}}$, and solve $1.645 \dfrac{800}{\sqrt{n}} \le 100$ for n. $n \ge \left[\dfrac{1.645 \cdot 800}{100} \right]^2$.

16.   (E)

Well-designed experiments are the only way to ensure a cause–effect relationship.

17.   (B)

This is a matched-pairs design with a sample of 10 individuals. You would calculate the 10 differences and use $n - 1 = 9$ degrees of freedom.

18.   (C)

If the proportion is 40%, then exactly 40% of the numbers must be assigned to Chemistry. Note that choice A does not assign zero.

19.   (E)

In a two-sided t-test with 27 degrees of freedom, any t-statistic over 2.052 (or less than –2.052) is significant at the 0.05 level. (The area in *one* tail of the t-distribution is 0.025.)

20.   (D)

The graph tells us nothing about raw numbers of students in each school, so choice A is wrong. There are about 10% of Franklin students in kindergarten, but 100% of Franklin students are at or below 11th grade, so there are no 12th grade students—choice B is incorrect. Choice C is incorrect—we cannot add percentages like it suggests. D is correct, because grade to grade (except 12th), a higher percentage of Franklin students are at that grade lower than Hillside. Choice E is incorrect because the cumulative frequency curve is nearly a straight line, indicating that the change in percentage of students, and therefore the number of students, is fairly constant from grade to grade.

21.   **(B)**

Choices A, D, and E are examples of undercoverage bias. Choice C is an example of nonresponse bias.

22.   **(E)**

A confidence interval for a proportion is centered at the sample proportion, in this case 188/416, so B and E are the only possibilities. E has the appropriate z^*-value for 95% confidence.

23.   **(D)**

The slope tells us how much the cost increases for a *one* unit increase in production. An increase in production cost for 100 units will be 100 times the slope.

24.   **(C)**

$P(E \text{ or } S) = P(E) + P(S) - P(E \text{ and } S) = 0.15 + 0.10 - 0.04 = 0.21.$

25.   **(E)**

Power is greatest for values of the parameter farthest from the hypothesized value, in the direction of the alternative hypothesis. We would correctly reject the null hypothesis if we have evidence that $p > 0.35$. The greatest value of p listed here would make it most probable to see that evidence.

26.   **(E)**

When we add or subtract independent random variables, we *add* their variances, not their standard deviations. $\sigma_{X-Y}^2 = \sigma_X^2 + \sigma_Y^2 = 149$. $\sigma_{X-Y} = \sqrt{149}$.

27.   **(C)**

The definition of a percentile is the proportion of measurements that are below the given individual's measurement.

28. **(C)**

A confidence interval for a proportion requires a few assumptions to be made. An SRS of the population of interest is assumed, with individual observations independent ($n < 10\%$ of population) and the sampling distribution of $\hat{p}$ to be normal ($np > 10$ and $n(1 - p) > 10$). Since this survey was a voluntary response survey, it is unreasonable to assume an SRS.

29. **(A)**

A purpose of blocking is *not* to test the effect of outside variables. This is a misconception.

30. **(C)**

Rescaling measurements does not affect correlation at all. Correlation is based on z-scores, which are free of units.

31. **(C)**

The expected value of a cell is given by $\dfrac{(\text{row total})(\text{column total})}{\text{grand total}}$.

32. **(B)**

A binomial setting requires a fixed number of trials. The number of trials is actually the variable of interest in this problem.

33. **(C)**

The null hypothesis should state that the parameter has one fixed value—a statement of equality. The alternative is the claim about which one is trying to find evidence.

34. **(B)**

Statement III is correct based on the central limit theorem. Statement II is false, as $\sigma_{\bar{x}} = \dfrac{\sigma}{\sqrt{n}}$, which is always less than σ. The mean of a sampling distribution is ALWAYS equal to the population mean.

35. **(B)**

Use the normal approximation to the binomial. Test H_0: $p = 0.474$ vs. H_A: $p > 0.474$. The standard deviation of the sample proportion is calculated with the value of p from the null hypothesis.

36.   **(C)**

A residual is calculated as $y - \hat{y}$. If this value is negative, it follows that $y - \hat{y} < 0$, or that $y < \hat{y}$, which means the prediction is greater than the observed value.

37.   **(A)**

The confidence interval for the population slope is
statistic $\pm$ (critical value)(standard error of statistic) or $b_1 \pm t^* \cdot SE(\beta_1)$ The sample size is 29, so the t-critical value is from the t-distribution with $n - 2 = 27$ degrees of freedom. The sample slope is the coefficient of NameLength and the standard error of the slope is in the Stdev column of NameLength.

38.   **(D)**

The expected winnings are

$$(\$10)\frac{30}{500} + (\$50)\frac{6}{500} + (\$100)\frac{2}{500} + (\$200)\frac{1}{500} = \$2. \text{ Since the ticket costs}$$

$5, our *net* expectation is $2 - $5 = -$3

39.   **(C)**

Choice A interprets the confidence level, not the interval itself. Choice B refers to all individuals in the population (an acre of land), not the mean. Choice D is similar to choice B except that it refers to one individual. Choice E is about the sample mean, not the population mean.

40.   **(E)**

A control group is needed to see if exercise is better than no exercise at all. Random assignment is needed in a good design in order to possibly conclude cause/effect and to balance out the effects of unknown variables. Other treatments are not necessary to answer the question at hand.

Free-Response Solutions

1. (a) The distribution of salaries is skewed right, as most have modest salaries and a few have very large salaries, so the mean will be higher than the median ($\bar{x}$ = 39,420, median = 27,000). The union will use the median to make it seem like the company is "robbing" the workers.

   (b) The company's attorney would use the mean, since in this skewed right distribution it is higher than the median. This would make it appear that salaries are more competitive than they may actually be.

   (c) If each of the 25 salaries increase by $3,000, then the mean and median will both increase accordingly by $3,000. The standard deviation will not change, since the spread of the salaries is not affected.

2. (a) **Bivariate Fit of Assessed Value (Thousands of dollars) by Selling Price (Thousands of dollars)**

   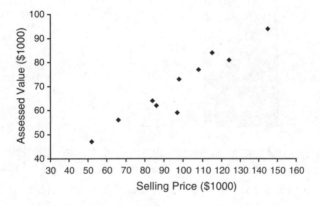

   (b) There is a strong, positive, linear relationship between the assessed value of homes in this area and their selling price. There does not appear to be any outliers.

   (c) *Predicted assessed value* = 20.354 + 0.50611 (*selling price*). For every additional dollar a home sells for, there is about a 50-cent increase in the assessed value.

   (d) 91.2% of the variation in assessed values can be explained by its linear relationship with selling price. 8.8% of the variation is due to other factors not under study.

3. (a) The parameter of interest is the mean reduction in systolic blood pressure with the new medication, μ.

    (b) $H_0: \mu = 10$

    $H_a: \mu > 10$.

    (c) A Type I error would occur if the company concludes that the mean reduction in systolic blood pressure with the new medication is greater than 10 when it really is not. The company would think the new medication is better and would mistakenly replace the old medication.

    (d) A Type II error would occur if the company fails to conclude that the mean reduction in systolic blood pressure with the new medication is greater than 10 when, in fact, it is. The company would fail to recognize the superiority of the new drug and mistakenly keep the old one on the market.

4. The diagram below shows the situation.

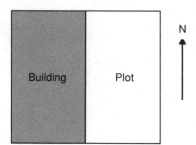

The south end of the plot will potentially get more sunlight than the north end—the plot will get the morning sun, but the building will block out the evening sun on the north end. Additionally, as the plants grow, those on the northern end will be shaded by those in the south. The plot should therefore be divided into blocks in order to take into account these ef-

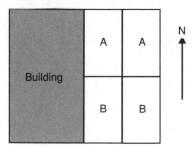

fects.

One example would be to divide the large plot into two blocks, A and B, of two plots each. The new fertilizer will be randomly assigned to one of the plots in block A; the other plot in block A receives the old fertilizer. The process is repeated for block B. The average number of blooms would be compared between the two fertilizers.

Since this lacks replication, one could create more blocks, each homogeneous with respect to changes in the north/south sunlight. An example of

10 blocks of two plots is provided.

Once the roses have grown to full bloom, the number of blooms should be recorded and then the blooms for each type of fertilizer will be compared.

5.   (a)   If it rains on Paradise Island on 40% of days, and we assume that rain on any given day is independent of rain on any other day, we can assign the digits 0, 1, 2, and 3 to represent days with rain. The digits 4, 5, 6, 7, 8, and 9 will represent days without rain. Five random digits will be selected in order, with replacement, to represent a 5-day span. We will record whether or not those 5 days had an instance of at least two consecutive days of rain. This process will be repeated several times.

     (b)   Key (R = rain, N = no rain)

           Trial 1 – 00233 = RRRRR   yes

           Trial 2 – 54830 = NNNRR   yes

           Trial 3 – 39108 = RNRRN   yes

           Trial 4 – 57935 = NNNRN   no

           Trial 5 – 28715 = RNNRN   no

           Trial 6 – 08996 = RNNNN   no

Trial 8 – 39280 = RNRNR   no

Trial 9 – 22222 = RRRRR   yes

Trial 10 – 31405 = RRNRN yes

(c)   In 10 trials of my simulation, 6 of the 5-day trips had at least two consecutive days of rain, so I estimate the probability of at least two consecutive days of rain in a 5-day period to be 60%.

6.   (a)   The grower should use a stratified sample to ensure equal representation from each level of the terrace. On each terrace, number the trees from 1 to 50. Then choose a random sample of five of these trees without replacement. Repeat this process for each level.

(b)   For any selected tree with more than one pineapple, number the pineapples on the tree and pick one at random. You do not want to always pick the easiest pineapple to reach.

(c)   The average weight of pineapples decreases by about 12.4 grams for each level one goes up the terrace.

(d)   The average change in mean pineapple weight per level is the slope, so we are asked for a confidence interval for the slope of the regression line. The t-score for a 95% CI with $n - 2 = 8$ degrees of freedom is 2.306. Our 95% CI is given by

$$-12.412 \pm 2.306(2.749) = (-18.751, -6.073).$$

We are 95% confident that the average loss in mean pineapple weight is between about 6.1 grams and 18.8 grams per level. Since zero is not in this interval, there is good evidence that weight indeed does decrease as one goes up in the terrace level.

(e)   Using individual pineapple weights would have produced a smaller r^2 value. Averaging the weights for each level removes much of the variation in weights. Removing this variation from our analysis would show a much stronger relationship between the two variables.

PRACTICE EXAM 4
AP Statistics

AP STATISTICS

PRACTICE EXAM 4

SECTION I

Time—1 hour and 30 minutes
Number of questions—40
Percent of total grade—50

(Answer sheets appear in the back of this book)

DIRECTIONS: Solve each of the following problems, using the available space for scratchwork. Decide which is the best of the choices given and fill in the corresponding oval on the answer sheet. No credit will be given for anything written in the test book. Do not spend too much time on any one problem.

---

1.   If one wanted to calculate summary statistics for salaries at a large company where there are many people with modest salaries and a few people with very high salaries, which would be the most appropriate measures of center and spread?

(A)   Mean and interquartile range

(B)   Median and interquartile range

(C)   Mean and standard deviation

(D)   Median and standard deviation

(E)   Mode and range

2.   A Gallup[*] poll conducted in February 2005 asked the question, "Who do you regard as the greatest United States president?" The most popular response was Ronald Reagan, given by 20% of the 1,008 respondents. The poll had a margin of error of 3%. Which of the following statements describes what is meant by 3%?

[*]Used with permission. *Source: www.gallup.com*

(A)   About 3% of the respondents had no opinion.

(B)   About 3% of the respondents were not of legal voting age.

(C)   About 3% of the respondents changed their minds during the course of the interview.

(D)   It is likely that between 17 and 23% of the entire population favors Ronald Reagan as greatest president.

(E)   The second place vote getter, Bill Clinton, was chosen as greatest by 17% of the respondents, 3% less than Ronald Reagan.

3.   In 1914, the passenger liner *Titanic* sank in the North Atlantic Ocean after striking an iceberg. Of the 1,323 passengers on board, 819 died. Females accounted for 466 of the passengers and 131 deaths.
  (a)   Are the events "dying" and "female" independent events?
  (b)   Are the events "dying" and "female" mutually exclusive (disjoint) events?

(A)   no; no

(B)   no; yes

(C)   yes; no

(D)   yes; yes

(E)   There is not enough information to determine if the events "dying" and "female" are independent and/or mutually exclusive.

4.   A glove manufacturer plans to conduct an experiment comparing two new types of materials for work gloves designated Material A and Material B. The gloves made from each of the materials look identical. One hundred construction workers in Las Vegas are recruited to test the gloves for durability. Workers are to wear a pair of work gloves as they normally would for 90 days, after which time the gloves will be evaluated by the company for wear.
    Which of the following methods will ensure that the assignment of gloves is independent and that equal quantities of the two types of materials are tested on each hand?

(A)   As workers report to receive their gloves, give the first 50 gloves of Material A and give the second 50 gloves of Material B.

(B)   As each worker reports to receive a pair of gloves, toss a coin. A result of heads means the worker will receive gloves of Material A; a result of tails means the worker receives gloves of Material B.

(C)   Assign the workers two-digit numbers from 00 to 99. Choose 50 two-digit numbers from a random number table, without duplicates. The workers having the 50 chosen numbers receive gloves of Material A and the remaining 50 receive gloves of Material B.

(D)   List the volunteers in alphabetical order by last name; then number the list from 1 to 100. Assign the odd-numbered names to receive gloves of Material A and the even-numbered names to receive gloves of Material B.

(E)   As workers report to receive their gloves, toss a coin. If the result is heads, give the worker a left-hand glove in Material A and a right-hand glove in Material B. A toss of tails reverses the assignment of gloves.

5.   A random sample has been drawn from a population and confidence interval computed for the population mean. All other things being equal, which of the following will increase the width of the interval?

   I.   Increasing sample size

   II.   Increasing confidence level

   III.   Using a t-critical value in place of a z-critical value

   (A)   II only

   (B)   I and II only

   (C)   I and III only

   (D)   II and III only

   (E)   I, II, and III

6.   A fair six-sided die has five faces painted green and one face painted red. The die is rolled repeatedly until the die lands red face up; let X be the number of rolls made. What is the most probable value of X?

   (A)   1

   (B)   2

   (C)   3

   (D)   4

   (E)   6

7.   Two students took different standardized college entrance exams last month. One student took the ABC exam and scored 45. Scores on the

ABC exam are approximately normally distributed with a mean of 40 and a standard deviation of 10. The second student took the XYZ exam and scored 88. Scores on the XYZ exam are approximately normally distributed with a mean of 80 and a standard deviation of 16. Which student did better on their respective test?

(A) The student taking the ABC exam.

(B) The student taking the XYZ exam.

(C) Both students did equally well.

(D) The exams are different, so there is no basis for comparison.

(E) The number of students taking the exam is not known, so there is insufficient information to compare.

8. A high school statistics class wants to conduct a student opinion survey at a local school. They want a sample of 40 of the school's 200 students, of which there 50 each in grades 9, 10, 11, and 12. The school's students are also divided into 10 homerooms, of 20 students each, alphabetically by last name. The class is entertaining three options for sampling.

   I. Assign each student in the school a number from 001 to 200. Then, generate three-digit random numbers from a random number table until 40 students are chosen for the survey.

   II. Assign each student in the school a number from 001 to 200, using 001–050 for 9th graders, 051–100 for 10th graders, 101–150 for 11th graders, and 151–200 for 12th graders. Then, generate three-digit random numbers from a random number table until 10 students are selected from each grade level.

   III. Assign each homeroom a one-digit number between 0 and 9. Then, generate two one-digit random numbers from a random number table and survey all 20 students in each of the two selected homerooms.

   Describe the type of sampling procedure for each option under consideration.

   (A) I, convenience sample; II, cluster sample; III, stratified random sample

   (B) I, convenience sample; II, multistage sample; III, simple random sample

   (C) I, simple random sample; II, cluster sample; III, stratified random sample

(D) I, simple random sample; II, stratified random sample; III, cluster sample

(E) I, systematic sample; II, stratified random sample; III, convenience sample

9. Child psychologists claim that babies who play with toys decorated with geometric patterns of black, white, and red develop cognitive abilities faster than those who do not. A study compared the mental skills of 72 randomly selected babies, half of whom routinely play with the special toys and half of whom do not. The summary statistics of the babies' mental scores are given in the table below.

Group	Sample Size	Mean	Standard Deviation
Special toys (S)	36	115	13
No special toys (N)	36	110	14

The researchers will use a hypothesis test to determine if there exists evidence that the mean mental score of babies using the special toys is significantly different than the mean mental score of babies not using the special toys. Which of the following is the correct set of hypotheses for the test?

(A) $H_0 : \mu_S = \mu_N$
$H_A : \mu_S \neq \mu_N$

(B) $H_0: \bar{x}_S = \bar{x}_N$
$H_A: \bar{x}_S \neq \bar{x}_N$

(C) $H_0: \mu_{S-N} = 0$
$H_A: \mu_{S-N} \neq 0$

(D) $H_0 : \beta_1 = 0$
$H_A : \beta_1 \neq 0$

(E) $H_0 : p_S = p_N$
$H_A : p_S \neq p_N$

10. A student wants to simulate the flipping of two coins by using a random digit table, recording outcomes as either zero, one, or two "heads." Which of the following assignments of digits 0 through 9 would be appropriate for modeling the outcome in this simulation?

(A) Assign "0" to zero heads, "1" to one head, "2" to two heads, and ignore digits "3, 4, 5, 6, 7, 8, 9."

(B)   Assign "0, 1, 2" to zero heads, "3, 4, 5" to one head, "6, 7, 8" to two heads, and ignore digit "9."

(C)   Assign "0, 1, 2" to zero heads, "3, 4, 5, 6" to one head, and "7, 8, 9" to two heads.

(D)   Assign "0, 1" to zero heads, "2, 3, 4" to one head, and "5, 6, 7, 8, 9" to two heads.

(E)   Assign "0, 1" to zero heads, "2, 3, 4, 5" to one head, "6, 7" to two heads, and ignore digits "8, 9."

11.   The owner of a chain of supermarkets notices that there is a positive correlation between monthly sales of sunscreen and monthly sales of ice cream over the course of the previous year. During months when sales of sunscreen were above average, sales of ice cream tended to be above average. Likewise, during seasons with below average sunscreen sales, ice cream sales were usually below average. Which of the following is a valid conclusion from these facts?

(A)   Using sunscreen makes one hungry for ice cream.

(B)   Eating ice cream makes one require more sunscreen.

(C)   A scatterplot of ice cream sales vs. sunscreen sales could look like this:

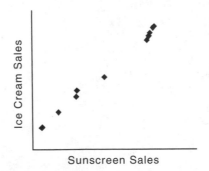

(D)   Sales records must be in error. There should be no association between sunscreen and ice cream sales.

(E)   No valid conclusion can be drawn; the sample size is too small.

12.   A teacher wanted to determine if students score higher on multiple-choice tests with four possible answers versus five possible answers. The teacher randomly assigned half of the students the exam with five choices, the other half the exam with four choices, and performed a statistical test comparing the mean scores of the two groups. The P-value for the test was 0.15. Which of the following statements is true?

(A)   The average score of one exam was 15% higher than the other exam.

(B)   If there really were no difference between the two exams, there is a 15% probability that the difference observed, or one more extreme, would be due to the chance assignment of the students to the two exams.

(C)   Fifteen percent of the students would score higher on one exam versus the other.

(D)   If the experiment were repeated, there is a 15% probability that the scores on the two tests would differ.

(E)   Only 15% of students passed the exam.

13.   A small construction company has two divisions that bid for contracts: commercial and residential. On the basis of past experience, the company has created the following table showing the probability of each division being awarded a certain number of contracts this year, and the typical profit on each contract.

Number of Contracts	Probability	
	Commercial Division	Residential Division
0	0.05	0.20
1	0.15	0.25
2	0.25	0.40
3	0.35	0.15
4	0.20	0
Typical profit per contract awarded	$250,000	$150,000

How much profit can the construction company expect to make this year?

(A) $400,000

(B) $600,000

(C) $850,000

(D) $1,050,000

(E) $4,000,000

14. Sarah is studying about climate in different parts of the world. She has the 365 daily high temperatures for last year from Kabul, Afghanistan. The data are given in units of degrees Celsius (°C). The mean high temperature is 19.3°C and the standard deviation of the high temperature is 9.8°C. Sarah converts each of the 365 temperatures to the Fahrenheit scale by using the formula $F = \frac{9}{5}C + 32$, where F is the temperature in degrees Fahrenheit (°F) and C is the temperature in °C. After making these conversions, what will be the new mean and standard deviation of daily high temperature in units of °F?

   (A) Mean: 34.7°F, standard deviation: 17.6°F

   (B) Mean: 34.7°F, standard deviation: 49.6°F

   (C) Mean: 51.3°F, standard deviation: 9.8°F

   (D) Mean: 66.7°F, standard deviation: 49.6°F

   (E) Mean: 66.7°F, standard deviation: 17.6°F

15. Arteriosclerosis is a disease where plaques made up of cholesterol deposits, calcium, and abnormal cells develop on the inner lining of the arteries. A pharmaceutical company has developed a new drug to reduce plaque buildup in the arteries. The new drug's effects will be compared to the company's existing drug. Volunteers who have a history of arteriosclerosis but are not on any medication are recruited to participate in the study. Since exercise can have an effect on the buildup of plaques, the volunteers will be placed into one of three blocks by exercise level (high, low, none) before randomly assigning the treatments (new drug, current drug). Throughout the study, the volunteers will visit doctors to have the buildup of their arterial plaque measured. Is it possible for this study to be double-blind?

   (A) Yes.

   (B) No, because the study uses volunteers.

   (C) No, because a placebo is not one of the treatments.

   (D) No, because the volunteers will know what block they are in.

   (E) No, because the doctors measuring plaque buildup will know which treatment each volunteer was given.

16. The regression analysis for two variables is shown below.

Predictor	Coef	StDev	T	P
Constant	5.782	1.106	5.23	0.000
Explanator	1.38573	0.09374	14.78	0.000

S = 3.546   R-Sq = 87.9%   R-Sq(adj) = 87.5%

32 – 2 = 30 degrees of freedom

Which of the following is the correct formula for a 90% confidence interval for the slope of the regression line?

(A) $1.38573 \pm 1.697 \,(1.106)$

(B) $1.38573 \pm 2.042 \,(0.09374)$

(C) $1.38573 \pm 1.645 \,(1.697)$

(D) $1.38573 \pm 1.697 \,(0.09374)$

(E) $1.38573 \pm 2.042 \,(1.106)$

17.   A reporter for a college newspaper wants to know the proportion of students who commute that are satisfied with parking on campus. The reporter initially sets out to randomly survey 500 students, but later believes that day students and night students could differ in their opinions because of the relative sizes of their groups and the amount of parking available. The reporter then randomly surveys 400 day students and 100 night students. What is/are the benefits of dividing the sample into two subgroups?

   I.   To reduce bias in the overall sample proportion due to the differences between the subgroups.

   II.   To reduce variability in the overall sample proportion due to the differences between the subgroups.

   III.   To allow comparison between the sample proportions of each subgroup.

(A)   I only

(B)   II only

(C)   I and III only

(D)   II and III only

(E)   I, II, and III

18. A significance test of $H_0: \mu = \mu_0$ vs. $H_a: \mu \neq \mu_0$ is to be performed with a significance level of α. The data will have sample size n. Which of the following will have the greatest effect on increasing the power of the test?

    (A) Decrease α, decrease n

    (B) Decrease α, increase n

    (C) Increase α, decrease n

    (D) Increase α, increase n

    (E) Increase n only. Changing α has no effect on power.

19. The relative frequency histograms below summarize test scores in two classes, A and B. Which of the following must be true?

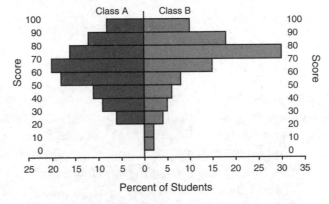

    (A) There are fewer students in class A than class B.

    (B) Fewer students scored between 70 and 80 in class A than class B.

    (C) The median of class A is larger than class B.

    (D) The standard deviation of class A is smaller than class B.

    (E) Neither class A nor class B contains outliers.

20. Which of the following is the best estimate of the standard deviation for the distribution shown in the diagram below?

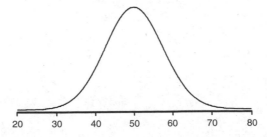

(A)   8

(B)   15

(C)   20

(D)   30

(E)   50

21.   A least-squares regression model of Y on X gives a correlation coefficient of 0.75. If the least-squares regression model of X on Y is done, the value of the correlation becomes

(A)   −0.75

(B)   −0.25

(C)   0.25

(D)   0.66

(E)   0.75

22.   A high school golf team of five players is to be in an upcoming tournament. Each of the players on the team will play a round of golf and the team score is the sum of the five individual scores. The individual player scores are independent of each other and approximately normally distributed with the following means and standard deviations.

Golfer	Mean	Standard Deviation
1	78	3
2	79	4
3	81	2
4	84	4
5	93	6

What are the mean and standard deviation of the team score?

(A)   Mean = 83, standard deviation = 3.8

(B)   Mean = 83, standard deviation = 9

(C)   Mean = 415, standard deviation = 6.0

(D)   Mean = 415, standard deviation = 9

(E)   Mean = 415, standard deviation = 19

23. A random sample of the cost of milk (per gallon) is taken at 30 grocery stores nationwide. The sample produced a mean price of $3.39 per gallon and a standard deviation of $0.38 per gallon. Which of the following is the correct 90% confidence interval for the mean cost of a gallon of milk nationwide?

(A) $\$3.39 \pm 1.645\dfrac{\$0.38}{\sqrt{30}}$

(B) $\$3.39 \pm 1.697\dfrac{\$0.38}{\sqrt{29}}$

(C) $\$3.39 \pm 1.697\dfrac{\$0.38}{\sqrt{30}}$

(D) $\$3.39 \pm 1.699\dfrac{\$0.38}{\sqrt{29}}$

(E) $\$3.39 \pm 1.699\dfrac{\$0.38}{\sqrt{30}}$

24. A manufacturer of major appliances (refrigerators, dishwashers, ovens, etc.) claims that only 3% of its appliances require major repairs during the first year of use. A major competitor disputes this claim, believing that the repair rate has been understated. Which of the following pairs of hypotheses should the competitor test?

(A) $H_0: p < 0.03$
    $H_a: p = 0.03$

(B) $H_0: p > 0.03$
    $H_a: p = 0.03$

(C) $H_0: p = 0.03$
    $H_a: p < 0.03$

(D) $H_0: p = 0.03$
    $H_a: p > 0.03$

(E) $H_0: p = 0.03$
    $H_a: p \neq 0.03$

25. The population of rolls on a single die is $\{1, 2, 3, 4, 5, 6\}$, which has a mean $\mu = 3.5$ and a standard deviation $\sigma = 1.71$. When rolling a die twice, there are 36 possible pairs. One case would be rolling a $(1, 4)$, which has a sample mean of 2.5. If the distribution of the sample means of all 36 possible pairs has a mean $\mu_{\bar{x}}$ and standard deviation $\sigma_{\bar{x}}$, which statement is true?

(A) $\mu_{\bar{x}} = 3.5,\ \sigma_{\bar{x}} > 1.71$

(B) $\mu_{\bar{x}} = 3.5,\ \sigma_{\bar{x}} < 1.71$

(C) $\mu_{\bar{x}} = 3.5,\ \sigma_{\bar{x}} = 1.71$

(D) $\mu_{\bar{x}} < 3.5,\ \sigma_{\bar{x}} = 1.71$

(E) $\mu_{\bar{x}} > 3.5,\ \sigma_{\bar{x}} < 1.71$

26.   In which of the following types of studies can a cause–effect relationship be established?

(A)   Observational study

(B)   Simple random sample

(C)   Comparative experiment

(D)   Census

(E)   Multistage survey

Use the information below for questions 27–28.

27.   The least-squares regression equation of the relationship between the sale price (in thousands of dollars) and the size (in square feet) for a randomly selected group of homes in a certain city is $\widehat{Price} = 0.118\ Size + 42.0$. Which of the following statements is the correct interpretation of the slope?

(A)   For each increase of one square foot in the home size, the price increases on average by $118.

(B)   For each increase of one square foot in the home size, the price increases on average by $42,000.

(C)   For each increase of $1,000 in the price of a home, the size increases on average by 0.118 square foot.

(D)   For each increase of $1,000 in the price of a home, the size increases on average by 42.000 square feet.

(E)   None of the above is a correct interpretation.

28.   One particular 2,500-square-foot house sold for $300,000. Compute its residual to the nearest thousand dollars.

(A)   –$337,000

(B)   –$37,000

(C) $0

(D) $37,000

(E) $337,000

29. A random sample of parents of incoming freshmen at a high school was asked before the beginning of the school year if they favored school uniforms. Of the 285 parents contacted, 168 favored uniforms. A second survey of 419 randomly selected parents was made halfway through the school year, in which 306 they indicated they favored school uniforms. The principal of the school wants to know if the proportion of parents favoring uniforms had changed significantly between the times of the two surveys.

Let p_1 = the true proportion of incoming freshmen parents favoring uniforms at the time of the first survey, and let p_2 = the true proportion of freshmen parents favoring uniforms at the time of the second survey. Which of the following is the correct test statistic to test H_0: $p_1 = p_2$ versus H_a: $p_1 \neq p_2$?

(A) $z = \dfrac{0.589 - 0.730}{\sqrt{\dfrac{0.673(1-0.673)}{285} + \dfrac{0.673(1-0.673)}{419}}}$

(B) $z = \dfrac{0.589 - 0.730}{\sqrt{\dfrac{0.589(1-0.589)}{285} + \dfrac{0.730(1-0.730)}{419}}}$

(C) $z = \dfrac{0.589 - 0.730}{\sqrt{\dfrac{0.589}{285} + \dfrac{0.730}{419}}}$

(D) $z = \dfrac{0.589 - 0.730}{\sqrt{\dfrac{0.660(1-0.660)}{285} + \dfrac{0.660(1-0.660)}{419}}}$

(E) $z = \dfrac{0.589 - 0.730}{\sqrt{\dfrac{0.589(1-0.589)+0.730(1-0.730)}{704}}}$

30. A lighting company purchases bulbs with a known defective rate of 2%. The bulbs come in packages of 20. Whether a bulb is defective or not is independent from bulb to bulb and package to package. The lighting company recently purchased two packages of bulbs and each had one defective bulb in it. What is the probability that each of the two packages of bulbs would have one or more defective bulbs in it?

(A) $1-(0.98)^{40}$

(B) $\left[1-(0.98)^{20}\right]^{2}$

(C) $P\left(z>\dfrac{1-(40)(0.02)}{\sqrt{40(0.02)(0.96)}}\right)$

(D) $\left[P\left(z>\dfrac{1-(20)(0.02)}{\sqrt{20(0.02)(0.96)}}\right)\right]^{2}$

(E) $1-\left[\left(\begin{array}{c}40\\1\end{array}\right)(0.02)^{1}(0.98)^{39}+\left(\begin{array}{c}40\\0\end{array}\right)(0.02)^{0}(0.98)^{40}\right]$

31. A nonlinear model $\hat{y}=f(x)$ has been fit to the bivariate data shown below.

x	2	4	5	7	9	10	12
y	5	11	15	27	35	43	63

The residual plot of the model is also shown.

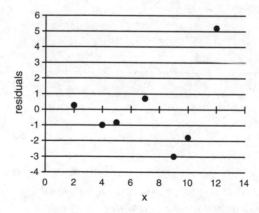

Which of the following is the model's predicted value of $\hat{y}$ for $x = 9$?

(A) −3

(B) 6

(C) 26

(D) 32

(E) 38

32. The probability distribution of the random variable x is shown below.

x	0	1	2	3	4	5
$p(x)$	0.40	0.25	0.15	0.10	0.08	0.02

Which statement is correct concerning the shape of this distribution?

(A) The distribution is uniform.

(B) The distribution is skewed to the left; therefore, the mean is greater than the median.

(C) The distribution is skewed to the right; therefore, the mean is greater than the median.

(D) The distribution is skewed to the right; therefore, the median is greater than the mean.

(E) The distribution is skewed to the left; therefore, the median is greater than the mean.

33. A national survey of people's attitudes toward prime time television was conducted in the years 2000, 2002, and 2004. Respondents were chosen at random and asked, "How often do you watch reality shows on television during prime time: never, sometimes, or often?" The results of the three surveys are shown in the table below.

	Never	Sometimes	Often	Total
2000	511	307	205	1,023
2002	471	346	230	1,047
2004	303	350	358	1,011
Total	1,285	1,003	793	3,081

If the null hypothesis, H_0: the distribution of responses is the same for 2000, 2002, and 2004, were true, then what would be the expected number of respondents in 2002 who answered "often"?

(A) $\dfrac{(1,047)(230)}{3,081}$

(B) $\dfrac{(1,047)(793)}{3,081}$

(C) $\dfrac{(793)(230)}{1,047}$

(D) $\dfrac{(1,047)(230)}{793}$

(E) $\dfrac{(793)(230)}{3,081}$

34. A swim team coach wants to compare mean race times of female swimmers using two different types of swim caps. He selects 30 swimmers from the county swim team and randomly selects which cap they will use for their race. Fifteen will swim with the old type of cap and the other 15 will swim with the new style of cap. The swimmers do not know which cap they have on when they swim their race. Which test of inference would be most useful for the swim coach?

   (A) One-sample t-test

   (B) Chi-square test of association

   (C) Matched-pairs t-test

   (D) Two-sample t-test

   (E) Two-sample z-test

35. The graph below shows the distribution of retail gasoline prices (per gallon) at randomly selected gas stations around Las Vegas, Nevada on the first day of June, July, August, and September 2005. Which of the following statements is NOT justified by the graphs?

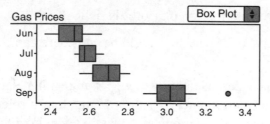

   (A) The price of gas tended to rise over time.

   (B) The lowest recorded price on September 1 was greater than the highest recorded price on August 1.

   (C) Prices were least variable on July 1.

   (D) More than half of the recorded prices in June were above $2.50 per gallon.

   (E) About twice as many stations were surveyed in June than July.

36. The back-to-back stemplots below give the number of points scored last season by two famous basketball players, Harry Hoops and Sam Shooter. Harry and Sam play for the same team and their team played 50 games.

Harry Hoops		Sam Shooter
4432211	0	4
9998876666	0	689999
444411110	1	0111222333344444444
87765	1	66666777788999
43311100	2	011222334
855	2	
4211	3	
87	3	5
1	4	
5	4	

stems: tens   leaves: ones

Which of the following statements is N T true?

(A) Harry outscored Sam in more games than Sam outscored Harry.

(B) Sam and Harry average about the same number of points per game.

(C) Sam is the more consistent scorer on the team.

(D) Harry's distribution of scores is right-skewed.

(E) Sam had one score that could be considered an outlier.

37. A politician concerned about winning an upcoming election commissions a poll of voter preference.   f the 627 randomly selected likely voters who were surveyed, 326 indicated that they would vote for the politician. Which of the following is the 95% confidence interval for the true proportion of voters who will vote for the politician?

(A) $0.520 \pm 1.960 \dfrac{0.520}{\sqrt{627}}$

(B) $0.480 \pm 1.960 \sqrt{\dfrac{(0.520)(0.480)}{627}}$

(C) $0.520 \pm 1.960\sqrt{\dfrac{(0.520)(0.480)}{627}}$

(D) $0.500 \pm 1.960\sqrt{\dfrac{(0.520)(0.480)}{627}}$

(E) $(0.520 - 0.480) \pm 1.960\sqrt{\dfrac{(0.520)(0.480)}{326} + \dfrac{(0.480)(0.520)}{301}}$

38. Sales of homes in a particular town were studied over the course of 1 month. Each time a home was sold, its floor area (in square feet), its selling price (in thousands of dollars), and its age (old or new) were recorded. A scatterplot of the selling price versus the floor area is shown below.

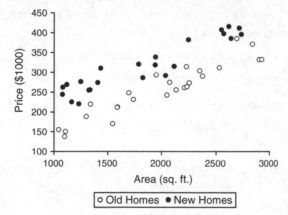

Which of the following statements is true about the relationship between the selling price and floor area?

   I.   New homes generally sell for a higher price than old homes of the same area.

   II. For a given increase in the area of a new home, the selling price generally increases more than it would for the same increase in the area of an old home.

   III. The area is strongly related to the price, regardless of the age of the home.

(A) I only

(B) II only

(C) III only

(D)   I and III only

(E)   I, II, and III

39.   In a study of engine size and fuel economy, 23 midsize cars were randomly selected and their fuel economy was determined using U.S. Government procedures. The least-squares regression line of fuel economy on engine size was *fuel economy* = 35.5 − 1.92 *engine size*, where fuel economy is measured in miles per gallon and engine size is measured in liters. The 95% confidence interval for the slope of the least-squares regression line is (−3.19, −0.65). Which of the following is a correct interpretation of this confidence interval?

(A)   If two engines are compared, there is a 95% chance that the larger engine gets lower gas mileage.

(B)   There is a 95% chance that the slope of the population regression line is between −3.19 and −0.65.

(C)   A line is the best model for the data because the slope of the least-squares regression line is in the interval.

(D)   It is unlikely that any two engines whose sizes differ by 1 liter will have a difference in fuel economy more than 3.19 mpg or less than 0.65 mpg.

(E)   About 95% of engines tested get poor fuel economy because both ends of the interval are negative.

40.   A classmate working on a research project for a statistics class has just reported to you that there is a correlation of −0.79 between gender and income among corporate executives. Which of the following is a correct conclusion that you can draw from your classmate's report?

(A)   For every dollar of income earned by males, females earn only 79 cents.

(B)   For every dollar of income earned by females, males earn $1.21.

(C)   Seventy-nine percent of female executives earn less than males doing the same job.

(D)   Females earn less than males because they work 21% fewer hours than males.

(E)   Your classmate's report is in error. There can be no correlation between gender and income.

SECTION II

Part A
Questions 1–5
Spend about 65 minutes on this part of the exam.
Percent of Section II grade—75

> **DIRECTIONS:** Show all your work. Indicate clearly the methods you use, because you will be graded on the correctness of your methods as well as on the accuracy of your results and explanation.

1. The box-and-whisker plots below show the distribution of the men's and women's times (in seconds) from the heats for the 100 m Butterfly swimming competitions at the 2004 Summer Olympic Games in Athens, Greece. There were five heats for women with 38 swimmers and eight heats for men with 59 swimmers. Heats are preliminary races that determine who competes in later races.

   The summary statistics are as follows:

	N	Min	Q_1	Median	Q_3	Max	Mean	Standard Deviation
Women	38	57.47	59.47	60.44	62.01	67.94	60.836	2.3096
Men	59	52.05	52.93	54.15	55.71	61.6	54.567	2.0281

   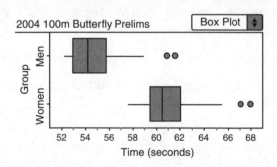

   (a) Compare the two distributions of swimming times.

   (b) *Approximately* what proportion of the men's times are faster than the women's fastest time?

   (c) *Approximately* what proportion of the women's times are faster than the men's slowest time?

2. A commuter airline uses 18-seat turbo-prop airplanes and it is important that the total weight of passengers and their bags does not exceed limits for safe take-off weight. It is known that the weights of passengers and their baggage are approximately normally distributed with the following means and standard deviations. Assume that the weights of a passenger and his or her baggage are independent, and that these weights are independent from passenger to passenger.

	Mean	Standard Deviation
Passenger Weight	175	25
Baggage Weight	70	13

    (a) What are the mean and standard deviation for the combined weight of a passenger and the passenger's baggage?

    (b) The allowed maximum weight of all passengers and their baggage is 4,700 pounds. What is the probability that a full flight of 18 passengers and their baggage will overload the aircraft? Show all work.

3. A homebuilder is planning a new housing development geared toward families with school-aged children. The builder needs to construct homes of various sizes (two bedroom, three bedroom, etc.) in quantities that take into account family sizes in the area.
    The builder contacts teachers at several local schools to implement a survey about family size. The teachers ask each of their students how many people presently live each student's home. The teachers then provide the information to the builder.

    (a) Describe the flaws in the design of this survey.

    (b) Describe a better design that still uses the student population as the sampling frame.

4. An association of county livestock ranchers is exploring the relationship between the size of a cattle herd and the cost of raising the cattle before going to market. Twenty ranchers from the county provided data to the association on the sizes of their cattle herds and the production cost per cow in dollars. The data are given in the table below.

Herd Size	12	30	40	45	53	56	149	161	171	188
Cost per Unit ($)	515	475	474	455	464	459	421	423	412	417
Herd Size	210	220	230	263	325	337	357	358	367	385
Cost per Unit ($)	406	416	411	410	390	400	401	386	391	394

A scatterplot of cost per unit versus herd size is shown below.

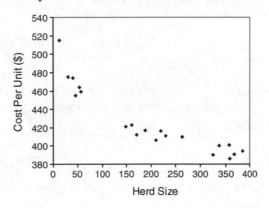

(a)　Describe the overall association between the herd size and the production cost per unit.

(b)　Ranches can be classified into three sizes: small (less than 100 cattle), medium (between 100 and 300 cattle), and large (more than 300 cattle). Describe the association between the herd size and the production cost per unit for each of the classifications: small, medium, and large.

The ranchers' association statistician transformed both cost per unit and herd size with logarithms. The following computer output and residual plot were created.

The regression equation is

Log Cost = 2.80 − 0.0784 Log Size

Predictor	Coef	StDev	T	P
Constant	2.79626	0.00640	436.82	0.000
Log Size	−0.078395	0.002926	−26.79	0.000

S = 0.005597　　　R-Sq = 97.6%　　　R-Sq(adj) = 97.4%

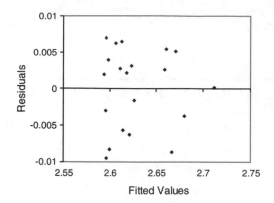

(c) Use the model to predict the cost per unit of a ranch with a herd size of 300 cattle.

(d) Comment on the validity and accuracy of your prediction in part (c), given the model of the relationship between the transformed variables.

5. The table below shows the numbers of randomly selected male and female college students who prefer various word processing software programs for their writing classes.

Choice of Word Processors by Male and Female Students

	Male Students	Female Students	Total
Software A	15	26	41
Software B	16	10	26
Software C	9	6	15
Total	40	42	82

Is there an association between preferred software type and gender? Give appropriate statistical support for your conclusion.

Part B
Questions 6
Spend about 25 minutes on this part of the exam.
Percent of Section II grade—25

> **DIRECTIONS:** Show all your work. Indicate clearly the methods you use, because you will be graded on the correctness of you methods as well as on the accuracy of your results and explanation.

6.   A pharmaceutical company is testing two new pain relievers to see which is more effective in reducing the pain of tension headaches. Twenty volunteers participate in the study.

The two medications, A and B, are given in randomly filled single-dose packages to the volunteers. Subjects are to take one of the medication packages when they experience a tension headache. The packages are labeled with code numbers in such a way that researchers will know which medication volunteers took for a given headache, but the volunteers cannot determine which.

After one-half hour, they are to rate their degree of pain relief on a scale of 0 to 5, with 0 meaning *no relief* and 5 representing *total relief*.

After six months, logs are collected from the volunteers and data compiled. The results of the study are in the table below:

		Relief Level							
Medication	Total Headaches	0	1	2	3	4	5	Mean	SD
A	228	21	46	57	56	29	19	2.36	1.40
B	263	18	27	64	95	49	10	2.61	1.21

(a)   Is there a significant difference between the two medications in terms of the mean level of relief? Conduct an appropriate statistical inference procedure.

(b)   Is there a significant difference between the two medications in terms of the proportion of headaches getting total relief? Conduct an appropriate statistical inference procedure.

(c)   If the company decided to market Medication A, what advertising claims should it make?

(d)   If the company decided to market Medication B, what advertising claims should it make?

AP STATISTICS

PRACTICE EXAM 4

Answer Key

1.	(B)	21.	(E)
2.	(D)	22.	(D)
3.	(A)	23.	(E)
4.	(C)	24.	(D)
5.	(D)	25.	(B)
6.	(A)	26.	(C)
7.	(C)	27.	(A)
8.	(D)	28.	(B)
9.	(A)	29.	(A)
10.	(E)	30.	(B)
11.	(C)	31.	(E)
12.	(B)	32.	(C)
13.	(C)	33.	(B)
14.	(E)	34.	(D)
15.	(A)	35.	(E)
16.	(D)	36.	(A)
17.	(D)	37.	(C)
18.	(D)	38.	(D)
19.	(D)	39.	(D)
20.	(A)	40.	(E)

DETAILED EXPLANATIONS
OF ANSWERS

PRACTICE EXAM 4

SECTION I

1.   **(B)**

Since a few people have very high salaries, the distribution of salaries is skewed. The median is the more appropriate measure of center for skewed distributions, since it is resistant to outliers. The interquartile range is reported with the median, and the standard deviation is reported with the mean.

2.   **(D)**

The margin of error accounts for using sample data to approximate a population parameter. It has nothing to do with nonresponse or second choices. It simply means we would be surprised if the true value of the parameter were not in our interval.

3.   **(A)**

The events would be independent if $P(\text{dying}) = P(\text{dying} \mid \text{female})$. Since $P(\text{dying}) = 819/1{,}323 = 0.619$ and $P(\text{dying} \mid \text{female}) = 131/466 = 0.281$, the events are not independent. Males were more likely to die than females. The events are certainly not disjoint, as 131 females did die. The events would only be disjoint if no females died at all.

4.   **(C)**

Choices A and D do not insure the assignment to be independent. Random assignment must be used for this purpose. Choice B does not guarantee equal quantities of the two types of materials tested, since in 100 coin flips, there will not always be exactly 50 heads. Choice C describes a completely randomized experiment design. Choice E describes a well-designed matched-pairs experiment, where the amount of materials will be the same, but not necessarily 50 left gloves and 50 right gloves for each material.

5. **(D)**

Increasing sample size will decrease the width, since n is in the denominator of the margin of error. Increasing confidence level does increase the width—to be 100% confident of capturing the parameter would require the widest of intervals. Given any confidence level, t-values are always greater than z-values, and thus would also give a wider interval.

6. **(A)**

With a fixed probability of a success and independent rolls, the number of rolls until a success is modeled by the geometric probability. The geometric probability distribution is always decreasing and always has a mode of 1, regardless of the probability of a success.

7. **(C)**

We can compare scores from different distributions by comparing the z-scores. $z_{ABC} = \dfrac{45 - 40}{10} = 0.5$ and $z_{XYZ} = \dfrac{88 - 80}{16} = 0.5$. Since the z-scores are equal, we conclude that the students did equally well.

8. **(D)**

Option I is a simple random sample. All students in the population are numbered and all possible groups of 40 have an equal chance of being chosen. Option II is a stratified random sample because 10 students are selected from each grade level. Option III is a cluster sample since entire homerooms are selected for study and all students in the selected homerooms are part of the sample.

9. **(A)**

The two groups are independent groups not paired in any way. The response variable is a mental score and means are to be compared. Choice B is bad since hypotheses are never about statistics like $\bar{x}$. Choice C would be used for a matched-pairs study. Choice D would be used for a linear regression t-test. Choice E would be used if we were comparing proportions.

10. **(E)**

In flips of two fair coins, the probability of observing two heads is $(0.5)(0.5) = 0.25$. The probability of observing zero heads is also 0.25. The probability of observing one head and one tail is therefore 0.50 (double the others since the head could occur first or second). So, the assignment of digits has to account for one head being twice as likely as the other two outcomes. Choice E is the only one that does this.

11.   **(C)**

An association does not mean causation, so choices A and B are out. Both of these factors are consequences of the temperature, so it is not surprising that they are associated. Choice D is therefore wrong. The scatterplot in choice C demonstrates a positive correlation.

12.   **(B)**

A P-value is the probability, if the null were true, of observing data at least as extreme as the given sample. The other choices are common misconceptions of a P-value.

13.   **(C)**

We need to calculate the expected profit for each of the divisions and add them together.

$$
\begin{aligned}
E\,(\text{Comm}) &= \$250,000\,[(0)\,(0.05)+(1)\,(0.15)+(2)\,(0.25)+(3)\,(0.35) \\
&\quad + (4)\,(0.20)] \\
&= \$625,000
\end{aligned}
$$

$$
\begin{aligned}
E\,(\text{Res}) &= \$150,000\,[(0)\,(0.20)+(1)\,(0.25)+(2)\,(0.40)+(3)\,(0.15)] \\
&= \$225,000
\end{aligned}
$$

The sum is \$850,000.

14.   **(E)**

Multiplying every value in a data set by a constant affects the mean and standard deviation both by the same factor. Adding a constant to every value affects the mean but not the standard deviation. So, the mean = (9/5)(19.3) + 32 = 66.7 and the standard deviation = (9/5)(9.8) = 17.6.

15.   **(A)**

Double blind means neither the subjects nor the doctors know which treatment was given; it has nothing to do with what block they are in. A placebo is not necessary for blinding, nor are volunteers. The doctor does not have to know the treatment to measure the plaque buildup.

16.   **(D)**

A 90% CI for the slope is given by

$b \pm t^{*}_{30df}\,(s_b) = 1.38573 \pm 1.697\,(0.09374)$. Note that choice B gives a 95% confidence interval instead of a 90% confidence interval. The other choices all have the wrong standard error of the slope.

17.   **(D)**

Choice I is not true—a simple random sample is unbiased even if there is a difference between the subgroups. But an SRS could disproportionately include members of one group over the other. Stratifying the sample guarantees the percentages of day/night students in the sample to match those of the population. Choice II is true. Taking a larger sample from the stratum with the greatest variability can help yield the least possible sampling variance. Choice III is also true. We now have data separated by the subgroups for easy comparison.

18.   **(D)**

Increasing α, the probability of a Type I error, increases power. While we may reject more true null hypotheses, we reject more of the false ones, too. Increasing n also increases power. The more representative the sample, the more chance the test has of making the correct decision.

19.   **(D)**

Since these are relative frequency histograms, we know nothing about sample sizes or numbers of students. We can add relative frequencies of the bars to see that the median of B is larger than the median of A. Class A's distribution clearly has a smaller spread, so its standard deviation must be smaller.

20.   **(A)**

The distribution is symmetric, so the mean is at the peak, around 50. The curve looks very close to that of a normal curve. In a normal distribution density curve, the inflection points are one standard deviation away from the mean. The inflection points appear to be around 42 and 58, making the standard deviation close to 8.

21.   **(E)**

Correlation is independent of which variable we call x and which we call y. In the formula for correlation, the x's and y's can be easily swapped.

22.   **(D)**

When we add independent random variables, we add their means and variances. The sum of the means is 415. We need to square the individual standard deviations to calculate the individual variances before adding them together. The sum of the five variances is 81, so the standard deviation of the sum is 9.

23.   **(E)**

With a sample size of 30, the confidence interval for the mean uses $30 - 1 = 29$ degrees of freedom. The t-critical value for a 90% confidence interval with 29 degrees of freedom is 1.699.

$$\bar{x} \pm 1.699 \frac{\sigma}{\sqrt{n}} = 3.39 \pm 1.699 \frac{0.38}{\sqrt{30}}.$$

24.   **(D)**

The null hypothesis should be an equation representing the advertised claim. The alternative should be an inequality that the competitor is trying to show. In this case, if they believe the repair rate has been understated, then they believe it is higher than 3%.

25.   **(B)**

We are looking at the sampling distribution of $\bar{x}$. The mean of a sampling distribution is always equal to the population mean, so $\mu_{\bar{x}} = 3.5$. Since the standard deviation of a sampling distribution is given by

$\sigma_{\bar{x}} = \dfrac{\sigma}{\sqrt{n}}$, we can see that $\sigma_{\bar{x}} < \sigma$.

26.   **(C)**

Well-designed experiments are the only way to ensure a cause–effect relationship.

27.   **(A)**

The slope is 0.118 and is measured in units y per unit x, or thousands of dollars per square foot. This means that for every additional square foot, the price increases by about $118.

28.   **(B)**

Residuals are calculated by taking the actual value minus predicted value. This home that sold for $300,000 was predicted by the least-squares regression line to sell for $0.118(2500) + 42.0 = \$337,000$. So the residual is $300,000 $- \$337,000 = -\$37,000$.

29.   **(A)**

Since the null hypothesis is that the true proportions are equal, we pool our surveys together for the calculation of the standard deviation of $p_1 - p_2$. This pooled proportion is $\dfrac{168+306}{285+419} = 0.673$. If we were doing a confidence interval, we would not be able to assume that they are equal, and we would use the denominator of choice B as our standard error.

30.   **(B)**

We want the probability of each of the two packages having at least one defective. The probability of at least one is $1 - P(\text{none})$. For one package, the probability of no defective bulbs is $(0.98)^{20}$. Therefore, the probability of at least one is $1 - (0.98)^{20}$. Since the packages are independent of each other, we just square this result for our answer. Choices C and D are wrong since we cannot use the normal approximation without having at least 10 expected defectives per package. Choices A and E are wrong because they are calculating the probability of at least one defective in 1 package of 40 instead of one defective in each of 2 packages of 20.

31.   **(E)**

The residual for $x = 9$ is -3. We see this from the graph. A residual is the actual y-value minus the predicted y-value. Since the actual y-value for $x = 9$ was 35, we have $-3 = 35 - \hat{y}$, so $\hat{y} = 38$.

32.   **(C)**

Since the probabilities decrease as x increases, the distribution is skewed right. Such distributions have the mean higher than the median, as the mean is more affected by the few high values of x.

33.   **(B)**

In a chi-square test for homogeneity (or for independence) the expected value of a cell is given by

$$\frac{(\text{row total})\,(\text{column total})}{\text{table total}} = \frac{(1{,}047)\,(793)}{3{,}081}.$$

34.   **(D)**

The coach is comparing means, so any chi-square test is out. There are two groups, so choice A is out. The 15 swimmers in each group are not paired in any way, so this is not a matched-pairs design. We cannot possibly know the values of the true standard deviations for each group, so we will be using the sample standard deviations instead. This means we are using a two-sample t-test.

35.   **(E)**

When we use a boxplot, we cannot tell how many observations were made. Any comparison about the number of observations is unwarranted. Choice A is clearly true as the medians increase. Choice B is clearly true as the boxplots for August and September do not overlap. Choice C is clearly true since July has the narrowest boxplot. Choice D is true since $2.50 is below the median for June.

36.   **(A)**

Even though we have all of Harry's and Sam's scores, they are not paired in any way that we can assess the truth of choice A. Harry's and Sam's medians are both equal, at 14. Sam is more consistent, as the spread of the distribution is narrower, even with Sam's outlier. Harry's distribution is right-skewed; it may look left-skewed because of the stemplot, but it is skewed toward larger values. (This is a common misinterpretation on back-to-back plots.)

37.   **(C)**

A 95% confidence interval for a proportion is given by

$$\hat{p} \pm 1.960\sqrt{\frac{\hat{p}(1-\hat{p})}{n}} = 0.520 \pm 1.960\sqrt{\frac{(0.520)(0.480)}{627}}.$$ Note that choice B

is a confidence interval for the true proportion of voters who will NOT vote for the politician.

38.   **(D)**

Choice I is correct since the new homes' points are generally above the old homes' points. Choice II is not true. The steepness of the patterns of points for the two ages of homes is about the same. Because new homes generally cost more than old homes of the same size, it does NOT mean that the increase in price per unit area is more. Choice III is true. The scatterplot shows a strong association as there is a clear pattern to the points.

39.   **(D)**

A confidence interval gives us a set of values that would not surprise us if they included the true value of the parameter. The slope can be interpreted as the average change in fuel economy for every additional liter in engine size. Choice D gives us this interpretation. The confidence level of 95% does not refer to a probability about the specific interval. Also, choice C is silly since the confidence interval always contains the sample slope because that is where it was centered.

40.   **(E)**

Gender is a categorical variable. Correlations are only calculated between two numeric variables.

Free-Response Solutions

1.   (a)   Women tend to have slower times for the 100 m Butterfly than men, averaging about 6.3 seconds longer. Both distributions are skewed right showing at least one swimmer of each gender with a time high above the mean—these are outliers. The women's times were a little more spread out overall, with a greater range and standard deviation, but the middle half of each group has about the same spread—the IQRs are about the same.

(b)   The fastest women's time of 57.47 seconds is slower than the men's third quartile time. We cannot assume a normal distribution of times given the skew; at least 75% of the men had times faster than the women's fastest time.

(c)   The men's slowest time of 61.6 seconds is slightly slower than the women's median time—almost to the third quartile. The proportion of women's times that are faster than this time is between 50 and 75%.

2.   (a)   Since the weights of the passengers and their luggage are combined, we can add means and variances to get the mean and variance of the total. $\mu_{total} = 175 + 70 = 245$ pounds and $\sigma^2_{total} = 25^2 + 13^2 = 794$. So, $\sigma_{total} = \sqrt{794} \approx 28.18$ pounds.

(b)   For 18 passengers, independent of each other, the mean weight is $18(245) = 4{,}410$ pounds and the variance is $(18)(794) = 14{,}292$, so the standard deviation of the total weight is about 119.55 pounds. Since the individual random variables had normal distributions, so will their sum. If X is the total weight of all passengers and luggage, we want

$$P(X > 4{,}700) = P\left(z > \frac{4{,}700 - 4{,}410}{119.55}\right) = P(z > 3.26) \approx 0.0078.$$

The plane is unlikely to be overloaded.

3. (a) By surveying students at schools about family size, we will double count many families that have multiple children in school. Their family sizes will be overrepresented in our sample. We will tend to get results that are higher than the truth.

   (b) To use the student population as the sampling frame, we could do a couple things. One possibility is asking the students if they are the oldest or only child in their family who attends school. We would then use data only from those children. Another possibility is to sample the children at the school and ask them how many siblings they have at the school. A child with one other sibling would have his data only weighted by half, since the other half would be counted if his sibling is sampled, too.

4. (a) There is a strong, negative, slightly curved relationship between herd size and production cost per unit among ranches in this county.

   (b) For the small herd size, the six points furthest left on the scatterplot show a strong, negative, linear relationship between the herd size and the production cost per unit. For the medium herd size, there is a strong, slightly negative, linear relationship between the herd size and the cost per unit. For the large herds, there is no visible relationship between the variables. If there is a relationship, it appears to be very weak.

   (c) For a herd size of 300 cattle, we have

   $$
   \begin{aligned}
   \log(cost) &= 2.80 - 0.0784\log(size) \\
   &= 2.80 - 0.0784\log(300) \\
   &= 2.80 - 0.0784(2.477) \\
   &= 2.80 - 0.194 \\
   &\approx 2.61.
   \end{aligned}
   $$

   So, $cost = 10^{2.61} \approx \$403.45$ per unit.

   (d) Because the residuals plot of the transformed data shows a random scatter and the r-squared value is so high, we can be comfortable with our new model. Our prediction is valid and probably quite accurate. The residuals on $\log(cost)$ are never more than 0.01 in absolute value, meaning that our prediction of log cost could be anywhere from 2.60 to 2.62, which yields a cost per unit between $398 and $417.

5. Step 1: State the parameter of interest and a correct pair of hypotheses: there is no parameter of interest here. We want to know if there is an association between preferred software and gender.

H₀: there is no association between preferred software type and gender.

H_a: there is an association between preferred software type and gender.

Step 2: Name the inference procedure and check assumptions/conditions: since the data are categorical, we will use a chi-square test of independence. We have a random sample of students and there are at least six counts in each cell, so the procedures will work fine. The expected values for each cell if the null hypothesis were true would be as follows.

	Male	Female	Total
A	20	21	41
B	12.68	13.32	26
C	7.32	7.68	15
Total	40	42	82

Step 3: Calculate the test statistic and *P*-value: the chi-square statistic is $\sum \frac{(\text{observed} - \text{expected})^2}{\text{expected}}$. That is,

$$\chi^2 = \frac{(15-20)^2}{20} + \frac{(26-21)^2}{21} + \frac{(16-12.68)^2}{12.68}$$
$$+ \frac{(10-13.32)^2}{13.32} + \frac{(9-7.32)^2}{7.32} + \frac{(6-7.68)^2}{7.68}$$
$$= 4.90.$$

The number of degrees of freedom is (rows − 1)(columns − 1) = 2. With 2 degrees of freedom, a chi-square value of 4.90 yields a *P*-value of between 0.05 and 0.10—the exact value is 0.086.

Step 4: Interpret the results in context. The *P*-value of 0.086 means that if there really were no association between gender and software preference, we would see a chi-square statistic at least as large as 4.90 about 8.6% of the time—about one chance in 11. This is fairly likely, so I will fail to reject the null hypothesis. Based on these data, there is insufficient evidence of an association between gender and software preference.

6. (a) **State Procedure and Parameter of Interest:**

The proper procedure is the two-sample t-test for the difference in mean level of pain relief between Medications A and B. (Note that the populations here are the headaches, not the volunteers.)

State Hypotheses:

H_0: $\mu_A - \mu_B = 0$, where μA is the mean level of pain relief for Medication A, and

H_A: $\mu_A - \mu_B \neq 0$, where μB is the mean level of pain relief for Medication B.

H_0: the mean level of pain relief for Medication A is equal to the mean level for Medication B

H_A: the mean level of pain relief for Medication A is different than the mean level for Medication B.

Check Assumptions/Conditions:

(1) The samples are independent: It is reasonable to assume this, since the treatments are randomly assigned to each headache.

(2) Data are from Simple Random Samples: Not samples, but the randomization condition is met by the random allocation of treatments.

(3) Both populations are Normally distributed: The sample sizes are large, both over 200, so the sampling distribution of the difference in sample means should be approximately Normal.

Calculate Test Statistic and P-value:

$$t = \frac{2.36 - 2.61}{\sqrt{\frac{s_A^2}{n_A} + \frac{s_B^2}{n_B}}} = \frac{-0.25}{\sqrt{\frac{1.4^2}{228} + \frac{1.21^2}{263}}} = \frac{-0.25}{0.119} = -2.10$$

with a minimum of 227 degrees of freedom (smaller of $n_A - 1$ and $n_B - 1$).

The P-value for the right-tailed test with $t \approx -2.10$ is between 0.02 and 0.04. (Graphing calculator output gives $t \approx 2.105$, $P \approx 0.036$, and $df \approx 452$.)

Interpret Test Evidence / Summarize in Context:

Since this P-value is small, we can reject the null hypothesis and conclude that there is a significant difference in mean level of relief.

(Solution using Confidence Interval acceptable since this is a two-sided test)

95% CI:

$$(\bar{x}_A - \bar{x}_B) \pm t^*_{227df, 95\%} \sqrt{\frac{s_A^2}{n_A} + \frac{s_B^2}{n_B}} \Rightarrow (2.36 - 2.61) \pm 1.984 \sqrt{\frac{1.4^2}{228} + \frac{1.21^2}{263}} \Rightarrow -0.25 \pm 0.236$$

$(-0.486 < \mu A - \mu B < -0.014)$ [Note: t^* is from 100 df line on t-table]

(Graphing calculator output gives $(-0.4839, -0.0161)$. $df \approx 452$.)

We are 95% confident that the true difference in mean level of pain relief between Medications A and B is between −0.48 and −0.02. That is, Medication B, on average, gives a higher mean pain relief by between 0.48 and 0.02. Since zero is not in the interval, we can conclude there is a significant difference in mean level of pain relief between Medications A and B.

(b) **State Procedure and Parameter of Interest:**

The proper procedure is the two-sample z-test for the difference in the proportion of headaches with total relief between Medications A and B. (Again, the populations here are the headaches, not the volunteers.)

State Hypotheses:

H_0: $p_A - p_B = 0$, where p_A is the proportion of headaches with total relief for Medication A, and

H_A: $p_A - p_B \neq 0$, where p_B is the proportion of headaches with total relief for Medication B.

H_0: the proportion of headaches with total relief for Medication A is equal to the proportion for Medication B

H_A: the proportion of headaches with total relief for Medication A is different than the proportion for Medication B.

Check Assumptions/Conditions:

The independence and randomization conditions were checked in part a.

(3) At least 10 successes and failures in each group: Yes, there were 19 successes and 209 failures in group A; there were 10 successes and 253 failures in group B.

(Note: some texts require these values to be at least 5 instead of 10.)

Calculate Test Statistic and P-value:

$$\hat{p}_A = \frac{19}{228}, \ \hat{p}_B = \frac{10}{263}, \text{ and the pooled proportion is } p_c = \frac{19+10}{228+263}$$

$$z = \frac{\hat{p}_A - \hat{p}_B}{\sqrt{p_c(1-p_c)\left(\frac{1}{n_a} + \frac{1}{n_b}\right)}} = \frac{0.083 - 0.038}{\sqrt{0.059(0.941)\left(\frac{1}{228} + \frac{1}{263}\right)}} = 2.12.$$

The P-value for the two-tailed test with $z \approx 2.12$ is 0.034.

Interpret Test Evidence / Summarize in Context:

Since the P-value is so small, we can reject the null hypothesis and conclude that there is also a significant difference in the proportion of patients getting total relief.

(Solution using Confidence Interval acceptable since this is a two-sided test)

95% CI:

$$(\hat{p}_A - \hat{p}_B) \pm z^* \sqrt{\frac{\hat{p}_A(1-\hat{p}_A)}{n_A} + \frac{\hat{p}_B(1-\hat{p}_B)}{n_B}}$$

$$\Rightarrow (0.0833 - 0.0380) \pm 1.960\sqrt{\frac{0.0833(0.9167)}{228} + \frac{0.0380(0.9620)}{263}}$$

$$\Rightarrow -0.045 \pm 0.0427$$

$$(0.0026 < p_A - p_B < 0.0880)$$

We are 95% confident that the true difference in the proportion of headaches with total relief between Medications A and B is between 0.003 and 0.088. That is, Medication A gives total pain relief between 0.3% and 8.8% more often than Medication B. Since zero is not in the interval, we can conclude there is a significant difference in the proportion of headaches with total relief between Medications A and B.

(c) Medication A has a higher proportion of patients getting total relief and should advertise that way. It has a significantly higher proportion of headaches experiencing total relief.

(d) Medication B has a higher mean pain relief rating. They should advertise that they have a significantly higher average relief rating when patients take this medication after a headache.

Appendices

FORMULAS AND TABLES

I. DESCRIPTIVE STATISTICS

$$\bar{x} = \frac{\sum x_i}{n}$$

$$s_x = \sqrt{\frac{1}{n-1}\sum (x_i - \bar{x})^2}$$

$$s_p = \sqrt{\frac{(n_1-1)s_1^2 + (n_2-1)s_2^2}{(n_1-1)+(n_2-1)}}$$

$$\hat{y} = b_0 + b_1 x$$

$$b_1 = \frac{\sum (x_i - \bar{x})(y_i - \bar{y})}{\sum (x_i - \bar{x})^2}$$

$$b_0 = \bar{y} - b_1 \bar{x}$$

$$r = \frac{1}{n-1}\sum \left(\frac{x_i - \bar{x}}{s_x}\right)\left(\frac{y_i - \bar{y}}{s_y}\right)$$

$$b_1 = r\frac{s_y}{s_x}$$

$$s_{b_1} = \frac{\sqrt{\frac{\sum(y_i - \hat{y}_i)^2}{n-2}}}{\sqrt{\sum(x_i - \bar{x})^2}}.$$

II. PROBABILITY

$$P(A \cup B) = P(A) + P(B) - P(A \cap B)$$

$$P(A|B) = \frac{P(A \cap B)}{P(B)}$$

$$E(X) = \mu_x = \sum x_i p_i$$

$$\text{Var}(X) = \sigma_x^2 = \sum(x_i - \mu_x)^2 p_i.$$

If X has a binomial distribution with parameters n and p, then

$$P(X = k) = \binom{n}{k} p^k (1-p)^{n-k}$$

$$\mu_x = np$$

$$\sigma_x = \sqrt{np(1-p)}$$

$$\mu_{\hat{p}} = p$$

$$\sigma_{\hat{p}} = \sqrt{\frac{p(1-p)}{n}}.$$

If $\bar{x}$ is the mean of a random sample of size n from an infinite population with mean μ and standard deviation σ, then

$$\mu_{\bar{x}} = \mu$$

$$\sigma_{\bar{x}} = \frac{\sigma}{\sqrt{n}}.$$

III. INFERENTIAL STATISTICS

$$\text{Standardized test statistic} = \frac{\text{statistic} - \text{parameter}}{\text{standard deviation of statistic}}$$

$$\text{Confidence interval} = \text{statistic} \pm (\text{critical value}) \cdot (\text{standard deviation of statistic}).$$

Single-Sample

Statistic	Standard Deviation of Statistic
Sample Mean	$\dfrac{\sigma}{\sqrt{n}}$
Sample Proportion	$\sqrt{\dfrac{p(1-p)}{n}}$

Two-Sample

Statistic	Standard Deviation of Statistic
Difference of sample means	$\sqrt{\dfrac{\sigma_1^2}{n_1} + \dfrac{\sigma_2^2}{n_2}}$ Special case when $\sigma_1 = \sigma_2$ $\sigma\sqrt{\dfrac{1}{n_1} + \dfrac{1}{n_2}}$
Difference of sample proportions	$\sqrt{\dfrac{p_1(1-p_1)}{n_1} + \dfrac{p_2(1-p_2)}{n_2}}$ Special case when $p_1 = p_2$ $\sqrt{p(1-p)}\sqrt{\dfrac{1}{n_1} + \dfrac{1}{n_2}}$

$$\text{Chi-square test statistic} = \sum \frac{(\text{observed} - \text{expected})^2}{\text{expected}}$$

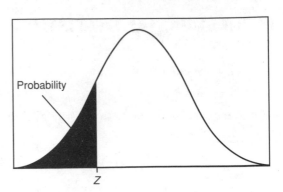

Table entry for z is the
probability lying below z.

Table A   Standard normal probabilities

Z	0.00	0.01	0.02	0.03	0.04	0.05	0.06	0.07	0.08	0.09
−3.4	0.0003	0.0003	0.0003	0.0003	0.0003	0.0003	0.0003	0.0003	0.0003	0.0002
−3.3	0.0005	0.0005	0.0005	0.0004	0.0004	0.0004	0.0004	0.0004	0.0004	0.0003
−3.2	0.0007	0.0007	0.0006	0.0006	0.0006	0.0006	0.0006	0.0005	0.0005	0.0005
−3.1	0.0010	0.0009	0.0009	0.0009	0.0008	0.0008	0.0008	0.0008	0.0007	0.0007
−3.0	0.0013	0.0013	0.0013	0.0012	0.0012	0.0011	0.0011	0.0011	0.0010	0.0010
−2.9	0.0019	0.0018	0.0018	0.0017	0.0016	0.0016	0.0015	0.0015	0.0014	0.0014
−2.8	0.0026	0.0025	0.0024	0.0023	0.0023	0.0022	0.0021	0.0021	0.0020	0.0019
−2.7	0.0035	0.0034	0.0033	0.0032	0.0031	0.0030	0.0029	0.0028	0.0027	0.0026
−2.6	0.0047	0.0045	0.0044	0.0043	0.0041	0.0040	0.0039	0.0038	0.0037	0.0036
−2.5	0.0062	0.0060	0.0059	0.0057	0.0055	0.0054	0.0052	0.0051	0.0049	0.0048
−2.4	0.0082	0.0080	0.0078	0.0075	0.0073	0.0071	0.0069	0.0068	0.0066	0.0064
−2.3	0.0107	0.0104	0.0102	0.0099	0.0096	0.0094	0.0091	0.0089	0.0087	0.0084
−2.2	0.0139	0.0136	0.0132	0.0129	0.0125	0.0122	0.0119	0.0116	0.0113	0.0110
−2.1	0.0179	0.0174	0.0170	0.0166	0.0162	0.0158	0.0154	0.0150	0.0146	0.0143
−2.0	0.0228	0.0222	0.0217	0.0212	0.0207	0.0202	0.0197	0.0192	0.0188	0.0183
−1.9	0.0287	0.0281	0.0274	0.0268	0.0262	0.0256	0.0250	0.0244	0.0239	0.0233
−1.8	0.0359	0.0351	0.0344	0.0336	0.0329	0.0322	0.0314	0.0307	0.0301	0.0294
−1.7	0.0446	0.0436	0.0427	0.0418	0.0409	0.0401	0.0392	0.0384	0.0375	0.0367
−1.6	0.0548	0.0537	0.0526	0.0516	0.0505	0.0495	0.0485	0.0475	0.0465	0.0455
−1.5	0.0668	0.0655	0.0643	0.0630	0.0618	0.0606	0.0594	0.0582	0.0571	0.0559
−1.4	0.0808	0.0793	0.0778	0.0764	0.0749	0.0735	0.0721	0.0708	0.0694	0.0681
−1.3	0.0968	0.0951	0.0934	0.0918	0.0901	0.0885	0.0869	0.0853	0.0838	0.0823
−1.2	0.1151	0.1131	0.1112	0.1093	0.1075	0.1056	0.1038	0.1020	0.1003	0.0985
−1.1	0.1357	0.1335	0.1314	0.1292	0.1271	0.1251	0.1230	0.1210	0.1190	0.1170
−1.0	0.1587	0.1562	0.1539	0.1515	0.1492	0.1469	0.1446	0.1423	0.1401	0.1379
−0.9	0.1841	0.1814	0.1788	0.1762	0.1736	0.1711	0.1685	0.1660	0.1635	0.1611
−0.8	0.2119	0.2090	0.2061	0.2033	0.2005	0.1977	0.1949	0.1922	0.1894	0.1867
−0.7	0.2420	0.2389	0.2358	0.2327	0.2296	0.2266	0.2236	0.2206	0.2177	0.2148
−0.6	0.2743	0.2709	0.2676	0.2643	0.2611	0.2578	0.2546	0.2514	0.2483	0.2451
−0.5	0.3085	0.3050	0.3015	0.2981	0.2946	0.2912	0.2877	0.2843	0.2810	0.2776
−0.4	0.3446	0.3409	0.3372	0.3336	0.3300	0.3264	0.3228	0.3192	0.3156	0.3121
−0.3	0.3821	0.3783	0.3745	0.3707	0.3669	0.3632	0.3594	0.3557	0.3520	0.3483
−0.2	0.4207	0.4168	0.4129	0.4090	0.4052	0.4013	0.3974	0.3936	0.3897	0.3859
−0.1	0.4602	0.4562	0.4522	0.4483	0.4443	0.4404	0.4364	0.4325	0.4286	0.4247
−0.0	0.5000	0.4960	0.4920	0.4880	0.4840	0.4801	0.4761	0.4721	0.4681	0.4641

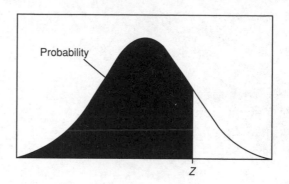

Table entry for z is the
probability lying below z.

Table A *(Continued)*

Z	0.00	0.01	0.02	0.03	0.04	0.05	0.06	0.07	0.08	0.09
0.0	0.5000	0.5040	0.5080	0.5120	0.5160	0.5199	0.5239	0.5279	0.5319	0.5359
0.1	0.5398	0.5438	0.5478	0.5517	0.5557	0.5596	0.5636	0.5675	0.5714	0.5753
0.2	0.5793	0.5832	0.5871	0.5910	0.5948	0.5987	0.6026	0.6064	0.6103	0.6141
0.3	0.6179	0.6217	0.6255	0.6293	0.6331	0.6368	0.6406	0.6443	0.6480	0.6517
0.4	0.6554	0.6591	0.6628	0.6664	0.6700	0.6736	0.6772	0.6808	0.6844	0.6879
0.5	0.6915	0.6950	0.6985	0.7019	0.7054	0.7088	0.7123	0.7157	0.7190	0.7224
0.6	0.7257	0.7291	0.7324	0.7357	0.7389	0.7422	0.7454	0.7486	0.7517	0.7549
0.7	0.7580	0.7611	0.7642	0.7673	0.7704	0.7734	0.7764	0.7794	0.7823	0.7852
0.8	0.7881	0.7910	0.7939	0.7967	0.7995	0.8023	0.8051	0.8078	0.8106	0.8133
0.9	0.8159	0.8186	0.8212	0.8238	0.8264	0.8289	0.8315	0.8340	0.8365	0.8389
1.0	0.8413	0.8438	0.8461	0.8485	0.8508	0.8531	0.8554	0.8577	0.8599	0.8621
1.1	0.8643	0.8665	0.8686	0.8708	0.8729	0.8749	0.8770	0.8790	0.8810	0.8830
1.2	0.8849	0.8869	0.8888	0.8907	0.8925	0.8944	0.8962	0.8980	0.8997	0.9015
1.3	0.9032	0.9049	0.9066	0.9082	0.9099	0.9115	0.9131	0.9147	0.9162	0.9177
1.4	0.9192	0.9207	0.9222	0.9236	0.9251	0.9265	0.9279	0.9292	0.9306	0.9319
1.5	0.9332	0.9345	0.9357	0.9370	0.9382	0.9394	0.9406	0.9418	0.9429	0.9441
1.6	0.9452	0.9463	0.9474	0.9484	0.9495	0.9505	0.9515	0.9525	0.9535	0.9545
1.7	0.9554	0.9564	0.9573	0.9582	0.9591	0.9599	0.9608	0.9616	0.9625	0.9633
1.8	0.9641	0.9649	0.9656	0.9664	0.9671	0.9678	0.9686	0.9693	0.9699	0.9706
1.9	0.9713	0.9719	0.9726	0.9732	0.9738	0.9744	0.9750	0.9756	0.9761	0.9767
2.0	0.9772	0.9778	0.9783	0.9788	0.9793	0.9798	0.9803	0.9808	0.9812	0.9817
2.1	0.9821	0.9826	0.9830	0.9834	0.9838	0.9842	0.9846	0.9850	0.9854	0.9857
2.2	0.9861	0.9864	0.9868	0.9871	0.9875	0.9878	0.9881	0.9884	0.9887	0.9890
2.3	0.9893	0.9896	0.9898	0.9901	0.9904	0.9906	0.9909	0.9911	0.9913	0.9916
2.4	0.9918	0.9920	0.9922	0.9925	0.9927	0.9929	0.9931	0.9932	0.9934	0.9936
2.5	0.9938	0.9940	0.9941	0.9943	0.9945	0.9946	0.9948	0.9949	0.9951	0.9952
2.6	0.9953	0.9955	0.9956	0.9957	0.9959	0.9960	0.9961	0.9962	0.9963	0.9964
2.7	0.9965	0.9966	0.9967	0.9968	0.9969	0.9970	0.9971	0.9972	0.9973	0.9974
2.8	0.9974	0.9975	0.9976	0.9977	0.9977	0.9978	0.9979	0.9979	0.9980	0.9981
2.9	0.9981	0.9982	0.9982	0.9983	0.9984	0.9984	0.9985	0.9985	0.9986	0.9986
3.0	0.9987	0.9987	0.9987	0.9988	0.9988	0.9989	0.9989	0.9989	0.9990	0.9990
3.1	0.9990	0.9991	0.9991	0.9991	0.9992	0.9992	0.9992	0.9992	0.9993	0.9993
3.2	0.9993	0.9993	0.9994	0.9994	0.9994	0.9994	0.9994	0.9995	0.9995	0.9995
3.3	0.9995	0.9995	0.9995	0.9996	0.9996	0.9996	0.9996	0.9996	0.9996	0.9997
3.4	0.9997	0.9997	0.9997	0.9997	0.9997	0.9997	0.9997	0.9997	0.9997	0.9998

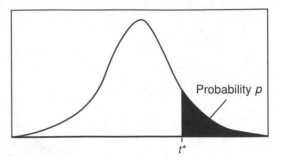

Table entry for p and C is the point t^* with probability p lying above it and probability C lying between $-t^*$ and t^*.

Probability p

t^*

Table B t-distribution critical values

df	0.25	0.20	0.15	0.10	0.05	0.025	0.02	0.01	0.005	0.0025	0.001	0.0005
1	1.000	1.376	1.963	3.078	6.314	12.71	15.89	31.82	63.66	127.3	318.3	636.6
2	0.816	1.061	1.386	1.886	2.920	4.303	4.849	6.965	9.925	14.09	22.33	31.60
3	0.765	0.978	1.250	1.638	2.353	3.182	3.482	4.541	5.841	7.453	10.21	12.92
4	0.741	0.941	1.190	1.533	2.132	2.776	2.999	3.747	4.604	5.598	7.173	8.610
5	0.727	0.920	1.156	1.476	2.015	2.571	2.757	3.365	4.032	4.773	5.893	6.869
6	0.718	0.906	1.134	1.440	1.943	2.447	2.612	3.143	3.707	4.317	5.208	5.959
7	0.711	0.896	1.119	1.415	1.895	2.365	2.517	2.998	3.499	4.029	4.785	5.408
8	0.706	0.889	1.108	1.397	1.860	2.306	2.449	2.896	3.355	3.833	4.501	5.041
9	0.703	0.883	1.100	1.383	1.833	2.262	2.398	2.821	3.250	3.690	4.297	4.781
10	0.700	0.879	1.093	1.372	1.812	2.228	2.359	2.764	3.169	3.581	4.144	4.587
11	0.697	0.876	1.088	1.363	1.796	2.201	2.328	2.718	3.106	3.497	4.025	4.437
12	0.695	0.873	1.083	1.356	1.782	2.179	2.303	2.681	3.055	3.428	3.930	4.318
13	0.694	0.870	1.079	1.350	1.771	2.160	2.282	2.650	3.012	3.372	3.852	4.221
14	0.692	0.868	1.076	1.345	1.761	2.145	2.264	2.624	2.977	3.326	3.787	4.140
15	0.691	0.866	1.074	1.341	1.753	2.131	2.249	2.602	2.947	3.286	3.733	4.073
16	0.690	0.865	1.071	1.337	1.746	2.120	2.235	2.583	2.921	3.252	3.686	4.015
17	0.689	0.863	1.069	1.333	1.740	2.110	2.224	2.567	2.898	3.222	3.646	3.965
18	0.688	0.862	1.067	1.330	1.734	2.101	2.214	2.552	2.878	3.197	3.611	3.922
19	0.688	0.861	1.066	1.328	1.729	2.093	2.205	2.539	2.861	3.174	3.579	3.883
20	0.687	0.860	1.064	1.325	1.725	2.086	2.197	2.528	2.845	3.153	3.552	3.850
21	0.686	0.859	1.063	1.323	1.721	2.080	2.189	2.518	2.831	3.135	3.527	3.819
22	0.686	0.858	1.061	1.321	1.717	2.074	2.183	2.508	2.819	3.119	3.505	3.792
23	0.685	0.858	1.060	1.319	1.714	2.069	2.177	2.500	2.807	3.104	3.485	3.768
24	0.685	0.857	1.059	1.318	1.711	2.064	2.172	2.492	2.797	3.091	3.467	3.745
25	0.684	0.856	1.058	1.316	1.708	2.060	2.167	2.485	2.787	3.078	3.450	3.725
26	0.684	0.856	1.058	1.315	1.706	2.056	2.162	2.479	2.779	3.067	3.435	3.707
27	0.684	0.855	1.057	1.314	1.703	2.052	2.158	2.473	2.771	3.057	3.421	3.690
28	0.683	0.855	1.056	1.313	1.701	2.048	2.154	2.467	2.763	3.047	3.408	3.674
29	0.683	0.854	1.055	1.311	1.699	2.045	2.150	2.462	2.756	3.038	3.396	3.659
30	0.683	0.854	1.055	1.310	1.697	2.042	2.147	2.457	2.750	3.030	3.385	3.646
40	0.681	0.851	1.050	1.303	1.684	2.021	2.123	2.423	2.704	2.971	3.307	3.551
50	0.679	0.849	1.047	1.299	1.676	2.009	2.109	2.403	2.678	2.937	3.261	3.496
60	0.679	0.848	1.045	1.296	1.671	2.000	2.099	2.390	2.660	2.915	3.232	3.460
80	0.678	0.846	1.043	1.292	1.664	1.990	2.088	2.374	2.639	2.887	3.195	3.416
100	0.677	0.845	1.042	1.290	1.660	1.984	2.081	2.364	2.626	2.871	3.174	3.390
1000	0.675	0.842	1.037	1.282	1.646	1.962	2.056	2.330	2.581	2.813	3.098	3.300
∞	0.674	0.841	1.036	1.282	1.645	1.960	2.054	2.326	2.576	2.807	3.091	3.291
	50%	60%	70%	80%	90%	95%	96%	98%	99%	99.5%	99.8%	99.9%

Tail probability p

Confidence level C

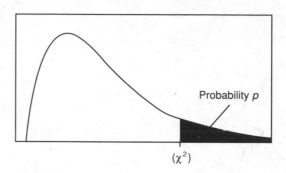

Table entry for p is the point (χ^2) with probability p lying above it

(χ^2)

Table C χ^2-critical values

df	0.25	0.20	0.15	0.10	0.05	0.025	0.02	0.01	0.005	0.0025	0.001
1	1.32	1.64	2.07	2.71	3.84	5.02	5.41	6.63	7.88	9.14	10.83
2	2.77	3.22	3.79	4.61	5.99	7.38	7.82	9.21	10.60	11.98	13.82
3	4.11	4.64	5.32	6.25	7.81	9.35	9.84	11.34	12.84	14.32	16.27
4	5.39	5.99	6.74	7.78	9.49	11.14	11.67	13.28	14.86	16.42	18.47
5	6.63	7.29	8.12	9.24	11.07	12.83	13.39	15.09	16.75	18.39	20.51
6	7.84	8.56	9.45	10.64	12.59	14.45	15.03	16.81	18.55	20.25	22.46
7	9.04	9.80	10.75	12.02	14.07	16.01	16.62	18.48	20.28	22.04	24.32
8	10.22	11.03	12.03	13.36	15.51	17.53	18.17	20.09	21.95	23.77	26.12
9	11.39	12.24	13.29	14.68	16.92	19.02	19.68	21.67	23.59	25.46	27.88
10	12.55	13.44	14.53	15.99	18.31	20.48	21.16	23.21	25.19	27.11	29.59
11	13.70	14.63	15.77	17.28	19.68	21.92	22.62	24.72	26.76	28.73	31.26
12	14.85	15.81	16.99	18.55	21.03	23.34	24.05	26.22	28.30	30.32	32.91
13	15.98	16.98	18.20	19.81	22.36	24.74	25.47	27.69	29.82	31.88	34.53
14	17.12	18.15	19.41	21.06	23.68	26.12	26.87	29.14	31.32	33.43	36.12
15	18.25	19.31	20.60	22.31	25.00	27.49	28.26	30.58	32.80	34.95	37.70
16	19.37	20.47	21.79	23.54	26.30	28.85	29.63	32.00	34.27	36.46	39.25
17	20.49	21.61	22.98	24.77	27.59	30.19	31.00	33.41	35.72	37.95	40.79
18	21.60	22.76	24.16	25.99	28.87	31.53	32.35	34.81	37.16	39.42	42.31
19	22.72	23.90	25.33	27.20	30.14	32.85	33.69	36.19	38.58	40.88	43.82
20	23.83	25.04	26.50	28.41	31.41	34.17	35.02	37.57	40.00	42.34	45.31
21	24.93	26.17	27.66	29.62	32.67	35.48	36.34	38.93	41.40	43.78	46.80
22	26.04	27.30	28.82	30.81	33.92	36.78	37.66	40.29	42.80	45.20	48.27
23	27.14	28.43	29.98	32.01	35.17	38.08	38.97	41.64	44.18	46.62	49.73
24	28.24	29.55	31.13	33.20	36.42	39.36	40.27	42.98	45.56	48.03	51.18
25	29.34	30.68	32.28	34.38	37.65	40.65	41.57	44.31	46.93	49.44	52.62
26	30.43	31.79	33.43	35.56	38.89	41.92	42.86	45.64	48.29	50.83	54.05
27	31.53	32.91	34.57	36.74	40.11	43.19	44.14	46.96	49.64	52.22	55.48
28	32.62	34.03	35.71	37.92	41.34	44.46	45.42	48.28	50.99	53.59	56.89
29	33.71	35.14	36.85	39.09	42.56	45.72	46.69	49.59	52.34	54.97	58.30
30	34.80	36.25	37.99	40.26	43.77	46.98	47.96	50.89	53.67	56.33	59.70
40	45.62	47.27	49.24	51.81	55.76	59.34	60.44	63.69	66.77	69.70	73.40
50	56.33	58.16	60.35	63.17	67.50	71.42	72.61	76.15	79.49	82.66	86.66
60	66.98	68.97	71.34	74.40	79.08	83.30	84.58	88.38	91.95	95.34	99.61
80	88.13	90.41	93.11	96.58	101.9	106.6	108.1	112.3	116.3	120.1	124.8
100	109.1	111.7	114.7	118.5	124.3	129.6	131.1	135.8	140.2	144.3	149.4

GLOSSARY

Addition rule: $P(A \cup B) = P(A) + P(B) - P(A \cap B)$ aids in computing the chances of one of several events occurring at a given time.

Alpha (α): the probability of a Type I error. See significance level.

Alternative hypothesis: the hypothesis stating what the researcher is seeking evidence of. A statement of inequality. It can be written looking for the difference or change in one direction from the null hypothesis or both.

Association: relationship between or among variables.

Back-transform: the process by which values are substituted into a model of transformed data, and then reversing the transforming process to obtain the predicted value or model for nontransformed data.

Bar chart: a graphical display used with categorical data, where frequencies for each category are shown in vertical bars.

Bell-shaped: often used to describe the normal distribution. See mound-shaped.

Beta (β): The probability of a Type II error. See power.

Bias: the term for systematic deviation from the truth (parameter), caused by systematically favoring some outcomes over others.

Biased: a sampling method is biased if it tends to produce samples that do not represent the population.

Bimodal: a distribution with two clear peaks.

Binomial distribution: the probability distribution of a binomial random variable.

Binomial random variable: a random variable X (a) that has a fixed number of trials of a random phenomenon n, (b) that has only two possible outcomes on each trial, (c) for which the probability of a success is constant for each trial, and (d) for which each trial is independent of other trials.

Bins: the intervals that define the "bars" of a histogram.

Bivariate data: consists of two variables, an explanatory and a response variable, usually quantitative.

Blinding: practice of denying knowledge to subjects about which treatment is imposed upon them.

Blocks: subgroups of the experimental units that are separated by some characteristic before treatments are assigned because they may respond differently to the treatments.

Box-and-whisker plot/boxplot: a graphical display of the five-number summary of a set of data, which also shows outliers.

Categorical variable: a variable recorded as labels, names, or other non-numerical outcomes.

Census: a study that observes, or attempts to observe, every individual in a population.

Central limit theorem: as the size n of a simple random sample increases, the shape of the sampling distribution of $\bar{x}$ tends toward being normally distributed.

Chance device: a mechanism used to determine random outcomes.

Cluster sample: a sample in which a simple random sample of heterogeneous subgroups of a population is selected.

Clusters: heterogeneous subgroups of a population.

Coefficient of determination (r^2): percent of variation in the response variable explained by its linear relationship with the explanatory variable.

Complement: the complement of an event is that event not occurring.

Complementary events: two events whose probabilities add up to 1.

Completely randomized design: one in which all experimental units are assigned treatments solely by chance.

Conditional distribution: see conditional frequencies.

Conditional frequencies: relative frequencies for each cell in a two-way table relative to one variable.

Conditional probability: the probability of an event occurring given that another has occurred. The probability of A given that B has occurred is denoted as $P(A|B)$.

Confidence intervals: give an estimated range that is likely to contain an unknown population parameter.

Confidence level: the level of certainty that a population parameter exists in the calculated confidence interval.

Confounding: the situation where the effects of two or more explanatory variables on the response variable cannot be separated.

Confounding variable: a variable whose effect on the response variable cannot be untangled from the effects of the treatment.

Contingency table: see two-way table.

Continuous random variables: those typically found by measuring, such as heights or temperatures.

Control group: a baseline group that may be given no treatment, a faux treatment like a placebo, or an accepted treatment that is to be compared to another.

Control: the principle that potential sources of variation due to variables not under consideration must be reduced.

Convenience sample: composed of individuals who are easily accessed or contacted.

Correlation coefficient (r): a measure of the strength of a linear relationship,
$$r = \frac{1}{n-1} \Sigma \left(\frac{x_i - \overline{x}}{s_x} \right) \left(\frac{y_i - \overline{y}}{s_y} \right).$$

Critical value: the value that the test statistic must exceed in order to reject the null hypothesis. When computing a confidence interval, the value of t^* (or z^*) where $\pm t^*$ (or $\pm z^*$) bounds the central $C\%$ of the t (or z) distribution.

Cumulative frequency: the sums of the frequencies of the data values from smallest to largest.

Data set: collection of observations from a sample or population.

Dependent events: two events are called dependent when they are related and the fact that one event has occurred changes the probability that the second event occurs.

Discrete random variables: those usually obtained by counting.

Disjoint events: events that cannot occur simultaneously.

Distribution: frequencies of values in a data set.

Dotplot: a graphical display used with univariate data. Each data point is shown as a dot located above its numerical value on the horizontal axis.

Double-blind: when both the subjects and data gatherers are ignorant about which treatment a subject received.

Empirical rule (68-95-99.7 rule): gives benchmarks for understanding how probability is distributed under a normal curve. In the normal distribution, 68% of the observations are within one standard deviation of the mean, 95% is within two standard deviations of the mean, and 99.7% is within three standard deviations of the mean.

Estimation: the process of determining the value of a population parameter from a sample statistic.

Expected value: the mean of a probability distribution.

Experiment: a study where the researcher deliberately influences individuals by imposing conditions and determining the individuals' responses to those conditions.

Experimental units: individuals in an experiment.

Explanatory variable: explains the response variable, sometimes known as the treatment variable.

Exponential model: a model of the form of $y = ab^x$.

Extrapolation: using a model to predict values far outside the range of the explanatory variable, which is prone to creating unreasonable predictions.

Factors: one or more explanatory variables in an experiment.

First quartile: symbolized Q_1, represents the median of the lower 50% of a data set.

Five-number summary: the minimum, first quartile (Q_1), median, third quartile (Q_3), and maximum values in a data set.

Frequency table: a display organizing categorical or numerical data and how often each occurs.

Geometric distribution: the probability distribution of a geometric random variable X. All possible outcomes of X before the first success is seen and their associated probabilities.

Geometric random variable: a random variable X (a) that has two possible outcomes of each trial, (b) for which the probability of a success is constant for each trial, and (c) for which each trial is independent of the other trials.

Graphical display: a visual representation of a distribution.

Histogram: used with univariate data, frequencies are shown on the vertical axis, and intervals or bins define the values on the horizontal axis.

Independent events: two events are called independent when knowing that one event has occurred does not change the probability that the second event occurs.

Independent random variables: if the values of one random variable have no association with the values of another, the two variables are called independent random variables.

Influential point: an extreme value whose removal would drastically change the slope of the least-squares regression model.

Interquartile range: describes the spread of middle 50% of a data set, $IQR = Q_3 - Q_1$.

Joint distribution: see joint frequencies.

Joint frequencies: frequencies for each cell in a two-way table relative to the total number of data.

Law of large numbers: the long-term relative frequency of an event gets closer to the true relative frequency as the number of trials of a random phenomenon increases.

Least-squares regression line (LSRL): the "best-fit" line that is calculated by minimizing the sum of the squares of the differences between the observed and predicted values of the line. The LSRL has the equation $\hat{y} = b_0 + b_1 x$.

Levels: the different quantities or categories of a factor in an experiment.

Linear regression: a method of finding the best model for a linear relationship between the explanatory and response variable.

Logarithmic transformation: procedure that changes a variable by taking the logarithm of each of its values.

Lurking variable: a variable that has an effect on the outcome of a study but was not part of the investigation.

Margin of error: a range of values to the left and right of a point estimate.

Marginal distribution: see marginal frequencies.

Marginal frequencies: row totals and column totals in a two-way table.

Matched-pairs design: the design of a study where experimental units are naturally paired by a common characteristic, or with themselves in a before–after type of study.

Maximum: the largest numerical value in a data set.

Mean: the arithmetic average of a data set; the sum of all the values divided by the number of values, $\bar{x} = \dfrac{\sum x_i}{n}$.

Mean of a binomial random variable X: $\mu_x = np$.

Mean of a discrete random variable: $\mu_x = \sum_{i=1}^{n} x_i P(x_i)$.

Mean of a geometric random variable: $\mu_x = \dfrac{1}{p}$.

Measures of center: these locate the middle of a distribution. The mean and median are measures of center.

Median: the middle value of a data set; the equal areas point, where 50% of the data are at or below this value, and 50% of the data are at or above this value.

Minimum: the smallest numerical value in a data set.

Mound-shaped: resembles a hill or mound; a distribution that is symmetric and unimodal.

Multiplication rule: $P(A \cap B) = P(A) \cdot P(B|A)$ is used when we are interested in the probability of two events occurring simultaneously, or in succession.

Multistage sample: a sample resulting from multiple applications of cluster, stratified, and/or simple random sampling.

Mutually exclusive events: see disjoint events.

Nonresponse bias: the situation where an individual selected to be in the sample is unwilling, or unable, to provide data.

Normal distribution: a continuous probability distribution that appears in many situations, both natural and man-made. It has a bell-shape and the area under the normal density curve is always equal to 1.

Null hypothesis: the hypothesis of no difference, no change, and no association. A statement of equality, usually written in the form H_0: *parameter* = hypothesized value.

Observational study: attempts to determine relationships between variables, but the researcher imposes no conditions as in an experiment.

Observed values: actual outcomes or data from a study or an experiment.

One-way table: a frequency table of one variable.

Outlier: an extreme value in a data set. Quantified by being less than $Q_1 - 1.5IQR$ or more than $Q_3 + 1.5IQR$.

Percentiles: divide the data set into 100 equal parts. An observation at the Pth percentile is higher than P percent of all observations.

Placebo: a faux treatment given in an experiment that resembles the real treatment under consideration.

Placebo effect: a phenomenon where subjects show a response to a treatment merely because the treatment is imposed regardless of its actual effect.

Point estimate: an approximate value that has been calculated for the unknown parameter.

Population: the collection of all individuals under consideration in a study.

Population parameter: a characteristic or measure of a population.

Position: location of a data value relative to the population.

Power: the probability of correctly rejecting the null hypothesis when it is in fact false. Equal to $1 - \beta$. See beta and Type II error.

Power model: a function in the form of $y = ax^b$.

Predicted value: the value of the response variable predicted by a model for a given explanatory variable.

Probability: describes the chance that a certain outcome of a random phenomenon will occur.

Probability distribution: a discrete random variable X is a function of all n possible outcomes of the random variable (x_i) and their associated probabilities $P(x_i)$.

Probability sample: composed of individuals selected by chance.

P-value: the probability of observing a test statistic as extreme as, or more extreme than, the statistic obtained from a sample, under the assumption that the null hypothesis is true.

Quantitative: a variable whose values are counts or measurements.

Random digit table: a chance device that is used to select experimental units or conduct simulations.

Random phenomena: those outcomes that are unpredictable in the short term, but nevertheless, have a long-term pattern.

Random sample: a sample composed of individuals selected by chance.

Random variables: numerical outcome of a random phenomenon.

Randomization: the process by which treatments are assigned by a chance mechanism to the experimental units.

Randomized block design: first, units are sorted into subgroups or blocks, and then treatments are randomly assigned within the blocks.

Range: calculated as the maximum value minus the minimum value in a data sct.

Relative frequency: percentage or proportion of the whole number of data.

Relative frequency segmented bar chart: a method of graphing a conditional distribution.

Replication: the practice of reducing chance variation by assigning each treatment to many experimental units.

Residual: observed value minus predicted value of the response variable.

Response bias: because of the manner in which an interview is conducted, because of the phrasing of questions, or because of the attitude of the respondent, inaccurate data are collected.

Response variable: measures the outcomes that have been observed.

Sample: a selected subset of a population from which data are gathered.

Sample statistic: result of a sample used to estimate a parameter.

Sample survey: a study that collects information from a sample of a population in order to determine one or more characteristics of the population.

Sampling distribution: the probability distribution of a sample statistic when a sample is drawn from a population.

Sampling distribution of the sample mean $\bar{x}$: the distribution of sample means from all possible simple random samples of size n taken from a population.

Sampling distribution of a sample proportion $\hat{p}$: the distribution of sample proportions from all possible simple random samples of size n taken from a population.

Sampling error: see sampling variability.

Sampling variability: natural variability due to the sampling process. Each possible random sample from a population will generate a different sample statistic.

Scatterplots: used to visualize bivariate data. The explanatory variable is shown on the horizontal axis and the response variable is shown on the vertical axis.

Significance level: the probability of a Type I error. A benchmark against which the P-value compared to determine if the null hypothesis will be rejected. See also alpha. (α).

Simple random sample (SRS): a sample where n individuals are selected from a population in a way that every possible combination of n individuals is equally likely.

Simulation: a method of modeling chance behavior that accurately mimics the situation being considered.

Skewed: a unimodal, asymmetric, distribution that tends to slant—most of the data are clustered on one side of the distribution and "tails" off on the other side.

Standard deviation of a binomial random variable X: $\sigma_x = \sqrt{np(1-p)}$.

Standard deviation of a discrete random variable X: $\sigma_x = \sqrt{\sigma_x^2}$.

Standard deviation: used to measure variability of a data set. It is calculated as the square root of the variance of a set of data, $s = \sqrt{\dfrac{\sum(x_i - \bar{x})^2}{n-1}}$.

Standard error: an estimate of the standard deviation of the sampling distribution of a statistic.

Standard normal probabilities: the probabilities calculated from values of the standard normal distribution.

Standardized score: the number of standard deviations an observation lies from the mean, $z = \dfrac{\text{observation} - \text{mean}}{\text{standard deviation}}$.

Statistically significant: when a sample statistic is shown to be far from a hypothesized parameter. When the P-value is less than the significance level.

Stemplot: also called a stem-and-leaf plot. Data are separated into a stem and a leaf by place value and organized in the form of a histogram.

Strata: subgroups of a population that are similar or homogenous.

Stratification: part of the sampling process where units of the study are separated into strata.

Stratified random sample: a sample in which simple random samples are selected from each of several homogenous subgroups of the population, known as strata.

Subjects: individuals in an experiment that are people.

Symmetric: the distribution that resembles a mirror image on either side of the center.

Systematic random sample: a sample where every kth individual is selected from a list or queue.

Test statistic: the number of standard deviations (standard errors) that a sample statistic lies from a hypothesized population parameter.

Third quartile: symbolized Q_3, represents the median of the upper 50% of a data set.

Transformation: changing the values of a data set using a mathematical operation.

Treatments: combinations of different levels of the factors in an experiment.

Two-way table: a frequency table that displays two categorical variables.

Type I error: rejecting a null hypothesis when it is in fact true.

Type II error: failing to reject a null hypothesis when it is in fact false.

Undercoverage: when some individuals of a population are not included in the sampling process.

Uniform: all data values in the distribution have the similar frequencies.

Unimodal: a distribution with a single, clearly defined, peak.

Univariate: one-variable data.

Variables: characteristics of the individuals under study.

Variability: the spread in a data set.

Variance: used to measure variability, the average of the squared deviations from the mean, $s_x^2 = \dfrac{\sum (x_i - \overline{x})^2}{n-1}$.

Variance of a binomial random variable X: $\sigma_x^2 = np(1-p)$.

Variance of a discrete random variable X: $\sigma_x^2 = \sum\limits_{i=1}^{n} (x_i - \mu_x)^2 \cdot P(x_i)$.

Venn diagram: graphical representation of sets or outcomes and how they intersect.

Voluntary response bias: bias due to the manner in which people choose to respond to voluntary surveys.

Voluntary response sample: composed of individuals who choose to respond to a survey because of interest in the subject.

z-score: see standardized score.

INDEX OF PRACTICE EXAM PROBLEMS

Following is a correlation of the problems on the four practice exams to the AP Statistics Topic Outline. Some questions may apply to more than one topic.

I: Exploring Data	Practice Exam			
	1	2	3	4
A. Constructing and interpreting graphical displays of distributions of univariate data	MC: 34 FR: 1	MC: 24 FR: 1	MC: 1	MC: 36 FR: 1
B. Summarizing distributions of univariate data	MC: 4, 17 FR: 1, 6	MC: 2, 11, 13 FR: 1	MC: 1, 10, 27 FR: 1	MC: 1, 7, 14
C. Comparing distributions of univariate data	MC: 16, 39 FR: 1	MC: 15, 31 FR: 1	MC: 20	MC: 19, 35, 36 FR: 1
D. Exploring bivariate data	MC: 7, 12, 28, 33 FR: 6	MC: 1, 7, 34, 37 FR: 3	MC: 6, 14, 23, 30, 36 FR: 2, 6	MC: 11, 21, 27, 28, 31, 38, 40 FR: 4
E. Exploring categorical data	MC: 23		MC: 5	

II. Sampling & Experimentation	Practice Exam			
	1	2	3	4
A. Overview of methods of data collection	Questions pertaining to this topic are included in B–D			
B. Planning and conducting surveys	MC: 5, 9, 30	MC: 30, 36 FR: 5	MC: 4, 21 FR: 6	MC: 8, 17 FR: 3
C. Planning and conducting experiments	MC: 19, 32 FR: 2, 4	MC: 6, 18, 25, 38	MC: 12, 29, 40 FR: 4	MC: 4, 15
D. Generalizability of results and types of conclusions that can be drawn	MC: 25, 29	MC: 12	MC: 16	MC: 11, 26

III: Anticipating Patterns	Practice Exam			
	1	2	3	4
A. Probability	MC: 8, 10, 24, 26, 36, 37 FR: 3	MC: 5, 16, 20, 26, 28, 39 FR: 2, 6	MC: 3, 9, 18, 24, 32, 38 FR: 5	MC: 3, 6, 10, 13, 30, 32
B. Combining independent random variables	MC: 14	MC: 9, 22	MC: 26	MC: 22 FR: 2
C. The Normal distribution	MC: 21, 27 FR: 3	MC: 9, 14, 22	MC: 13, 28	MC: 20 FR: 2
D. Sampling distributions	MC: 2	MC: 14, 40	MC: 2, 34	MC: 25

IV: Statistical Inference	Practice Exam			
	1	2	3	4
A. Estimation (point estimators and confidence intervals	MC: 6, 11, 13, 18, 38 FR: 2,5	MC: 3, 4, 17, 29, 32, 33, 37 FR: 4	MC: 7, 8, 15, 22, 28, 37, 39 FR: 6	MC: 2, 5, 16, 23, 37, 39, FR:6
B. Tests of significance	MC: 1, 3, 15, 18, 20, 22, 31, 35, 40 FR: 2, 5	MC: 8, 10, 19, 21, 22, 27, 32, 33, 35, 37	MC: 8, 11, 17, 19, 25, 31, 33, 35 FR: 2, 3	MC: 9, 12, 18, 24, 29, 33, 34 FR: 5, 6

REFERENCES

Bock, David E., Velleman, Paul F., & Deveaux, Richard D. (2004). *Stats: Modeling the World*. Boston: Pearson/Addison-Wesley.

Cobb, George W. (1998). *Introduction to Design and Analysis of Experiments*. New York: Springer.

Everitt, B.S. (2002). *The Cambridge Dictionary of Statistics*, 2nd ed. New York: Cambridge University Press.

Peck, Roxy, Olsen, Chris, & Devore, Jay. (2005). *Introduction to Statistics and Data Analysis*. Belmont, CA: Brooks/Cole.

Scheaffer, Richard L., Mendenhall III, William, & Ott, R. Lyman. (1996). *Elementary Survey Sampling*, 5th ed. Belmont, CA: Wadsworth.

Utts, Jessica M., & Heckard, Robert F. (2002). *Mind on Statistics*. Pacific Grove, CA: Wadsworth.

Watkins, Ann E., Scheaffer, Richard L., & Cobb, George W. (2004). *Statistics in Action: Understanding a World of Data*. Emeryville, CA: Key Curriculum Press.

Yates, Daniel S., Moore, David S., & Starnes, Daren S. (2003). *The Practice of Statistics*, 2nd ed. New York: Freeman.

Websites

Centers for Disease Control and Prevention: www.cdc.gov

The College Board: www.collegeboard.com/student/testing/ap/about.html and www.collegeboard.com/student/testing/ap/sub_stats.html?stats

The Gallup Organization: www.gallup.com

keepkidshealty.com: www.keepkidshealthy.com/growthcharts

National Oceanic and Atmospheric Administration: www.noaa.gov

Polling Report.com: www.pollingreport.com

U.S. Environmental Protection Agency: www.epa.gov

U.S.D.A. Agricultural Marketing Service: www.ams.usda.gov

Answer Sheets

AP STATISTICS
PRACTICE EXAM 1

ANSWER SHEET

1. Ⓐ Ⓑ Ⓒ Ⓓ Ⓔ		21. Ⓐ Ⓑ Ⓒ Ⓓ Ⓔ
2. Ⓐ Ⓑ Ⓒ Ⓓ Ⓔ		22. Ⓐ Ⓑ Ⓒ Ⓓ Ⓔ
3. Ⓐ Ⓑ Ⓒ Ⓓ Ⓔ		23. Ⓐ Ⓑ Ⓒ Ⓓ Ⓔ
4. Ⓐ Ⓑ Ⓒ Ⓓ Ⓔ		24. Ⓐ Ⓑ Ⓒ Ⓓ Ⓔ
5. Ⓐ Ⓑ Ⓒ Ⓓ Ⓔ		25. Ⓐ Ⓑ Ⓒ Ⓓ Ⓔ
6. Ⓐ Ⓑ Ⓒ Ⓓ Ⓔ		26. Ⓐ Ⓑ Ⓒ Ⓓ Ⓔ
7. Ⓐ Ⓑ Ⓒ Ⓓ Ⓔ		27. Ⓐ Ⓑ Ⓒ Ⓓ Ⓔ
8. Ⓐ Ⓑ Ⓒ Ⓓ Ⓔ		28. Ⓐ Ⓑ Ⓒ Ⓓ Ⓔ
9. Ⓐ Ⓑ Ⓒ Ⓓ Ⓔ		29. Ⓐ Ⓑ Ⓒ Ⓓ Ⓔ
10. Ⓐ Ⓑ Ⓒ Ⓓ Ⓔ		30. Ⓐ Ⓑ Ⓒ Ⓓ Ⓔ
11. Ⓐ Ⓑ Ⓒ Ⓓ Ⓔ		31. Ⓐ Ⓑ Ⓒ Ⓓ Ⓔ
12. Ⓐ Ⓑ Ⓒ Ⓓ Ⓔ		32. Ⓐ Ⓑ Ⓒ Ⓓ Ⓔ
13. Ⓐ Ⓑ Ⓒ Ⓓ Ⓔ		33. Ⓐ Ⓑ Ⓒ Ⓓ Ⓔ
14. Ⓐ Ⓑ Ⓒ Ⓓ Ⓔ		34. Ⓐ Ⓑ Ⓒ Ⓓ Ⓔ
15. Ⓐ Ⓑ Ⓒ Ⓓ Ⓔ		35. Ⓐ Ⓑ Ⓒ Ⓓ Ⓔ
16. Ⓐ Ⓑ Ⓒ Ⓓ Ⓔ		36. Ⓐ Ⓑ Ⓒ Ⓓ Ⓔ
17. Ⓐ Ⓑ Ⓒ Ⓓ Ⓔ		37. Ⓐ Ⓑ Ⓒ Ⓓ Ⓔ
18. Ⓐ Ⓑ Ⓒ Ⓓ Ⓔ		38. Ⓐ Ⓑ Ⓒ Ⓓ Ⓔ
19. Ⓐ Ⓑ Ⓒ Ⓓ Ⓔ		39. Ⓐ Ⓑ Ⓒ Ⓓ Ⓔ
20. Ⓐ Ⓑ Ⓒ Ⓓ Ⓔ		40. Ⓐ Ⓑ Ⓒ Ⓓ Ⓔ

FREE-RESPONSE ANSWER SHEET

For the free-response section, write your answers on sheets of blank paper.

A grid for Question 1 is provided below.

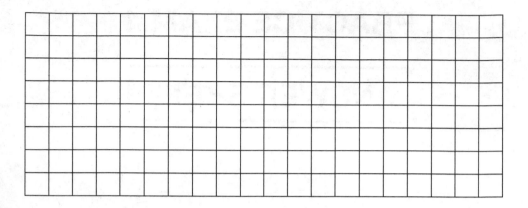

AP STATISTICS
PRACTICE EXAM 2

ANSWER SHEET

1. Ⓐ Ⓑ Ⓒ Ⓓ Ⓔ   21. Ⓐ Ⓑ Ⓒ Ⓓ Ⓔ
2. Ⓐ Ⓑ Ⓒ Ⓓ Ⓔ   22. Ⓐ Ⓑ Ⓒ Ⓓ Ⓔ
3. Ⓐ Ⓑ Ⓒ Ⓓ Ⓔ   23. Ⓐ Ⓑ Ⓒ Ⓓ Ⓔ
4. Ⓐ Ⓑ Ⓒ Ⓓ Ⓔ   24. Ⓐ Ⓑ Ⓒ Ⓓ Ⓔ
5. Ⓐ Ⓑ Ⓒ Ⓓ Ⓔ   25. Ⓐ Ⓑ Ⓒ Ⓓ Ⓔ
6. Ⓐ Ⓑ Ⓒ Ⓓ Ⓔ   26. Ⓐ Ⓑ Ⓒ Ⓓ Ⓔ
7. Ⓐ Ⓑ Ⓒ Ⓓ Ⓔ   27. Ⓐ Ⓑ Ⓒ Ⓓ Ⓔ
8. Ⓐ Ⓑ Ⓒ Ⓓ Ⓔ   28. Ⓐ Ⓑ Ⓒ Ⓓ Ⓔ
9. Ⓐ Ⓑ Ⓒ Ⓓ Ⓔ   29. Ⓐ Ⓑ Ⓒ Ⓓ Ⓔ
10. Ⓐ Ⓑ Ⓒ Ⓓ Ⓔ   30. Ⓐ Ⓑ Ⓒ Ⓓ Ⓔ
11. Ⓐ Ⓑ Ⓒ Ⓓ Ⓔ   31. Ⓐ Ⓑ Ⓒ Ⓓ Ⓔ
12. Ⓐ Ⓑ Ⓒ Ⓓ Ⓔ   32. Ⓐ Ⓑ Ⓒ Ⓓ Ⓔ
13. Ⓐ Ⓑ Ⓒ Ⓓ Ⓔ   33. Ⓐ Ⓑ Ⓒ Ⓓ Ⓔ
14. Ⓐ Ⓑ Ⓒ Ⓓ Ⓔ   34. Ⓐ Ⓑ Ⓒ Ⓓ Ⓔ
15. Ⓐ Ⓑ Ⓒ Ⓓ Ⓔ   35. Ⓐ Ⓑ Ⓒ Ⓓ Ⓔ
16. Ⓐ Ⓑ Ⓒ Ⓓ Ⓔ   36. Ⓐ Ⓑ Ⓒ Ⓓ Ⓔ
17. Ⓐ Ⓑ Ⓒ Ⓓ Ⓔ   37. Ⓐ Ⓑ Ⓒ Ⓓ Ⓔ
18. Ⓐ Ⓑ Ⓒ Ⓓ Ⓔ   38. Ⓐ Ⓑ Ⓒ Ⓓ Ⓔ
19. Ⓐ Ⓑ Ⓒ Ⓓ Ⓔ   39. Ⓐ Ⓑ Ⓒ Ⓓ Ⓔ
20. Ⓐ Ⓑ Ⓒ Ⓓ Ⓔ   40. Ⓐ Ⓑ Ⓒ Ⓓ Ⓔ

FREE-RESPONSE ANSWER SHEET

For the free-response section, write your answers on sheets of blank paper.

A grid for Question 1 and the random digit table for Question 6 are provided below.

<table>
<tr><td></td><td></td><td></td><td></td><td></td><td></td><td></td><td></td><td></td><td></td><td></td><td></td><td></td><td></td><td></td><td></td><td></td><td></td><td></td></tr>
<tr><td></td><td></td><td></td><td></td><td></td><td></td><td></td><td></td><td></td><td></td><td></td><td></td><td></td><td></td><td></td><td></td><td></td><td></td><td></td></tr>
<tr><td></td><td></td><td></td><td></td><td></td><td></td><td></td><td></td><td></td><td></td><td></td><td></td><td></td><td></td><td></td><td></td><td></td><td></td><td></td></tr>
<tr><td></td><td></td><td></td><td></td><td></td><td></td><td></td><td></td><td></td><td></td><td></td><td></td><td></td><td></td><td></td><td></td><td></td><td></td><td></td></tr>
<tr><td></td><td></td><td></td><td></td><td></td><td></td><td></td><td></td><td></td><td></td><td></td><td></td><td></td><td></td><td></td><td></td><td></td><td></td><td></td></tr>
<tr><td></td><td></td><td></td><td></td><td></td><td></td><td></td><td></td><td></td><td></td><td></td><td></td><td></td><td></td><td></td><td></td><td></td><td></td><td></td></tr>
<tr><td></td><td></td><td></td><td></td><td></td><td></td><td></td><td></td><td></td><td></td><td></td><td></td><td></td><td></td><td></td><td></td><td></td><td></td><td></td></tr>
<tr><td></td><td></td><td></td><td></td><td></td><td></td><td></td><td></td><td></td><td></td><td></td><td></td><td></td><td></td><td></td><td></td><td></td><td></td><td></td></tr>
</table>

93015	93615	03413	72295	97291
36377	14756	03768	53840	55333
63186	77781	69103	43259	01660
23825	65704	49525	84121	44856
97187	05901	61053	04173	07717

AP STATISTICS
PRACTICE EXAM 3

ANSWER SHEET

1. Ⓐ Ⓑ Ⓒ Ⓓ Ⓔ   21. Ⓐ Ⓑ Ⓒ Ⓓ Ⓔ
2. Ⓐ Ⓑ Ⓒ Ⓓ Ⓔ   22. Ⓐ Ⓑ Ⓒ Ⓓ Ⓔ
3. Ⓐ Ⓑ Ⓒ Ⓓ Ⓔ   23. Ⓐ Ⓑ Ⓒ Ⓓ Ⓔ
4. Ⓐ Ⓑ Ⓒ Ⓓ Ⓔ   24. Ⓐ Ⓑ Ⓒ Ⓓ Ⓔ
5. Ⓐ Ⓑ Ⓒ Ⓓ Ⓔ   25. Ⓐ Ⓑ Ⓒ Ⓓ Ⓔ
6. Ⓐ Ⓑ Ⓒ Ⓓ Ⓔ   26. Ⓐ Ⓑ Ⓒ Ⓓ Ⓔ
7. Ⓐ Ⓑ Ⓒ Ⓓ Ⓔ   27. Ⓐ Ⓑ Ⓒ Ⓓ Ⓔ
8. Ⓐ Ⓑ Ⓒ Ⓓ Ⓔ   28. Ⓐ Ⓑ Ⓒ Ⓓ Ⓔ
9. Ⓐ Ⓑ Ⓒ Ⓓ Ⓔ   29. Ⓐ Ⓑ Ⓒ Ⓓ Ⓔ
10. Ⓐ Ⓑ Ⓒ Ⓓ Ⓔ   30. Ⓐ Ⓑ Ⓒ Ⓓ Ⓔ
11. Ⓐ Ⓑ Ⓒ Ⓓ Ⓔ   31. Ⓐ Ⓑ Ⓒ Ⓓ Ⓔ
12. Ⓐ Ⓑ Ⓒ Ⓓ Ⓔ   32. Ⓐ Ⓑ Ⓒ Ⓓ Ⓔ
13. Ⓐ Ⓑ Ⓒ Ⓓ Ⓔ   33. Ⓐ Ⓑ Ⓒ Ⓓ Ⓔ
14. Ⓐ Ⓑ Ⓒ Ⓓ Ⓔ   34. Ⓐ Ⓑ Ⓒ Ⓓ Ⓔ
15. Ⓐ Ⓑ Ⓒ Ⓓ Ⓔ   35. Ⓐ Ⓑ Ⓒ Ⓓ Ⓔ
16. Ⓐ Ⓑ Ⓒ Ⓓ Ⓔ   36. Ⓐ Ⓑ Ⓒ Ⓓ Ⓔ
17. Ⓐ Ⓑ Ⓒ Ⓓ Ⓔ   37. Ⓐ Ⓑ Ⓒ Ⓓ Ⓔ
18. Ⓐ Ⓑ Ⓒ Ⓓ Ⓔ   38. Ⓐ Ⓑ Ⓒ Ⓓ Ⓔ
19. Ⓐ Ⓑ Ⓒ Ⓓ Ⓔ   39. Ⓐ Ⓑ Ⓒ Ⓓ Ⓔ
20. Ⓐ Ⓑ Ⓒ Ⓓ Ⓔ   40. Ⓐ Ⓑ Ⓒ Ⓓ Ⓔ

FREE-RESPONSE ANSWER SHEET

For the free-response section, write your answers on sheets of blank paper.

A grid for Question 2 is provided below.

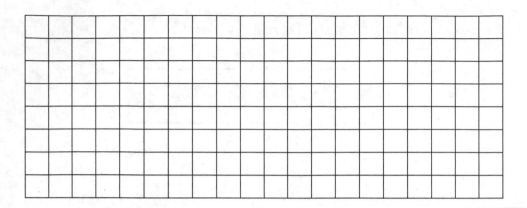

AP STATISTICS
PRACTICE EXAM 4

ANSWER SHEET

1. (A) (B) (C) (D) (E)
2. (A) (B) (C) (D) (E)
3. (A) (B) (C) (D) (E)
4. (A) (B) (C) (D) (E)
5. (A) (B) (C) (D) (E)
6. (A) (B) (C) (D) (E)
7. (A) (B) (C) (D) (E)
8. (A) (B) (C) (D) (E)
9. (A) (B) (C) (D) (E)
10. (A) (B) (C) (D) (E)
11. (A) (B) (C) (D) (E)
12. (A) (B) (C) (D) (E)
13. (A) (B) (C) (D) (E)
14. (A) (B) (C) (D) (E)
15. (A) (B) (C) (D) (E)
16. (A) (B) (C) (D) (E)
17. (A) (B) (C) (D) (E)
18. (A) (B) (C) (D) (E)
19. (A) (B) (C) (D) (E)
20. (A) (B) (C) (D) (E)

21. (A) (B) (C) (D) (E)
22. (A) (B) (C) (D) (E)
23. (A) (B) (C) (D) (E)
24. (A) (B) (C) (D) (E)
25. (A) (B) (C) (D) (E)
26. (A) (B) (C) (D) (E)
27. (A) (B) (C) (D) (E)
28. (A) (B) (C) (D) (E)
29. (A) (B) (C) (D) (E)
30. (A) (B) (C) (D) (E)
31. (A) (B) (C) (D) (E)
32. (A) (B) (C) (D) (E)
33. (A) (B) (C) (D) (E)
34. (A) (B) (C) (D) (E)
35. (A) (B) (C) (D) (E)
36. (A) (B) (C) (D) (E)
37. (A) (B) (C) (D) (E)
38. (A) (B) (C) (D) (E)
39. (A) (B) (C) (D) (E)
40. (A) (B) (C) (D) (E)

FREE-RESPONSE ANSWER SHEET

For the free-response section, write your answers on sheets of blank paper.

INDEX

Index

NOTES

NOTES

NOTES

NOTES

NOTES

NOTES